Migrants and Minorities

Migrants and Minorities: The European Response

Edited by

Adam Luedtke

CAMBRIDGE SCHOLARS

PUBLISHING

Migrants and Minorities: The European Response,
Edited by Adam Luedtke

This book first published 2010

Cambridge Scholars Publishing

12 Back Chapman Street, Newcastle upon Tyne, NE6 2XX, UK

British Library Cataloguing in Publication Data
A catalogue record for this book is available from the British Library

ISBN (10): 1-4438-2111-X, ISBN (13): 978-1-4438-2111-7

To Afton

TABLE OF CONTENTS

LIST OF TABLES AND FIGURES

PART I

THE EUROPEANISATION OF IMMIGRATION POLICY?

CHAPTER ONE

INTRODUCTION: REGULATING THE NEW FACE OF EUROPE

ADAM LUEDTKE, CARRIE HUMPHREYS, TERRI E. GIVENS AND RHONDA EVANS CASE

Europe stands on the brink of a new era of diversity and immigration. Although many Europeans would prefer to ignore this fact, the signs are everywhere. Societies and politics are being irrevocably changed by encounters with migrants, both recent and settled. European governments increasingly experiment with a range of policy responses—both restrictive and liberal—from visas for skilled workers to bans on religious garb. But beyond a solemn acknowledgment of the importance of the "problem" (in reality a maze of interrelated problems and opportunities stemming from European encounters with migrants and minorities), analysts of EU immigration must pinpoint specific trends and emerging patterns if we hope to understand what this change means for the future of Europe, and for broader questions such as Islam/West relations, or how democracies deal with diversity. Two decades after the end of the Cold War and the revitalization of European integration, we must go beyond sensationalistic and simplistic accounts of headscarves, riots and radical right-wing parties, so that we can illustrate the everyday interactions and dialogues between European states, societies, migrants and minorities. On the ground level, institutions like schools and local governments have charted unique courses for dealing with diversity. And from above, the institutions of Brussels become ever more important for regulating the big picture. The passage of the Lisbon Treaty means that common EU rules on immigration will now be easier to achieve (and more likely). But what exact role is played by the institutions of the EU in Brussels, and how does this vary across policy areas? How are Europeans on all levels dealing with the sensitive questions raised by Islam, and how are migrants and minorities dealing with the hostility and xenophobia they routinely encounter? And finally, how have the experiences of different European countries in integrating their immigrants and minorities changed our comparative understanding of race, ethnicity and citizenship? These three sets of issues—EU-level regulations, Islam and xenophobia, and comparative integration policy—are the topics that motivate and structure this book.

This introductory chapter will first illustrate the increasing influence of Brussels in regulating immigration and diversity, but will also show how differences between EU rules on how to coordinate anti-discrimination policy, and EU rules on how to coordinate immigration policy, have led to very different outcomes in these two policy areas. In general, anti-discrimination policy is more "Europeanised" than immigration policy, though the passage of the EU's Lisbon Treaty will lead to more Europeanisation of immigration policy. Also, most EU-level immigration policy has been relatively "restrictive" towards the rights and freedoms of immigrants, while most EU-level anti-discrimination policy has been relatively "liberal", or expansive towards the rights and freedoms of immigrants.

After an analysis of how immigration and anti-discrimination policy are regulated at EU level, we close with a plan of the book and a summary of each individual chapter.

Introduction: New European Faces, Common European Rules?

Immigration has played an important role in the postwar economic development of Europe. Ostensibly "temporary" labourers were integral to the labour force in Europe during periods of strong economic growth in the 1950s and 1960s. Despite the general stop of the mass importation of labour in the early 1970s, immigration continues to play a role in the labour markets and social policies of European countries. Countries are dealing with not only the issues of family reunification, asylum seekers, and illegal immigration, but also with aging populations and declining birthrates, and potentially crippling skilled and/or unskilled labour shortages in some sectors. To prevent future crises, political elites now generally agree that these issues need to be addressed proactively, as opposed to the traditional method of attempting to ignore the problem (Givens 2007, 68; Euractiv 2007a). Immigration has created a new face for Europe, which has had to confront the challenge of incorporating millions of immigrants from outside the continent, including many Muslims. It is estimated that 680,000 legal immigrants and 500,000 illegal immigrants enter Europe every year (Euractiv 2005; Euractiv 2007b; Vucheva 2007). This influx has led to new difficulties for the receiving countries, most of whom had considered themselves homogenous rather than multi-ethnic states. One example is the Netherlands, which has been steadily moving away from its multicultural policies (Givens 2007; Groenendijk 2004; Ireland 2004) in the climate of fear generated by the murder of Theo van Gogh. Incidents like these, along with the London and Madrid bombings, have led countries to seriously reconsider their immigration and integration policies.

Despite calls for harmonisation of policy at the EU level, the ongoing influx of immigrants and issues of integration have not, for the most part, led to concrete new policies in Brussels (Green 2007; Lavenex 2006; Spongenberg 2007c; Velluti 2007). Immigrants are faced with a broad range of policies depending upon the country in which they reside. Some countries such as France and Britain have made it relatively easy for immigrants to naturalize while others such as Germany and Austria have historically made it more difficult. While Germany has changed its citizenship policy to be more in line with its fellow member states, the EU's new Lisbon Treaty leaves citizenship as a national issue (Green 2007).

European integration has led to a push by certain member states for more harmonisation in the areas of immigration and social policies that affect immigrants (Burnett 2007; Spongenberg 2007a; Spongenberg 2007b). Policy proposals have come in many areas, including asylum policy, illegal immigration, visas and border control, labour recruitment and anti-discrimination policy. We will show below that the first three policy areas have seen a great deal of harmonisation, although this was often due to the restrictive goals of such policies at EU level, emphasizing control over liberalization. However, labour recruitment, particularly for third country nationals[1] (TCNs), is an area in which the EU has been hesitant to make major policy initiatives and where the few successful initiatives are more often restrictive in nature (Lahav 2004; Givens & Luedtke 2004). By contrast, in 2000, the EU adopted the relatively liberal Racial Equality Directive (RED), which applies to (non-TCN) immigrants

[1] A "third country national" is an immigrant residing in one EU member state who is not a citizen of another EU member state.

holding nationality in an EU member state. It obligates member states to enact anti-discrimination laws that protect individuals from discriminatory acts committed by government as well as a range of private entities. The most highly developed anti-discrimination regimes—those of Britain and the Netherlands—served as models for the RED (Geddes 2003; Geddes & Guiraudon 2004). Thus, in this particular policy area, developments more closely approximate a "race to the top" rather than a "race to the bottom."[2] The literature on federalism uses the term "race to the bottom" to indicate that when policy is harmonised, the result is often a lowest common denominator policy, with minimal protections (e.g. in the areas of the environment or human rights). This is because of competition between jurisdictions to attract business, repel immigrants, or whatever the policy goal may be (Tiebout 1956; Oates 1999). However, with anti-discrimination policy, the EU used its institutional advantages to adopt the strongest regime available from the menu of national choices. It will be explained below that key factors explaining this divergence between immigration and anti-discrimination policy were NGOs, in combination with the European Parliament, who were essential to developing the legislation (Lavenex 2006, 1288).

Another area where the EU has taken steps is in policy towards TCNs who are long-term residents. In November 2003, the European Council adopted the Directive on the status of third-country nationals who are long-term residents. This directive, with required transposition into national law by 2006, allows TCNs with five years of residence to have a special secure residence status, equal treatment as nationals in areas of employment and welfare benefits, and perhaps most importantly, the freedom to work and live in other EU member states.[3] However, as Groenendijk notes, "It is a status with rights comparable but not equal to those of Union citizens" (Groenendijk 2004, 121; Lavenex 2006). The directive contains many caveats and national exceptions that restrict TCN rights in practice. At the EU level, both immigration and anti-discrimination policy are determined through largely the same institutional

---

[2] This is *not* to say that civil society proponents of the RED got everything they wanted. Importantly, protection for TCNs was explicitly rejected by member states and excluded from the Directive in its final form.

[3] Directive 2003/109/EC of 25 November 2003, OJ 2004, L 16/44. As of June 2007, this directive is being amended to extend LTR rights to other beneficiaries of international protection: refugees and beneficiaries of subsidiary protection.

structures, namely the EU's primary legislative body, the Council[4]; yet, we see divergent policy outcomes—generally restrictive immigration policy, and liberal anti-discrimination policy.

In terms of theoretical explanations for immigration's "lag" as an integrated policy area, Givens and Luedtke (2004) have analyzed immigration policy at the EU level, showing that "restrictionist national executives protect de facto national sovereignty over immigration (to maximize political capital), either by blocking supranational harmonisation of immigration policy, or making sure that the harmonisation that *does* occur is weighted in favour of law-and-order and security, and is not subject to the scrutiny of supranational institutions and courts" (Givens & Luedtke 2004, 150). Overall, in terms of immigration policy, the longstanding unanimity voting requirement[5] meant that a single member state could block harmonisation, which in turn often led to no harmonisation, or to a race to the bottom regarding immigrant rights and freedoms (Lavenex 2006, 1285). Another key difference between immigration policy and most other areas of EU policy was that until 2004 the European Commission did not have the sole right of initiative to propose a policy (which it normally does in other policy areas), meaning that until 2005 harmonisation proceeded in a more bottom-up manner, in line with national interests (Geddes 2000; Moravcsik 1998).

Coupled with the unanimity voting requirement on the Council, the lack of sole right of initiative for the Commission meant that it was easier for countries to either block harmonisation of controversial immigration issues, or to propose *restrictive* harmonisation of controversial immigration issues, since the Commission normally proposes extensive and relatively expansive harmonisation of immigration policies (Geddes 2000; Euractiv 2007a). Also, the United Kingdom, Ireland and Denmark have opt-outs from most EU immigration laws, leaving them free to implement restrictive policies if they so choose (Green 2007; Euractiv 2007b).[6]

---

[4] This area of policy will from unanimity to qualified majority voting (QMV) under the Lisbon Treaty.

[5] The use of unanimity voting changed in 2005 with The Hague Programme. While legal migration issues were still decided by unanimity, illegal migration and asylum moved to QMV. Ultimately, though, Lisbon moves all areas to QMV.

[6] The UK has mainly opted-in to more restrictive measures on asylum and illegal immigration (Givens & Luedtke 2004, Geddes 2003).

The European Parliament, which has been a proponent of rights-expansive harmonisation, has seen its influence minimized in the area of immigration policy through the use of the "consultation" procedure as opposed to the "co-decision" procedure (which applies to most other areas of EU policy). In the more common co-decision procedure, which will apply to immigration and asylum under Lisbon, the Council and Parliament must both give consent for a particular policy, and if they cannot reach agreement then a "conciliation committee" is formed to hammer out a deal. This institutional arrangement gives the European Parliament a great deal of influence in many matters of EU policy (Wallace, Wallace & Pollack 2005). In the weaker consultation procedure, however, which applied to immigration (and other sensitive policy areas like law enforcement), the Council is merely required to "examine" the opinion of the Parliament, which is non-binding and cannot block a decision. This gave the Council, which is made up of national executives, a freer hand in implementing policy away from judicial and democratic constraints, which might require a more expansive harmonisation of immigration policies, protecting immigrant rights and ensuring the free flow of labour in the single market.

Based on the types of policies that have been adopted by the Council, we argue that politics at the national level continue to determine the success of harmonisation proposals, by determining the positions of member states when negotiating in the European Council. However, on certain proposals, as we will show in the case of the RED and some immigration directives, supranational pressures do have an impact on the policies of individual member states. And these pressures will only increase with the passage of the Lisbon Treaty.

This analysis begins by describing policy developments in the EU in the area of immigration and asylum. We then discuss whether the policy initiatives that have been adopted indicate a greater role for the EU in immigration and integration policy. The subsequent section of the chapter will focus on a detailed analysis of the RED, one of the few areas where we have seen the development of rights-expansive policy relating to immigrants. We then close with an outline of the book.

EU-Level Immigration Policy Developments

As mentioned above, it is widely agreed that immigration harmonisation has lagged behind other EU policy areas (Geddes 2000, Guiraudon 2000,

Lahav 2004). In their analysis, Givens and Luedtke (2004, 146) point out that:

> The economic and institutional imperatives of European integration have led to two contradictory political developments: 1) a push by EU institutions . . . to develop a common, "harmonised" EU immigration policy that includes TCNs; and 2) a resistance on the part of some member states to this development.

All EU policy developments in the areas of immigration and anti-discrimination policy are listed in Table 1. Proposals have been broken down into five areas: asylum, legal migration, visas and border control, illegal migration and anti-discrimination policy. As the table indicates, the Council has been selective in its adoption of this legislation. Following Givens and Luedtke (2004), we argue that harmonisation proposals in controversial policy areas are less likely to be successful, and if they are successful they are more likely to be restrictive.

TABLE 1-1: Proposed EU Immigration Policies and Their Outcomes

Policy Area	EU Proposal	Adopted by Council?	If Adopted, Restrictive or Expansive?
Asylum	Common Asylum Procedure (COM(2000)755)	Yes	Restrictive
	Minimum Standards for Conditions for the Reception of Asylum-Seekers (COM(2001)181)	Yes	Restrictive
	Determining the Member State Responsible for Examining an Asylum Application (COM(2001)447)	Yes	Restrictive
	Council Directive 2005/85/EC of 1 December 2005 on Minimum Standards on Procedures in Member States for Granting and Withdrawing Refugee Status.	Yes	Restrictive
	Council Directive 2004/83/EC of 29 April 2004 on Minimum Standards for the Qualification and Status of Third Country Nationals or Stateless Persons as Refugees or as Persons Who Otherwise Need International Protection and the Content of the Protection Granted	Yes	Restrictive
	Granting Temporary Protection In Case of Mass Influx (COM(2000)303)	Yes	Restrictive
	Council Regulation No 2725/2000, the Establishment of "Eurodac" for the Comparison of Fingerprints	Yes	Restrictive
	European Refugee Fund (COM(1999)686)	Yes	Neither

Legal migration	Family Reunification (COM(2002)225)	Yes	Restrictive
	Status of Third Country Nationals who are Long Term Residents (COM(2001)127)	Yes	Restrictive
	Coordination of Social Security Benefits (COM(2002)59)	No	
	Conditions of Entry and Residence of TCNs for Paid Employment (COM(2001)386)	No	
	"Blue Card": Council Directive on the Conditions of Entry and Residence of Third-Country Nationals for the Purposes of Highly Qualified Employment, COM(2007) 637	Yes	Expansive
	Council Regulation (EC) No 2424/2001, Development of Schengen Information System II (fingerprint database)	Yes	Restrictive
	Proposal for a Council Directive on a Single Application Procedure for a Single Permit for Third-Country Nationals to Reside and Work in the Territory of a Member State and on a Common Set of Rights for Third Country Workers Legally Residing in a Member State, COM(2007) 638 final.	No	
	Admission for Scientific Research (COM(2004)178)	Yes	Expansive
	Admission for Study/Training (COM(2002)548)	Yes	Expansive
Visas and border control	Council Regulation Amending Regulation 1683/95 Uniform Format for Visas (2002/C 51 E/03) (COM(2001)577)	Yes	Neither
	Listing Third Countries Whose Nationals Must Possess Visas (COM(2002)679)	Yes	Restrictive
	Proposal for a Regulation of the European Parliament and of the Council amending the Common Consular Instructions on Visas for Diplomatic Missions and Consular Posts in Relation to the Introduction of Biometrics Including Provisions on the Organization of the Reception and Processing of Visa Applications, COM(2006) 269 final.	No	

	Common Border Guard Manual (2001/C 73)	Yes	Restrictive
	Regulation (EC) No 562/2006 of the European Parliament and of the Council of 15 March 2006 Establishing a Community Code on the Rules Governing the Movement of Persons Across Borders (Schengen Borders Code), OJ L 105, 13.4.2006, p. 1.	Yes	Restrictive
	Regulation (EC) No 767/2008 of the European Parliament and of the Council of 9 July 2008 Concerning the Visa Information System (VIS) and the exchange of data between Member States on Short-Stay Visas (VIS Regulation), OJ L 218, 13.8.2008, p. 60; and Council Decision 2008/633/JHA of 23 June 2008 Concerning Access for Consultation of the Visa Information System (VIS) by Designated Authorities of Member States and by Europol for the Purposes of the Prevention, Detection and Investigation of Terrorist Offences and of Other Serious Criminal Offences, OJ L 218, 13.8.2008, p. 129.	Yes	Restrictive
	Council Decision 2008/633/JHA of 23 June 2008 Concerning Access for Consultation of the Visa Information System (VIS) by Designated Authorities of Member States and by Europol for the Purposes of the Prevention, Detection and Investigation of Terrorist Offences and of Other Serious Criminal Offences, OJ L 218, 13.8.2008, p. 129.	Yes	Restrictive
	Travel by Nationals Exempt from the Visa Requirement (2000/C 164)	No	

Illegal Immigration	Transit Assistance for Removal by Air (2003/C 4)	No	
	Mutual Recognition of Expulsion Orders (2000/C 243)	Yes	Restrictive
	Directive 2008/115/EC of the European Parliament and of the Council of 16 December 2008 on Common Standards and Procedures in Member States for Returning Illegally Staying Third-Country Nationals, OJ L 348, 24.12.2008, p. 98.	Yes	Restrictive
	2004/191/EC: Council Decision of 23 February 2004 Setting out the Criteria and Practical Arrangements for the Compensation of the Financial Imbalances Resulting from the Application of Directive 2001/40/EC on the Mutual Recognition of Decisions on the Expulsion of Third-Country Nationals	Yes	Restrictive
	Council Directive 2004/81/EC on the Residence Permit Issued to Non-EU Member Country Nationals Who are Victims of Trafficking in Human Beings or Who Have Been the Subject of an Action to Facilitate Illegal Immigration, who Cooperate with the Competent Authorities.	Yes	Mixed
	Penalties for Carriers of Illegal Immigrants (2000/C 269)	Yes	Restrictive
	Council Directive 2004/82/EC of 29 April 2004 on the Obligation of Carriers to Communicate Passenger Data.	Yes	Restrictive
	Proposal for a Directive of the European Parliament and of the Council Providing for Sanctions Against Employers of Illegally Staying Third-Country Nationals, COM(2007) 249 final.	No	
	Combating Human Trafficking (COM(2000)854)	Yes	Restrictive
	Strengthening of Penal Framework (2000/C 253)	Yes	Restrictive

Anti-discrimination	Compliance with the Charter of Fundamental Rights in Commission Legislative Proposals - Methodology for Systematic and Rigorous Monitoring, COM(2005) 172 final.	Yes	Expansive
	Council Regulation (EC) No 168/2007 of 15 February 2007 establishing a European Union Agency for Fundamental Rights, OJ L 53, 22.2.2007, p. 1.	Yes	Expansive
	Council Framework Decision 2008/913/JHA of 28 November 2008 on combating certain forms and expressions of racism and xenophobia by means of criminal law, OJ L 328, 6.12.2008, p. 55.	Yes	Expansive
	Racial Equality Directive (COM(1999)566)	Yes	Expansive
	Council Decision 2007/435/EC of 25 June 2007 establishing the European Fund for the Integration of Third Country Nationals for the Period 2007 to 2013 as Part of the General Program Solidarity and Management of Migration Flows, OJ L 168, 28.6.2007, p. 18.	Yes	Expansive
	Community Action Program to Combat Discrimination (COM(1999)649)	Yes	Expansive
	Common Basic Principles, Council document 14615/04, p. 15; A Common Agenda for Integration: Framework for the Integration of Third-Country Nationals in the European Union, COM(2005) 389 final.	Yes	Mixed

As the table indicates, with the exception of anti-discrimination policy, only three of the policies that have been adopted by the Council are expansive towards immigrant rights and freedoms. These are the directives on the admission of students, researchers, and highly-skilled workers (the "Blue Card") who obviously trigger less public alarm than other categories of immigrants. As already mentioned, some harmonisation *restricts* immigrant rights, by standardizing policy at the lowest common denominator. These policies allow member states to lower their standards for the protection of immigrant rights and do not provide judicial remedies. Other harmonisation obligates members to raise their standards and is *expansive* towards immigrant rights. The main example in this area is the RED (Lavenex 2006). While this directive does not protect all immigrants (since it is based on race and not nationality), it does provide judicial remedies for ethnic minority immigrants, and obligates all member states (including those who previously had no racial discrimination legislation) to implement the RED into national law (Niessen 2001).

One of the main concerns of NGOs that work in the area of immigration and integration is that policy-making at the EU level will become a "race to the bottom" meaning that policy will match the level of those member states with the most restrictive policies. This has proven particularly true in the areas of asylum policy and illegal immigration. Several examples illustrate this point.

First, in looking at asylum, as shown in Table 1, policies adopted under the Amsterdam process related to asylum seekers include: determining the member state responsible for an asylum application, the EURODAC fingerprinting system, temporary protection, minimum standards for the reception of asylum seekers and the establishment of a European Refugee Fund (ERF) (Lindstrom 2005, 598-600). In addition, a directive on creating uniform procedural standards in the examination of asylum claims, and access to law and a fair trial, was finally adopted in December 2005 after a series of delays (Lavenex 2006, 1295). While a step towards harmonised asylum standards would seem like a positive development, it has actually been treated by the European Parliament (EP) and international organizations like the United Nations as a breach of international refugee law. The EP, in decrying the downgrading of established standards in many countries, challenged this directive before the ECJ in 2006. With the exception of the ERF, these measures have allowed member states to lower their standards of refugee protection (van der Klaauw 2004).

Illegal immigration, like asylum, has yet to encounter an expansive European-wide policy, but instead focuses on restrictions (Lindstrom 2005). For example, there is a push to crack down on companies that hire illegal immigrants. Member states have been required to increase the number of companies that are annually inspected for the employment of illegal immigrants from 2% to 10% (Euractiv 2007c). In addition they have committed themselves to conducting spot checks and any companies in violation could face criminal charges. Overall, EU-level policy has aided national politicians in enacting stringent measures to deal with illegal immigrants (Velluti 2007).

As Lavenex sums it up, "The metaphor of 'fortress of Europe' expresses well this emphasis which has so far consisted more in downgrading existing domestic rights, for example, through limiting access to territory and full asylum procedures, than in creating common European standards" (2006, 1292).

Visas and border control is another area in which several measures have been adopted but initial successes in harmonisation actually resulted from intergovernmental agreements. Major agreements like the Schengen and the Dublin Conventions helped create a uniform format for visas, and a common border guard manual to assist agents at border crossings to determine the status of an immigrant, whether they are coming legally for work, illegally, or as an asylum seeker. These requirements are being expanded to new member states from Central and Eastern Europe. Border checks were scheduled to stop at the end of 2007 and airport checks in early 2008 (Kubosova 2007). With the Lisbon Treaty and movement away from a solely intergovernmental approach, there have also been newer developments such as directives that require the listing of third countries whose nationals must possess visas, and common Consular instructions for examining visa applications. This change also impacts several categories of immigrants, and requiring Schengen visas may push more immigrants to seek asylum or to enter a country illegally.

In the area of legal migration, the Commission has provided numerous proposals. Most recently, there were a series of proposals from former EU Justice and Home Affairs Commissioner Franco Frattini that focused on economic migrants. The central component is the blue card. As Mahony explains, "The blue card – the blue comes from the EU flag – would allow skilled workers to work in an EU member state for an initial two-year period. They would then be able to move to another EU country" (2007a).

This proposal was an attempt to proactively deal with looming labour shortages and had the support of the EP (*Economist* 2007, 54; Euractiv 2007a). Even with this support, the proposal was been highly contested and does not necessarily create clear European standards.

In summary, despite the large number of Commission proposals, few have been adopted, and those few pieces of legislation that are tend to be highly restrictive, harmonise only weakly, and leave many options to national discretion[1] (Mahony 2007b). All of the measures in the four areas described above indicate that the main emphasis of the European Council up to this point has been to provide member states with restrictive measures, while avoiding regulations that would limit a country's sovereignty in the area of immigration. It is the area of anti-discrimination policy where we see some cracks in this position.

EU-Level Anti-Discrimination Policy

As in the area of immigration, anti-discrimination policy also demonstrates the importance of national political concerns in the push for harmonisation of policy related to Europe's changing demographic profile. Here, however, the resultant policy, the RED, constitutes a dramatic change in the way that at least some countries approach anti-discrimination policy. This is curious because, as with citizenship and immigration policy, the Council dominates the policymaking process in this area. Indeed, the process through which the RED was achieved was even more onerous than standard modes of EU policymaking because it entailed amending the Treaty of Amsterdam in order to empower the EU to act in this area. In this section, we discuss the developments that led up to the RED, the preferences of nongovernmental organizations (NGOs) supporting the directive, and the specific terms of RED in its final form.

An Institutional History of the Racial Equality Directive (RED)

Beginning in 1985, the European Parliament played a key role in putting and keeping the issue of racism on the European agenda.[2] The

---

[1] Even though legal migration moves to QMV under Lisbon, national governments still have significant discretion, like determining the volume/quantity of immigrants that are allowed to enter their countries.

[2] That year, a Committee of Inquiry produced the so-called "Evrigenis report" that documented the growing problem of xenophobia among Member States.

following year, after a series of dramatic electoral gains by extreme right parties, most notably in France, the European Commission, the Council and the Parliament signed the *Joint Declaration against racism and xenophobia*.[3] Over the ensuing years, however, the Council refused to enact anti-discrimination legislation covering racial discrimination, despite repeated requests by the European Parliament. Although there was consensus that racism and xenophobia presented serious problems requiring redress, within the Council there was disagreement as to the appropriate form of that redress and the legal competence of European institutions to deliver it.

As a new decade dawned, the European Parliament redoubled its efforts and was joined by a coalition of NGOs. Foremost among these was the Starting Line Group (SLG), formed by the British Commission for Racial Equality (CRE), the Dutch National Bureau against Racism, and the Churches Commission for Migrants in Europe (CCME).[4] It promptly organized a group of legal experts from across member states to draft a directive targeting racial discrimination, and by 1993, its draft was endorsed by more than 200 NGOs and submitted to the European Parliament, which explicitly approved it in two separate resolutions.[5] The original measure proposed by SLG relied upon Article 308 (formerly Article 235) as its legal basis. That Article empowers the European Community (EC) to take actions not explicitly authorized in the EC Treaty

---

[3] Joint Declaration by the European Parliament, the Council and the Commission against racism and xenophobia, 11 June 1986 (OJ C 158, 25.6.1986).

[4] The SLG's activities are discussed in Isabelle Chopin, "The Starting Line: A harmonised approach to the fight against racism and to promote equal treatment," *European Journal of Migration and Law* 1: 1999. Founded in 1964, the CCME is an organization of churches and ecumenical councils from Austria, Belgium, Czech Republic, Finland, France, Germany, Greece, Italy, the Netherlands, Norway, Romania Switzerland, Spain, Sweden, the United Kingdom and Ireland. There are contacts with the Ecumenical Patriarchate (Brussels/Istanbul) and with church partners in Denmark, and Russia. The General Assembly of CCME, October 1999 in Järvenpää/Finland, decided in conjunction with the Conference of European Churches and the World Council of Churches to expand its mandate to cover the whole area of migration and integration, refugees and asylum, and racism and xenophobia. The General Assembly welcomed four new members from the above listed countries. CCME holds official observer status with the Council of Europe in Strasbourg http://www.coe.int/T/E/Social_Cohesion/Migration/ and observes the Committee on Migration of the Council of Ministers.

[5] 1993 resolution, OJ 1993 C 342/19, 20.12.93; 1994 resolution, para. 0, OJ 1994 C 323/154, 20.11.94.

if such action is proven "necessary to attain, in the course of the operation of the common market, one of the objectives of the Community." When it became clear in 1993 that there was insufficient political will to use Article 308, the SLG shifted its strategy and sought an amendment to the EC Treaty that would provide clear authority for a directive on racial discrimination.

To that pressure, the Council of Ministers initially responded with a series of symbolic gestures rather than substantive legislative proposals.[6] In 1994, however, more consequential action was taken by the Council with the establishment of the Consultative Commission on Racism and Xenophobia, or "Kahn Commission" as it came to be known after its chair, Jean Kahn, President of the European Jewish Congress. In its final report, the Kahn Commission issued a number of recommendations, three of which are of particular importance here. First, it recommended that the EC Treaty be amended to authorize the EC to fight racial discrimination, thereby resolving uncertainties concerning the EC's legal competence.[7] Second, borrowing largely from the EC's sex equality legislation, the Commission recommended a policy model based upon the use of directives.[8] And third, the Kahn Commission concluded that the effective implementation of new anti-discrimination policy would require record keeping and monitoring.[9] The last of these recommendations proved quite controversial among several countries, most notably France, which argued that such record keeping would actually reinforce difference.

Both the Parliament and Commission subsequently endorsed the first two recommendations, and at the 1996 intergovernmental conference,

---

[6] Resolution on the Fight against Racism and Xenophobia in the fields of Employment and Social Affairs (OJ 1995 C 296/13); Resolution on the Response of Educational Systems to the Problems of Racism and Xenophobia (OJ 1995 C 312/1); and, Declaration by the Council and the Representatives of the Governments of the Member States, meeting within the Council of 24 November 1997 on the fight against racism, xenophobia and anti-Semitism in the youth field, OJC 368/1, 5.12.97.

[7] European Council Consultative Commission on Racism and Xenophobia, "Final Report" Ref. 6906/1/95 Rev 1 Limite RAXEN 24 Brussels: General Secretariat of the Council of the European Union (1995).

[8] European Council Consultative Commission on Racism and Xenophobia (1995) "Final Report" Ref. 6906/1/95 Rev 1 Limite RAXEN 24, at p. 39.

[9] European Council Consultative Commission on Racism and Xenophobia (1995) "Final Report" Ref. 6906/1/95 Rev 1 Limite RAXEN 24, at p. 40.

member states took the important step of amending the EC Treaty.[10] As a result, in 1997, the Treaty of Amsterdam was amended to provide for a new Article 6a (subsequently known as Article 13).[11] Article 13, which took effect in 1999, provides:

> Without prejudice to the other provisions of this Treaty and within the limits of the powers conferred by it upon the Community, the Council, acting unanimously on a proposal from the Commission and after consulting the European Parliament, may take appropriate action to combat discrimination based on sex, racial or ethnic origin, religion or belief, disability, age or sexual orientation.[12]

Although it did not fulfil all of the activists' wishes, this reform does represent "a turning point" in EU anti-discrimination policy (Bell 1997, 49). The SLG had hoped that the new Article would possess direct effect as does Article 119, which requires equal pay between women and men,[13] for that would have enabled individuals to invoke the Article in national legal proceedings and ultimately to appeal to the European Court of Justice. Instead, Article 13 "simply provides a discretionary power to the Council to adopt measures as they see fit."[14] Given the past reluctance of the Council to make policy in the area of racial discrimination, the SLG's disappointment in this regard was understandable. Yet, only thirteen months after the Treaty of Amsterdam was ratified – record speed for the EU – the European Council unanimously adopted the RED[15] in June of 2000.

---

[10] See Jan Niessen, "The Amsterdam Treaty and NGO responses," *European Journal of Migration and Law* 2: 2000; and, Isabelle Chopin, "Possible harmonisation of anti-discrimination legislation in the European Union. European and non-governmental proposals," *European Journal of Migration and Law* 1: 2001.

[11] Importantly, the Treaty of Amsterdam also provides for the renumbering of the articles of the Treaty. Consequently, Article 6a became Article 13 and shall be referred to as such throughout the remainder of this article.

[12] The Treaty entered into force in May 1999.

[13] Isabelle Chopin, *Campaigning against racism and xenophobia: from a legislative perspective at European level* (ENAR, November 1999), p. 3.

[14] Mark Bell, EU *Antidiscrimination Policy: from equal opportunities between women and men to combating racism* (Brussels: European Parliament Directorate General for Research, 1997), p. 12.

[15] Council Directive 2000/43/EC of 29 June 2000 implementing the principle of equal treatment between persons irrespective of racial or ethnic origin, Official Journal (OJ) L 180/22, 19 July 2000.

During the negotiations that preceded the directive's adoption, an array of NGOs played a key role in shaping the terms of debate (Lavenex 2006). Members of the SLG, including the European Roma Rights Centre (ERRC), the Migration Policy Group, and Interights played especially important roles in the RED negotiations. They published comprehensive analyses of the domestic anti-discrimination legislation in twenty-six countries. The ERRC co-organized three transnational workshops on legal standards, legal advocacy, and litigation strategies that brought national and EU level stakeholders together. The ERRC "made campaigning for comprehensive anti-discrimination law a cornerstone of its advocacy at international fora."[16]

Although each country had various types of anti-discrimination measures on their law books, in most instances, very few cases challenging racial discrimination ever made it into the courts. Most existing national laws were therefore deemed deficient by interested observers, who characterized them as "dead letters." The NGOs thus pursued three main types of reforms, inspired by the experience of other countries, especially that of Great Britain, with more elaborate anti-discrimination legal regimes. First, they sought a specific set of legal innovations. These included a shift in the burden of proof that would favour complainants[17] and liberalization of the requirements for *locus standi*, "legal standing," i.e. the right to pursue a case in court. Typically, only aggrieved *individuals* can pursue legal action. Members of the SLG, as well as other commentators (Bell 1997, 30; Forbes & Mead 1992, 24), believed it was critical to provide NGOs with legal standing so that such organizations might directly support or represent victims of discrimination, particularly in the more costly and expensive cases involving institutional discrimination. Prior to the RED, this issue of standing was a national rather than a Community issue.

Second, NGOs sought additional policies that would facilitate what Charles Epp has called "support structures for legal mobilization" (1998, 3). These support structures include "rights-advocacy organizations, rights-advocacy lawyers, and sources of financing, particularly government-supported financing" (Epp 1998: 3). Based upon the experience of particular

---

[16] *ERRC Biannual Report 2001-2002*, p. 11 accessed at http://www.errc.org/Biannual_index.php on 18 July 2004.

[17] In 1997, a Directive was issued that reversed the burden of proof in cases of sex discrimination.

countries, such as Great Britain,[18] proponents of anti-discrimination legislation advocated the creation of "an independent public body, in each state, specifically responsible for the provision of legal and financial assistance to individuals who feel they have been the victim of discrimination" (Bell 1998, 27). Such independent bodies are thought especially useful in facilitating "strategic litigation" as a means of "maximis[ing] the impact of individual cases" and developing the law where it is unclear or ambiguous (Bell 1998, 29). The third set of reforms involved empowering the state to promote positive action, known as "affirmative action" in the U.S., in order to address indirect, or institutional, discrimination. These types of polices already existed, to varying degrees, in Great Britain and the Netherlands, but for most member states they would constitute a significant change.

The Terms of the RED

The RED is comprised of a lengthy preamble, twenty-eight paragraphs that articulate its genesis and rationale, followed by nineteen Articles that set forth its specific terms. In this section, we discuss important points in the preamble and identify three main sets of reforms mandated by the RED, namely the definition of discrimination, the scope of the directive's coverage, and the requisite enforcement structure.

The preamble begins by observing that "the Treaty on European Union marks a new stage in the process of creating an ever closer union among the peoples of Europe,"[19] a union "founded on the principles of liberty, democracy, respect for human rights and fundamental freedoms, and the rule of law."[20] It asserts that racial and ethnic discrimination threaten the attainment of EU objectives, among them those of "social cohesion and

---

[18] In addition, Northern Ireland (Commission for Racial Equality, est. 1997), Belgium (*Centre pour l'Egalité des Chances et la Lutte contre le Racisme*, est. 1993), the Netherlands (Dutch Commission for Equal Treatment, est. 1980, responsible for racial discrimination since 1994), and Sweden (Ombudsman for Ethnic Discrimination, est. 1986) have independent public bodies. Bell distinguishes those from the Danish Board for Ethnic Equality and the Finnish Advisory Board for Refugee and Migration Affairs on the grounds that the latter combat discrimination writ large rather than assisting individual victims of discrimination (Bell 1998, 77).

[19] Para. 1, RED..

[20] Para.2, RED.

solidarity."[21] The RED recognizes a "right to equality before the law and protection against discrimination for all persons," both of which are enshrined in a number of United Nations and European instruments.[22] It asserts that "the development of democratic and tolerant societies" requires anti-discrimination measures that "go beyond" access to employment, the traditional sphere of EU regulation.[23] The RED can thus be seen as a polity-building instrument, but it is one with limits. Although it protects TCNs from racial or ethnic discrimination, it "does not cover differences of treatment based on nationality" and does not affect "provisions governing the entry and residence of third-country nationals and their access to employment and to occupation."[24] This is a significant omission, one that was contested by most NGO representatives[25] but was ultimately essential to member state acceptance of the RED.

Article 2 of the RED defines racial and ethnic discrimination along four lines. First, discrimination can be *direct*, meaning that a person "is treated less favourably than another is, has been or would be treated in a comparable situation on grounds of racial or ethnic origin." Or, second, it can be *indirect*, "where an apparently neutral provision, criterion or practice" would particularly disadvantage persons of a racial or ethnic origin vis-à-vis other persons, "unless that provision, criterion or practice is objectively justified by a legitimate aim and the means of achieving that aim are appropriate and necessary." Third, *harassment* also constitutes discrimination. It is defined as "unwanted conduct related to racial or ethnic origin" that occurs "with the purpose or effect of violating the dignity of a person and of creating an intimidating, hostile, degrading, humiliating or offensive environment."[26] Lastly, instructions to discriminate, which most frequently arise in relation to employment placement agencies, are also deemed to constitute discrimination.

The scope of the RED is set forth in Article 3. It encompasses "both the public and private sectors, including public bodies," in relation to a list

---

[21] Para. 9, RED.
[22] Para. 3, RED.
[23] Para. 12, RED.
[24] Para. 13, RED. See also Article 3(2).
[25] See Patrick Yu and Isabelle Chopin, "Introduction" in Isabelle Chopin and Jan Niessen (eds.), *The Starting Line and the Incorporation of the Racial Equality Directive into the National Laws of the EU Member States and Accession States* (London: Commission for Racial Equality), pp. 5-6, 6.
[26] Article 2(3), RED.

of specified areas. These include access to employment, including promotion, working conditions, pay, and dismissals; access to vocational training, membership and involvement in professional, workers', or employers' organizations; social protection, including social security and healthcare; social advantages; education; and, access to goods and services, including housing. Moreover, the principle of equal treatment continues to apply "even after the relationship in which the discrimination is alleged to have occurred has ended."[27] Aside from its general inapplicability to discrimination based upon nationality, the RED permits differential treatment in two instances. With regard to employment, Article 4 provides for racial or ethnic distinctions where, "by reason of the nature of the particular occupational activities concerned or the context in which they are carried out," a racial or ethnic characteristic "constitutes a genuine and determining occupational requirement, provided that the objective is legitimate and the requirement proportionate." More generally, Article 5 permits member states to deviate from "the principle of equal treatment" in order to maintain or adopt "specific measures to prevent or compensate for disadvantages linked to racial or ethnic origin."

The RED requires the creation of a national enforcement framework. Aggrieved individuals must be given access to judicial and/or administrative procedures,[28] and they must be protected by law against adverse consequences, i.e. "victimization," as retribution for availing themselves of those procedures.[29] Recognizing the difficulty of proving discrimination—for example, in 2001 only 16% of racial discrimination cases brought before Great Britain's employment tribunals were successful—Article 8 shifts the burden of proof from the complainant to the respondent once sufficient evidence has been presented to establish a presumption that discrimination has occurred.[30] In successful cases, complainants must be entitled to sanctions that are "effective, proportionate and dissuasive."[31] The Directive also legitimates institutional support for complainants. Member states must permit "associations, organizations or other legal entities" with "a legitimate interest" in

---

[27] Article 7(1), RED.

[28] Article 7(1), RED.

[29] Article 9, RED.

[30] See Barbara Cohen, *Executive Summary on Racial Equality Directive, State of Play in the United Kingdom* (30 September 2003), accessed at http://www.stop-discrimination.info/fileadmin/pdfs/Reports/Reports_on_Racial_Equality/RacialEqualityReport_UK.pdf.

[31] Article 15, RED.

ensuring compliance with the RED to "engage, either on behalf of or in support of the complainant, with his or her approval," in enforcement proceedings.[32] More generally, they must "encourage dialogue" with such NGOs.[33] Finally, Article 13 provides for the creation of a national institution devoted to promoting equal treatment, conducting research on discrimination, and "providing independent assistance to victims of discrimination in pursuing their complaints."[34]

Member states were required to enact the foregoing reforms, as well as to abolish unlawful discrimination from their laws, regulations, and administrative provisions and render null and void unlawful discrimination from provisions included in a set of private rules,[35] by 19 July 2003. Five countries were initially placed in infringement proceedings with the ECJ by the European Commission at the end of 2004 for failing to transpose the Directive into national law: Germany, Luxembourg, Greece, Austria and Finland. These countries have slowly complied; Germany, for example, finally transposed the RED into national law in 2006 (EU Commission 2006: 7-14; Green 2007, 107; Lavenex 2006, 1288). To monitor compliance, states are required to report every five years to the Commission on their progress, which will be taking place next year (2008). The RED represents a significant development as it involves issues of race, immigration, and European integration, all of which can serve as lightening rods within national politics. Whereas the push for laws prohibiting sex discrimination was driven by labour market considerations (Bell 2002, 8-9, 30), the adoption of the RED in 2000 was largely driven by an elite reaction to Joerg Haider's rise to power in Austria (Geddes & Guiraudon 2004; Lavenex 2006, 1290). As such, it represents a rejection of radical right demagoguery and a new commitment to fostering greater "social cohesion and solidarity" in the face of demographic shifts attributable to immigration.[36] The RED essentially promotes the adoption of a model of legal protection that recognizes and penalizes racial discrimination in the areas of social protection, housing, education, and associations, as well as in employment. In terms of its reach into the non-state sphere, it thus represents a significant advance in European

[32] Article 7(2), RED.
[33] Article 12, RED.
[34] Article 13(2), RED.
[35] Article 14(a) and 14(b), RED.
[36] Anna Diamantopoulou, "Fighting Discrimination: from Theory to Practice," Italian Presidency Conference (21 July 2003).

integration. Further, reaching beyond employment, it recognizes the socio-cultural dimension of racial and ethnic discrimination.

Although its proponents frequently note that the RED enjoyed the support of over 400 NGOs, the directive was nevertheless *not* a response to a large-scale movement comparable to the civil rights movement in the U.S. The development of the RED was mainly driven by nongovernmental legal elites well versed in anti-discrimination law and policy. By contrast, governmental representatives in the negotiations were far less informed about their own country's existing laws as well as the implications of the RED. This is not, however, to say government officials did not know what they were doing in adopting the RED. For the NGOs, the RED represents an opportunity to pursue long-term interests in sociopolitical change, whereas for government representatives, it represented a short-term, and largely symbolic, fix to a nasty diplomatic problem. Partisan politics also played a role in the passage of the RED. The presence of a large number of social democratic governments in the European Council in 2000 was another important factor that led the directive's passage.

Although members of the SLG did not get everything they wanted out of the RED, it does represent a major departure for most EU countries. It has forced countries like France, which had primarily relied upon a criminal law approach, to make major changes to the way they approach anti-discrimination policy. France has, however, succeeded in getting the appropriate legislation passed and a new quasi-governmental organization (High Authority on the Fight Against Discrimination and for Equality – HALDE) to deal with issues of discrimination was in place as of May 2005. This marks a potentially monumental change in that country's approach to immigrants and discrimination.

In the years since the passage and subsequent adoption of the RED, anti-discrimination has continued to be an important topic. While no new directives have been adopted, 2007 has been designated as the European Year of Equal Opportunities for All. The Commission hopes to build on the success of the RED with the goals of further combating discrimination and making equal treatment a reality for everyone in the EU (EU Commission 2006, 7; EU Commission 2007).

Conclusion: The Impact of Supranationalism on Immigration and Integration Policy

Is the European Union playing a role in immigration policy and in policies to integrate immigrants? A look at overall immigration policy would suggest that only small inroads have been made, with a heavy bias towards security and restriction. However, the case of the RED demonstrates that despite resistance to particular measures, opportunities can open for the passage of directives that lead to greater supranationalism and immigrant rights and freedoms. Clearly the Council has resisted measures which would lead to any kind of expansiveness in the area of immigration policy; however, it is possible for measures that give greater rights to immigrants may succeed, leading to "spillovers" in other areas of immigration politics. The political nature and timing of the RED were crucial in its passage, and the lower visibility of the issue may also have played a role. In general, the nature of anti-discrimination policy may lead one to think that it has less impact on the sovereignty of nation states than policies related to asylum or illegal immigration. However, one difference may be that the "threat" of anti-discrimination policy (to national politicians) is less immediate than that of immigration policies, since court cases which might make the issue salient to the public will take time to work their way through the European judicial system. This time lag has been identified as a key causal mechanism by which the European Union gains "creeping sovereignty" under the radar of oblivious national governments (Pierson 1996; Stone Sweet and Caporaso 1998)

Thus far, however, the EU has often played a marginal role in immigration politics, and it is difficult to see major changes occurring in the near future, for the freedom of movement of TCNs or easing of restrictions on asylum seekers. Even the EU's bold new "blue card" scheme applies only to a narrow category of highly skilled workers and will probably be subject to a large degree of national discretion. However, with the Lisbon Treaty instituting majority voting in the Council and an EP veto on immigration policy, and as the European Court of Justice begins to play a greater role in the development of anti-discrimination policy, it is possible that TCNs will eventually gain an increased level of rights regardless of country of residence. These rights, if granted, will lead to cracks in the current restrictions on free movement of persons, and put the issue of anti-discrimination policy higher on the public agenda. Of course, like any other EU issue, this may provoke a public backlash. As immigration policy is determined more and more at EU level, perhaps the politicians in Brussels will be forced to openly adopt populist measures to stem a new wave of far-Right voting. In October 2009 a collection of far-Right parties formed an alliance in the European Parliament. Thus far, however, Brussels has been able to maintain a relatively liberal and pro-immigrant orientation, in spite of Europe's consistently xenophobic public opinion.

The Plan of the Book

The remainder of Part One is devoted to the topic of immigration and anti-discrimination policy being made at EU level, and the causes and effects of EU-level policy in domestic politics.

In the next chapter, Maarten P. Vink attempts to determine whether and how "Europe" actually influences national immigration policies. To do so, he analyzes how European asylum and citizenship policies have affected domestic policies in the Netherlands. Vink thus investigates how relevant European requirements found their way into domestic legislation in a more or less technical manner, and he determines to what extent Europe was a decisive factor in solving domestic policy issues. The main argument is that even though both cases show a broad European process of convergence, and plausible mechanisms of Europeanisation can account for domestic changes, counterfactual reasoning is necessary to prevent us from overestimating the significance of the European factor.

In Chapter Three, Alexander Caviedes looks at the increasingly important topic of immigration for skilled labour migrants. Caviedes argues that while something of a "best practice" has emerged in Europe around the concept of Canadian-style "points" systems, which award points to migrants based on skills, education and other desirable characteristics, this utilitarian system has not been compatible with the philosophies of most continental European countries. A series of brief case studies of the varying fortunes of the UK, Germany, the Netherlands, and Austria highlights why certain countries adopted a version of the points model, while others struggle politically to integrate such a policy. This struggle is mirrored in the policy initiatives that have been advanced at the European level as well. Following the survey of the national policies, Caviedes considers EU policy in this area, from the ignominious demise of the open method of coordination (OMC), to the more focused "Blue Card" program. The chapter closes with an explanation of why this latest EU initiative remains somewhat modest in its promise.

Chapter Four turns to the politically contentious issue of how EU countries coordinate the management of refugee and asylum-seeker flows and settlement. Eiko Thielemann finds that the distribution of asylum seekers and refugees in European countries appears highly inequitable. Moreover, earlier attempts at EU burden sharing in this area have not been particularly effective. From this starting point, Thielemann shows how this limited effectiveness stems from specific shortcomings in the institutional design of existing EU burden sharing instruments. However, even a far-reaching reform of the existing instruments, even though it should be welcomed, is unlikely to achieve the objective of equalizing responsibilities across Member States in this area. Thielemann argues strongly that the EU needs a more comprehensive burden-sharing approach. He proposes that such a new approach should be based on a new conception of burden sharing which entails both reactive and proactive elements.

The final chapter in Part One, by Meng-Hsuan Chou, looks at a relatively hidden category in EU labour markets; namely, those working in the sex trade. To what degree has the EU's promotion of free movement for labour been extended to these underground sectors? Chapter Five takes stock of this development and advances the proposition that the evolution of European integration has contributed to increasing the levels of global inequality by marginalizing those already at the economic and political fringes of society. Chou argues that such an outcome directly contradicts the democratic ethos underpinning the unification project and should be cause for concern. Using the example of sex workers, Chou demonstrates how EU member states' efforts to "manage" migration flows contributed to increasing the vulnerability of non-EU migrants who are sex workers within an internally borderless Europe. While recent developments at the supranational level confirmed that there has been a concerted effort to address the growing divide between "insiders" and "outsiders", these endeavours face multiple challenges. Hence, the chapter concludes by considering ways that the EU and its member states could narrow the inequality gap through a three-pronged strategy consisting of "universal principle, comprehensive policy and good practice".

Part Two of the book turns to the politically controversial issues of Islam, xenophobia, and how the politicization of religious and ethnic diversity affects immigrant integration policies.

In Chapter Six, Raymond Taras looks at the degree to which European secularism drives xenophobia, i.e. whether anti-migrant attitudes are part of—and not distinct from—a more general EU antipathy towards religious groups of any kind. To answer this question, Taras considers the cases of Islamophobia in France, "Orthodoxophobia" in Poland, and "sectophobia" in Russia. In the individual cases, he asks whether all Muslims in France have been re-defined as "strangers", whether Russia's past brutal occupation of Poland has produced Polish antipathy towards Eastern Orthodox minorities, and whether recent Russian hostility to largely Protestant American missionary groups operating in the country arises from a more general dislike of religiously-defined Western foreigners. Taras reviews a variety of data to find that French Islamophobia is driven by a dislike of the Islamic faith that has become politically salient over the past two decades. Social constructions of the migrant and foreigner are inspired by the conviction that Islam and its followers are alien to France. However, Islam is not necessarily repudiated because it is not Catholicism. Taras concludes with the insight that minorities, migrants, and missionaries espousing different religious beliefs regularly face hostility in countries such as Poland and Russia. But proposing secularism as the antidote is facile, for a secular godless Europe is equally capable of becoming one of fear, intolerance, and hatred of the "other".

Kathryn L. Gardner remains in the theme of religion in Chapter Seven, looking at how Europe's governing structures have shaped and moulded the rise and politicization of a "Euro-Islam". Gardner departs from the conventional wisdom that pre-existing church-state relations in European countries determined the level and degree of accommodation of Muslim needs. Her analysis accounts for changes in how the government has viewed their domestic Muslim population and "problem" over time, by tracing the history of policy toward Muslims in two cases, Great Britain and France, and providing evidence that religion was not the primary focus of governments. Muslims were not defined initially or primarily by their religious characteristics – they were foreign, non-European, and different. It was not until the late 1980s and early 1990s that the category of "Muslim" gained a high level of resonance both as an identity marker for the population and as a political category. Nor did Church-state legacies exert a similar level of influence across cases; in France, church-state relationships were predominant, particularly the concept of *laïcité*, while in Great Britain, the Labour government modelled its policy response on its race relations framework.

In Chapter Eight, Alessandra Beasley Von Burg offers a view of Islam's "place" in Europe from the standpoint of normative political theory. Drawing upon Hannah Arendt, Beasley Von Burg describes why the EU is uniquely positioned to contribute to the understanding and possible solution of the Muslim "problem", on both the backdrop of their vision of unity, equality and respect of difference, and for the several institutional efforts to reach out to the Muslim population. The analysis separates the spheres of understanding Muslim private and public space, positioning religion as an individual matter that needs not be hidden but can be used as motivation to reach out to others and recognize what is common. Beasley Von Burg also addresses the need for both spheres to create opportunities for the permanence and continuity of culture and religion. Finally, the chapter concludes with a redefinition of multiculturalism as a multiplicity of people and ideas, so that they may come together for their commonalities rather than differences, to recognize that what appears different is often not, so that EU institutions, the member states, their citizens and others around the world listen to multiple Muslim voices and do not silence what it is often misrepresented as one uniform group.

Bihter Tomen's chapter, Chapter Nine, focuses in on the case of France, looking at the interplay between identity and state policy in issues such as the headscarf debate. Tomen first conceptualizes the notion of identity, which is often used carelessly in the literature, and thus requires a clear definition. Tomen then discusses the emergence and significance of national identity. The relationship between French national identity, Jacobinism and secularism is analyzed in detail to demonstrate how the cultural practices of minorities are limited. Tomen then explores the limits of cultural pluralism within the French education system and in society. Lastly, the chapter points out how definitions of integration and assimilation are used interchangeably in France, and why this disposition is closely linked to the Jacobin, republican political culture.

The final chapter in Part Two looks at the European country perhaps most marked by the aftermath of September 11th and the new furore over Islam: the Netherlands. Willem Maas begins Chapter Ten with the observation that by the 1990s, the Netherlands had become famous as one of the few countries whose public policies reflected a genuine commitment to multiculturalism. Then, within the space of a few years we saw terrorist attacks and war in Afghanistan and Iraq, an anti-immigrant politician assassinated and his upstart political party posthumously becoming the second largest in parliament, a filmmaker murdered gruesomely, repressive policies causing asylum applications to plummet and the best-educated non-western immigrants leaving the Netherlands. Maas uses citizenship policy as a test case, since the complete toleration of dual nationality in the Netherlands resulted in large-scale naturalizations, peaking at over 80,000 in 1996. The openness towards dual nationality then waned, and policies once again became more restrictionist. By 2009, naturalization was more difficult, dual nationality had become more restricted, and new laws even made it possible to strip individuals of their Dutch citizenship for engaging in activities such as terrorism. However, the increase in the numbers of residents of the Netherlands who hold both Dutch nationality and one or more foreign nationalities is significant: from barely four hundred thousand (2.6% of the total population) to over one million (6.4% of the total population) in the space of twelve years. Because only Dutch citizens can vote, this means that roughly 6.7% of the Dutch electorate now holds more than one nationality. At least partially because of the extreme proportionality of the Dutch electoral system, issues relating to citizenship and nationality can be expected to remain sensitive.

The book's final part, Part Three, compares countries on the policies they use to integrate immigrants. Most importantly, the authors in Part Three lay out theoretical frameworks and case studies that can help guide future studies of immigrant integration.

The chapter by Jacobs et al. reminds us that measuring immigrant origin or ethnicity is not as easy as some may suspect, and that this shortcoming hinders integration efforts. The chapter studies how immigrant background and immigration-related ethnicity are measured by national statistical institutes in European countries. The scope of the chapter is restricted to an exploratory study of the existence (and non existence) of official definitions and related usages. Applications of statistical data on foreign origin and ethnic background have strong implications for both politics and academic research. The authors close by reflecting on the question of what kind of data should be collected in the future.

Hubert Peres then asks whether national "models" of immigrant integration are still pertinent as focal categories of analysis. In assessing the persistence of national integration models, Peres argues that we must distinguish between the specificity of the frames, the range of policies involved, and the "national" feature. In this perspective, the chapter asks whether the convergence of paradigms of integration policies in Europe mean that they are less connected with the idiosyncratic nature of national identities and politics. To answer this question, the study focuses on the cases of Britain, France and Spain. First, Peres reviews the different national models in these countries. Then he demonstrates that there is both a convergence of paradigms and a resilience of national idiosyncrasies and identities, a phenomenon which seems to limit the consequences of rhetorical changes on policies and demands.

In Chapter 13, Jeannette Money presents a general theory of citizenship politics. According to Money, although there is no unique definition of citizenship, most researchers would agree that, in the contemporary context of (nation) states, citizenship offers a set of rights and responsibilities to individuals who meet the criteria. And these rights may be more or less distinctive from the rights of non-citizens. Money argues that politicians evaluate the costs and benefits arising from these definitions and modify citizenship laws accordingly. In other words, the incentives that politicians face in making citizenship access easier or more difficult vary based on potential gains deriving from obligations that citizens must fulfil, and the costs that these gains represent in terms of rights offered. The important element of this definition is that the set of rights and responsibilities varies across countries, as does the treatment of citizen and non-citizen, thus providing the basis for a generic theory of citizenship change.

In Chapter 14, Elizabeth M. Wright analyzes the interplay between federalism and immigration policy in the case of Spain. Wright argues that in a federal system like Spain's, political actors at the central and sub-central levels of government face important political costs and benefits by centralizing or decentralizing certain aspects of immigration policy—specifically, sub-central actors seek to gain control over policies dealing with the social integration of immigrants for both economic and "nation"-preserving reasons (language, culture, identity, etc.), while central actors seek to gain control over policies dealing with immigration control (borders, visas, work permits, security). Wright uses the Spanish case to argue that there are important reasons for the nation-preserving aspect of the theory taking the lead in Spain as opposed to the economic, market-preserving aspect. The Spanish division of responsibility of the different classifications of immigration policy is more firmly rooted in nation-preserving motivations because of the historical, cultural, and linguistic particularities of the individual regions within the federation.

Finally, Jacqueline S. Gehring closes out the book with an intriguing comparison across the Atlantic, asking whether France is following an American trajectory of race relations. Gehring proposes that the 2005 riots in France, and their fallout, were not the only events in France that are similar to historical experiences in the United States. Instead, the chapter argues that there are a number of similarities between current developments in French racial policy and the development of American racial policy in the 1960s and 1970s. By considering some of the similarities and differences between the French and American experiences, Gehring sheds light on current debates in France over the efficacy of new anti-discrimination institutions, as well as the possible development of other policy changes.

Works Cited

Bell, Mark. 1997. *EU anti-discrimination policy: From equal opportunities between women and men to combating racism.* Brussels: European Parliament Directorate for Research.

—. 1998. *EU anti-discrimination policy: From equal opportunities between women and men to combating racism.* Brussels: European Union DG12 Public Liberties Series No: LIBE 102 EN.

—. 2002. *Anti-discrimination law and the European Union.* Oxford: Oxford University Press.

Burnett, Victoria. 2007. To curb illegal immigration, Spain offers a legal route. *The New York Times* [Online]. 11 August. Available online at: http://www.nytimes.com/2007/08/11/world/europe/11spain.html [11 August 2007].

Cohen, Barbara. 2003. *Executive summary on Racial Equality Directive, state of play in the United Kingdom.* 30 September. Available online at: www.stopdiscrimination.info/fileadmin/pdfs/Reports/Reports_on_Racial_Equality/RacialEqualityReport_UK.pdf

Economist, The. 2007. In search of an immigration policy. 2 June. 383(8540): 54.

Epp, Charles R. 1998. *The rights revolution: Lawyers, activists, and supreme courts in comparative perspective.* Chicago: University of Chicago Press.

EU Commission. 2006. *Equality and non-discrimination: Annual report 2006.* Luxembourg: Office for Official Publications of the European Communities. Available online at:

www.ec.europa.eu/employment_social/fundamental_rights/pdf/pubst/poldoc/annualrep06_en.pdf [5 October 2007].

—. 2007. 2007-European year of equal opportunities for all [website]. Available online at: www.ec.europa.eu/employment_social/eyeq/index.cfm?language=EN [12 October 2007].

Euractiv.com. 2005. EU immigration, asylum and visa policy. (2005). Available online at: http://www.euractiv.com/Article?tcmuri=tcm:29-117508-16&type=LinksDossier [27 January 2005].

—. 2007a. Parliament backs EU 'blue card.' 27 September. Available online at: www.euractiv.com/en/justice/parliament-backs-eu-blue-card/article-167135 [1 October 2007].

—. 2007b. Illegal immigration, asylum and border control. 24 April. Available online at: www.euractiv.com/en/justice/illegal-immigration-asylum-border-control/article-117508 [11 August 2007].

—. 2007c. EU toughens stance on illegal-immigrant employers. 18 May. Available online at: www.euractiv.com/en/security/eu-toughens-stance-illegal-immigrant-employers/article-163851 [11 August 2007].

European Parliament. 2001. 13-movement and residence of EU citizens. *Official Journal of the European Communities* C 135: 44.

Forbes, Ian and Geoffrey Mead. 1992. *Measure for measure: A comparative analysis of measures to combat racial discrimination in the Member Countries of the European Community.* Equal Opportunities Studies Group University of Southampton 1992, Research Series No. 1

Geddes, Andrew. 2000. *Immigration and European integration: Towards Fortress Europe?* Manchester: University Press.

—. 2003. *The politics of migration and immigration in Europe.* London: Sage.

Geddes, Andrew and Virginie Guiraudon. 2004. The emergence of a European Union policy paradigm amidst contrasting national models: Britain, France and EU anti-discrimination policy. *West European Politics* 27(2): 334-53.

Givens, Terri E. and Adam Luedtke. 2004. European Union immigration policy: Institutions, salience and harmonisation. *Policy Studies Journal* 32(1): 145-65.

Givens, Terri E. 2007. Immigrant integration in Europe: Empirical research. *Annual Review of Political Science* 10: 67-83.

Green, Simon. 2007. Divergent traditions, converging responses: Immigration and integration policy in the UK and Germany. *German Politics* 16(1): 95-115.

Groenendijk, Kees. 2004. Legal concepts of integration in EU migration law. *European Journal of Migration and Law* 6: 111-26.

Guiraudon, Virginie. 2000. European integration and migration policy: Vertical policy-making as venue shopping. *Journal of Common Market Studies* 38(2): 251-71.

Ireland, Patrick. 2004. *Becoming Europe: Immigration, Integration and the Welfare State*. Pittsburgh: University of Pittsburgh Press.

Kubosova, Lucia. 2007. New Europeans ready to join Schengen passport-free zone. *EU Observer* [Online]. 4 September. Available online at: www.euobserver.com/9/24688 [5 September 2007].

Lahav, Gallya. 2004. *Immigration and Politics in the New Europe: Reinventing Borders*. Cambridge: University Press.

Lavenex, Sandra. 2006. Towards the constitutionalisation of aliens' rights in the European Union? *Journal of European Public Policy* 13(8): 1284-1301.

Lindstrom, Channe. 2005. European Union policy on asylum and immigration. Addressing the root causes of forced migration: A Justice and Home Affairs policy of freedom, security and justice? *Social Policy & Administration* 39(6): 587-605.

Mahony, Honor. 2007a. EU to propose 'blue card' for skilled immigrants. *EU Observer* [Online]. 14 September. Available online at: www.euobserver.com/9/24761 [24 September 2007].

—. 2007b. French deputies tighten immigration rules. *EU Observer* [Online]. 20 September. Available online at: www.euobserver.com/9/24802 [24 September 2007].

Moravcsik, Andrew. 1998. *The choice for Europe: Social purpose and state power from Messina to Maastricht*. Ithaca: Cornell University Press.

Niessen, Jan. 2001. The further development of European anti-discrimination policies. In *The starting line and the incorporation of the Racial Equality Directive into the national laws of the EU member states and accession states*, ed. Isabelle Chopin and Jan Niessen, 7-21. London: Commission for Racial Equality.

Oates, Wallace E. 1999. An essay on fiscal federalism. *Journal of Economic Literature* 37: 1120–49.

Pierson, Paul. 1996. The path to European integration: A historical institutionalist analysis. *Comparative Political Studies* 29(2): 123-63.

Spongenberg, Helena. 2007a. Lisbon stops legalization of immigrants after avalanche of applications. *EU Observer* [Online]. 31 August. Available online at: www.euobserver.com/9/24668 [5 September 2007].

—. 2007b. Spain and Portugal seek common EU immigration policy. *EU Observer* [Online]. 4 October. Available online at: www.euobserver .com/844/24917 [4 October 2007].

—. 2007c. EU states could do much more for immigrants, says report. *EU Observer* [Online]. 15 October. Available online at: www.euobserver .com/9/24973 [16 October 2007].

Stone Sweet, Alec and James A. Caporaso. 1998. From free trade to supranational polity: The European Court and integration. In *European Integration and Supranational Governance*, ed. Wayne Sandholtz and Alec Stone Sweet, 92-133. Oxford: Oxford University Press.

Tiebout, Charles M. 1956. A pure theory of local expenditures. *Journal of Political Economy* 64: 416-24.

van der Klaauw, Johannes. 2004. The future common asylum system: Between a closed-circuit and an open-ended scheme? In *Justice and Home Affairs in the EU: Liberty and Security Issues after Enlargement*, ed. Joanna Apap, 235-58. Northampton: Edward Elgar.

Velluti, Samantha. 2007. What European Union strategy for integrating migrants? The role of OMC soft mechanisms in the development of an EU immigration policy. *European Journal of Migration and Law* 9(1): 53-82.

Vucheva, Elitsa. 2007. EU sees numbers of asylum seekers drop. *EU Observer* [Online]. 8 October. Available online at: www.euobserver. com/9/24923 [9 October 2007].

Wallace, Helen, William Wallace, and Mark A. Pollack. 2005. *Policy-making in the European Union* (5th ed.). New York: Oxford University Press.

CHAPTER TWO

EUROPEAN INTEGRATION AND DOMESTIC IMMIGRATION POLICIES: CONVERGENCE, CAUSALITY AND COUNTERFACTUALS

MAARTEN P. VINK

Europeanisation

How do various processes of European integration, in the European Union as well as the Council of Europe, impact on domestic immigration policies, and how can we measure such a "Europeanisation" effect? This chapter relates closely to what has become known since the late 1990s as the research agenda of "Europeanisation" (cf. Green Cowles *et al* 2001; Featherstone and Radaelli 2003; Vink 2003; Graziano and Vink 2007). This new research agenda has enriched the field of European integration studies in at least two dimensions. First, not only has a 'Europeanisation' focus added a distinctively comparative perspective to a field that was previously dominated strongly by IR approaches (see Hix 1994; Mair 2004). Second, we also see much more explicit questioning of the substantial changes that are often attributed to European integration processes, as well as theorizing on the mechanisms through which such changes might occur (see e.g. Knill and Lehmkuhl 2002; Börzel and Risse 2003).

Scholars thus go to great lengths to explain the differences in transposition rates of European directives in EU member states (e.g. Börzel 2002; Mastenbroek 2004), and domestic implementation processes are characteristically studied in great detail in such fields as environmental policy (Haverland 2000) or transport policy (Héritier *et al* 2001). More generally on Europe's impact on political systems, another branch of studies focuses on wider changes in the 'organisational logic of national politics and policy-making' (Ladrech 1994: 70; cf. Börzel 1999; Harmsen 1999; Schmidt 1999; Falkner 2001). Moreover, scholars increasingly study aspects of national politics that have traditionally been assumed less subject to European influence, such as party systems (Mair 2000) or political parties (Ladrech 2002). Here we can now also see studies on the Europeanisation of immigration policies (Favell 2000; Guiraudon 2001; Givens and Luedtke 2004), or on migration-related policies of asylum (Lavenex 2001; Thielemann this volume) or citizenship (Checkel 2001; Vink 2001). Finally, it has become common wisdom that processes of Europeanisation are not restricted to EU member states, but also take place in non-members Switzerland and Norway (Mach *et al* 2002; Brochman and Lavenex 2002), in candidate countries like those of Central and Eastern Europe (Goetz 2001; Grabbe 2001), as well as in countries from neighbouring regions like the Mediterranean area (Pastore 2002).

As for the domain of immigration, the claim that national immigration policies are increasingly subject to external influences from an ongoing process of legal, socioeconomic and political integration between European countries will not raise many eyebrows. Not only do dynamics of human rights proliferation and internal market-building pose an ever stronger constraint on national autonomy over the domestic control of the entry and residence of non-nationals, but moreover states are increasingly formulating a common response towards the challenges related to the movement of persons across borders. Within the European Union (EU), as one of the four key freedoms, the free movement of workers/persons has been established in an expanding body of secondary legislation since the 1960s in order to guarantee a functioning internal market –thereby limiting possibilities for preferential treatment of national citizens vis-à-vis Community nationals. As for border controls, the communitarisation of immigration and asylum policy by the Treaty of Amsterdam, as consolidated by the Lisbon Treaty, has given a strong impetus to the development of legal instruments at the Community level. Outside the European Union, the construction of a human rights regime within the Council of Europe (CoE) has provided a very important external constraint of national policies vis-à-vis non-citizens.

But how to determine whether and how "Europe" actually influences national immigration policies? In this chapter I present a study of how European policies with regard to asylum and citizenship have affected domestic policies in the Netherlands. These empirical analyses focus on

Dutch legislation as well as parliamentary debates in the 1990s. I investigate how relevant European requirements found their way into domestic legislation in a more or less technical manner and determine to what extent Europe was a decisive factor in solving domestic policy issues. In the two case studies presented in this chapter I thus present in more detail not only the technical domestic implementation of European provisions but also the analyses of how 'Europe' affects political opportunity structures as well as, more substantially, the political inclusion of citizens and non-citizens (see Maas in this volume for a broader discussion of Dutch citizenship and integration policy). My main argument is that even though in both cases empirical data show a broad European process of convergence, and plausible mechanisms of Europeanisation can account for domestic changes, counterfactual reasoning is necessary to prevent us from overestimating the significance of the European factor (see Vink 2005 for a more extensive account of the impact of European integration on domestic immigration policies in the Netherlands).

Some Methodological Concerns

In doing empirical research on the case of the Netherlands, my research methods consisted of analyzing policy proposals, legislative texts, and judicial rulings -both European and national; studying parliamentary proceedings; and interviewing key domestic actors. Before going to the actual empirical evidence from the Netherlands, there are some important methodological questions that demand specific reflection with regard to determining the linkage between European and domestic events, in other words with regard to the crucial issue of *causality*. Three aspects of the research strategy need to be clarified with regard to methodology and causality: case selection, reliability and counterfactuals.

Case Selection

This chapter presents a study of Europeanisation in the case of the Netherlands. But what can we conclude on the basis of this one case? What makes it worthwhile bringing to the attention of more generalized discussions? First of all there is the empirical interest of in-depth description of a process of Europeanisation in a policy field where national states are, at most, only hesitantly giving way to Europe. There has been abundant attention for developments in immigration policy at the European level (see e.g. Koslowski 1998; Kostakopoulou 2000; Geddes 2000) as well as at the domestic level (e.g. Joppke 1998; Van Selm 2000;

Marshall 2000; Green 2001). Yet apart from important studies on the conceptualization of mechanisms of change in the field of immigration (see Favell 1998; Guiraudon 2000; Checkel 2001), there is still relatively little systematic empirical research on how European developments 'hit home' at the national level (see e.g. Lavenex 1999 and Jileva 2002 on migration policy in Central and Eastern Europe; Lavenex 2001 on refugee policy in France and Germany; and Guiraudon 2001 on migration control policies in France, Germany and the Netherlands). Secondly, and although it is often seen as a problem to draw general conclusions on the basis of only one case, a case study allows for broader conclusions beyond the limited scope of the specific case under scrutiny (King *et al* 1994: 43-46).

Particularly in those studies that are known as theory-infirming and theory-confirming case studies, single cases may be used to test propositions derived from established generalizations (Lijphart 1971: 692). One may think of a *crucial* case where 'it must be extremely difficult, or clearly petulant, to dismiss any finding contrary to the theory as simply "deviant" (…) and equally difficult to hold that any finding confirming theory might just as well express quite different regularities' (Eckstein 1975: 118). Alternatively, and less extreme with regard to the relevant characteristics of the case, *most-likely* and *least-likely* cases may also serve to invalidate or confirm established generalizations, 'if any cases can be expected to do so' (ibid.). In this light our case study becomes particularly relevant if we consider the Netherlands as a most-likely case for European integration to have an impact on domestic immigration policies. There are three reasons to do so.

First of all, the Dutch attitude towards European integration might be summarized as 'instrumental supranationalism', due to the fact that the Dutch from the start favoured supranational powers at the European level to support market integration in Europe and to protect the smaller member states against dominance of the larger ones (Harryvan *et al* 2001: 20). Originally foremost with a focus on agriculture, but in the 1990s also strongly supporting monetary integration, the Dutch may be seen as a good example of a small nation whose influence has actually increased rather than decreased through European integration (Andeweg and Irwin 2002: 168; cf. Milward 1994). Secondly, the Dutch legal system has long been characterized by monism, resulting in a general openness of the Dutch legal system towards European legislation. This forces the legislator to great alertness for the question of compatibility of national with European legislation, because there is a real danger that national legislation will not be upheld in national courts. This makes the constitutional setting in the Netherlands optimal for Europeanisation, and should particularly not be underestimated when taking into account European international law as deriving from the Council of Europe and its Court of Human Rights.

Thirdly, besides being generally receptive to external (European) influences, the Netherlands has often taken a positive or even a proactive attitude towards European integration in the field of immigration policy. This is particularly the case for asylum policy, where Dutch governments have consistently tried to push for more European integration, as exemplified by its successful initiative in 1998 for the institution of a High Level Working Group on Asylum and Migration (HLWG). The Netherlands has also supported the change towards a more permissive attitude on multiple nationality in the Council of Europe, by actively promoting the 1993 Second Protocol to the 1963 Strasbourg Convention, and pushed forward the agenda of non-discrimination and equal treatment. It goes without saying that this positive attitude towards European immigration policies does not preclude the fact that the Netherlands may not always live up to European standards, and in fact like other countries it has more than occasionally found itself in defence before the European Commission in Brussels, the European Court of Justice in Luxembourg, or the European Commission of Human Rights in Strasbourg. Yet, more than in other countries such as Britain or France, this may be seen as occasionally cheating the European rules rather than a principal hesitance to play the European game at all.

One could of course object to these arguments that, in fact, much more change can be expected in countries – mainly in the Mediterranean area or in Central and Eastern Europe – with immigration policies that are historically much less pronounced and developed than in the Netherlands. Not only will states with already firmly established policies be more resistant to change, and thus be less receptive to European influences, but vice versa one may also expect new immigration countries to look more quickly to the European level for domestic policy solutions. Yet here one should remember that in as far as we can indeed see a stronger process of Europeanisation in such countries, this is largely to be explained by the 'conditionality' factor, and thus a process of domestic change principally different from the 'normal' politics of Europeanisation (on 'conditionality' see Grabbe 2001). A well-known example is Spain, where in the run up to the country's 1986 accession to the EC, the first immigration law was adopted in 1985 'under pressure to conform to EC legislation that restricted non-EC citizen immigration' (Ortega Pérez 2003: 4; see also Wright this volume). In subsequent years, this quite straightforward European influence became less visible. The extraordinary regularization processes that formed a key aspect of Spain's immigration policy in the 1990s, and in fact still did in early 2005 when the Spanish government 'surprised' other member states with a new regularization announcement, cannot be associated with a direct 'European' influence –it signifies perhaps rather the lack of a strong influence. The still relatively low numbers of asylum seekers in Spain also make asylum policy, one of the key immigration issues at the European level, much less relevant in that country. If European integration should be expected to impact on domestic immigration policies, it should at least be visible in the Netherlands. And, conversely, should there be only limited Europeanisation in the Netherlands, then it is not likely to be more substantial in other countries.

Reliability

The main focus in my study of the Dutch case is on parliamentary decision-making, and in particular on the domestic and European arguments brought into debates between government and parliament on the issues under scrutiny. There are two reasons why I decided to put parliamentary politics at the centre of my analysis. First, the actual output in terms of domestic public policy is explained most directly by looking at the parliamentary debate, in that it is, after all, the national parliament that has to approve new laws. Looking at the arguments used by national MPs in these debates allows measuring the evidence for Europeanisation against the evidence for counterfactual, domestic considerations. Second, because MPs have a clear electoral interest in voicing the concerns of their voters on these debates, the parliamentary debate is a residual of wider societal debates. Thus, focusing on parliamentary politics should also enable us to pin down changing domestic attitudes on these specific issues beyond the mere arena of the parliament. Even though such a perspective is relatively narrow in the sense that it focuses on a very specific part of the domestic political system (and thereby neglects other potentially relevant parts of the system such as policy implementation, interest representation or civic attitudes), it provides a potentially solid ground for empirical research on disentangling the European and national systems that influence a politically contested issue like immigration policy.

The second methodological problem concerns the *reliability* of these sources, particularly with regard to statements made by parliamentarians in plenary debates. In other words, how 'honest' are national politicians when they discuss the importance of European politics? Two points can be highlighted in dealing with this reliability problem. A) It is unlikely that there is a univocal and systematic bias in statements made by politicians towards either underestimating or inflating the European impact on domestic politics. After all, there may at times be an inclination to minimize the importance of 'Europe' in order not to make national politics look irrelevant, but at other times 'Europe' may equally be used as a scapegoat to legitimize unpopular policy decisions. B) In order to look beyond merely rhetorical arguments, the reliability of statements made by parliamentarians in plenary debates can be checked by looking at the consistency with previous lines of argument, and also by pushing the actors in interviews to clarify their position on specific policy issues and debates. With regard to the decisive European influence in these political debates, and foremost because politicians often refer to the straightforward legally binding effect of European legislation, one can precisely assess such claims more objectively by looking at the specific legal provisions and jurisprudence on an issue.

Counterfactuals

This is, of course, exactly where the real difficulty of measuring Europeanisation begins. The crucial methodological problem of all Europeanisation research, that of causality, is after all particularly acute in a policy domain as immigration where many European instruments and initiatives are *not* legally binding, and where it is often very difficult to assess the decisive effect of European integration for domestic policy change (or at least has been so far). Thus even when we are able to formulate an elegant theory of soft Europeanisation, which is a prerequisite for any convincing causal explanation of policy change, the empirical question is yet to be answered of whether domestic changes would not have occurred in the absence of European integration. In other words, *counterfactual reasoning* is in my view a vital part of any research strategy on complex issues such as these where a large number of variables interact and a whole policy sector is our unit of analysis; it helps to strengthen our argument by controlling for other potentially important variables (Haverland 2004: 4). But how to construct a good counterfactual?

By its very nature, because a counterfactual in essence is a thought experiment, one could object that we are on slippery ground here with this kind of hypothetical reasoning. How can we know what would have happened if we leave out the European element, and wouldn't we find ourselves in a completely different –and incomparable- situation without the presence of the process of European integration? This may be true, indeed, yet one very important criterion for a compelling counterfactual is that we 'should rewrite history as little as possible' (Haverland 2004: 5). We might, for example, assume that the London Resolutions on manifestly unfounded applications were not adopted by JHA ministers in 1992, and wonder whether Germany would nevertheless have managed to construct its ´asylum compromise´, but if we reason from a scenario where the European Union as such would be absent our hypothetical situation would become too speculative. Moreover, the same critique of being too hypothetical can perhaps be said to apply also when we rely too much on a theoretical – and thus also hypothetical- construct to explain domestic policy change without finding the necessary 'key evidence' to convince the jury. What we often see here is that 'Europe' is attributed a vital importance because European countries have been moving in the same – often restrictive – direction. Hence the empirical evidence is then a process of convergence that assumes an explanatory role for one common variable: the European element. We see this in the field of asylum policy, but also for example in the field of citizenship policy where 'Europe' (in this case mainly the Council of Europe) is attributed a liberalizing role on such issues as dual nationality and citizenship for second-generation immigrants. In the latter case, a liberal trend common to all or many European countries is often used as key evidence for a causal link between European and domestic policy change (see e.g. Groenendijk and Heijs 2001: 162-164; cf. Hansen and Weil 2001: 13). The problem here is that *convergence* can be a consequence of European integration, but it must not be used synonymously with Europeanisation because there is a difference between a process and its consequences (Radaelli 2003: 33). European regimes may be converging, as in the case of citizenship policies, however not as a result of initiatives emanating from Brussels, but as a response to domestic considerations (Freeman and Ögelman 1998). Counterfactual reasoning can thus help to prevent making the mistake inherent in Europeanisation research of overestimating the explanatory power of the European variable.

In the following two sections I will illustrate these methodological considerations by going into the cases of asylum policy and citizenship policy: two cases where we clearly see a process of convergence between European countries, but where in my view it is equally problematic to attribute (too) much significance to the European factor. In both cases I will only briefly set out the background of the policy domain and with a view to limited space assume a basic knowledge of the European and domestic developments in this field (for more on asylum policy, see Thielemann in this volume, and for more on citizenship policy, see Money in this volume). I will then concentrate, first, on showing how indeed one can make a good case for Europeanisation on the basis of commonly applied theoretical notions combined with empirical data; and, second, by going into more empirical detail on my Dutch parliamentary debates, show how counterfactual scenarios in both cases make a strong Europeanisation explanation hard to sustain.

Asylum Reform

As a consequence of disparities between European countries, in terms of severely divergent relative numbers of asylum applications per country over the past twenty-five years, the need for burden-sharing is one of the driving forces behind asylum co-operation in the EU (cf. Suhrke 1998; Thielemann this volume). The most direct forms of burden-sharing are sharing people and sharing resources. Thus one can think of a redistribution of asylum seekers along a distributive key based on such criteria as population size or GDP (Suhrke 1988) or, alternatively, of financial compensation of main receiving countries for taking a disproportionately high number of asylum applications (Schuster 2000: 129). In the EU such direct mechanisms of burden-sharing are highly contentious and the available instruments related to this form of burden-sharing – the Temporary Protection Directive and the European Refugee Fund– are of minor importance in terms of effectively influencing a redistribution (see Thielemann in this volume). More indirectly, however, burden-sharing could also be achieved through harmonisation of European asylum policies. Burden-sharing would then be conceived as the sharing of norms. 'Harmonisation is seen particularly by Germany and Sweden as a means to ensure burden-sharing –a "fairer" distribution of asylum seekers around Europe, or at least a fairer sharing of the financial burden' (Schuster 2000: 129). Precisely because of this underlying redistributive logic, however, harmonisation has always been less attractive to countries with traditionally less developed asylum systems. The result is quite well-known, namely that European asylum co-operation has been driven by a minority of countries only (in particular Germany, Sweden, the Netherlands), and that states were mostly forced to implement unilateral solutions. Under the unanimity rule of the Maastricht Treaty, European asylum co-operation was limited to lowest common denominator policies, which were often non-binding (joint positions) or not very effective (Dublin Convention). Yet, as Lavenex (2001: 863; emphasis added) argues, even these 'minimal' policies were not without results: "Although the idea of establishing a system of burden-sharing at the EU level continues to encounter strong opposition from several Member States, domestic reforms in the main refugee-receiving countries and the coming into force of the Schengen and Dublin conventions have led to a redistribution of asylum seekers 'by default'. (...) Coupled with the restriction of formerly liberal asylum provisions in the main receiving countries, *these measures have changed the relative shares of asylum-seekers in Europe*."

More implicitly, the Dublin Convention –later replaced by the Dublin Regulation- together with some non-binding resolutions may be considered as an attempt to legitimize a restrictive policy changeover in the EU member states. 'Though the ratification of the Dublin Convention was a slow and difficult process, now that it has come into force, its significance in terms of burden-sharing is growing' (Schuster 2000: 129). At a more informal level, with regard to 'discouraging' asylum shopping, the most relevant instruments enacted under the third pillar are two 1992 Council resolutions, which were largely inspired by Germany, and by now have seemingly found their way into most domestic asylum policies. These so-called 'London Resolutions' argued that domestic 'asylum policies should give no encouragement to the misuse of asylum procedures,' and substantially redefined the idea of refugee protection. When asylum-seekers travel through transit countries where they could have claimed asylum (safe third countries), they are excluded from the asylum procedure altogether (Bunyan 1997, doc. 26). And, when asylum seekers originate from countries in which there is generally no serious risk of persecution (safe countries of origin), their applications are considered 'manifestly unfounded' (Bunyan 1997, docs 27-28). It is often argued that European support contributed to the resolution of German difficulties to cope with an ever growing stream of asylum seekers. Shifting the blame to Europe allowed the SPD to agree in the 1992 asylum compromise, and the Constitutional Court to approve of the necessary constitutional amendment (Lavenex 2001: 862; cf. Marshall 2000: 91; but see Koslowski 2000: 162). Hence it is the sharing of, admittedly rather soft, norms that potentially leads to a process that could be termed 'implicit burden-sharing' (Vink and Meijerink 2003).

Figure 2.1 Distribution of asylum applications in EU15 (1985-2007)

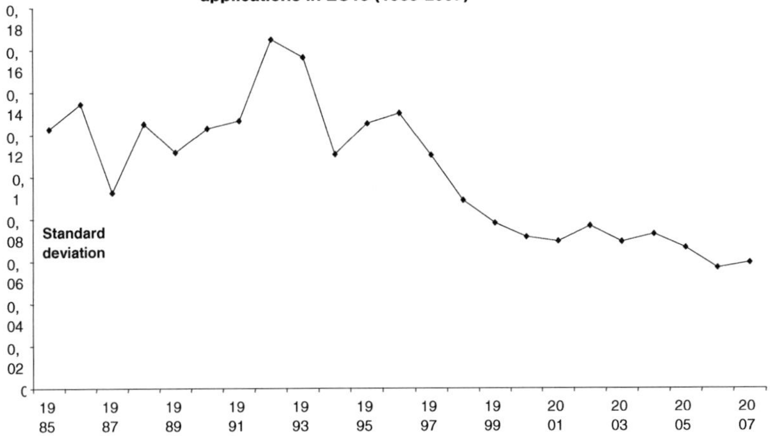

Source: Eurostat

So much for the mechanisms of Europeanisation, but what about the data? First, in order to determine whether there is indeed a common process of convergence between EU member states, we can look at the distribution of asylum seekers in terms of numbers of asylum applications per country. In order to correct for the increase of the total number of applications over time, we divide all annual numbers of applications per country by the aggregate number of applications in the EU15 in that year. This results in the proportional distribution of applications in the EU per year (note that, for this example, we use absolute number of applications per country per year and do not correct for country size). We then use the standard deviation as a very straightforward measure of dispersion to indicate to what extent the asylum burdens of all fifteen member states are converging. The results presented in Figure x.1 show an unequivocal picture: after a peak in 1992, visualizing Germany´s share of over 65% of the total asylum ´burden´ for the EU15 countries, the overall trend is clearly one of decreasing disproportionality in the distribution of asylum applications.

The second –and crucial– empirical question would subsequently be whether we can indeed explain this changed distribution of asylum applications over time by a "European" effect? Can we see this indeed as evidence for a process of Europeanisation of asylum policy? When studying the Europeanisation of Dutch asylum policy, can the redefinition of asylum policy in the mid-1990s in the Netherlands by way of a Safe Countries of Origin Act (1994) and a Safe Third Countries Act (1995) be viewed as being the result of Schengen/Dublin co-operation? Despite clearly resonating with the two 1992 London Resolutions, which specify the principles of manifestly unfounded applications, the link between European and domestic policy is far from straightforward. In fact, after studying the explanatory notes and parliamentary proceedings from that period, it becomes clear that the Dutch (restrictive) policy shift was basically a reaction to similar changes in Germany, rather than the institutional adaptation to European policy. Both the Safe Countries of Origin Act and the Safe Third Countries Act explicitly, and almost exclusively, refer to the respective German terms of *sichere Herkunftsstaaten* and *sichere Drittstaaten*.

In 1993 and 1994, in contrast with decreasing numbers in Germany, the number of asylum seekers in the Netherlands increased significantly. Dutch MPs fearing 'asylum-tourism' explicitly demanded that Dutch policy would not deviate from German policy. The government explains in the explanatory note to the Safe Countries of Origin Act that 'in order to counteract forum-shopping of asylum seekers (…), Dutch legislation must connect as closely as possible to the asylum legislation of the Federal Republic of Germany on this point' (*Tweede Kamer* 1993-1994, file 23588, no. 3, p. 1). An explanatory note to the Safe Third Countries Act is equally unambiguous: 'The most important intention of the introduction of a regulation concerning safe third countries was to improve the connection with the German asylum policy, in order to end in this way the phenomenon of 'asylum-shopping' in the direction of the Netherlands' (*Staatsblad* 1995, no. 356, p. 3). These explicit references to Germany, together with the almost complete ignorance of the London resolutions, are striking for two reasons: first, given the fact that in general the Dutch attitude towards more European asylum co-operation has been very proactive. Second, it is noteworthy to the extent that in the literature it is widely accepted that the London Resolutions, although not legally binding, have been very influential (cf. Lavenex 2001).

The same kind of 'domestic' considerations can be seen again during the adoption of the Aliens Act 2000, which was a matter of much political prestige for the governmental coalition, and revised the asylum system. The detailed enshrining in the 1998 government coalition agreement, long before the actual plenary debate in parliament in June 2000, of a compromise between the traditionally more permissive (social-) democrats on the one hand, and the more restrictive liberals on the other, indicates the political salience of the matter. The stakes were apparently too high to allow dissent within the government coalition to surface. In fact, opposition parties complained loudly, for example in the words of a Green MP, of a 'pre-arranged' debate which left little room for meaningful discussion (*Handelingen Tweede Kamer* 1999-2000, no. 83, p. 5347). This bargaining is probably also reflected in the outcome where, simply said, the liberals achieved a more efficient system (one status) with early distinction between real refugees and bogus asylum seekers, reduced safeguards and a tougher expulsion policy, and the social democrats achieved a maximum to the period of uncertainty for applicants and a uniform status after three years. For as much as the international environment was relevant for this compromise, it is hard to see a strong, if any, influence of European policies on the outcome in substantial terms. Rather, and similar to the case of the safe countries in the early 1990s, the fear of being more 'generous' than neighbouring countries clearly dominated the discussions and confirmed that the idea of a common European asylum system did not hit home, yet.

With regard to the decisiveness of the European argument in domestic political debates, the evidence from the Netherlands thus points at the importance of asking the counterfactual. In other words, what would have happened without European integration? What if –during the 1990s- the ‘soft’ (yet restrictive) European norms would not have been there? Although this hypothetical question is by nature difficult to answer, looking closely at the domestic argumentation between government and legislature suggests that in the case of the Netherlands the decisive criterion for restricting the access to asylum procedures for asylum seekers from safe countries of origin and, particularly, safe third countries in 1993 and 1994 had everything to do with reacting to Germany's policy change. In more general terms, one could say that –due to increasing numbers of asylum applications– we would surely also have seen an intensified policy competition between countries that would have inevitably also have lead to more restrictive policies being enacted across Europe (or at least in the main receiving countries).

One final caveat is necessary, though. In the Dutch case we saw that the government in the end did not really need Europe to ‘get away with’ restrictive policies because the need to ‘do something’ was shared at least among a parliamentary majority (and more contested in the early 1990s than in the late 1990s). In the German case, however, this *could* of course have been different, particularly because the 1993 constitutional amendment required a qualified majority and thus the support of the parliamentary opposition. Hence, even though in the German case there is much to say for the counterfactual idea that the extremely high number of asylum applications in 1992 induced a wide support to restrict policies, the European 'justification' might have been crucial for the domestic about-face of the social democrats –and thus indirectly also for policy change in the Netherlands. It is important to see here that –somewhat contrary to the Europeanisation literature– Europe actually becomes more important exactly *because* of a strong 'domestic veto point' (cf. Risse et al 2001: 9).

Citizenship Reform

My second case is the European impact on domestic policy regarding citizenship acquisition. I take the question of whether or not to allow applicants for naturalization to retain their original nationality as a test-case for Europeanisation. This dilemma on whether or not to permit "dual nationality" was at the centre of a long-lasting parliamentary debate in the Netherlands. The comprehensively revised Dutch Nationality Act only entered into force in 2003 after more than a decade of discussions. As a considerable number of "European" arguments were brought in the discussion pro and contra the principle of multiple nationality, the attempt to reform the Nationality Act provides us with an interesting case to study the Europeanisation of citizenship policy.

I concentrate here on the 'European' impact of the Council of Europe. In addition to its involvement with human rights issues in general, the Council of Europe has also dealt more specifically with issues relating to nationality since the 1960s. In particular the Convention on the Reduction of Cases of Multiple Nationality and on Military Obligations in Cases of Multiple Nationality (Strasbourg, 1963) should be mentioned here as a key legal instrument for the international coordination of citizenship policies. The 1963 Convention aims at reducing the number of people with a multiple nationality and reflect the idea –broadly accepted at the time- that nationality should be the recognition of a fundamental link between the individual and the political community, endowing the state with the duty to protect the interests of its citizens and the individual with the duty of loyalty towards the state. However, nowadays, nationality is increasingly seen as a medium to obtain access to the labour market and social security, whilst on the other hand military service is increasingly being abolished across Europe. The so-called 1993 Second Protocol signalled a fundamental change in the European attitude towards multiple nationality. It became widely accepted that, from the perspective of both the individual and the host state, the acquisition of nationality may be crucial for a person's integration in society, even when retaining the nationality of origin. Three new paragraphs were added to Article 1 of the 1963 Convention making exceptions to the rule of one nationality for second-generation migrants, spouses of mixed marriages, and their children.

This 'liberal' line was continued in the European Convention on Nationality (ECN) that was signed in Strasbourg on 6 November 1997. With respect to multiple nationality the ECN is neutral; it neither obliges nor forbids signatory states to demand applicants for voluntary naturalization to give up their former nationality. Although the ECN respects that 'each State shall determine under its own law who are its nationals' (Article 3(1)), it explicitly aims at a harmonisation of nationality laws of its member states. Some commentators note a striking correlation between processes of liberalization of citizenship policy at both the European as well as at the domestic level: 'The Second Protocol (...) allows states to adopt a more liberal attitude towards dual nationality for spouses and children of mixed marriages and second-generation migrants, and this has strongly influenced the [Dutch] parliamentary debate on the issue in recent years. A similar effect [was] expected of the new Convention on Nationality, adopted by the Committee of Ministers of the Council of Europe in November 1997' (Groenendijk and Heijs 2001: 163). The Council of Europe as a forum where national representatives regularly meet to exchange information, particularly in the Committee of Experts on Nationality, could well be an explanation for such convergence. According to Hansen and Weil (2001: 13), 'such meetings (…) provide venues for the sharing of ideas and experiences among member states (…). Although its precise causal effect cannot be proven, the thinking of participants cannot but have been affected by the experience.'

Given the fact that the Council of Europe is often depicted as being not much more than a 'talking club', one would however need to ask the counterfactual question of what would have happened without Council of Europe involvement (cf. Checkel 2001: 192). In other words: how decisive is international, and particularly European, coordination in the field of citizenship policy for the explanation of domestic policy changes? Recent comparative work also shows that despite a converging trend between countries, with regard to the acceptance of dual citizenship, great differences persist in terms of birth-right based acquisition of citizenship. Moreover, the introduction of new civic integration tests and the tightening of residency requirements make it impossible to speak of a unidirectional liberalization trend (Howard 2005; Goodman Wallace 2010; Vink and De Groot 2010; and see also Money in this volume).

Equally, in terms of actual acquisition of citizenship by resident non-nationals, European states display great variation. The average percentage of resident non-nationals that acquired the citizenship of one of the fifteen old EU member states in the period 195 to 2004 ranges between less than two percent in Germany, Greece, Ireland, Italy, Luxembourg and Portugal to more than five percent in the Netherlands and Sweden (Waldrauch 2006: 298-299).

So how does this play out in a domestic context? Particularly in a case such as the Netherlands, where citizenship policy has indeed been liberalized in the 1990s seemingly in line with changing European norms, but changing government coalitions have also contributed to liberal and restrictive policy changes, a more detailed look into domestic debates is the only sane basis for more conclusive insights in the entanglement of European and national events. The constraints posed by the 1963 Strasbourg Convention and the 1993 Second Protocol are a central concern throughout the parliamentary debate on citizenship in the Netherlands. Parliamentary proceedings and appendices often refer to these European norms from the Council of Europe, which can surely be seen as a sign of relevance. This European side of the parliamentary debate revolves around the question whether the 1993 Second Protocol allows or even demands neglect of the 1963 Strasbourg Convention by abolishing the rule of one nationality. The Dutch government had anticipated the Second Protocol and the consequent shift in European norms by the permissive citizenship policy it had undertaken since 1992. This policy was similarly based on the idea of integrating non-national residents more fully in society by allowing naturalization without asking them to give up their original nationality.

When talking about Europeanisation in this case the first important caveat is the fact that there were essentially different views on dual nationality between leftwing and rightwing political parties. From the five largest parliamentary factions in the period 1989-2002, the Social-Democrats (PVDA), the Democrats (D66) and the Greens (Groen Links) were in favour of multiple nationality; the Christian Democrats (CDA) and the Liberals (VVD) were against. Generally speaking, the first view sees naturalization as an *instrument* in the process of integrating migrants in society, where it is assumed that without possessing formal citizenship migrants will never fully integrate in society. The latter view sees naturalization rather as the *award* of being well integrated, and argues that without giving up their former citizenship migrants are allowed as it were to have the best of both worlds and will never fully integrate in the host society. These two essentially different views remind us that parliamentary debates about dual nationality always refer to a more general debate about how to integrate migrants in the host society.

From interviews it appears that the initial liberal policy shift in 1992 is explained more by a deal that was made between the social democrats and the Christian democrats with respect to non-national long-term residents, rather than by the anticipating impact of the 1993 Second Protocol (see Vink 2005, Ch. 7 for list of interviews). Both the PVDA and the CDA, who formed a government coalition from 1989 to 1994, aimed at societal integration of immigrants, yet had a fundamentally different view on how to achieve that goal as explained above. With regard to voting rights, for example, in the late 1980s long-term residents were given the right to vote for local elections as a means to integrate them more fully in Dutch society. The PVDA wanted to go one step further, however, and proposed also giving long-term resident non-nationals the right to vote for national elections. The CDA strongly opposed extending suffrage to non-nationals in national elections and committed itself to a compromise. A less restrictive citizenship policy would still make it easier for immigrants to participate more fully in Dutch society, because as Dutch nationals they could vote for national elections, without necessarily 'devaluing' national citizenship by making its traditional prerogatives less exclusive.

So were European-level developments in the Council of Europe not relevant at all for domestic citizenship policy changes in the Netherlands? In order to study that question more closely we need to look at the actual parliamentary debates on the formal amendment of the 1985 Nationality Act, as proposed by the 1993 government bill, and see how the 'European' arguments were used. A first contextual point of crucial political importance is that the 1993 government bill was not actually dealt with in parliament before 1995. By that time the Christian democrats were no longer part of the government coalition with the social democrats. After the elections of 1994, the coalition was formed by PVDA, VVD and D66.

The liberal VVD had always been fervently against the principle of multiple nationality. Consequently the government bill depended crucially on the support of the CDA, which it got in the Lower House, perhaps because the Christian democrats felt responsible as 'spiritual father' of the bill (it was introduced by the Christian democratic Minister of Justice Hirsch Ballin in 1993). However, in November 1996, it appeared that the bill could not count on the support of the CDA in the Senate. The Christian democratic senators felt free to oppose the government bill as they were, and had always been, against the principle of multiple nationality and saw fundamental difficulties with the 1963 Strasbourg Convention. In their eyes the government bill simply went too far because the 1993 Second Protocol only argues for exceptions to the rule of one nationality and not for a new rule of multiple nationality. Moreover, the Christian democrats had become much more sceptical on the whole about the process of integrating immigrants into Dutch society.

Despite the fact that the Second Protocol was ratified by the Netherlands in 1996, the Dutch government could not get enough parliamentary support to formalize the permissive policy that had been undertaken since 1992, and had to withdraw its bill. The 1991 circular, putting the renunciation demand on hold, was also abrogated in 1997. In setting the terms of the parliamentary discourse the Council of Europe has played an important role, but it could not decisively direct Dutch citizenship policy one way or the other. This could only be explained by the fact that the Council of Europe altered the strategic behaviour of domestic actors, but not their preferences. The preferences of MPs towards multiple nationality have remained stable throughout the 1990s and the policy shift that lasted from 1992 to 1997 was only possible because of a political compromise made between the social democrats and the Christian democrats. The PVDA tried to gain from the momentum and push through a reform bill of the 1985 Nationality Act. Thereby they relied heavily on the Second Protocol, which was clearly seen as a strategic opportunity to influence citizenship policy in a more permissive direction; or rather, as an opportunity to legitimize the policy shift *post hoc*. The 1963 Strasbourg Convention has, however, been used as a strategic opportunity by the parties preferring the principle of one nationality. Due to this unresolved conflict between the 1963 Convention and the 1993 Second Protocol, there was *de facto* autonomy for the national legislature.

The attempt to "Europeanise" Dutch citizenship policy thus derailed on the conservative unwillingness to abandon the principle of one nationality.

The counterfactual question, of whether domestic (liberal) changes would also have happened without the mechanisms of 'policy learning' through the involvement of political and bureaucratic elites within the framework of the Council of Europe, has to be answered negatively –tentatively at least. The Dutch case is a good illustration of how changing domestic coalitions are probably the most decisive factor for changing domestic citizenship policies throughout the 1990s (cf. Joppke 2003). Particularly on such a politically contested issue as dual citizenship, it is crucial to know which parties actually are in the majority in parliament (see Money and in this volume, for a comparable account based of German case).

Conclusion

In the cases of asylum and nationality in the Netherlands we saw that although European policies and norms were surely relevant they did not decisively affect domestic politics. This limited European impact was explained by the opportunity structure that particularly focused on Germany for 'burden-sharing' reasons (asylum), and by the fact that domestic support for dual nationality disappeared after the about-turn of the Christian democrats in the Senate, or after a change of government, for that matter (nationality). Even though in both cases we can determine a European process of convergence, and also mechanisms of Europeanisation can be theoretically specified, the counterfactual question of what would have happened without specific European involvement warns us not to overestimate the role of "Europe".

When thinking about counterfactual explanations for domestic change, one unmistakable trend is of course demographic change. In the Netherlands, not atypical for many other countries in this respect, post-war decolonization, labour migration from the 1960s, and increased numbers of asylum seekers since the 1980s literally altered the face of the population. Declining birth rates together with economic growth certainly constituted important pull factors for such migration, but other root causes or facilitating factors may be seen in cheaper intercontinental transportation, new modes of communication, and the power vacuum and political disorder around the globe after the end of the Cold War.

These changes in the structure of populations are mirrored by changes in the political system that occurred more or less apart from processes of European integration, by means of reactive attempts to control and dam the 'influx' of immigrants, but also more positively by recognizing the increased diversity in the population. To put it in more dramatic terms, host societies were forced to rethink and redefine the nature of their citizenship. In the 'affaire du foulard', for example, a row about wearing headscarves at school challenged the idea of '*laïcité*' underlying the French republican notion of citizenship (see Tomen this volume). In the Netherlands, undoubtedly with greater conviction than in most European countries, full attention was given to the agenda of minority integration since the late-1970s. In 1986 this resulted, for instance, in the right to participate in local elections for non-nationals residing in the country for at least five years. The introduction of dual nationality in the early 1990s that would make it easier for immigrants to integrate fully in Dutch society (as they would not have to give up their former nationality) may also be seen as a core aspect of the Dutch minorities policy.

Such changes in the political system were clearly seen, by some at least, as part of an unavoidable process of undermining the institution of national citizenship (Soysal 1994; Jacobson 1996). With guestworkers and their offspring becoming increasingly part of host societies, but at the same time retaining links with their countries of origin, for instance via marriage, education and military service, there is indeed an unmistakable transnational element in contemporary politics (Bauböck 1994). The standard interpretation of these events follows the idea that global processes of unification, in terms of economy, politics or culture, of which European integration would be viewed as a regional manifestation, result in local particularistic responses (Barber 1995). Following such dialectical views, a community under threat from ongoing immigration and shifting powers to supranational institutions such as the European Union or the Council of Europe is eager to reaffirm its own uniqueness and identity.

True, there are many things going on in Brussels and in Strasbourg that strongly relate to the policy domain of immigration, and particularly with an ever-progressing process of communitarisation of immigration policy, Europe's role in domestic immigration policies will increase. Particularly in the field of asylum policy, we now have a much more developed Common European Asylum Policy, with a whole set of Minimum Directives on procedures, qualification and reception, that together with the Dublin and Eurodac Regulations clearly pose a much stronger external constraint on domestic asylum policies. The Lisbon Treaty, by consolidating *and* completing that process will only strengthen that integration process. Before that, and particularly when looking back at some of the developments in the 1990s that took place within a mainly intergovernmental and non-binding framework, the significance of European integration for domestic policy changes is indeed easily exaggerated. Moreover, when analyzing such changes across Europe in terms of trends and convergence, we could well overemphasize the unidirectional aspect of such processes. In the Dutch parliament, for example, the long-standing discussion on the desirability of dual nationality, which resulted first in the abolition of the traditional prohibition and later in the reintroduction of the rule of one nationality, is a fine example of how changes in societal discourse affect immigration policies. In the wake of the Van Gogh murder many calls were made in cabinet and parliamentary circles to decrease the number of exceptions to the formal ban on dual nationality in Dutch citizenship, and to actively remove the Dutch nationality of terrorists with dual nationality. New government proposals to restrict the occurrence of multiple nationality were being discussed in parliament mid-2009. If this would be a forebode of what is to come in other countries, this could well reverse the liberal trend that we saw during the 1990s –in the Netherlands as well as in Europe. However, with even traditionally restrictive Luxembourg abolishing its renunciation demand in 2009, and introducing new ´double jus soli´ provisions for third generation immigrants, the Dutch debate manifests a reluctance to go along with the broader European trend of accepting double nationality as an unavoidable part of modern societies, rather than signify a reversal of that trend. The lesson for Europeanisation studies: convergence is hardly ever a uniform and uncontested process, and may well result from other factors than a straightforward ´European´ influence.

Works Cited

Börzel, Tanja A. 1999. Towards convergence in Europe? Institutional adaptation to Europeanisation in Germany and Spain. *Journal of Common Market Studies* 37(4): 573-96.

Börzel, Tanja A. and Thomas Risse. 2000. When Europe hits home: Europeanisation and Domestic Change. *European Integration Online Papers* 4(15). Available online at http://eiop.or.at/eiop/texte/2000-015a.htm.

Börzel, Tanja. 2002. Pace-setting, foot-dragging, and fence-sitting: Member State responses to Europeanisation. *Journal of Common Market Studies* 40(2): 193-214.

Bunyan, Tony, ed. 1997. *Key texts on justice and home affairs in the European Union*, Vol. 1 (1976-1993). London: Statewatch.

Checkel, Jeffrey T. 2001. The Europeanisation of citizenship? In *Transforming Europe: Europeanisation and domestic change*, ed. Maria Green Cowles, James A. Caporaso and Thomas Risse, 180-197. Ithaca: Cornell University Press.

Coalition Agreement. 1998. *Regeerakkoord 1998* [only available in Dutch] http://www.parlement.nl/odp/regakko/docs/regak1998-10.html.

Geddes, Andrew. 2000. *Immigration and European integration: Towards fortress Europe?* Manchester: Manchester University Press.

Givens, Terri and Adam Luedtke. 2004. The politics of European Union immigration policy: Institutions, salience and harmonisation. *Policy Studies Journal* 32(1): 145-65.

Goetz, Klaus and Simon Hix, eds. 2000. Europeanised politics? European Integration and national political systems. Special issue of *West European Politics* 23(4).

Goodman Wallace, Sara. 2010. Integration requirements for integration's sake? Identifying, categorizing, and comparing civic integration policies. *Journal of Ethnic and Migration Studies* 36(4), 753-72.

Graziano, Paolo and Maarten P. Vink, eds. 2007. *Europeanisation: New research agendas*. Basingstoke: Palgrave Macmillan.

Green Cowles, Maria, James A. Caporaso and Thomas Risse, eds. 2001. *Transforming Europe: Europeanisation and domestic change*. Ithaca and London: Cornell University Press.

Guiraudon, Virginie. 2000. European integration and migration policy: Vertical policy-making as venue shopping. *Journal of Common Market Studies* 38(2): 251-71.

—. 2001. Seeking new venues: The Europeanisation of migration-related policies. *Swiss Political Science Review* 7(3): 100-06.

Hansen, R. and P. Weil (2001) Introduction: Citizenship, Immigration and Nationality: Towards a Convergence in Europe? In *Towards a European nationality: Citizenship, immigration and nationality law in the EU*, ed. Randall Hansen and Patrick Weil, 1-23. Basingstoke: Palgrave.

Haverland, Markus. 2005. Does the EU cause domestic developments? The problem of case selection in Europeanisation research. *European Integration Online Papers* 9(2), available online at: http://eiop.or.at/eiop/texte/2005-002a.htm.

Howard, Marc Morje. 2005. Variation in dual citizenship policies in the countries of the EU. *International Migration Review* 39(3): 697-720.

Joppke, Christian. 1998. Asylum and state sovereignty: A comparison of the United States, Germany, and Britain. In *Challenge to the Nation-*

State: Immigration in Western Europe and North America, ed. Christian Joppke, 109-52. Oxford: Oxford University Press.

—. 2003. Citizenship between de- and re-ethnicisation. *Archives européennes de sociologie* 44(3): 429-58.

King, Gary, Robert O. Keohane and Sidney Verba. 1994. *Designing social inquiry: Scientific inference in qualitative research*. Princeton: Princeton University Press.

Knill, Christoph and Dirk Lehmkuhl. 2002. The national impact of European Union regulatory policy: Three Europeanisation mechanisms. *European Journal of Political Research* 41(2): 255-80.

Ladrech, Robert. 1994. Europeanisation of domestic politics and institutions: The case of France. *Journal of Common Market Studies* 32(1): 69-88.

Lavenex, Sandra. 2001. The Europeanisation of refugee policies: Normative challenges and institutional legacies. *Journal of Common Market Studies* 39(5): 851-974.

Lijphart, Arend. 1971. Comparative politics and the comparative method. *American Political Science Review* 65(3): 682-93.

Maas, Willem. 2010. Citizenship and Immigrant Integration in the Netherlands. In *Migrants and minorities: The European response*, ed. Adam Luedtke. Newcastle upon Tyne: Cambridge Scholars Publishing.

Marshall, Barbara. 2000. *The new Germany and migration in Europe*. Manchester and New York: Manchester University Press.

Radaelli, Claudio. 2000. Whither Europeanisation? Concept stretching and substantive change. *European Integration Online Papers* 4(8). Available online at: http://eiop.or.at/eiop/texte/2000-008a.htm.

—. (2004) Europeanisation: Solution or problem? *European Integration Online Papers* 8(16). Available online at: http://eiop.or.at/eiop/texte/2004-016a.htm.

Risse, Thomas, Maria Green Cowles and James A. Caporaso. 2001. Europeanisation and domestic change: Introduction. In *Transforming Europe: Europeanisation and domestic change*, ed. Maria Green Cowles, James A. Caporaso and Thomas Risse, 1-20. Ithaca: Cornell University Press.

Schuster, Liza. 2000. A comparative analysis of the asylum policy of seven European governments. *Journal of Refugee Studies* 13(1): 118-32.

Thielemann, Eiko. 2010. The common European asylum system: In need of a more comprehensive burden-sharing approach. In *Migrants and minorities: The European response*, ed. Adam Luedtke. Newcastle upon Tyne: Cambridge Scholars Publishing.

Van Selm, Joanne. 2000a. Asylum in the Netherlands: A hazy shade of purple. *Journal of Refugee Studies* 13(1): 74-90.

—. 2000b. The Netherlands: The few who made it "won't be staying". In *Kosovo's refugees in the European Union*, ed. Joanne Van Selm, 43-66. London/New York: Pinter.

Vink, Maarten P. 2001. The limited Europeanisation of domestic citizenship policy: Evidence from the Netherlands. *Journal of Common Market Studies* 39(5): 875-96.

—. 2003. What is Europeanisation? And other questions on a new research agenda. *European Political Science* 3(1): 63-74.

—. 2005. *Limits of European citizenship: European integration and domestic immigration policies*. Basingstoke: Palgrave Macmillan.

Vink, Maarten P. and Gerard-Rene de Groot. 2010. Citizenship attribution across Europe: International framework and domestic trends. *Journal of Ethnic and Migration Studies* 36(5), 713-34.

Vink, Maarten and Frits G.J. Meijerink. 2003. Asylum applications and recognition rates in EU Member States 1982-2001: A quantitative analysis. *Journal of Refugee Studies* 16(3): 297-315.

CHAPTER THREE

TOWARDS A EUROPEAN MODEL FOR HIGH SKILLED LABOR MIGRATION?

ALEXANDER CAVIEDES

One of the ground stones of the European Economic Community (EEC) at the time of its formation in the latter 1950s was the principle of free movement of labour. This reflected burgeoning widespread labour shortages that, though rooted in the expansion of industrial manufacturing, were manifesting themselves across various sectors including agriculture and mining. Nevertheless, it was not until 1968 that EEC workers could truly exercise this freedom of movement, and instead European countries including EEC members such as Germany, Belgium and the Netherlands, continued to utilize bilateral agreements with Southern European and Mediterranean countries where lagging development created high unemployment. This pattern has remained unchanged, as almost every European country still hosts a higher percentage of non-European Union foreign workers than those from fellow EU countries.[1]

In the era of guest worker recruitment programs, most European governments did not foresee that eventually their need for predominantly unskilled or semi-skilled workers would be eclipsed by urgent skills shortages in areas that only the highly skilled or advanced educated could assuage. However, to characterize the labour migration developments of the last decades as predominantly focused on the highly skilled would be incorrect, since countries have also pursued policies to address labour shortages in the agriculture, food processing, care-giving, and hospitality branches. Following a period of mass recruitment in the 1960s, and a period of relative closure in the 1970s and 1980s, a new paradigm has

---

[1] An example of an industry where a shift from non-EU to EU workers is taking place is dealt with in this volume in the chapter by Chou on sex-trade workers (Chou, "this volume").

developed in which countries target particular types of foreign workers at both the high and low end of the skills spectrum.

National strategies to attract less skilled workers have ranged from continued bilateral agreements to tacit acceptance of undocumented workers, but greater innovation has been necessary in the area of high skilled workers, due in large part to the competition that has ensued among advanced industrialized countries for such workers. In particular, the growth of information technology (IT) has heightened the sense that Europe's future lies in generating a highly skilled workforce. This is reflected by the European Union's (EU) Lisbon Strategy 2000, which had the goal of transforming Europe into the "most competitive and dynamic knowledge-based economy in the world" by 2010. Such rhetoric not only fuels the belief that skills are in urgent demand, but that governments must be prepared to implement various means to ensure the vitality of those sectors employing the highly skilled.

This chapter argues that while something of a 'best practice' has emerged around the concept of points systems, this system has not been deemed compatible with the political economic philosophies of most continental European countries. A series of brief case studies of the varying fortunes of the UK, Germany, the Netherlands, and Austria highlights why it is that certain countries adopted a version of the points model, while others struggle politically to integrate such a policy within their labour migration schemes. The struggle between what seems efficacious and politically acceptable is mirrored in the policy initiatives that have been advanced at the European level as well. Following the survey of the national policies, consideration is given to EU policy in this area, from the ignominious demise of the open method of coordination (OMC) to the more focused Blue Card program, closing with an explanation of why this latest EU initiative remains somewhat modest in its promise.

Attracting Highly Skilled Workers

In advanced industrial countries, policy for bringing in skilled labour has developed along three lines. The first of these has developed parallel with the WTO regime on services. The 1994 Global Agreement on Trade and Services' Annex on Movement of Natural Persons is designed to ease restrictions upon skilled people such as accountants, doctors or teachers. While countries are still free to choose which service sectors to liberalize, and to set qualification requirements, once they do so, such benefits must be extended without discriminating based on country of origin. In practice, this has hastened the proliferation of policies that relax the flow of workers in the upper echelons of multinational corporations through policies that facilitate intra-company transfers throughout most of the world (Lavenex 2006). However, few countries have extended the reach of these policies beyond the highest level of managers or technicians, thus they remain a mechanism for attracting international firms through the promise of allowing them to seamlessly shuttle key personnel across borders, rather than offering a springboard for permanent immigration or a means of filling skills gaps.

To meet such broader economic needs, a second option that countries increasingly resort to are sector-specific policies. A common format is to establish quotas for foreign specialists whose entry conditions are relaxed either through a reduced qualifications review or by bypassing the examination of local labour conditions. Limiting the procedural obstacles to securing work permits allows employers to rapidly access foreign workers in those sectors or occupations where skills shortages have been identified, yet a modicum of government control is maintained through definite limits to the number of permits available. As will be illustrated in the case studies, this option has produced mixed results, sometimes providing swift temporary relief, yet in other instances it has proven inflexible in adjusting to shifting needs or in compensating for national labour market rigidities that reduce the attractiveness of this option.

The third and most radical option is that of the points-system. In its purest form, this system is not limited to only certain sectors or professions, but is open to foreigners who amass a minimum score on a point system that rewards various criteria that can include age, command of the language, professional qualifications, previous work experience, and a minimum salary at their current position. Australia, New Zealand and Canada employ the archetypes of such policies, which sometimes do not even require the applicant to have secured a job offer in the host country. Unlike most sectoral visas that are of limited duration, these programs generally carry the prospect of permanent residence after a probationary period. The idea is that an infusion of young, highly educated or well-experienced immigrants will enrich the national labour market without displacing the local workforce, provided that the qualification criteria are sufficiently rigorous. Unlike sector-specific programs whose prime motivation is to address specific skills shortages, points-systems are generally integrated into a larger immigration strategy through which countries intend to raise the general skills profile and competitiveness of the national workforce. Variations that afford the host country greater control over entry may require a concrete job offer, set numerical limits, be geographically limited, or offer more points for specific enumerated occupations, thus rendering them something of a hybrid between the sector-specific and general high skilled migrant programs. While this model is often held up as somewhat of a benchmark, it often proves difficult to reconcile politically with more regulated labour markets or societies that still have misgivings over whether further immigration is to be encouraged.

National Policy Responses

In Europe the response has been varied. Viewed as a whole, the majority of countries have not engaged in major policy changes, but among those countries that have experience with immigration – especially those that utilized guest worker programs – the common response has been to liberalize the ingress of the highly skilled. In particular, the immigration responses have been triggered by the rapid and uneven expansion of the information technology industry. However, the cases demonstrate that common needs or intentions have not translated into identical programs, and more importantly, contrasting political economic philosophies have produced greater liberalization or policy experimentation in countries with liberal market economies than those designated as coordinated market economies.[2]

[2] Coordinated and liberal market economies are the vocabulary of the 'varieties of capitalism' framework (Hall and Soskice 2001). Essentially, coordinated economies such as Germany or Austria feature more regulated labour markets, greater coordination between firms, and the involvement of the social partners in policy formation and implementation. Conversely, in liberal economies such as the UK or US, labour and financial markets are less regulated, firms transact at arm's length, and the business stance to government policy is more voluntaristic and accomplished though lobbying rather than more institutionalized fora.

The UK: Highly Skilled Worker Programs Sprouting from Sector-Based Initiatives

Beginning in the 1960s, and capped off by the Immigration Law of 1971, the UK moved from a migration system that tolerated labour movements from the commonwealths towards a virtual closure to all unskilled workers. After 1971, permits were only available for employers seeking to employ skilled workers. With the most internationalized information technology sector in Europe, one would expect British firms to take advantage of intra-company transfer policies. While this is true, these internal labour market chains have proven insufficient to meet demand, with the number of permits issued to the computing science industry between 1995 and 2000 increasing almost six-fold from 1827 to 12,726 (Dobson and Salt 2004, 137).

In a bid to provide greater flexibility to the information technology and communications (ITC) branch, in 2000, the Home Office placed several professions on the shortage occupation list, which allows employers to apply for work permits on behalf of foreign specialists without first advertising the position domestically. Moreover, existing postgraduate experience requirements were waived and the duration of the permit was extended by one year to five years. This change was in response to a study published by the ITCE Skills Strategy Group within the Department for Education and Employment – in consultation with sector business and labour organizations – that confirmed increasingly grave skills shortages within the branch (DfEE 1999).

To monitor the needs of the sector, an IT Sector Panel was also established in the government's Work Permits office through which union - Amicus and the Trades Union Conference (TUC) - and employer - Intellect and the Professional Contractors Group (PCG) - representatives could proffer information and arguments. By 2002, the bursting of the 'dot.com' bubble led even some employers to doubt the necessity of work permits when supposedly 26% of the branch was unemployed (personal communication with PCG and Confederation of British Industry (CBI), 2003). A twenty percent decline in permits issued in computer services (Clarke and Salt 2003, 567) made the decision easier for the government, which removed IT jobs from the skills shortage list in 2002.

With the procedures for intra-company transfers remaining intact, large firms did not complain (personal communication with Intellect, 2003), yet the government did recognize continued demand for top-level talent. Understanding the inflexibility of approaches that only liberalize migration in specific enumerated sectors and professions, the government introduced the Highly Skilled Migrant Programme (HSMP) in 2002 that provided a track toward permanent residence for scientists and business and finance professionals rated on a points system, who could enter even without wielding a concrete job offer. Not used extensively by businesses (personal communication with the CBI and Intellect, 2003), there were only 1,300 successful applicants in its first year (TUC 2003). Nevertheless, this limited stream of applicants signalled that initiating a points-system need not trigger large-scale immigration beyond the control of the government.

This has led to the revamping of the labour migration system toward a multi-tiered system whose upper tier employs a points-system to grade an expanded class of professionals including doctors, scientists, engineers, entrepreneurs, innovators and graduates of certain MBA programs. While the top tier is the successor of the HSMP, a second tier retains the shortage occupation option for skilled employer-sponsored applicants. One could argue that by avoiding formal quotas, the new system surrenders a degree of control, but it would be more appropriate to point out that the skills advisory bodies that integrate the input of employers and trade unions in deciding what is considered a shortage occupation retain a degree of control over the process. Further, the experience with the HSMP has given the British government the impression that it can gauge the demand for such permits.

The British labour migration regime for the highly skilled is the most extensive in Europe. The presence of a substantial number of firms engaged in work requiring the highly skilled, together with a less guarded attitude toward labour market economics, has enabled the UK to most closely approximate the policies of the full-blown countries of immigration that were – not coincidentally – formerly parts of the British commonwealth. As the other cases illustrate, most European countries' views of labour market and labour migration regulation are considerably more cautious and incremental.

Germany: The Green Card Fails to Take Root

West Germany had an extensive labour migration experience beginning in the mid-fifties. Millions of guest workers arrived in Germany during the 1960s and 1970s, but this ended in 1973 with the *Anwerbestopp*, or recruitment termination. Similar to the British situation, this signalled the end of non-skilled labour migration save for some seasonal labour in agriculture or hospitality. To hire a skilled foreign worker, employers were required to show that after advertising the position, they could not find a suitable domestic or EU applicant. Those who thought that reunification would solve labour shortages were mistaken, and almost immediately, Germany entered into a series of bilateral agreements with Eastern European countries to bring in mostly unskilled labour.

However, as in the UK, it was the growth of the IT branch that first exposed serious shortcomings with the existing permit system. Given the intense growth of the industry and the rapid fluctuations in what are considered essential skills for its various professions, the standard individualized work permit process was pilloried as being too cumbersome at the dawn of the new millennium. Though German firms make use of intra-company transfer provisions for high-level management and technicians, this only benefits larger companies. With a less internationalized information technology sector than in the British case, numerous small and mid-sized firms were left clamouring for IT specialists.

In February of 2000, no lesser personage than German Chancellor Gerhard Schröder announced the administration's plan to introduce a specialized program facilitating the recruitment of IT workers. Unlike the similar British program, the so-called Green Card program passed that July featured an annual quota of 10,000. Under this relaxation of the standard work permit process, employers were no longer required to demonstrate individual need, and applicants merely needed a two-year diploma in the field, or absent that, a prospective annual salary of over €51,000.

The time between announcement of the policy and its passage into law was short by German standards, illustrating that the measure not only enjoyed the support of employers such as the Federal Union of German Employers' Associations (BDA), Bitkom (representing the IT industry), and Gesamtmetall, but had also received the approval of labour in the form of support from the Federation of Trade Unions (DGB) and IG Metall (personal communication with BDA, Bitkom, Gesamtmetall, DGB and IG Metall, 2003). The need to honour the input of these various interests explains the relatively more rigorous provisions of the German proposal. After two years, less than 70% of the quota had even been filled. While this is due in part to the aforementioned bursting of the global dot-com bubble, it also reflects that for many businesses – especially in former East Germany, which was the destination of only 4% of applicants – the income requirements constitute an considerable constraint (Hillman 2003, 583).

Riding the initial consensus and momentum behind the Green Card, in 2000 the Ministry of Interior announced its intention to further reform German immigration law. A major component of its labour migration aspect was a points system to attract the highly skilled. The proposed law enjoyed the support both of business and labour, as well as other important elements of civil society including churches and academics. However, dissatisfaction from the opposition Christian Democrats concerning some provisions dealing with asylum and deportation derailed the legislation. When the *Zuwanderungsgesetz* finally passed in 2005, the points system was one of its casualties, with the remaining nod to the highly skilled being a provision voiding the necessity of performing a local labour-needs tests in the case of highly qualified scientists, teachers or researchers or specialists and managers whose prospective salaries were at least double the minimum measure used by the public health insurer: €85,000. The law also phased out the Green Card provision itself, which was retired without much comment from employers who had long since come to see that it was not resoundingly successful in attracting computer professionals to Germany.

Business needs in IT are no longer trumpeted as urgently as in the past, yet the current provision has come under increasing attack from the business community as the German economy began experiencing steady growth in 2007 and 2008. The response of the government has been *ad hoc*. In response to severe shortages of engineers, in August of 2007 the government proclaimed that it would ease free movement restrictions for electrical and mechanical engineers from the new Eastern European EU members. This limited adjustment has employers in other industries within the service sector clamouring for more workers (Dempsy 2007). The government response of lowering the income requirements for highly qualified immigrants to €63,600 and to allow East European graduates from German universities to look for work in certain technical professions have met with measured approval, as firms complain that this salary is still well above the industry standard.

In comparison with policy in countries such as Canada or Australia, the Germans have evinced distaste for loosening controls over access to the labour market. While the Labour Ministry flippantly broached placing a points-system back on the drawing board (*Deutsche Welle* 2007), this is not being contemplated in earnest (personal communication with Ministry of Interior, 2008). Instead, the strength of the social partners that generally eschew new infusions of unregulated or simply less-regulated labour will probably ensure that German policy remains conservative, at the most comprising sectoral initiatives.

The Netherlands: Struggling to Compete for the "Top Minds"

Labour migration to the Netherlands has been something of a hybrid between the British and Germany experience. Similar to the UK, many immigrants hail from former colonies, yet this did not prevent the Dutch from utilizing a guest worker system that was terminated in 1974, one year later than Germany's policy.

The growth of jobs in computer services/ICT from 1995 to 2000 was explosive, more than doubling from 47,500 to 115,900 (Kolb et al. 2004, 152). From 1996 to 2000, the number of work permits issued to foreigners in IT rose by over 400% from 414 to 2,209, comprising nearly 10% of all permits issued (Dobson and Salt 2004, 135). This did not satisfy the needs of industry during a time when the industry's growth was at its zenith, especially since Dutch firms have difficulty retaining foreign workers in these branches since Dutch wages are relatively modest and many skilled foreign nationals treat the Netherlands as a proving ground before passing on to more lucrative employment in other countries (OECD 2005). Furthermore, Dutch provisions for inter-company transfers do not extend to workers with technical skills, so that even large firms are relatively more reliant on standard work permits than is the case in Germany or the UK (personal communication with VNO-NCW, 2003).

In 2000, a coalition of the peak employers' association, VNO-NCW, the Federation of Dutch IT Firms (FENIT), and a few individual large firms including Germany's Siemens and the Netherland's own Phillips, began lobbying the government for relief. Citing the EU's Lisbon Agenda, they pointed to the German announcement of the Green Card initiative, in the hope that the Dutch government would also introduce a quota system for foreign IT workers, and that the government would assist business in recruitment through some form of centralized coordination (Interview VNO-NCW). The government's response was almost immediate. As of May 1, 2000, Article 13 of the Aliens law (*Vreemdelingenwet*) was altered to eliminate the existing requirement that employers first engage in a domestic job search for IT workers. A further regulation (the *AD-regeling*) that went into effect on February 22, 2001, exempted employers from the duty to advertise their vacancies for ICT jobs at the higher vocational education level. However, this victory for employers was somewhat short-lived, since the ensuing economic downturn in the IT sector led the government to terminate the program as of January 1, 2003.

Nevertheless, the unique situation of the IT sector was re-affirmed on October 1, 2004, when Immigration Minister Verdonk introduced the knowledge worker regulation (*kennismigrantenregeling*), an accelerated procedure for issuing permits to highly skilled workers. Foreign 'knowledge workers' earning more than € 45,000 (2009: € 49,097) no longer require a work permit and need merely qualify for residence. Recognizing the important role that foreign instructors play in the information technology field, the regulation also considers postgraduates and university teachers under the age of 30 to be 'knowledge workers' if their income exceeds € 32,600 (2009: € 35,997).[3] A special sub-office within the IND is responsible solely for these applications, with the set goal of processing the applications within two weeks.

A half-year into the program, roughly 400 foreigners had taken advantage of the procedure (*Expatica News* 2005) suggesting that if there is truly a dearth of high skilled workers, then it is not at the top wage level, else one would certainly have to expect a greater number of applicants. To suggest that the skills shortage situation in the Netherlands is resolved and that all that remains is some fine-tuning would be incorrect. Even the more restrictionist Minister Verdonk acknowledged that the Netherlands is losing the battle to attract the top minds, and hinted that the Netherlands might consider instituting a points-based system that offers rapid entry and the possibility for permanent residence as incentives (*Dagblad Tubantia/Twentsche Courant* 2004). This has not come to fruition, and the Dutch continue to actively recruit foreign IT talent (*Economic Times* 2009).

[3] Those who obtain their diploma in the Netherlands merely need an annual salary of € 25,800.

The more pluralistic system of interest representation that exists in the IT sector has meant that the employers' greater resources have been parlayed into new policies under which business was afforded access to potentially large numbers of foreign IT specialists. The domestic constraints that are often in place in the form of established patterns of industrial relations are less relevant for highly skilled workers. Nevertheless, with its long processing times, the initial work permit program was not attuned to the needs of the dynamic, internationalized IT branch. In a country like the Netherlands that already possesses a relatively fluid labour market, there is a disjuncture with the expectations of employers and a system of labour migration system that struggles to provide rapid access to workers. The second attempt to draft a policy to meet the needs of employers provided swift processing times, but by reducing the capacity to also generate wage flexibility with its relatively high wage requirements, the program has proven inadequate for comprehensively resolving the skills shortages in the Dutch IT sector, even if some engineers and top-level researchers have been able to enter since they can command such high salaries. Factors such as the relatively lower Dutch wage structure, compared with Germany, the UK or the US, together with the desire of smaller employers to have Dutch-speaking applicants have rendered the knowledge worker provisions rather toothless with respect to the Netherlands' most urgent IT needs.

Austria: Rigidities in the Land of Corporatism

Austrian labour migration initially patterned itself after that of Germany, but Austria exhibits far greater rigor in controlling the entry of foreign workers. While Austrian recruitment of guest workers ended formally with the Foreign Employment Law of 1975 that signalled a return to individual work permits, employers are still able to secure permits for foreign workers fairly easily within a system through which the social partners set annual quotas for individual economic branches or classes of occupations. Under this system, a certain number of permits are always allotted for skilled workers, whose professions are enumerated in federal regulations.

Germany's Green Card program in 2000 triggered similar discussions in Austria. Before this time, computer experts were subject to the general quota allocated to skilled workers, which meant that their access to Austrian labour market was limited, and there were no special conditions facilitating their entry. Already in 1998, employers in the IT sector complained that Austria's 283,400 computer specialists still fell 20,000 workers short of firms' needs (*Der Standard* 2000), and in 1996, the peak business association, the *Industriellenvereinigung* (IV) worried aloud that there were not sufficient possibilities to bring in biotechnologists or computer specialists under provisions that only exempted top-level management from immigration control (Foggensteiner 1996). With one-quarter of all firms facing skilled worker shortages (Leitner 2001), it is clear that Austria has difficulties in producing and/or attracting such workers. Unlike German employers who criticized their own Green Card program for its failure to offer IT workers a long-term perspective, employers in Austria are well aware of the short-term nature of foreign employment in the Austrian high tech branches (personal communication with IV, 2003).

Within a few weeks after the German proclamation of the Green Card program, a joint report from the Austrian market research firm, IDC, and Microsoft prognosticated that within three years a shortage in the order of 85,000 IT specialists would develop (*Der Standard* 2000). With this report in hand, the IV was soon canvassing the Ministry of Economics to develop some manner of labour migration proposal for the IT branch. The response was not long in coming: in August of 2000, the Ministry classified IT specialists as 'key workers' (*Schlüsselkräfte*), meaning that employers seeking a work permit were freed from demonstrating that they had sought such a worker domestically or within the EU. This reduced the processing time for such a permit from four to six weeks. To prevent this program from becoming a tool to undercut local wage demands, key workers must receive a minimum of € 2100 per month, while workers without degrees could only be employed if their monthly salary exceeded € 3240.

Agreement among both employers and unions that there was a skills shortage emboldened the administration to re-allocate 600 permits formerly allotted to refugees from Kosovo or normal work permit applicants to the quota for IT workers in 2001. This number appears minor, yet considering that the total immigrant permits for the year was only 8518 (with the lion's share of 5490 allotted to family reunification), and that in the previous year only 250 applications were made out of a possible 1000, it is a brazen step by Austrian standards. Though in 2001 and 2002 fewer IT workers were brought in than the quotas permitted, firms still insisted that their needs were not being addressed. Frustrated that its attempts to solve the needs of the branch were not having the desired effect of attracting foreign workers, the government reduced its allocation of key worker permits for the year of 2004 (Asamer 2003), and then once again in 2005. While the unions claim that the slack demand proves that employers' claims were unfounded, business continue to protest that shortages persist, but that Austria is simply not proving a sufficiently attractive destination for IT workers (personal communication with IV and WKÖ-IT, 2005). Recognizing that shortages could not be solved in the long-term simply through immigration policy, the peak employers' association, WKÖ, and IV both encouraged the government to invest in higher education, with the WKÖ allocating € 1.5 million to firms that commit to providing internships in the IT field (Unterhuber 2000).

The unparalleled control of the social partners over labour market policy in Austria's strong corporatist configuration has proven to be a double-edged sword in the pursuit of high skilled workers. Attempts to rapidly introduce a large-scale migration program for highly skilled workers foundered due to the presence of a vigilant and sceptical labour movement and the fact that the government is accustomed to incremental changes in labour migration policy that require the consent of both capital and labour. As Germany learned as well, simply having a labour migration policy in place is no guarantee that it effectively meets the exact needs of branches that seek highly educated specialists who are familiar with cutting edge technologies and procedures. While social partner cooperation on labour migration policy has opened the door to sectoral labour migration policies that provide special exemptions for the highly skilled, the rigid, measured nature of labour market policy prohibits any discussion of a points-system in which such control is relinquished. As such, Austrian employers must be content with the negotiated quota systems as the sole mechanism for attracting high skilled workers.

Greater Policy Change at the European level?

While labour immigration policy towards non-EU citizens remains the ambit of national policy-makers, in other related immigration policy areas such as asylum or border enforcement the European Union has begun to develop common policies (Thielemann, "this volume"). As the institutions of the EU accrue greater competences in this area, some see it as inevitable that labour migration will also become subject to common EU guidelines (Stetter 2000). The pattern of policy development in this area is difficult to gauge, since member state attitudes fluctuate from apparent consensus to apathy, but this can certainly not be put down to a lack of initiative from Brussels. Instead, it appears that while member states accept that European level policies in certain areas – usually those having to do with physical borders – enhance national control over migration, there is still doubt whether a European policy would be able to assuage worker shortages to a greater degree than the existing panoply of national policies.

Within the EU, the free movement of workers is mandated by the Treaty of the European Economic Community, and is one of the cornerstones of the European Single Market. However, the status of workers from countries outside the EU remains a nation-state prerogative. Prior to the 1986 Single European Act, there was no EC policy toward third country nationals, and even in its wake, policy has advanced sporadically through a series of directives that have incrementally increased the freedom of movement and other rights of long-term permanent residents. After Maastricht and the Treaty on European Union, immigration policy was limited to cooperation in the areas of asylum and reciprocal recognition of transit visas under the Justice and Home Affairs pillar where decisions require member state unanimity and the European Court of Justice cannot rule on the validity of provisions nor act to enforce them. A necessary step towards a more supranational policy was taken under the 1997 Treaty of Amsterdam, which introduced Title IV on 'Visas, Asylum, Immigration and Other Policies Related to the Free Movement of Persons,' which transferred these areas to the 'first pillar' where EU legislation becomes a possibility. Beyond immigration and asylum, Title IV includes external border controls, visas and other rights of third country nationals. During the first five years, member states and the Commission shared the right of initiative, but the European Council, representing the interests of the individual member states, still had to approve such legislation unanimously. Since 2003, the member states decide whether any of the areas in Title IV will be further "Europeanised" and subjected to the qualified majority voting procedure, but there was no profound qualitative break from the existing EU immigration paradigm. The Lisbon Treaty stands to change this upon entering into force, as Title V's new "Area of Freedom, Security and Justice" promises that the EU will develop a common immigration policy with regard to "the conditions of entry and residence, and standards on the issue by Member States of long-term visas and residence permits," and since this chapter is subject to qualified majority voting, there is no veto (though the UK, Ireland and Denmark can opt out).

The 1999 Tampere European Council concluded with the Presidency announcing that the creation of the EU's new "union of freedom, security and justice" would require a common asylum and immigration policy.[4] The policy was mapped out into four separate elements: partnership with countries of origin, a common European asylum system, fair treatment of third country nationals, and management of labour migration flows. The commission crystallized this proclamation through a general statement on immigration policy and asylum (Commission 2000), and in the following year suggested that in the field of immigration, European policy be advanced through the soft-law coordinative process known as the open method of coordination, or OMC (Commission 2001). The intention was to create a European immigration regime based on coordination, absent the imposition of binding external conditions or quotas. The proposed areas included cooperation with countries of origin and the pooling of information to hinder flows of illegal migration, but given the skills shortages of the time, the real carrot being dangled before the member states was the economic migration component that contemplated establishing a coherent and transparent procedure for accessing the labour market that would be allied to the European employment strategy (Caviedes 2004).

The failure of the Council to act on this communication led to years of inaction regarding labour migration, with the most successful initiatives on migration being those that are instead restrictive in nature (Moraes 2003; Givens and Luedtke 2004). As the individual country cases illustrate, the contraction and plateauing of growth in the IT sector meant that one of the prime motivations for liberalizing labour migration policy had dissolved. The 2005 publication of a Green Paper on managing economic migration signals that the Commission is still interested, and that it is attentive to national trends, since it proposed introducing sector-specific programs or common fast-track procedures to admit migrants in cases of specific labour or skills shortages (Commission 2005).

The latest and most concrete initiative goes by the name of the Blue Card, and picks up the latter logic of the Green Paper, namely the need to address skills shortages. While the Commission's intention as late as spring 2007 was to create various sectoral visas, the focus of the directive proposal of fall 2007 is limited to highly skilled foreign nationals. Lobbying the member states to embrace this initiative, EU Justice Commissioner Frattini pointed out that the EU is being crowded out

---

[4] SN 200/99 (Presidency Conclusions of the Tampere European Council 15 & 16 October 1999).

globally in the competition for skilled workers, 55% of which go to the US, while only 5% have the EU as their destination (Charter 2007). For this reason, while 3.5% of the American and 10% of the Australian foreign workforce are highly skilled, less than one percent falls under that category in the EU (Bilefsky 2007). While many member states have adopted national policies to tackle these skills gaps, the cases of Germany, Austria and the Netherlands are indicative of their modest success. The Commission argues that the key missing ingredients to individual national policies are that they often lack long-term perspectives for those who wish to stay, or conversely, that those foreign workers who desire mobility are not empowered to move freely within the single EU labour market.

The agreement passed by the Council in May of 2009 provides entry for highly skilled foreign nationals, who are then able to circulate throughout the European Union following an 18-month probation period, and who may then apply for permanent residence after five years. Conscious of the tendency of member states to guard their prerogative to control labour migration in the face of centralized European level quotas, the Commission's proposal (Commission 2007) makes it clear that rather than replacing national policy, it is merely seeking to add an additional entry track designed to make migration to Europe more attractive through the possibility to seek employment throughout the EU. In fact, initial entry is subject to obtaining at least a one-year contract through one of the existing national schemes. Thus, while the policy expands the options of those who can already enter the EU, it does not follow the points-system logic that simply rewards the qualifications of the highly skilled. Moreover, those who simply enter through national points-based programs would not become eligible unless they also secure employment.

Despite the cautious nature of the proposal, the public responses by most national governments were even more guarded. In Germany, the Minister of Labour and Minister of Economics, though from the rival Social and Christian Democrats, agree that such decisions must remain the responsibility of national governments. In particular, given the different job market situations and salaries within Germany compared to Southern or Eastern Europe, the prospect of common standards seems utopian (personal communication with the Department of the Interior, 2008). Austria and the Netherlands have also insisted that labour migration should remain in the hands of national governments, with Dutch Deputy Justice Minister Albayrak even questioning the necessity for common policy, unless the priority were to ensure rapid and flexible procedures (Brand 2007).

While it is understandable that coordinated market economies with their more regulated labour markets would be less supportive of the new proposal, they are not the only critics. Spain has pointed out that the focus on the highly skilled risks exacerbating brain drain effects to the developing world, while Eastern European countries such as the Czech republic point out the hypocrisy of recruiting workers from outside the EU at a time when workers from the newly acceded members from the East are barred from working in follow member states such as Germany, Austria, or France (Goldirova 2007). Even in the UK, which has shown the least reticence in opening its labour markets to migration flows over which it does not have complete control – whether through its points-system or in its immediate conferral of freedom of movement rights to East European workers – Immigration Minister Liam Byrne has expressly not supported the proposal (Charter 2007). However, since the UK has secured an opt-in for Title V (immigration) measures, it is not bound by common policies unless it expressly chooses to do so. Regardless of British attitudes, the limited extent of the Blue Card provisions reflects that most European Union countries are coordinated market economies that generally exhibit caution with regard to liberalizing the labour market.

Indeed, after being subjected to the scrutiny of the Council and the European Parliament (EP), the Blue Card proposal has been altered to address many of these member state concerns. Blue Card holders' salaries must be at least 1.5 times the average in a given country, though this may be lowered to 1.2 in certain shortage professions. Further, if they wish to move to a different member state (after 18 months) they have to apply anew, and countries can set absolute quotas to limit access, and beyond that, even deny applications based on local labour market conditions. The objections of the newly acceded countries threatened to postpone the adoption of the program until 2011, but the Czech delegation delivered on its promise to move forward in 2009. The final result is a potentially ambitious program, but risks providing little value-added beyond existing national policies since countries may effectively opt out of any obligation to admit even a single applicant. This speaks volumes as to the limited consensus behind creating an actual common policy for highly skilled immigrants.

Conclusion

If there is a global race for the most talented and highly skilled, Europe's pursuit of such a class of workers is not being carried out in a coherent fashion in terms of converging national or common European level policy. What initially blossomed as the identification of common challenges and fairly similar responses through sector-specific work permit programs throughout several European countries, branched out into different policy directions rather quickly. The migration of the highly skilled has been identified as a relevant phenomenon by no lesser entity than the OECD, which published the *International Mobility of the Highly Skilled* in 2002. One rationale behind the OECD is to compare national economic policies in the effort to facilitate coordination as well as promote the identification and furtherance of what it distils as benchmark practices. In this realm, the points-system is heralded as the most successful policy, and indeed there is an unspoken suggestion that most national policy will 'evolve' in this direction. However, as Peres points out in this volume, there are numerous pressures that militate against a smooth convergence among national policies (Peres, "this volume").

One of the most influential theorists of European integration was Ernst Haas whose concept of neo-functionalism (Haas 1964) contemplated the transference of policy authority from the national to the supranational level. Once a policy area falls under the control of the European Commission, interest groups whose primary focus was on influencing the policy-making process through contacts to their national governments will be tempted transfer their attention and loyalties to the level at which decisions are being made. Under this logic, it might be possible that interest groups – such as the German Chamber of Commerce, DIHK, or BITKOM, which are enthusiastic supporters of the Blue Card (*Der Spiegel* 2007) – may overcome the objections of their national governments and act as powerful allies for the Commission in bringing about deeper policy change.

In this light, the OECD and an actively supranational EU are at the heart of efforts that could lead to a greater convergence of policy regarding the highly skilled. However, what both the OECD and neo-functionalists often underestimate are the political factors that often militate against solutions that at first glance possess universal appeal. Clearly, there is competition for the highly skilled amongst OECD countries, yet not every member is likely to weigh the balance between the pursuit of the highly skilled versus the political costs of relinquishing control over migration flows or regulation of the labour markets in the same way. Whether the desire for such control resides in the institutions of government itself, or whether it is societal forces such as trade unions, conservative business interests, or anti-immigration lobbies that are able to impose themselves upon the decision-making process, there remain plenty of motivations for European countries to remain cautious and incremental in their choice of labour migration policy for the highly skilled. While a path has been laid out for the development of a points-based policy, in Europe for the time being it remains the road less travelled.

Works Cited

Asamer, Florian. 2003. Viele saisonniers, wenig Schlüsselkräfte. *Economist* (*Die Presse* Insert) (November 27).

Bilefsky, Dan. 2007. Europe tries to attract migrants it prefers. *New York Times*, October 24.

Brand, Constant. 2007. EU plan to set to set up U.S.-style Green Card to lure skilled labour to Europe gets lukewarm support. *Associated Press Worldstream*, November 8.

Caviedes, Alexander. 2004. The open method of coordination in immigration policy: A tool for prying open fortress Europe? *Journal of European Public Policy* 11(2): 289-310.

Charter, David. 2007. Blue card scheme will lure qualified workers to ply EU skills gap. *The Times*, October 24.

Chou, Meng-Hsuan. 2010. The free movement of sex workers in the European Union: Excluding the excluded. In *Migrants and minorities: The European response*. Newcastle upon Tyne: Cambridge Scholars Publishing.

Clarke, James and John Salt. 2003. Work permits and foreign labour in the UK: a statistical review. *Labour Market Trends* (November): 563-74.

Commission of the European Communities. 2000. Communication on a community immigration policy, COM (2000) 757 final, November 22.

—. 2001. Communication on an open method of co-ordination for the community immigration policy, COM (2001) 387 final, July 11.

—. 2005. Green paper on an EU approach to managing economic migration, COM (2004) 811 final, January 11.

—. 2007. Proposal for a Council directive on the conditions of entry and residence of third-country nationals for the purposes of highly qualified employment, COM (2007) 637 final, October 23.

Dagblad Tubantia / Twentsche Courant. 2004. Opgeleide migrant mijdt Nederland, July 15.

Dempsy, Judy. 2007. Germany to ease limits on some foreign workers. *New York Times*, August 25.

Department for Education and Employment. 1999. *Skills for the information age: Final report from the Information Technology, Communications and Electronics Skills Strategy Group*. Nottingham: DfEE Publications.

Der Spiegel. 2007. Germans reject EU fast-track immigration scheme, October 24. Available online at: http://www.spiegel.de/international/europe/0,1518,513241,00.html.

Der Standard. 2000. Bartenstein will erst prüfen, March 14.

Deutsche Welle. 2007. Germany to open job market to Eastern European engineers, September 19. Available online at: http://www.dw-world.de/dwarticle/0,2144,2789244,00html.

Dobson, Janet and John Salt. 2004. Review of migration statistics. In *Organisational recruitment and patterns of migration: Interdependencies in an integrating Europe*, ed. Michael Bommes, Kirsten Hoesch, Uwe Hunger and Holger Kolb, 99-140. Osnabrück: Institut für Migrationsforschung und Interkulterelle Studien.

Economic Times. 2009. Netherlands eyes more skilled Indian professionals, May 1. Available online at: http:/economictimes.indiatimes.com/Jobs?Netherlands-eyes-more-skilled-Indian-professionals-/articleshow/4469912.cms.

Expatica News. 2005. Netherlands faces mass shortage of top expats, May 4. Available online at: http:/www.expatica.com/source/site_article.asp?subchannel_id=1&story_id=19772.

Foggensteiner, Alexander. 1996. Industrie für liberale Ausländergesetze. *Wirtschafts Blatt*, June 13.

Givens, Terri and Adam Luedtke. 2004. The politics of European Union immigration policy: Institutions, salience, and harmonisation. *Policy Studies Journal* 32(1): 145-65.

Goldirova, Renata. 2007. EU work permit 'blue card' faces opposition. *euobserver.com*, December 7. Available online at: http://euoberver.com/9/25292.

Haas, Ernst B. 1964. *Beyond the nation state: Functionalism and international organization*. Stanford: Stanford University Press.

Hall, Peter and David Soskice, eds. 2001. *Varieties of capitalism: The institutional foundations of comparative advantage*. Oxford: Oxford University Press.

Hillmann, Felicitas. 2002. Zuwanderung und arbeitsmarkt: alter zopf mit neuem muster? *WSI Mitteilungen* 10(2002): 578-85.

Kolb, Holger, Susana Murteira, João Peixoto and Catarina Sabino. 2004. Recruitment and migration in the ICT sector. In *Organisational recruitment and patterns of migration: Interdependencies in an integrating Europe*, ed. Michael Bommes, Kirsten Hoesch, Uwe Hunger and Holger Kolb, 147-78. Osnabrück: Institut für Migrationsforschung und Interkulterelle Studien.

Lavenex, Sandra. 2006. The competition state and the multilateral liberalization of skilled migration. In *The Human Face of Global Mobility: International Highly Skilled Migration in Europe, North America, and the Asia-Pacific*, ed. Adrian Favell, 29-52. New Brunswick, NJ: Transaction Publishers.

Leitner, Karin. 2001. Wirtschaft will mehr ausländische Arbeitskräfte. *Der Kurier*, March 22.

Moraes, Claude. 2003. The politics of European Union migration policy. *Political Quarterly* 74(4): 116-31.

OECD (2002) *International Mobility of the Highly Skilled*. Paris: OECD.

—. (2005) *Science, Technology and Industry Scoreboard*. Paris: OECD.

Peres, Hubert. 2010. Towards the end of national models for the integration of immigrants in Europe? Britain, France and Spain in comparative perspective. In *Migrants and minorities: The European response*, ed. Adam Luedtke. Newcastle upon Tyne: Cambridge Scholars Publishing.

Stetter, Stephan. 2000. Regulating migration: Authority delegation in justice and home affairs. *Journal of European Public Policy* 7(1): 80-103.

Thielemann, Eiko. 2010. The future of the common European asylum system: In need of a more comprehensive burden-sharing approach. In *Migrants and minorities: The European response* ed. Adam Luedtke. Newcastle upon Tyne: Cambridge Scholars Publishing.

Unterhuber, Wolfgang. 2000. Facharbeitermangel: Die wirtschaft muss sich selbst helfen. *Wirtschafts Blatt*, November 8.

CHAPTER FOUR

THE COMMON EUROPEAN ASYLUM SYSTEM: IN NEED OF A MORE COMPREHENSIVE BURDEN-SHARING APPROACH

EIKO THIELEMANN

Asylum Responsibilities and Types of Burden-Sharing Mechanisms

The recent Commission Green Paper on the Future of the European Asylum System (Commission 2007a) shows that European policy-makers continue to be concerned about the numbers of asylum seekers arriving in Europe. In part, this concern is linked to the fact that most refugees in Europe arrive in their host countries, not on the basis of an offer of resettlement, but as "spontaneous" asylum seekers – over which states have only limited influence given a volatile international system and obligations under international law.[1] However, policy makers are not just worried about the overall inflow of persons asking for refugee status on their territory; they are also concerned about the distribution of asylum applications between states, in particular when they feel that restrictive policy measures adopted in neighbouring states shift responsibilities and are in part responsible for increasing their own asylum burden.[2] Recent

---

[1] All EU Member States are signatories of the Geneva Convention (UN Convention on the Status of Refugees 1951, as amended by the 1967 New York Protocol) under which they are under an obligation not to return a person who "owing to a well-founded fear of being persecuted for reasons of race, religion, nationality, membership of a particular social group, or political opinion, is outside the country of his nationality, and is unable to or, owing to such fear, is unwilling to avail himself of the protection of that country."

[2] Like in the Green Paper, the focus here is on intra-EU solidarity and burden-sharing. The Green Paper also mentions the need for South-North responsibility sharing in its chapter on the 'External Dimension of Asylum'. The question of

developments towards a common asylum policy in Europe have therefore been closely linked with the perceived need for *burden-* or *responsibility-sharing* in this area.[3] The ambitions for an EU burden-sharing system were already made explicit in the text of the Amsterdam Treaty of October 1997, Article 63 (ex 73k), which states that the Council shall adopt measures "promoting a balance of effort between Member States in receiving and bearing the consequences of receiving refugees and displaced persons".

In other EU documents we find even more concrete calls for solidarity and fairness in this area. A recent Commission document states that "the implementation of such a [EU asylum] policy should be based on solidarity between Member States and requires the existence of mechanisms intended to promote a balance in the efforts made by the Member States in receiving and bearing the consequences of receiving refugees and displaced persons".[4] The commitment of Member States in this regard was perhaps most clearly stated at the Brussels European Council meeting in November 2004. In their final declaration, EU leaders stressed that the development of a common policy in the field of asylum, migration and borders "should be based on solidarity and fair sharing of responsibility including its financial implications and closer practical co-operation between Member States."[5] The United Nations High Commissioner for Refugees (UNHCR) echoes this concern because "… burden-sharing is a key to the protection of refugees and the resolution of the refugee problem."[6] In 2005, the then UNHCR High Commissioner Lubbers stated that "[t]here is a need for responsibility and burden-sharing within the EU… I fear that high protection standards will be difficult to maintain in a system which shifts responsibility to states located on the

---

global burden-sharing, however, raises a set of different issues that cannot be adequately addressed within the scope of this paper. For such North-South issues, see e.g. Schuck (1997).

[3] For an overview of the debate this has sparked in the academic literature, see Thielemann (2003).

[4] 2004/904/EC: Council Decision of 2 December 2004 establishing the European Refugee Fund for the period 2005 to 2010.

[5] Brussels European Council, 4/5 November 2004, Presidency Conclusions, page 18.

[6] Official Documents Burden-Sharing - Discussion Paper Submitted By UNHCR Fifth Annual Plenary Meeting Of The APC; ISIL Year Book of International Humanitarian and Refugee Law, Vol. 17 (2001); URL: http://www.worldlii.org/int/journals/ISILYBIHRL/2001/17.html

external border of the EU, many of which have limited asylum capacity."[7] In its recent Green Paper the Commission echoes this concern and emphasizes that "there is a pressing need for increased solidarity in the area of asylum, so as to ensure that responsibility for processing asylum applications and granting protection in the EU is shared equitably" (Commission 2007a: 10), while the Council in its recent 'European Pact on Immigration and Asylum' states that external border control should be exercised 'in a spirit of joint responsibility on behalf of all Member States' [...] 'Those Member States whose geographical location exposes them to influxes of immigrants, or whose resources are limited, should be able to count on the effective solidarity of the European Union' (Council 2008: 9).

How (Un)Equal is the Distribution of Asylum Burdens?

When analyzing the development of asylum applications across EU countries, the distribution of asylum applications appears highly unbalanced (see also Vink, this volume). Attention was first drawn to this in 1992 when Germany received over 438,000 asylum applications, which constituted more than 62 percent of all applications registered in Europe at the time (UNHCR 1997). In more recent years the UK and France have topped the table in terms of the absolute number of asylum applications in the EU. Over the past decade, the largest numbers of asylum seekers have originated from former Yugoslavia, Afghanistan, Iraq and most recently Russia (Chechnya). However, analyzing reception burdens by comparing *absolute* asylum figures is often misleading. When using the more meaningful measure of *relative* burdens, that is, one which takes account of differences in states' reception capacity, the unevenness in distribution becomes much clearer. The available data suggests that between 1994 and 2002 some smaller EU countries such as the Netherlands, Belgium and Sweden were among those EU states bearing the highest relative (per capita) asylum burdens (see Table 4.1).[8]

---

[7] United Nations High Commissioner for Refugees, Mr. Ruud Lubbers, Talking Points for the Informal Justice and Home Affairs Council (Luxembourg, 29 January 2005).

[8] Even if one expanded the table to include responsibilities for refugees and individuals granted subsidiary protection status, the ranking of countries in the table would not look very different (Thielemann and Dewan 2006: 355).

Table 4.1: Average Number of Asylum Applications per Year in selected OECD countries, 1994-2002 (per thousand of population)

HIGHEST						LOWEST	
Switzerland	3.5	Norway	1.8	UK	1.0	Spain	0.2
Netherlands	2.2	Denmark	1.6	Australia	0.5	Italy	0.2
Belgium	2.1	Germany	1.2	France	0.5	Japan	0
Sweden	1.8	Canada	1.0	US	0.3		

In more recent years some new Member States such as Malta and Cyprus have had to deal with the highest per capita burdens. High relative burdens have constituted a considerable domestic challenge in many of these countries, in particular those with little previous experience of dealing with large inflows of asylum seekers. When thinking about how it might be possible to address the challenges of unequal responsibilities in this area through multilateral policy measures, several different types of burden-sharing mechanisms can be usefully distinguished.

Types of International Burden-Sharing Regimes

One can identify two substantively different types of international burden-sharing regimes and four principal burden-sharing mechanisms (see table 4.2).

Table 4.2: Types of Burden-Sharing Mechanisms

		Dimensionality	
		One Dimensional	**Multi Dimensional**
Distribution Rule	**Hard**	Binding Rules	Explicit Compensation
	Soft	Voluntary Pledging	Implicit Trade

First, there are *one-dimensional* burden-sharing regimes that aim to equalize the efforts of states on one particular contribution dimension, usually by seeking to equalize the number of asylum seekers and refugees that states have to deal with. This tends to be done in two ways – through binding rules or through voluntary pledging mechanisms. Policy harmonisation would be an example of the former method as it is based on the assumption that agreeing on a common set of rules will overcome burden inequalities. By obliging states to harmonise their policies or to comply with a set of common international rules, we may expect that individual countries will face converging burdens. The core idea of such a mechanism is that common rules will reduce the need for corrective action. Redistributive quotas are also classic examples of such "binding rules" mechanisms as they try to equalize observed imbalances or inequities in burdens through some agreed distribution key (which is usually based on one or several fairness principles such as responsibility, capacity, benefit or cost).[9] Germany, for example, operates such a quota regime for asylum seekers on its territory. Individuals who seek refugee status in Germany are initially processed in centralized reception centres, before they get distributed across the sixteen *Länder* of the Federal Republic according to the *Länder's* population size (a capacity based distribution key).

A second type of one-dimensional burden-sharing mechanisms are those which are based on non-binding "pledging" mechanisms. If states cannot agree on a binding distribution key, they can make appeals which ask states with smaller responsibilities to alleviate some of the high burdens that other states are being faced with. During the Kosovo crisis in 1999, the UNHCR operated such a system through which it encouraged countries to alleviate the burdens of bordering countries, such as Macedonia, by agreeing to resettle refugees in their territory. A more institutionalized EU system exists (at least on paper) since 2001, when the Council agreed to set up a Council Directive on Temporary Protection in the Case of Mass Influx.[10] The directive develops a range of ultimately

---

[9] The "responsibility" principle is commonly used in environmental regimes and also known as the "polluter pays" principle. The "capacity" principle refers to a state's "ability to pay" (and is often linked to relative GDP). The "benefit" principle proposes that states should contribute to a particular regime in relation to the benefit they gain from it and the "cost" principle suggests that states' relative costs in making certain contributions should be taken into account when establishing burden-sharing regimes.

[10] Council Directive 2001/55/EC of 20 July 2001.

non-binding mechanisms based on the principle of *double voluntarism* which means that the agreement of both the recipient state and the individuals concerned is required before protection seekers can be moved from one country to another. In its efforts to enhance solidarity and equalize responsibilities across the Member States, existing EU burden-sharing initiatives in this area have until recently largely relied on a one-dimensional burden-sharing logic.

Multi-dimensional burden-sharing regimes are those that do not seek to equalize burdens or responsibilities on one particular contribution dimension alone, but instead operate across several contribution dimensions. On the one hand, some multi-dimensional regimes are based on an explicit compensation logic. In these cases, a country's disproportionate efforts in one contribution dimension are recognized and that country gets compensated (through benefits or cost reductions) on other dimensions. An example of this is Schuck's "decentralized, market-based refugee sharing system," (Schuck 1997) which is similar to the Kyoto emission trading scheme. According to this model, an international agency would assign a refugee protection quota to each participating state on the basis of which states would then be allowed to trade their quota by paying others (with money or in kind) to fulfil their obligations.

A second type of a multi-dimensional burden-sharing mechanism is based on an implicit trading logic which recognizes that states contribute to international collective goods such as refugee protection in different ways (Thielemann and Dewan 2006). In the refugee context, these include what might be called *pro-active* measures, which attempt to halt the escalation of potential refugee problems by, for instance, sending peacekeeping troops to a region in order to prevent or contain forced migration. Another set of contributions are those which can be called *reactive* measures. The latter measures deal with the consequences of refugee problems once they have occurred, in particular by admitting protection seekers to a host country's territory. During the negotiations of recent EU refugee burden-sharing initiatives, the British and French governments expressed their wishes that their participation in peacekeeping operations should be taken into account when assessing the burdens borne by individual Member States.[11] This suggestion, however, has not been followed up in the more recent EU discussions.

[11] Council resolution of 25 September 1995 "on burden-sharing with regard to the admission and residence of displaced persons on a temporary basis" (OJ No C 262/1, 7 October 1995).

Existing EU Asylum Burden-Sharing Initiatives

There have been several European burden-sharing initiatives in the area of asylum. Following Noll's categorization (Noll 2000), there are essentially three ways to address the unequal distribution of protection seekers that states are faced with: (1) physical burden-sharing (sharing people); (2) harmonising of asylum legislation (sharing policy) and (3) financial burden-sharing (sharing money).

Sharing People

The idea of "people sharing", i.e. the physical transfer of protection seekers from one host territory to another, is perhaps the most obvious method to address disparities in refugee burdens. The Dublin Convention is often regarded as the flagship of the EU's asylum acquis. It provides the rules that determine the responsible Member State for dealing with a particular asylum claim. In essence, the rule states that asylum seekers who move to another member state as a secondary movement can be sent back to the "state of first entry". Its principal aim is to 'establish which Member State is responsible for the examination of an asylum application lodged on EU territory [...] and to prevent secondary movements between Member States' (Commission 2007a: 10). Other more recent EU initiatives based on the idea of people-sharing have been influenced not only by the recent experience with the refugee crises in Bosnia and Kosovo but also by people-sharing arrangements found in the refugee regimes of several Member States (see e.g. Boswell 2003). Particularly noteworthy in this context is the 2001 Council Directive on Temporary Protection in the Case of Mass Influx.[12]

Sharing Policy

A further possible way to achieve a more equitable distribution of asylum burdens is to take a common policy approach through the harmonisation of domestic refugee legislation. The EU has worked towards the convergence of Member States' laws on forced migration since the mid-1980s. What started with initially non-binding intergovernmental instruments has since then been followed by developments in Community law. Most noteworthy here are several directives that have aimed to level the asylum playing field and to lay the

[12] Council Directive 2001/55/EC of 20 July 2001.

foundations for a Common European Asylum System.[13] The 2003 Reception Conditions Directive guarantees minimum standards for the reception of asylum-seekers, including housing, education and health. The 2004 Qualification Directive contains a clear set of criteria for qualifying either for refugee or subsidiary protection status and sets out what rights are attached to each status. The 2005 Asylum Procedures Directive seeks to ensure that, throughout the EU, all procedures at first instance are subject to the same minimum standards. The Commission Green paper summarizes the underlying logic of EU policy harmonisation as a burden-sharing instrument as follows: "Further approximation of national asylum procedures, legal standards and reception conditions, as envisaged in creating a Common European Asylum System, is bound to reduce those secondary movements of asylum seekers which are mainly due to the diversity of applicable rules, and could thus result in a more fair [sic] overall distribution of asylum applications between Member States" (Commission 2007a: 11).

Sharing Money

More recently, the EU has started to introduce multi-dimensional burden-sharing elements in order to address existing disparities. It has done so through the payment of financial compensation to the most popular destination countries for asylum seekers. This kind of explicit financial burden-sharing has been taking place since the establishment of the European Refugee Fund (ERF), which was put in place to support and encourage efforts of the Member States in receiving and bearing the consequences of receiving refugees and displaced persons (for a more extensive analysis on this, see Thielemann 2005). Created on the basis of Article 63(2) (b) of the EC Treaty, the Council Decision of 28 September 2000 established the European Refugee Fund (ERF).[14] The ERF is to allocate resources proportionately to the burden on each Member State by reason of their efforts in receiving refugees and displaced persons. This Fund, which is jointly financed by the Member States, seeks to support special projects for the reception, integration and repatriation of refugees and displaced persons. Its rationale is "to demonstrate solidarity between Member States by achieving a balance in the efforts made by those Member States". The decision's text states as its rationale that "it is fair to

[13] Council Directive 2003/9/EC of 27 January 2003; Council Directive 2004/83/EC of 29 April 2004 and Council Directive 2005/85/EC of 1 December 2005.
[14] OJ L 252/12 of 6 October 2000.

allocate [EU] resources proportionately to the burden on each Member State by reason of its efforts in receiving refugees and displaced persons".[15] For its first funding period (2000-2004), the ERF had at its disposal a total budget of €216 million. In 2004, the Council adopted a European Commission proposal to extend ERF for the period 2005–2010.[16] At the same time, it was agreed to triple the size of the Fund to just under €700 million.

Criticism and Proposals for Reform

EU burden-sharing initiatives have attracted criticism, not just in terms their impact on individual asylum seekers and refugees, but also with regard to their effectiveness from a burden-sharing perspective which will be the focus of the analysis here.

Dublin

In its Green Paper, the Commission acknowledges that "the Dublin System may *de facto* result in additional burdens on Member States that have limited reception and absorption capacities and that find themselves under particular migratory pressures because of their geographical location" (Commission 2007a: 10). Nonetheless, the Commission re-emphasizes the need for a system that clearly allocates responsibility for the examination of an asylum claim among the Member States in order to avoid the phenomena of "asylum shopping" (individuals making multiple asylum claims in different countries) and "refugees in orbit" (no country taking responsibility for a displaced person). However, the Commission does see the need to establish "corrective burden-sharing mechanisms" that are complementary to the Dublin system (Commission 2007a: 11). In particular, it advocates the development of an intra-EU resettlement system without making clear how such a system might operate.

The UNHCR is more critical of the Dublin system. It laments that the system is based on the flawed assumption that the asylum laws and practices of the participating states are based on common standards and produce comparable results. "In reality, asylum legislation and practice still vary widely from country to country, and as a result, asylum-seekers receive different treatment from one Dublin State to another" (UNHCR

[15] OJ L 252/12 of 6 October 2000, para. 11.

[16] 2004/904/EC; OJ381/52 of 28/12/2004.

2007: .38). From a human rights perspective, UNHCR would favour a system that allocates responsibility for an asylum seeker to the Member State in which the first application for asylum was made. However, in the short-term it advocates two changes to the existing "people-sharing" arrangements. First, it would like to see more flexibility in the management of the Dublin system, with the possibility of States facing disproportionate pressures being released from their responsibility for the examination of asylum requests, with the responsibility being transferred to the State in which the asylum application is first lodged. Second, like the Commission, the UNHCR would like to complement the Dublin system with new reallocation arrangements for both asylum-seekers and refugees that are aimed at helping States which are facing pressures exceeding their reception capacities. Again, few detailed proposals regarding the operation of such systems are made, but the UNHCR insists that any transfer under such a new mechanism would require the consent of the individuals concerned.

The European Council on Refugees and Exiles (ECRE) also questions the track-record of the Dublin system, given the significant human and financial costs incurred as a result of its operation. It highlights the findings of the recent Commission report, which shows that in recent years, transfer of responsibility was requested in 17% of all asylum applications lodged across the EU, with 30% of accepted requests for transfer being effected (Commission 2007b). ECRE advocates a revised system that "delivers quick, efficient and fair status determination, wherever a claim is lodged, followed by an opportunity for recognized refugees and those who have been granted subsidiary protection to relocate within the EU" (ECRE 2007: 37).

Policy Harmonisation

The Green Paper recognizes that even the establishment of a common asylum procedure and a uniform status will not completely eradicate all reasons why asylum seekers may find some Member States more attractive than others (ECRE 2007: 11). Policy harmonisation can only address imbalances due to differences in domestic legislation in the first place. It is well established that policy differences are only one of several determinants for a protection seeker's choice of host country, with structural factors such as historic networks, employment opportunities, geography or a host country's reputation being at least equally, if not more, important. The Commission's belief in the equalizing effect of policy harmonisation might therefore be exaggerated. If structural pull factors are indeed crucial for the scale of a countries' asylum and refugee burdens, then policy harmonisation might actually do more harm than good to the EU's efforts to achieve a more equitable distribution of asylum seekers across the Member States. EU policy harmonisation curtails Member States' ability to use national asylum policies to counterbalance their country's unique structural pull-factors (language, colonial ties, etc.). This is why policy harmonisation might in fact undermine rather than facilitate efforts to achieve to more equitable responsibility sharing (Thielemann 2004). There appears to be an emerging agreement that the moves towards EU policy harmonisation at the very least need to be complemented by initiatives that tackle disparities through intra-EU resettlement or the development of more effective financial compensation mechanisms.

The European Refugee Fund

The Commission emphasizes the need to identify ways to better use ERF funding "to reduce disparities and to raise standards" (Commission 2007a: 11). The Green Paper suggests setting up new information-sharing mechanisms to identify more effective projects and programs that could be funded by the ERF. However, this focus seems rather narrow, as it does not address the crucial issue; namely that the ERF has so far failed to provide for effective incentives that would make states with smaller asylum and refugee burdens accept greater responsibilities. While much of the UNHCR's response on this issue engages with the question of how allocated resources from the ERF could be spent better in the future, it does raise the issue of existing allocation mechanisms that go the heart of the ERF's functioning as a burden-sharing mechanism. The UNHCR expresses its concern about the fact 'that the current allocation based on [the absolute] numbers of asylum claims tends to favour larger Member States with well-established asylum systems' (UNHCR 2007: 11). It therefore supports higher minimum allocations for new Member States that will help them to build up their reception capacities.

ECRE also stresses this point, stating that in order to develop into a more effective burden-sharing instrument, "the ERF should target a greater proportion of its funding at states with historically less developed asylum systems while at the same time continuing to compensate states which receive a higher volume of asylum applications" (ECRE 2007). Instead of supporting an expansion of the fixed dispensing element of the Fund, it advocates the development of "a mechanism that is specifically designed to allow states with less developed asylum systems to catch up with more developed states". The ECRE paper also argues that ERF funding should be allocated by taking account of Member States relative (rather than absolute) protection responsibilities. This means that resources should be distributed 'according to the degree of relative efforts required by different states', taking account of differences in states' size, wealth, etc. Finally, ECRE emphasizes that a more effective ERF would need to be large enough to realistically reflect the financial responsibilities faced by States, if it is to provide some States with incentives to accept increased responsibilities in this area (for all these proposals, see also Thielemann 2005). To put the ERF's resources in perspective, it is instructive to compare them with costs incurred at the national level. According to UK Home Office estimates, Britain spent just under €30,000 per asylum-seeker in 2002, if one includes administrative costs, legal bills, accommodation and subsistence. According to figures from the ERF's mid-term review, the UK was the second largest recipient of the fund in 2002, and received just over €100 ERF money per asylum application received that year. It therefore seems clear that, on their own, the reforms discussed above should not be expected to achieve an equitable distribution of asylum and refugee burdens across Europe. To achieve this aim, the EU will need to develop a broader burden-sharing regime in this area.

The Need for a More Comprehensive Burden-Sharing Approach

Given the limitations of the existing EU refugee-sharing initiatives, it might be time to further explore the fourth burden-sharing mechanism discussed above: trade. The Member States have not yet used this mechanism in their burden-sharing efforts. Several objections have been made against a Kyoto-style refugee burden-sharing regime based on the idea of "explicit burden trading", as proposed by Schuck, which raised "unease about treating refugees as commodities in inter-state transactions" (Anker, Fitzpatrick and Shacknove 1998). An alternative "implicit trade" model suggests that countries can be expected to specialize according to their comparative advantage as to the type and level of contribution they make to international collective goods. Applied to the area of forced migration, Thielemann and Dewan suggest that countries contribute to refugee protection in two principal ways: proactively (e.g. through peace-keeping/making, aid, trade or investment in regions of origin) and reactively (most commonly through providing protection for displaced persons on a host state's territory (Thielemann and Dewan 2006). While pro-active measures seek to alleviate push-factors and aim at preventing a refugee crisis to develop in the first place, re-active measures aim at dealing with the crisis once it has occurred. Empirically, one indeed finds evidence that some countries make disproportionate contributions in "pro-active" refugee protection contributions (such as through peace-keeping efforts) while other countries contribute disproportionately with "reactive" measures related to refugee reception. It therefore appears that some implicit trading in refugee protection contributions is already taking place.

From a theoretical perspective, it is not difficult to see why such a division of labour occurs as countries can be expected to have a comparative advantage in providing certain types of collective goods over others which means that every country can contribute to some collective goods *relatively* more cheaply than another country.[17] It seems perfectly reasonable to assume that countries are not equally well placed to contribute to refugee protection in same way. From an economic efficiency of countries specific contributions differ. For example, from such a perspective, one might expect a country with well established asylum/refugee institutions to be relatively more efficient in processing and offering refuge to protection seekers than a country without such institutions. In contrast, a country with a large army and experience in interventions abroad can be expected to be more efficient in pro-active refugee protection efforts than a country with a small army and no such experience. One can extend this argument to the political realm (Boyer 1993). A country's political comparative advantage is determined by its political environment, with national policy-makers being constrained by the preferences of their constituents. To remain in power, policy-makers will usually take such preferences into account. In a country where public attitudes are strongly opposed to its army's intervention abroad but where there is general support for refugee protection in general, granting refuge to displaced persons (i.e. re-active rather than pro-active refugee protection measures) might be a government's policy of choice.[18] Take the

---

[17] Individual countries need only have a relative (not an absolute) advantage in the production of a particular good to be able to reap benefits from specialisation and trade. Even if a country can produce every good more efficiently than other countries, it will still be better off when it specialises in the production of goods in which it holds the greatest relative advantage.

[18] Even in the case when the people of a country and by extension its policy-makers are reluctant to engage in either pro-active and re-active forms of refugee protection, a government the wants to react to its concerns about irregular flows of

example of post-war Germany. Given its historical legacy, for much of the post-war period, the German public insisted on a policy of non-intervention by the German security forces, which constitutionally prohibited 'out of area' operations by the German army. The resulting policy choices became most obvious during the time of the Bosnian conflict in the early 1990s, when Germany chose not to participate in NATO-led military action against the Bosnian Serbs. Instead it provided refuge to very large numbers of Bosnian asylum seekers.

The specialisation in countries' contributions suggested by the implicit trade model has potentially important implications for attempts to develop multi-lateral burden-sharing initiatives that are perceived to advance states' interests in providing more equitable, efficient and effective refugee protection. First, evidence of inter-country specialisation suggests that overall refugee protection contributions are perhaps not as inequitable as often assumed. Second, it is possible that burden-sharing initiatives that attempt to force all nations to increase contributions into any particular category of provision are likely to be counterproductive for the efficient provision of collective goods such as refugee protection. It can then be argued that the provision of this collective good is closer to optimum when countries are able to specialise with regard to their contributions.

Allowing for specialization in states' contributions can help to increase the efficiency of refugee protection efforts. While it might be tempting to conclude from the exclusive analysis of reactive protection contributions (as most current EU burden-sharing initiatives do) that some countries should be brought in line with others, such a conclusion would be simplistic and misleading. It appears reasonable to expect that attempts to impose exclusively one-dimensional burden-sharing mechanisms can constitute a hindrance for greater specialization and trade which will have adverse overall effects on states' willingness to contribute. EU burden-sharing initiatives, if they are to more effectively strengthen refugee protection, need to be aware of variations in states' preferences as to how to contribute in this area and need to recognize the comparative advantages individual states possess with regard to making certain kinds of

---

displaced persons will favour the less costly type of contributions. Of course, like in the case of international trade where a country can choose not to trade with other countries, an isolationist state could also decide not to make contribution to refugee protection, being prepared to accept the cost of such 'non-action'.

contributions. If they do not, they risk undermining the search for more effective refugee protection efforts.

Works Cited

Anker, Deborah, Joan Fitzpatrick and Andrew Shacknove. 1998. Crisis and cure: A reply to Hathaway/Neve and Schuck. *Harvard Human Rights Journal* 11: 295-310.

Boswell, Christina. 2003. Burden-sharing in the EU: Lessons from the German and UK experience. *Journal of Refugee Studies* 16(3): 316-35.

Boyer, Mark. 1993. *International cooperation and public goods.* Baltimore and London: John Hopkins University Press.

Commission of the European Communities. 2007a. *Green paper on the future common asylum system*, COM (2007) 301 final.

Commission of the European Communities. 2007b. *Report from the Commission to the European Parliament and the Council on the evaluation of the Dublin system*, COM (2007) 299 final.

Council of the European Union. 2008. *European pact on immigration and asylum*, 13189/08 ASIM 68, Brussels, 24 September 2008, available online at: http://register.consilium.europa.eu/pdf/en/08/st13/st13440.en08.pdf

ECRE (European Council on Refugees and Exiles). 2007. *Submission from the European Council on Refugees and Exiles in response to the Commission's Green Paper on the Future Common European Asylum System*, 2007, available online at: http://www.ecre.org/resources/Policy_papers/952 (accessed 24/7/09).

Noll Gregor. 2000. *Negotiating asylum, the EU acquis, extraterritorial asylum and the common market of deflection.* The Hague: Kluwer Law International.

Schuck, Peter. 1997. Refugee burden-sharing: A modest proposal. *Yale Journal of International Law* 23: 243-97.

Thielemann, Eiko. 2004. Why European policy harmonisation undermines refugee burden-sharing. *European Journal of Migration and Law* 6(3): 43–61.

—. 2005 Symbolic politics or effective burden-sharing? Redistribution, side-payments and the European Refugee Fund. *Journal of Common Market Studies* 43(4): 807–24.

Thielemann, Eiko and Torun Dewan. 2006. The myth of free-riding: Refugee protection and implicit burden-sharing. *West European Politics* 29(2): 351-69.

Thielemann, Eiko. 2003. European burden-sharing and forced migration. *Journal of Refugee Studies* 16(3): 223-35.

UNHCR. 1999. *UNHCR statistical yearbook.* Geneva: UNHCR.

UNHCR 2007. *Response to the European Commission's Green Paper on the Future Common European Asylum System*, September 2007, available at: http://www.unhcr.org/46e53de52.html (accessed 24/7/09).

Vink, Maarten P. 2010. European integration and domestic immigration policies: Convergence, causality and counterfactuals. In *Migrants and minorities: The European response*, ed. Adam Luedtke. Newcastle upon Tyne: Cambridge Scholars Publishing.

CHAPTER FIVE

THE FREE MOVEMENT OF SEX WORKERS IN THE EUROPEAN UNION: EXCLUDING THE EXCLUDED

MENG-HSUAN CHOU

Introduction

The principle of free movement has been central to the process of European unification. The 1957 Treaty of Rome identified four 'factors of production' that would be eligible for free movement, namely, goods, capital, services and labour (i.e. the 'four freedoms'). Creators of the European Economic Community, as the EU[1] was then known, believed that after pooling resources in key policy areas, the four freedoms would result in greater economic interdependence between the participant states. This economic tie would then in turn generate prosperity and peace between the historically warring European nations. Over fifty years have elapsed since the European countries agreed to remove internal barriers between their common territories, and the exercise now involves more than 27 sovereign states. Whilst the integration process did enter a period

[1] The EU is the current manifestation of over fifty years of close economic, and then subsequently political and social, cooperation between a group of European countries. It officially came into existence after its member states signed the Treaty on European Union (TEU), also known as the Maastricht Treaty, in 1992. Before 1992, it was variably refer to as the European Community (EC), European Communities or European Economic Community (EEC) depending on the policy area and treaty in reference. The 1957 Rome Treaty established the EEC, one of the three European Communities. The Maastricht Treaty changed the name of the EEC to EC in an attempt to differentiate existing cooperation from defence and police cooperation. In this chapter, I will generally use the terms 'European Community' to refer to pre-1992 cooperation and 'European Union' for post-1992 activities.

of "Eurosclerosis" shortly after the 1973 Oil Crisis, it has been relaunched in the 1980s with free movement, or 'mobility' as it is now more commonly referred to by EU officials, as both the key strategy and objective of the integration process. This chapter takes stock of this development and advances the proposition that the evolution[2] of European integration has contributed to increasing the levels of global inequality by marginalizing those already at the economic and political fringes of society. Such outcome directly contradicts the democratic ethos underpinning the unification project and should be cause for concern.

To develop the argument, it first explains how, as they strived to achieve the four freedoms through market regulation, the member states had created legal categories of which persons were entitled to exercise mobility and, by implication, those who would be excluded from enjoying the privilege. Thus, an 'insider' and 'outsider' divide has been established (Ugur 1995). Next, to illustrate how such categorization became more pronounced as the integration process widened and deepened, I situate this development within the context of the emerging common European migration policy. As the member states intensified the removal of internal barriers against free movement, they also strengthened their external borders against what they considered as 'unauthorized' and 'undesirable' migration. The immediate result of this exercise has been that some of the 'persons' who were previously and implicitly excluded from free movement now became explicit. Moreover, the heterogeneity of the member states' migration preferences had led to the successful adoption of policies concerning irregular migration but not labour migration. This means that the European migration regime, whilst empowering the authorities to remove irregular migrants from their common territories, do not offer any viable labour migration channels for entry and residence. Using sex workers as a case study, I demonstrate how EU member states' efforts to 'manage' migration flows contributed to increasing the vulnerability of third country nationals who are sex workers within an internally borderless Europe. Whilst recent developments at the supranational-level confirmed that there has been a concerted effort to address the growing divide between 'insiders' and 'outsiders', these endeavours face multiple challenges. Hence, the chapter concludes by considering ways that the EU and its member states could narrow the

[2] By evolution, I refer to the adaptive changes that the EU and member states had made in order to advance the integration project; changes could be internally or externally induced (see Lewis and Steinmo 2008).

inequality gap through a three-pronged strategy consisting of 'universal principle, comprehensive policy and good practice'.

Free Movement for Whom?

The founders of the European Community defined 'free movement of persons' in a limited way in the 1957 Rome Treaty. According to Callovi (1992: 355), the Rome Treaty 'did not set out any obligation for implementing it [free movement of persons], whereas it did make provisions for implementations in regard to workers'. This was so even though the creators used the phrase 'free movement of persons' throughout. For instance, article 3(c) stated that Community activities shall include 'the abolition, as between Member States, of obstacles to freedom of movement for *persons*, services and capital', and Title III was concerned with 'Free movement of *persons*, services and capital' (emphases added). Reading further, we find a detailed explanation of what the founders meant by free movement in article 48(2), which stipulated that 'Such freedom of movement shall entail the abolition of any discrimination based on nationality between *workers* of the Member States as regards employment, remuneration and other conditions of work and employment' (emphasis added). Through selective omission and specification, the European member states initially identified workers as the primary category of 'persons' with whom they were concerned within the context of free movement.

A comparative reading between the 1951 Paris Treaty, which established the European Coal and Steel Community, and the 1957 Rome Treaty suggests that workers can also be divided into European and non-EC nationals. Article 69(1) of the Paris Treaty declared that 'Member states undertake to remove any restriction based on nationality upon the employment in the coal and steel industries of workers who are nationals of Member states'. Whilst the articles concerning free movement of workers in both the Paris and Rome Treaties were similarly phrased, close examination reveals some difference. For instance, whereas the Paris Treaty explicitly stressed that workers must be nationals of participant states – this was not the case in the Rome Treaty. Indeed, article 59 of the Rome Treaty asserted that 'The Council may, acting unanimously on a proposal from the Commission, extend the provisions of this Chapter [on free movement of services] to nationals of a third country who provide services and who are established within the Community'. Whilst one may argue that free movement of persons and services are two distinct fields of cooperation, such distinction is not necessarily obvious considering that some ‘services’ are provided by ‘persons’. Undoubtedly, as service providers, these ‘persons’ were certainly ‘workers’.

The case of Rush Portuguesa is particularly illustrative in this regard (European Court of Justice 1990b). Rush Portuguesa was a construction and public works company that brought its Portuguese workers to France to fulfil a contract. According to article L341.9 of French Labour Code, the *Office National d’Immigration* had the exclusive right to recruit non-French nationals. From the viewpoint of *Office National d’Immigration*, Rush Portuguesa violated French law and a fine ensued. Rush Portuguesa refused to pay because it argued that it was exercising freedom to provide services as permitted under the Act of Accession for Portugal, which joined the EC on 1 January 1986. ONI countered by arguing that free movement of services did not extend to all employees. The case was referred to the ECJ, which opined that articles 59 and 60 of the Rome Treaty and articles 215 and 216 of the Accession Act must be interpreted to mean that Rush Portuguesa should be allowed to bring its Portuguese employees to France. Yet the Court of Justice asserted that these workers must leave once the job had been completed. The case of Rush Portuguesa revealed that third country nationals contracted as service providers by companies established within the Community was another category of ‘persons’ to whom free movement provisions would apply.

Subsequent EC legislation created additional groupings of ‘persons’ eligible to exercise mobility when free movement and associated benefits were extended to spouses and dependants of Community workers. Council Regulation 1612/68 on freedom of movement for workers stipulated that their spouses and dependants enjoy ‘derived’ rights, or privileges, such as access to ‘install themselves with a worker…in the territory of another Member State’ (Council Document 1968: article 10). Moreover, it asserted that this must be so ‘irrespective of their [workers’ family members’] nationality’ (ibid). These privileges were reaffirmed and expanded by later Community legislation and ECJ rulings. For instance, Commission Regulation 1251/70 identified rights of workers and their families to remain in the territory of a host member state continuously and permanently (European Commission 1970). The Court confirmed these rights in the case of *Dzodzi vs. Belgium* (Cases C-297/88 and C-197/89, European Court of Justice 1990a), where it implied that family members of Community nationals could remain permanently in another member state even after the demise of EC workers if the Community nationals were exercising free movement at the time. Council Regulation 1408/71 outlined social security schemes for workers and their families (Council Document 1971). These privileges were upheld by the Court in *Fiorini vs. SNCF* (Case 32/75, European Court of Justice 1975) and *Forcheri vs. Belgium* (Case 152/82, European Court of Justice 1983). In both cases, the ECJ ruled that workers and their families residing in a host member state must be entitled to all social and tax advantages equal to those of national workers. Thus, spouses and dependants of EC-nationals who exercise free movement constitute another category of 'persons' who may practise mobility.

The bilateral and multilateral agreements concluded between the European Community and third countries also introduced another group of 'persons' who may exercise free movement.[3] For instance, the 1963 Association Agreement (the 'Ankara Agreement') between Turkey and the Community permitted Turkish nationals to enter and reside in the EC without going through the ordinary immigration procedure. Indeed, article 12 of the Ankara Agreement stipulated that the pre-accession partnership was to be guided by articles 48, 49 and 50 of the Rome Treaty 'for the purpose of progressively securing freedom of movement for workers between [Turkey and the Community]'. However, developments[4] since the conclusion of the Ankara Agreement have placed the free movement of Turkish nationals within a legally ambiguous context (see also Aral 1997; 2005). To be sure, Turkish nationals occupy the grey area where free movement is theoretically possible; but, in practice, neither the EC nor its member states had enforced the mobility of Turkish workers as originally stipulated by the Ankara Agreement. By contrast, citizens of Iceland, Norway and Liechtenstein are allowed to exercise free movement as the result of the European Economic Area Agreement (EEA) that their governments had signed with the EU within the institutional context of the European Free Trade Association (EFTA). Similarly, Swiss nationals are

---

[3] This brief discussion is limited to agreements concluded between the EC/EU and third countries and thus does not consider agreements such as the Saarbrücken Convention, nor those that had resulted in the Benelux Economic Union (the Benelux countries are Belgium, the Netherlands and Luxembourg), Nordic Passport Union and the common travel area between the UK and Ireland.

[4] Such as the 1973 economic recession, two decisions taken in 1976 and 1980 by the Council of Association created to execute the Ankara Agreement, the 1987 ruling from the Court on *Demirel* (European Court of Justice 1987), and the qualified rejection of the Turkish application by the Community in 1989 and the current ongoing political wrangling over Turkish membership to the EU.

also entitled to free movement as part of the Schengen arrangement, which also applies to the other three EFTA members. Hence, third country nationals whose governments have concluded agreements with the EU that explicitly permit mobility for workers make up a new category of 'persons'.

Finally, the transition period that 'old' member states imposed on 'new' members artificially creates an additional category of 'persons' who may exercise mobility. When the Treaty of Maastricht introduced the concept of EU citizenship, it also codified free movement as an inalienable right of all EU national. However, when eight[5] of the ten Central and Eastern European countries joined the Union on 1 May 2004, their citizens faced multiple transition periods – known as the '2+3+2 scheme' – during which their right to free movement has been limited. For instance, only Ireland, Sweden and the UK lifted their reservations on mobility of workers from the new member states on 1 May 2004. Finland, Greece, Italy, Portugal and Spain withdrew their reservations on 1 May 2006, which marked the conclusion of the first transition period. France, Belgium, Denmark, Luxembourg, and the Netherlands decided to progressively remove their reservations until 2009; Austria and Germany will maintain their right to bar nationals from the eight new member states to enter and reside in their countries for work until at least 2009. When Romania and Bulgaria became EU members on 1 January 2007, their nationals were also subjected to the '2+3+2 scheme' concerning free movement. It should be stressed that the practice of restricting mobility of citizens from 'new' member states, whilst appearing to be discriminatory, has been traditional. For instance, when Greece, Spain and Portugal joined the Community in the 1980s, existing member states had imposed a transition period of seven years on their nationals (Steering Group on Enlargement 1992). Indeed, because over a quarter of its population in 1979 were Portuguese (Statec Luxembourg 1990), the Luxembourger government sought and received a ten-years transition period against the free movement of Portuguese workers. In sum, the completion of various transition periods added new groups of 'persons' who were previously ineligible for mobility to those who could now fully exercise free movement.

Developments concerning free movement have shown the concept to be constantly evolving. From the limited legal basis in the 1957 Rome

[5] They were Poland, Lithuania, Latvia, Estonia, the Czech Republic, Slovakia, Hungary and Slovenia. Cypriots and Maltese were exempted from these transitional measures.

Treaty emerged diverse categories of 'persons' who were either entitled to exercise free movement or were given the privilege to do so. If we were to place these groupings of 'persons' along a continuum stretching from an end-point of 'free movement without conditions' to the mid-point of 'free movement with conditions' and then to the opposite end-point of 'no free movement', we find them to be evenly scattered along this spectrum. For instance, EU citizens of member states which have completed their transition periods (if any were originally placed) and nationals of EFTA countries may exercise 'free movement without conditions'. Under the wider range of 'free movement with conditions', EU nationals of 'new' member states which are currently finishing their transition periods temporarily co-exist with third country nationals who are service providers within the Union and family members of EU citizens who practise mobility. The legal ambiguity concerning the status of Turkish nationals would place them on the edge of this category and closer to the end-point of 'no free movement'. Because the Rome Treaty and EC legislation have not been overtly explicit[6] in distinguishing between 'persons' who may not exercise mobility, one may assume that those 'persons' not mentioned above could be placed near the end-point of 'no free movement'. As we shall discuss next, EU member states' ongoing efforts to establish a common migration policy contributed to clarifying which 'persons' were explicitly prohibited from exercising mobility. Thus, if we juxtaposed the distinct categories of 'persons' according to their access of free movement within the EU, we find an obvious inequality gap between those entitled and those excluded. Put simply, free movement of persons did not apply equally to all persons.

Toward a Common European Migration Policy: A Brief Overview

Migration reached the top of the European agenda when the Maastricht Treaty established immigration and asylum as two policy fields that were of 'common interest' for EU member states (OJ C 191/1 1992). Considering that border control has been integral to the Weberian conception of the sovereign state, this development was remarkable and a brief examination reveals how 'free movement of persons' has been

[6] The only exception to this has been a 1964 Council Declaration, which excluded 'refugees from free movement, but declare[d] that refugees should be considered with special favour' (Niessen 1992: 678); but it did not elaborate on what 'special favour' entailed or how it would be achieved.

central to this process. By signing the Single European Act (SEA) in February 1986, the member states had committed themselves to transforming Europe into 'an area without internal frontiers' – a direct reference to free movement. According to Adrian Fortescue (2002), the first Commission Director-General for justice and home affairs, the unanimity rule prevalent in European decision-making at the time was a significant factor behind the lack of advancement in implementing the four freedoms. Thus, to address the legislative stalemate, the SEA stipulated that for all issues relating to free movement the Council was to decide via qualified majority voting (QMV); with, however, one exception. For free movement of 'persons', the Council would reach a decision after consensus has been reached among the members. The member states were eager to ensure that the SEA did not infringe on their right to adopt 'necessary' border control measures. However, the member states were also anxious to give impetus to the integration process. To this end, the European states annexed several declarations to the SEA that were contradictory in terms of their intended effects. For instance, whereas 'Political Declaration (No. 2) by the Governments of the Member States on the free movement of persons' showed that the member states would do their utmost to implement free movement 'without prejudice to the powers of the Community', 'General Declaration (No. 6) on Articles 13 to 19 of the Single European Act' stipulated that the free movement provisions shall not affect the 'right of Member States to take such measures as they consider necessary'. This outcome can be seen as the result of the member states' 'agreement to disagree' with regards to the removal of internal borders against free movement of persons, how this could be achieved, and the roles to be accorded to the central institutions in this process.

The 'agreement to disagree' is key to explaining the evolution of European migration cooperation and the current diverse categorization of 'persons' eligible for mobility. Whilst member states such as Germany, France, and the Benelux countries viewed that within an internally borderless Europe all persons legally present should be entitled to free movement, other EC members such as Britain wanted only EC nationals to have access to mobility (Pallett 2001). Divergence in their approach had led the Community members to pursue two distinct institutional paths with regards to border control. The first path was created in June 1985 when the Benelux, France and Germany signed the Schengen Convention. Whilst it has now been incorporated into the European legal framework, Schengen cooperation up until 1999 was conducted exclusively outside the purview of the EU. Schengen cooperation has been crucial for EU migration cooperation because it explicitly identified free movement and external migration as inseparable developments that must be addressed simultaneously. Next, after the SEA declared that the Community was to be 'an area without internal frontiers', Britain proposed in 1986 the creation of the Ad Hoc Group on Immigration. An intergovernmental body, the Ad Hoc Group was tasked to examine how the Community could stop unauthorized migration (de Lobkowicz 2002: 29).[7] The timing of the British initiative and its initial resistance against treaty revision suggest that the Ad Hoc Group was the British attempt to re-set the migration agenda after the Schengen endeavour. In contrast to Schengen, the Ad Hoc Group on Immigration was established within the European framework but the central institutions exercised limited decision-making powers. To assist the Ad Hoc Group, the member states created the Group of Coordinators in 1988 to give 'impetus to and unblock the whole complex of intergovernmental and Community work in the fields of free movement of persons' (House of Lords 1989: Appendix 5). The Group of Coordinators became a key decision-maker when the Maastricht Treaty provided a legal basis for existing European migration cooperation. Indeed, rather than introduce new institutional arrangements, the Maastricht Treaty formalized the member states' 'agreement to disagree'.

Changing migratory trends shortly after the collapse of the Soviet Union prompted European states to engage in regulatory competition so as to minimize 'unwanted' migration, and their failure to independently affect a 'solution' exerted significant pressures for EU constitutional change (Barbou des Places 2003; Thielemann and Dewan 2006). Moreover, the minimal advancement in migration cooperation at the European-level also provided the appropriate institutional context for treaty revision. For EU migration cooperation, the entry into force of the Amsterdam Treaty in 1999 marked the transition of external migration regulation from an exclusive national prerogative to a shared competence between the European institutions and the member states. Such institutional change also widened the range of legal instruments that were available for EU migration cooperation. In addition to joint positions, joint actions and conventions, the member states now have the possibility to achieve their migration objectives by using Council directives and

[7] The mandate of the Ad Hoc Group on Immigration reflected its genesis as an offshoot of the Trevi Group. Established in the 1970s and also a British initiative, Trevi was a forum within which interior ministers exchanged information and views concerning police training and how to prevent terrorism, drug trafficking and organised crime (House of Lords 1993: 65).

regulations, which are enforceable under Community law. Yet, because it incorporated the Schengen framework into the EU legal order, the Amsterdam Treaty had to accommodate the ongoing 'agreement to disagree' between the member states. To this end, two distinct 'opt-out' mechanisms were adopted for three European countries, namely the UK, Ireland and Denmark. Whilst their rationales for wanting to remain outside of existing EU migration cooperation were different, the outcome was the same: the national authorities of these three member states would individually determine which third country national were permitted to cross their external borders (den Boer and Corrado 1999). To execute the Amsterdam Treaty and its goal of 'establish[ing] progressively an area of freedom, security and justice', the European heads of state and government adopted an ambitious working program at Tampere, Finland in October 1999 (Council Document 1999b). The Tampere program served as the blueprint for the way forward in justice and home affairs issues (see Vink this volume).

A common European migration policy was identified as one of the four critical 'milestones' of the Tampere agenda and it was to be realized through a three-pronged strategy. Firstly, the European Council argued that 'partnership with countries of origin' would be essential. Here, they advocated the 'comprehensive approach', which would address the 'political, human rights and development issues in countries and regions of origin and transit' (Council Document 1999b: paragraph 11). Specifically, EU efforts would contribute to 'combating poverty, improving living conditions and job opportunities, preventing conflicts and consolidating democratic states and ensuring respect for human rights, in particular rights of minorities, women and children' (ibid). Whilst the Tampere program did not outline which measures the EU could and would adopt in this regard, it did acknowledge the contribution from the High Level Working Group on Asylum and Immigration (HLWG).[8] Secondly, the European heads of state and government announced that the EU would enforce 'fair treatment of third country nationals' by drawing on best practices and experiences concerning how to combat racism and xenophobia. To this end, the Commission was invited to propose how article 13 of the Rome Treaty on anti-racism and anti-xenophobia could be implemented. Moreover, the EU was to adopt measures approximating

[8] A Dutch initiative, the HLWG was created in 1998 to 'help reduce the influx of asylum seekers into the Member States of the European Union. Its main aim is to analyse and combat the reasons for flight taking account of the political and human rights situation' (Council Document 1999a).

national legislations concerning the admission and residence of third country nationals and the 'rights' to be given accordingly. Finally, the EU would establish a common migration policy through the 'management of migration flows' by developing 'information campaigns on the actual possibilities for legal immigration, and for the prevention of all forms of trafficking in human beings' (Council Document 1999b: paragraph 22). Essential to an effective campaign, it was argued, would be an active policy on visa and false documents with the legal possibility to readmit migrants to their countries of origin. EU measures imposing 'severe sanctions' against 'trafficking in human beings and economic exploitation of migrants', and readmission agreements between the Union and third countries were also foreseen.

The results achieved at the completion of the Tampere program were impressive. To start, in the area of illegal migration, the EU had concluded readmission agreements with several third countries and territories; for instance, with Hong Kong (in 2002), Macao (2003), Sri Lanka (2004), and Albania (2005). Negotiations have been underway with Morocco, Pakistan, and Russia since February 2000, with Ukraine since March 2002, and with Algeria, China and Turkey since October 2002 (Chou 2006: 8). Three Council directives had also been adopted concerning illegal immigration: mutual recognition of decisions taken by the member states to expel third country nationals (Council Document 2001a), approximation of carrier liability[9] (Council Document 2001b), and short-term residence permits to be issued to 'victims' of illegal migration or trafficking who cooperate with authorities[10] (European Commission 2002). In the area of legal migration, the member states reached an agreement on two Council directives for study and vocational training; more specifically, they concerned the procedures and conditions for admitting third country nationals for scientific research (Council Document 2005), and for pupil

[9] By implementing a policy concerning 'carrier liability', the member states were able to fine carriers if they brought into the country any undocumented third country nationals (Barbou des Places 2003: 12; Collinson 1996: 80). Also commonly referred to as 'carrier sanctions', it was first enacted by Denmark in 1983, with Germany, Belgium and the UK introducing the concept into their national legislation four years later.

[10] An extensive critique of the victims directive is provided in Chou (2008), in which I argued that in its current form the victims directive will not affect the human trafficking phenomenon because, even when they do cooperate with the competent authorities, victims remains vulnerable to deportation and subsequent re-trafficking.

exchange, studies, voluntary service and unremunerated training (Council Document 2004a). Continuing, the EU adopted two Council directives concerning third country nationals who are or have the prospects of becoming long-term residents in an EU member state. One of the directives sought to approximate their positions by stipulating the duration of residence, conditions for acquiring long-term resident status and the rights to which recognized migrants are entitled (Council Document 2003b). The second directive outlined the right to family reunification for long-term residents or a migrant who holds a residence permit valid for at least one year and 'who has reasonable prospects of obtaining the right of permanent residence' (Council Document 2003a). By contrast, the EU has not adopted any measures with regards to labour migration. Whilst the Commission did propose a Council directive on the conditions of entry and residence of migrants for paid and self-employment in 2001, the member states failed to reach an agreement on the draft proposal, which was withdrawn by the Commission on 17 March 2006. With regards to visas, the EU adopted regulations concerning uniform visa formats (Council Document 2002), the conditions for issuing visas for stays shorter than three months, and the lists of third countries whose nationals required or did not need to obtain visas to enter the Union (i.e. the so-called 'black' and 'white' lists) (Council Document 2001c).[11] In sum, during the short space of five years, the EU adopted multiple measures with regards to illegal and legal migration.

The adopted migration policies under the Tampere agenda, whilst substantial, contribute to widening the existing inequality gap between those entitled or privileged to exercise mobility within the Union and those ordinarily excluded. Indeed, by explicitly dividing third country nationals into categories of those who required a visa to enter the EU and those who did not, the European states further differentiated between 'persons' not traditionally eligible for free movement. For instance, those migrants from third countries belonging to the 'black' list have to overcome the initial hurdle of obtaining entry into an EU member state before they could even contemplate the possibility of free movement. Whilst the member states did facilitate this process by adopting provisions governing the common conditions for visa issuance and mobility of visa-holders within the EU, the non-applicability of these provisions in the case of Ireland and the UK meant that some migrants remained excluded. For example, a third country national on the 'black' visa list who has entry clearance for the UK would

[11] The 'black' and 'white' lists were amended in December 2001 to remove Romania from the 'black' list (Council Document 2001d).

need to obtain a visa for Ireland and another for the Schengen territory before they would be permitted to cross the external borders of these countries. By contrast, migrants belonging to countries on the 'white' list could move freely within the EU for a period of less than 90 days. Thus, we could also view recent efforts in establishing a common European visa policy as introducing another category of 'persons' who qualify for 'free movement with conditions'. Yet for 'persons' who remain within the category of 'no free movement', the successful conclusion and introduction of readmission agreements[12] and clauses[13] between the EU and third countries, and the adoption of the mutual recognition of expulsion orders, provided legal recourse for European states to remove them from the Union territory should they fail to obtain prior authorization to reside or enter the EU. Whilst integral to any robust migration regime, expulsion policies must co-exist with viable legal migratory routes so as to ensure the credibility of such regime. The EU did make significant advances in the area of legal migration when the member states adopted Council directives concerning the right of family reunification, study and research, but their failure to agree on any policies with regards to labour migration undermines the credibility of the current EU migration regime. Beyond family reunification, the only alternative and legal route for settlement is through labour migration.[14] Taking sex workers as a case study, the following section shows how the lack of a common approach

---

[12] However, both Bouteillet-Paquet (2003) and Ellermann (2008) question the effectiveness of these readmission agreements in practice by demonstrating the difficulties that European officials faced in convincing their counterparts in third countries to accept their own nationals. Moreover, Bouteillet-Paquet (2003) argues that the combined usage of these readmission agreements with the notion of 'safe third countries' seriously violate the right of asylum seekers to seek refuge according to the Geneva Convention.

[13] Readmission clauses carry the same legal effect as a readmission agreement, but are ordinarily inserted into an agreement not explicitly about migration. For instance, the 'migration clause' outlined in article 13 of the Cotonou Agreement obliges the signatories – European states and the ACP (African, Caribbean and Pacific) countries – to readmit their nationals should any be considered irregularly present in their respective states. The Cotonou Agreement, which replaced the Lomé Convention in June 2000, is more concerned with poverty reduction, financial cooperation and trade.

[14] For instance, to satisfy the residency requirement migrants need to demonstrate that they have resided in the host country for a pre-determined period. Ordinarily, the years that a third country national has resided for non-labour purposes such as study are either not taken into consideration or only a fraction of which can be used to fulfil the residency requirement.

toward labour migration creates the capacity to further marginalize those third country nationals already ineligible for mobility within the context of an internally borderless Europe.

Sex Workers in the EU: Mobility of Service Providers vs. Movement of Illegal Migrants

As the oldest profession in human history, sex work is regulated differentially, if at all, among the EU member states.[15] Whilst no ideal 'model' exists to capture the complexity of the diverse national approaches toward sex work, three general legislative categories have often been suggested, and they are prohibitionism, regulationism, and abolitionism (Askola 2007). For prohibitionist states such as the UK and Ireland, sex work is seen as immoral and illegal; persons who offer or purchase sexual services are punishable by law. Regulationist countries such as the Netherlands and Sweden view the exchange of sexual services for financial gain differently. Whilst morally condemning the nature of such work, states which are regulationist tolerate sex work as a 'necessary evil'. Thus, rather than criminalize (nearly) all aspects of sex work, regulationist countries attempt to control it by adopting legislation that monitor the sale of sex and the health of the providers. By contrast, states such as Italy which are classically considered abolitionist do not see women who engage in sex work as morally corrupt. Indeed, abolitionist governments perceive these women as victims needing to be rescued. Reflective of the feminist approach, abolitionist states view sex work as degrading for women and seek to punish those who engage in the act of trafficking, which has been the primary channel through which sex workers enter Europe, and pimping. In practice, however, distinctions blur between the countries officially categorized as one of the three legislative models. For instance, formally prohibitionist, Britain allows a sex worker to work indoors given that he or she is providing the services without the assistance of a pimp and has not advertised such services (Danna 2003). Thus, for Askola (2006), the UK is 'officially abolitionist' but with 'a semi-prohibitionist tinge'. The aim of this discussion is not to categorize

---

[15] The following discussion will not debate the question of 'choice' concerning a worker's decision to engage in sexual activities in exchange for money (see Chou 2008). Rather, the focus is placed on those who are currently in the profession and examines how EU free movement provisions distinguishes between European and non-EU workers in this regard. Undoubtedly, the European approach toward sex providers affects such 'choice' and we return to this in the final section.

the various national approaches toward sex workers. Instead, it offers an alternative perspective to the categorization exercise by focusing on how, within the context of free movement, sex providers who are EU citizens or nationals of the then candidate members are treated differently than those who are third country nationals. The brief examination demonstrates the starkness of the inequality gap between those entitled, privileged or barred from mobility outlined in the previous two sections.

The EU has no explicit competence to regulate sex work, but it has the authority to intervene if a member state permits its own nationals to work as sex providers. In such a scenario, EU nationals who are sex workers would be entitled to work in the sex industry of the permissive member state within the framework of free movement of persons. Moreover, under Community law all EU nationals who are sex workers are to be accorded the same rights and social benefits as those of the host member state. This principle has been famously upheld by the Court of Justice in 1982. In the joint cases of *Andoui and Cornuaille vs. Belgium*, the Belgian authorities refused to issue residence permits to two French nationals on the grounds that they 'were waitresses in a bar which was suspect from the point of view of morals' (European court of Justice 1982); both women repeatedly denied that they were prostitutes. Invoking the public policy exception clause concerning free movement, which would allow a member state to derogate from treaty obligations, the Belgian authorities sought to deport Andoui and Cornuaille. The Court ruled that Belgium could only do so if 'it took repressive measures or other genuine and effective measures intended to combat such conduct against its own nationals' (Flynn 1996: 312). Given that Belgium only 'banned soliciting, incitement to debauchery, exploitation of prostitution, keeping a disorderly house and living on immoral earnings' but not prostitution (Askola 2007: 53-54), it was unable to expel Andoui and Cornuaille on grounds of public policy. The Court reaffirmed its opinion twenty years later in the case of *Jany and Others vs. the Netherlands* (European Court of Justice 2001). The case, however, involved sex workers who were nationals of Poland and the Czech Republic, which only became EU members in May 2004. The Association Agreements concluded between the Union and these two countries expressly privileged the nationals from the latter to the 'right of establishment' in the EU if they intended to 'take up an activity as a self-employed person' (European Court of Justice 2001: paragraph 3). The Dutch officials argued that since sex work was not 'socially acceptable', Jany and others were eligible for deportation (Askola 2007: 54). To this the Court responded that, since it did not explicitly prohibit its own citizens from sex work, the Netherlands could not legally act against these Polish and Czech nationals in accordance to the provisions contained within the Association Agreements. In sum, workers who are allowed to exercise free movement within the EU may do so as providers of sexual services in member states where such acts had not been explicitly prohibited or tolerated in practice.

By contrast, third country nationals are not permitted to enter the EU legally as sex workers. The notion of legality for migrants here is defined by the European authorities as possessing the appropriate work and residence permit to practice in the sex industry. Since most member states straddle between the official position of prohibiting (some form of) sex work but permissively allowing it in practice, no formal channels exist for non-EU sex workers to gain entry into the Union and reside legally. Take for example Belgium and France; both countries criminalize the active procurement of sex but prostitution is allowed in both states. More specifically, in Belgium, sex workers must not be a nuisance to the public order or make 'abnormal profits' from their trade; in France, sex work could only be carried out in specified locations and the authorities have criminalized the act of purchasing sexual services from persons who are under eighteen or those who are disabled (European Parliament 2004). Similar provisions and practices exist throughout the EU. In the event that third country nationals have been found to be working as sex providers, the authorities could deport them on the grounds that they violated their conditions of entry and residence even though sex work is tolerated in their country. Indeed, this applies equally to both long-term residents and those on a short-term visa (i.e. less than 90 days). For long-term residents, their authorization to remain in a host member state – either through family reunification or employment[16] – would exclude their working in the sex industry; for 'tourists', their conditions of entry would preclude any possibility of work. For migrant sex workers who are irregularly present in the EU, their deportation is seemingly automatic. The exception to this has been the practical approach adopted by Austrian authorities in Graz and Vienna. The police in Graz and Vienna have willingly registered unauthorized foreign sex workers for weekly health checks and, in so

[16] Authorisation to work in an EU member state could be given for purposes of paid or self-employment. Work permits issued to employees of a European company are ordinarily non-transferable in the first instance and for a limited duration. For entrepreneurs, permission to be working in Europe would only be given after a rigorous demonstration of sufficient financial means and also a business plan.

doing, recognize and tolerate their presence (IOM 1996). Such exception aside, there is no legal route for third country nationals to enter the EU on a work permit that would allow them to work as sex providers, and those who are tolerated are present in the EU under extremely precarious conditions and are susceptible to exploitation. The lack of a legal labour migration route for migrant sex workers certainly does not decrease the demand of their services. Actually, as Anderson and Davidson (2003) argue, the unregulated nature of such work, coupled with the nonexistence of a viable labour migration channel, contributes to the exploitation of sex workers who are third country nationals by unscrupulous persons (see also Chou 2008). This outcome certainly challenges the democratic ethos of the European integration process and in the following section we examine potential ways to tackle this policy dilemma.

European Union: Market Politics or a Political Market?

In the preamble of the Lisbon Treaty, EU member states declared that European integration will proceed by 'drawing inspiration on the cultural, religious and humanist inheritance of Europe, from which have developed the universal values of the inviolable and inalienable rights of the human person, freedom, democracy, equality and the rule of law'. This statement revealed that, whilst the European unification process has previously been dominated by market politics inherent within the logic of economic integration, the European project has since moved on to grander aspirations. This chapter has shown that, however, the EU remains a highly politicized market where all 'persons' are not equal before a court of law. Indeed, as the member states strived to realize the four freedoms, they distinguished between different categories of persons who were entitled or privileged to exercise mobility and those who would be excluded. These categories became more defined as the European states strengthen their external borders through the formation of a common migration policy. By erecting legal barriers against what they considered as 'unauthorized' entry and residence the European heads of state and government confirmed that some 'persons' already under the category of 'no free movement' would be explicitly criminalized if they attempt to exercise mobility within the EU. However, such designation has not been unproblematic, not least with regards to both the economic logic and moral aspirations of European integration. For instance, the free movement of sex workers as service providers within the Union illustrated the starkness of the widening divide of inequality simply as the result of EU member states' unilateral decision to consider certain activities criminal only for particular individuals. Given that equality remains an inherent objective of the unification process, this recent development is a cause for concern.

It is proposed that a three-pronged strategy of 'universal principle, comprehensive policy and good practice' would contribute to narrowing the inequality gap established by the existing categorizations of 'persons' entitled, privileged or prevented from exercising mobility within the EU. To start, the 'universal principle' approach refers to codifying a set of rights that would be applicable to all persons undifferentiated by any sets of criteria such as gender, nationality or age. Most of these rights already exist at the European-level (for instance, the European Charter of Fundamental Rights) and also in the member states (European Convention on Human Rights and the Geneva Convention…etc.). Thus, rather than reiterate these rights, the focus should be placed on extending their applicability beyond the core constituent to whom these rights originally addressed. Put simply, to realize the universality of these principles. That is to say, not only should EU citizens and third country nationals who are long-term residents in a European member state be entitled to these rights; but all persons. The aim is to minimize the multiplicity of differentiation between 'persons', which could be achieved in two ways: by removing qualifying statements such as 'nationals of third countries who are authorized to work…' (Article 15.5 of the EU Charter) and simplifying the recipient to 'all persons', or by introducing similar statements to every article that makes a distinction between 'everyone' and 'EU citizens'. Whilst the latter appears redundant, the explicitness of the statements may be easier to enforce in a court of law that has jurisdiction. Next, in order to give effect to the universal principles, the EU and its member states must introduce a comprehensive migration policy. By comprehensive, I mean policies with regards to both removal and entry-residence. As mentioned earlier, a robust migration regime consists of expulsion policies and legislation allowing for legal entry and stay. It follows that a 'comprehensive' EU migration strategy would mean enacting illegal and labour migration policies. Lastly, the 'good practice' component of the strategy pertains to compliance with adopted policies. The effectiveness of this latter approach can be measured by the minimal frequency or lack of infringement cases the Commission brings against some member states. In sum, if the EU and its member states are serious about addressing the inequality gap, they must simultaneously address the three components of the proposed strategy.

It should be stressed that since the member states failed to adopt any EU-wide policy with regards to labour migration at the 'completion' of the Tampere program, the Commission has been actively engaged in generating interest in this area.[17] For instance, in January 2005, the Commission launched a public debate on an EU approach to managing economic migration (European Commission 2005b). This was followed in December 2005 by a Commission communication on a 'policy plan on legal migration', which advocated a strategy based on responses to the 'green paper' (European Commission 2005a). In this communication, the Commission outlined five new legislative measures on labour migration: a general framework directive[18] setting out a 'single application for a joint permit' and the rights for migrants legally employed within the EU but who had not acquired long-term residence (scheduled to be ready in 2007); four Council directives on the conditions of entry and residence of highly skilled workers (i.e. the 'Blue Card' initiative presented in October 2007), seasonal workers (2008), intra-corporate transferees (2009), and remunerated trainees (2009). In 2006, the nexus between migration and development reached the top of the European agenda (European Commission 2006). Here, the so-called 'global approach to migration' was debated by the EU member states with regards to the eradication of the 'root causes' behind involuntary migration (see Chou 2006). Continuing, in 2007 the Commission examined the possibility of introducing 'circular migration', which would allow nationals of third countries to legally enter and reside in the EU for a pre-determined period, through 'mobility partnerships' between certain member states and some third countries (Chou 2008; European Commission 2007a; 2007b). At the time of writing, the prospects for implementing the three-pronged strategy advocated in

---

[17] The member states endorsed the successor to the Tampere agenda – the Hague programme – in November 2004 without much fanfare. It will remain operational until 2010 (see Council Document 2004b).

[18] Commission officials tasked to prepare the directives indicated that it was unlikely that the EU member states would endorse the framework directive (interview conducted on 30 March 2006, Brussels, Belgium). Whilst the EU has in place two Council directives setting out a 'general framework for equal treatment in employment and occupation' (Council Document 2000b) and stipulating the 'principle of equal treatment between persons irrespective of racial or ethnic origin' (Council Document 2000a), these two directives were careful in noting that their legal effects were not applicable to migrants with regards to their entry, residence, and access to employment and occupation. Thus, the framework directive essentially tried to achieve what the failed Council directive concerning labour migration sought to do; it would be applicable to the four specific directives that follow.

this chapter are not promising. For instance, in November 2008, the UK tabled a proposal in the Council to curtail access to free movement for persons who have been found to 'abuse' and 'misuse' the rights (Council Document 2008a; 2008b). The British proposal aims to reverse the ruling of *Metock* in which the ECJ opined that the family members of EU citizens who are third country nationals need not be legally resident in the Union to access family reunion rights (such as mobility) enshrined in Community law (see OJ C 236/4 2008). If enforced, the British initiative will introduce another category of 'persons' who would fall under the end-point of 'no free movement'. To conclude, it is worth recalling that the EU heads of state and government endorsed the 'European Pact on Immigration and Asylum' at its meeting in 15 October 2008. At the heart of the Immigration Pact is the so-called 'ten common principles' proposed by the Commission and the first principle declared that the EU would establish 'clear rules and a level playing field' (European Commission 2008). For migrants continuously and explicitly excluded from exercising mobility within the Union, this would indeed be a welcome objective and should be the way forward.

Works Cited

Anderson, Bridget and Julia O'Connell Davidson. 2003. *Is trafficking in human beings demand driven? A multi-country pilot study*. Geneva: International Organization for Migration.

Aral, Berdal. 1997. The case of free movement for workers between Turkey and the European Union. *The Turkish Yearbook* 27: 1-11.

—. 2005. Making sense of the anomalies in Turkish-European Union relations. *Journal of Economic and Social Research* 7(1): 99-120.

Askola, Heli. 2006. Globalised sexual labour in the EU: Challenging domestic debates. Paper presented at 2006 Biennial Conference of the European Community Studies Association – Canada, May 19-20, in Victoria, Canada.

—. 2007. *Legal responses to trafficking in women for sexual exploitation in the European Union*. Oxford and Portland: Hart Publishing.

Barbou des Places, Segolene. 2003. Evolution of asylum legislation in the EU: Insights from regulatory competition theory (RSC No. 2003/16), EUI Working Papers. Florence: Robert Schuman Centre for Advanced Studies.

Bouteillet-Paquet, Daphne. 2003. Passing the buck: A critical analysis of the readmission policy implemented by the European Union and its Member States. *European Journal of Migration and Law* 5: 359-77.

Callovi, Giuseppe. 1992. Regulation of immigration in 1993: Pieces of the European Community jig-saw puzzle. *International Migration Review* 26(2): 353-372.

Chou, Meng-Hsuan. 2006. EU and the migration-development nexus: What prospects for EU-wide policies? *Centre on Migration, Policy and Society, Working Paper* WP-06-37.

—. 2008. The European Union and the fight against human trafficking: Comprehensive or contradicting? *St Antony's International Review* 4(1): 76-95.

Collinson, Sarah. 1996. Visa requirements, carrier sanctions, "safe third countries" and "readmission": The development of an asylum "buffer zone" in Europe. *Transactions of the Institute of British Geographers* 21(1): 76-90.

Council of the European Union. 1968. *Regulation (EEC) No. 1612/68 of the Council of 15 October 1968 on freedom of movement for workers within the Community*. Brussels: Council of the European Union.

—. 1971. *Regulation (EEC) No 1408/71 of the Council of 14 June 1971 on the application of social security schemes to employed persons and their families moving within the Community*. Brussels: Council of the European Union.

—. 1999a. *Strategy on migration and migration policy, Brussels, 19 January 1999, Limite, CK4 4 ASIM3, from the Presidency to the K4 Committee*. Brussels: Council of the European Union.

—. 1999b. Tampere European Council Conclusions, 15-16 October 1999. Available online at: http://europa.eu.int/european_council/conclusions/index_en.htm.

—. 2000a. *Council Directive 2000/43/EC of 29 June 2000 implementing the principle of equal treatment between persons irrespective of racial or ethnic origin (OJ L 180, 19.07.2000, p.22-26)*. Brussels: Council of the European Union.

—. 2000b. *Council Directive 2000/78/EC of 27 November 2000 establishing a general framework for equal treatment in employment and occupation (OJ L 303, 02.12.2000, p.16-22)*. Brussels: Council of the European Union.

—. 2001a. *Council Directive 2001/40/EC of 28 May 2001 on the mutual recognition of decisions on the expulsion of third country nationals (OJ L 149, 02/06/2001, p.0034-0036)*. Brussels: Council of the European Union.

—. 2001b. *Council Directive 2001/51/EC of 28 June 2001 supplementing the provisions of Article 26 of the Convention implementing the*

Schengen Agreement of 14 June 1985 (OJ L 187 of 10.07.2001, page 45). Brussels: Council of the European Union.

—. 2001c. *Council Regulation (EC) No 539/2001 of 15 March 2001 listing the third countries whose nationals must be in possession of visas when crossing the external borders and those whose nationals are exempt from that requirement* (OJ L 81, 21.3.2001, p.1-7). Brussels: Council of the European Union.

—. 2001d. *Council Regulation (EC) No 2414/2001 of 7 December 2001 amending Regulation (EC) No 539/2001 listing the third countries whose nationals must be in possession of visas when crossing the external borders of Member States and those whose nationals are exempt from that requirement (OJ L 327, 12.12.2001, p.1-2).* Brussels: Council of the European Union.

—. 2002. *Council Regulation (EC) No 334/2002 of 18 February 2002 amending Regulation (EC) No 1683/95 laying down a uniform format for visas (OJ L 053, 23.02.2002, p. 7-8).* Brussels: Council of the European Union.

—. 2003a. *Council Directive 2003/86/EC of 22 September 2003 on the right to family reunification (OJ L 251, 3.10.2003, p.12-18).* Brussels: Council of the European Union.

—. 2003b. *Council Directive 2003/109/EC of 25 November 2003 concerning the status of third-country nationals who are long-term residents (OJ L 16, 23.1.2004, p. 44-53).* Brussels: Council of the European Union.

—. 2004a. *(114/04) Council Directive on the admission of third country nationals for the purposes of studies, pupil exchanges, unremunerated training or voluntary services.* Brussels: Commission of the European Communities.

—. 2004b. *(16054/04) The Hague Programme: strengthening freedom, security and justice in the European Union.* Brussels: Council of the European Union.

—. 2005. *Council Directive 2005/71/EC on a specific procedure for admitting third-country nationals for the purposes of scientific research (OJ L 289, 3/11/2005, p.0015).* Brussels: Commission of the European Communities.

—. 2008a. *Free movement of persons: abuses and substantive problems - Draft Council conclusions on abuses and misuses of the right to free movement of persons, 16151/1/08 REV 1, 26 November 2008.* Brussels: Council of the European Union.

—. 2008b. *Free movement of persons: abuses and substantive problems - Draft Council Conclusions, 15903/08, 18 November 2008*. Brussels: Council of the European Union.

Danna, Daniella. 2003. Trafficking and prostitution of foreigners in the context of the EU countries' policy about prostitution. Paper presented at the NEWR Workshop on Trafficking, April 25-26, in Amsterdam, the Netherlands.

de Lobkowicz, Wenceslas. 2002. *L'Europe et la sécurité intérieure*. Paris: La Documentation Française.

den Boer, Monica and Laura Corrado. 1999. For the record or off the record: Comments about the incorporation of Schengen into the EU. *European Journal of Migration and Law* 1: 397-418.

Ellermann, Antje. 2008. The limits of unilateral migration control: Deportation and inter-state cooperation. *Government and Opposition* 43(2): 168-89.

European Commission. 1970. *Regulation (EEC) No 1251/170 of the Commission of 29 June 1970 on the right of workers to remain in the territory of a Member State after having been employed in that State*. Brussels: Commission of the European Communities.

—. 2002. *Proposal for a Council Directive on the short-term residence permit issued to victims of action to facilitate illegal immigration or trafficking in human beings who cooperate with the competent authorities, 71 final.* Brussels: Office for Official Publications of the European Communities.

—. 2005a. *Communication from the Commission: Policy plan on legal migration, 669 final.* Brussels: Office for Official Publications of the European Communities.

—. 2005b. *Green Paper on an EU approach to managing economic migration, 811 final.* Brussels: Office for Official Publications of the European Communities.

—. 2006. *Communication from the Commission to the European Parliament and the Council. The global approach to migration one year on: towards a comprehensive European migration policy, 735 final.* Brussels: Office for Official Publications of the European Communities.

—. 2007a. *Circular migration and mobility partnerships between the European Union and third countries, MEMO/07/197*. Brussels: Office for Official Publications of the European Communities.

—. 2007b. *Communication from the Commission to the European Parliament, the Council, the European Economic and Social Committee and the Committee of the Regions on circular migration and mobility partnerships between the European Union and third countries, 248 final.* Brussels: Office for Official Publications of the European Communities.

—. 2008. *Questions and answers on the EU common immigration policy, Memo/08/404, Brussels, 17 June 2008.* Brussels: Commission of the European Union.

European Court of Justice. 1975. *Anita Cristini v Société nationale des chemins de fer français, Case 32/75 of 30 September 1975, Reference for a preliminary ruling: Cour d'appel de Paris – France.* Available online at: http://europa.eu.int/smartapi/cgi/sga_doc?smartapi!celexplus!prod!CELEXnumdoc&lg=en&numdoc=61975J0032.

—. 1982. *Judgment of the Court of 18 May 1982, Rezguia Adoui v Belgian State and City of Liège, Dominique Cornuaille v Belgian State, joined cases 115 and 116/81.* Brussels: Office for Official Publications of the European Communities.

—. 1983. *Sandro Forcheri and his wife Marisa Forcheri, née Marino, v Belgian State and asbl Institut Supérieur de Sciences Humaines Appliquées - Ecole Ouvrière Supérieure, Case 152/82 of 13 July 1983, Reference for a preliminary ruling: Justice de paix de Bruxelles (4e canton) – Belgium.* Available online at: http://europa.eu.int/smartapi/cgi/sga_doc?smartapi!celexplus!prod!CELEXnumdoc&lg=en&numdoc=61982J0152.

—. 1987. *Meryem Demirel v Stadt Schwäbisch Gmünd, Case 12/86 of 30 September 1987, Reference for a preliminary ruling: Verwaltungsgericht Stuttgart – Germany.* Available online at: http://europa.eu.int/smartapi/cgi/sga_doc?smartapi!celexplus!prod!CELEXnumdoc&lg=en&numdoc=61986J0012.

—. 1990a. *Massam Dzodzi v Belgian State, Joined cases C-297/88 and C-197/89 of 18 October 1990, References for a preliminary ruling: Tribunal de première instance de Bruxelles et Cour d'appel de Bruxelles - Belgium, Preliminary rulings - Jurisdiction of the Court - Reference in national legislation to provisions of Community law - Right of residence - Right to remain - Directive 64/221/EEC.* Available online at: http://europa.eu.int/smartapi/cgi/sga_doc?smartapi!celexplus!prod!CELEXnumdoc&lg=en&numdoc=61988J0297.

—. 1990b. *Rush Portuguesa Lda v Office national d'immigration, Case C-113/89 of 27 March 1990, Reference for a preliminary ruling: Tribunal administratif de Versailles – France.* Available online at:

http://europa.eu.int/smartapi/cgi/sga_doc?smartapi!celexplus!prod!CELEXnumdoc&lg=en&numdoc=61989J0113.

—. 2001. *Judgment of the Court of 20 November 2001, in Case C-268/99 (reference for a preliminary ruling from the Arrondissementsrechtbank te's-Gravenhage): Aldona Malgorzata Jany and Others v Staatssecretaris van Justitie.* Brussels: Office for Official Publications of the European Communities.

European Parliament. 2004. *Public hearing on the consequences of the sex industry in the EU, a summary of the prostitution regulations in the EU Member States, Monday, 19 January 2004, Committee on Women's Rights and Equal Opportunities.* Brussels: European Parliament.

Flynn, Leo. 1996. The body politic(s) of EC law. In *Sex equality law in the European Union*, ed. Tamara K. Hervey and David O'Keeffe. Chichester: John Wiley & Sons.

Fortescue, Adrian. 2002. *Justice and Home Affairs DG moving into the mainstream of European Commission work.* Available online at: http://europa.eu.int/comm/dgs/justice_home/director/dg_fortescue_adrian_en.htm).

House of Lords. 1989. *1992: Border control of people (Twenty-Second Report, Session 1988-1989, HL 90).* London: Her Majesty's Stationery Office.

—. 1993. *House of Lords Scrutiny of the Inter-Governmental Pillars of the European Union (Twenty-Eighth Report, Session 1992-1993, HL 124).* London: Her Majesty's Stationery Office.

IOM. 1996. *Trafficking in women to Austria for sexual exploitation, Migration Information Programme.* Brussels: International Organization for Migration.

Lewis, Orion and Sven Steinmo. 2008. Taking Evolution seriously. ARENA Working Paper #19.

Niessen, Jan. 1992. European Community legislation and intergovernmental cooperation in migration. *International Migration Review* 26(2): 676-84.

OJ C 191/1. 1992. *Treaty on European Union.* Brussels: European Communities.

OJ C 236/4. 2008. *Judgment of the Court (Grand Chamber) of 25 July 2008 (reference for a preliminary ruling from the High Court of Ireland) - Blaise Baheten Metock et al. v Minister for Justice, Equality and Law Reform, Case C-127/08.* Brussels: Official Journal of the European Communities.

Pallett, Lesley. 2001. The United Kingdom position: Implementing the Schengen Protocol. In *Asylum, immigration and Schengen post-*

Amsterdam, ed. Clotilde Marinho, 91-105. Maastricht: European Institute of Public Administration.

Statec Luxembourg. 1990. *Statistiques historiques 1839-1989*. Luxembourg: Service Central de la Statistique et des Etudes Economiques.

Steering Group on Enlargement. 1992. Document for information, chronology of previous enlargements, DG I Enlargement Task Force. *Archives historiques des Communautés européennes*. Florence: Villa Il Poggiolo, Deposits, DEP. Graham JL Avery, GJLA, GJLA-000280.

Thielemann, Eiko and Torun Dewan. 2006. The myth of free-riding: Refugee protection and implicit burden-sharing. *West European Politics* 29(2): 351-69.

Ugur, Mehmet. 1995. Freedom of movement vs. exclusion: A reinterpretation of the "insider"-"outsider" divide in the European Union. *International Migration Review* 29(4): 964-99.

PART II

ISLAM, XENOPHOBIA AND IMMIGRANT INTEGRATION POLICIES

CHAPTER SIX

SECULAR AND RELIGIOUS GROUNDINGS OF EUROPEAN XENOPHOBIA: DISTINGUISHING FRENCH, POLISH, AND RUSSIAN PREJUDICES

RAYMOND TARAS

Fears, Migrants, and Religion

There have been alarming indications in Europe of the spread of xenophobic attitudes in the first decade of the new century. A number of studies have documented the rise of xenophobic politics (Lahav 2004; Messina 2007; Mudde 2007; Norris 2005; Roemer, Lee, and Van der Straeten 2007; Saideman and Ayres 2008; Taras 2009) Right-wing parties, and even mainstream ones campaigning on anti-migrant platforms, have recorded electoral inroads and gained influence in Austria, Belgium, Denmark, Greece, Italy, and Switzerland. In such recent accession states as Hungary, Poland and Romania, political attacks on the "other"—minority groups, neighbouring nations, as well as migrants from the east—were becoming more commonplace. The 2009 elections to the European Parliament—the first cross-national barometer of how the global financial crisis may have impacted citizen attitudes towards outsider groups—registered gains for anti-immigrant movements. Given the emphasis that the European Union has placed on setting standards of tolerance, inclusion, and incorporation, the news has not been good.

Xenophobia in a society can make its state lurch towards illiberal and undemocratic practices. While much of the xenophobia in Europe today represents an anti-immigrant backlash, it is also in part a backlash against Euro-elite discourse that is viewed as privileging civic rights for migrants over their civic obligations while, conversely, for ethnic majorities, underscoring their civic obligations at the expense of rights—national identity, language, lifestyle, and values.

The battle over rights and obligations is not confined to the nation-state but to the supranationalising European Union. In striving to deepen integration among 27 national identities and a myriad of minority and migrant groups, the dilemma facing Europe is straightforward: "Should the European public succumb to the threat of losing their unique cultures and identities for a viable European Union to exist or should the potential of this supranational force be dismissed for the preservation of national identity?" (Lahav 2004: 104).

Understated in dominant Euro-discourse on identity has been the role of religion in the process of supranational identity formation. This is largely explained by the EU's construction of an identity based on secularism. What follows logically from this is the defining of the stranger, the other, as someone who *is* religious.

Equating *homo religio* with the stranger is, paradoxically, not always self-evident in the case of migrants. Migrants are typed as not belonging for many other reasons (see Beaseley von Burg, Gardner, and Tomen in this volume). They are visible minorities who generally do not have European origins. They speak non-European languages and embrace non-European customs and traditions. Their values commonly are at odds with European norms governing democratic and liberal practices. A process of migrant integration into European society will, it is believed, narrow these differences. It would be too provocative to state openly, however, that abandoning religious practices is also a prerequisite for assuming a pan-European (secular) identity. So it is not said.

Is the EU's strident secularism the root cause of European phobias of strangers? Should Islamophobia—today the most attention-getting of antipathies in Europe—be placed alongside other religiously anchored phobias, for example, dislike of Eastern Orthodoxy, of Eastern European Roman Catholicism, of Judaism? Is the secular EU even Christophobic, as some observers have suggested?

In short, are anti-migrant attitudes part of—and not distinct from—a more general EU antipathy towards religious groups of any kind? Does a process of foreignisation take place whereby religious adherents become Europe's strangers? To address these questions this Chapter considers the cases of Islamophobia in France, Orthodoxophobia in Poland, and "sectophobia" in Russia. Have all Muslims in France been re-defined as strangers? Has Russia's brutal occupation of Poland at different times in history produced Polish antipathy towards Eastern Orthodox minorities? In turn, is recent Russian hostility to largely Protestant American missionary groups operating in the country part of a more general dislike of religiously-defined foreigners from the West?

The Liminal Nature of Xenophobia

Why citizens come to fear and even hate foreigners has been the subject of extensive research. Fear of foreigners may be self-induced but it may also be incited by ethnic entrepreneurs to serve their interests. The mere act of defining a group as foreign can be an insidious act prompting a xenophobic response to it. Nearly a century ago Russian literary critic Mikhail Bakhtin advanced the notion of "official fear," which he identified as an offshoot of a cosmic fear felt by a helpless humanity confronting the forces of nature (discussed by Bauman 2004: 46-53). Political elites everywhere know the power of spreading fear among their citizens.

Having the status of stranger may *eo ipso* evoke a hostile reaction. German sociologist Georg Simmel explained how "a stranger is not one who comes today and goes tomorrow, but rather as the person who comes today and stays tomorrow" (Simmel 1950: 402). Polish social theorist Zygmunt Bauman concluded that strangers are "always uninvited guests" undermining the host-guest principle (Bauman 1997: 6). Turkish scholar Meyda Yegenoglu elaborated further: "Because they trespass over the allowed borders of guest status, migrants engender uncertainty and ambivalence. By refusing to accept the termination of their allowed period of stay and thereby turning their temporary status into an unexpected permanency, they remain 'stubbornly and infuriatingly indeterminate,' to use a phase from Bauman" (Yegenoglu 2005: 143-44; Bauman 1991: 65). It seems that being categorized as a stranger can take place at any stage in the process leading from sojourner to settler—and even beyond it.

The nature of the stranger is liminal, characterized by ambiguity, opaqueness, fluidity, and indeterminacy. *Dislike* of the stranger is, correspondingly, also liminal, operating without fixed categories, structured in an open ended way, and ever ready to change target. Pretexts for disliking strangers that have overstayed their welcome are multiple. "Immigrants, and particularly foreigners, are presented as the persons responsible for the deterioration of security conditions, terrorism, unemployment and increased public expenditure. This process of stigmatization and criminalization provides a breeding ground for racial discrimination" (European Commission 2006).

The distinction between migrants and minorities can be ambiguous, even capricious. Generally, migrant refers to recent arrivals to a receiving society. The term minority has several possible meanings. The European Convention on Human Rights' definition is a technical one: "a group inferior in number to the rest of the population and whose members share in their will to hold on to their culture, traditions, religion, or language" (European Convention on Human Rights, art. 29, 1; Kastoryano 1999: 83). To be sure, what group constitutes a minority is never really that straightforward—even in Europe. There are officially recognized minorities (Catalans in Spain), officially unrecognized minorities (Bretons in France), officially recognized immigrant communities (Moluccans in Holland), officially unrecognized immigrant communities (Poles in Britain), ethnic kin returning to their "homeland" (German speakers who originate from outside Germany, like Volga Germans), a variety of diasporas (such as Jewish), and indigenous peoples (Sami in the Nordic states).

An astonishing phenomenon is that just about any country's longstanding minority—whatever its nature—can be othered and transformed in the public view into strangers. Once they are seen as not belonging to a society, they come to be regarded as alien regardless of their citizenship status or length of residence in the country. Ascribing a cosmological difference to majority versus minority is an effective way of turning the minority into aliens. Within the EU, the question arises whether this cosmological difference is based on a Christian Europe versus a non-Christian one—a much-debated subject in Turkey's application for EU membership—or whether this difference is grounded in a modal Europe of secular values opposed to a really-existing Europe of religious adherents, most of whom have limited experience living in the EU.

France's *Laicité* and Islamophobia

French psychiatrist Patrick Declerck admits: "I hate Islam.... I invoke the right to hate Islam and the right to express it in public. In public—even if it means transgressing the laws of the Republic. Because today to denounce the vicious stupidities of religious beliefs is more than a pleasure. It is an obligation" (Declerk 2004a). We might add that in secular France it is also a virtue.

Declerck's principal objection is to the discursive taboo on criticizing Islam *qua* religion. Instead, the politically correct practice is to "target not Islam but Islamism, not religion but fanaticism, not racism but communitarianism." While he acknowledges that the majority of Muslims disapproves of organizing terrorism, slitting throats, and decapitating people, Declerck persists in declaring his hatred of Islam because, as a system of thought, it countenances holy war and embraces Sharia law (Declerk 2004b).

As in other European nations, anti-Muslim views can be traced back centuries. A leading nineteenth century scholar of the nation, Ernest Renan, gave a celebrated lecture at the Sorbonne in 1883. In addition to stating that nation building involves a daily plebiscite, he added: "Any person with some education about current affairs clearly discerns the actual inferiority of Muslim countries, the decadence in states ruled by Islam, the intellectual nullity of races which behold exclusively their culture and education to this religion" (Renan 2003: 16).

After the terrorist attacks in the U.S. in 2001, in Madrid in 2004, and in London in 2005, political elites began to make passing, then ever more direct references to the threat posed by Islamic communities. One report sounded an apocalyptic tone. "Europe appears to be crossing an invisible line regarding its Muslim minorities: more people in the political mainstream are arguing that Islam cannot be reconciled with European values." Political leaders were taking their cue from public attitudes. "For years those who raised their voices were mostly on the far right. Now those normally seen as moderates—ordinary people as well as politicians—are asking whether once unquestioned values of tolerance and multiculturalism should have limits" (Bilefsky and Fisher 2006). In 2006, the year this report was published, Pope Benedict XVI called aspects of Islam evil and inhuman.

The fear of an Islamicisation of Europe is not merely a psychological phenomenon. Existential concerns are also involved. Eurostat has predicted significant decreases in the size of European populations by 2050. European leaders' miscalculation about the impact Muslim migrants would have on European demographics contributed further to the fanning of existential fears. Historian Walter Lacquer underscored the naïveté of

European governments in trying to accommodate large groups of Muslim migrants, which eventually triggering an Islamophobic backlash. “The host governments were quite unaware of the social, cultural, and political consequences of welcoming people whose customs and values were so different from their own—immigrants who thought their values were superior and would want eventually, as their numbers grew stronger, to impose these values on the host countries. Nor did the Europeans foresee that these ambitions on the part of the immigrants would generate opposition, strengthen radical xenophobic parties, and add greatly to domestic tensions” (Lacquer 2007: 79).

Lacquer also railed against the powerful lobby groups that Muslim migrants had created. “Turks in Belgium and Arabs in Britain have acquired influence out of proportion to the size of the ethnic group to which they belong” (Lacquer 2007: 209). The fear of the emergence of Eurabia was the result.

In France the Muslim population totals somewhere between two and four million, about half of whom come from Morocco, Algeria, and Tunisia. A 2005 national survey found that about five percent of respondents identified Islam as their religion of origin or membership; this would place the total Muslim population of France at over 2 million. The survey reported that 80 percent (about 35 million people) identified Catholicism as their religion of origin or membership—a high figure given France’s emphasis on secularism and the decline in numbers of practicing Catholics. About two percent (just under one million people) identified themselves as Protestant—about the same number as those proclaiming other faiths (there are close to 600,000 Jews in France). Finally 11 percent (five million) stated they did not belong to any denomination (*Le Figaro* 2008).

Antipathy towards Muslims in France has a distinctive historical basis. According to Vincent Geisser, a CNRS specialist on Islam, “If in other European countries attacks on Muslim people and property resonate mainly along traditional registers of anti-immigrant xenophobia and the rejection of the stranger, Islamophobia *à la française* is grafted onto a contentious history in which Islam is considered at one and the same time a religion in the process of *francisation* and a national problem” (Geisser 2003: 10).

Contemporary French Islamophobia has contributed to a re-categorization of Muslims living in the country (see Gardner this volume). One popular perception is that many of the radical youth from city outskirts have been re-Islamicised by fundamentalist movements, including Algeria's notorious GIA ("Armed Islamic Group"). These radicals supposedly often hold French citizenship and are *not* recent migrants from the Maghreb. The result is a bizarre process of reversal which converts French Muslim nationals into migrants and foreigners. Xenophobia is now directed at French people of Muslim background who are seen as constituting both an internal and external danger at the same time (Blanchard and Bancel 1998).

For Geisser, then, "Islamophobia is not simply a transposition of racism that is anti-Arab, anti-Maghrebi, and anti-*jeunes de banlieues,* it is also *religiophobia*" (Geisser 2003: 11). What has happened in France is "a progressive abandonment of traditional anti-immigrant and anti-stranger registers in favour of exclusively Islamophobic registers, so that the hatred of Islam and Muslims becomes the rallying point of ultranationalists" Geisser 2003: 12).

A fundamental contradiction lies at the heart of French Islamophobia: "even though the vast majority of children originating in African, Maghreb, and Turkish immigration are today French nationals, taxonomies continue to designate them as 'young Arab Muslims'—a process of stigmatization that simultaneously combines an ethnic referential (Arab) with a religious one (Muslim)" Geisser 2003: 11). Invoking their young age further demeans them. Anti-Muslim attitudes and behaviour undergo a process of homogenization, essentialisation, and commmunitarianisation. It is as if Muslims think and act as one on all matters.

Has Islamophobia peaked in France? The 2007 report of the National Consultative Commission for Human Rights (CNCDH), first set up by the French legislature in 1990, noted that incidents of racist and xenophobic threats and violence had declined from their highest point in 2004. As in the past people of Maghrebi origin were the primary targets of racist violence—representing 68 percent of all violent acts—as well as racist threats (60 percent). About one-third of violence and threats against people of Maghreb background had a specifically anti-Islamic character, with mosques, memorials, and believers as the targets. (Commission nationale 2008: 35-38).

A 2007 national survey investigated public attitudes towards racial and religious minorities living in France. While 82 percent said the insult "dirty Black" should be condemned by the courts and 78 percent said the same for use of "dirty Jew," only 69 percent agreed with such action for using the "dirty Arab" slur (Commission nationale 2008: 316-18). In addition, while 90 percent regarded not giving a job to a qualified Black as a serious matter, only 83 percent agreed this was the case for someone of Maghreb origin. Finally, 67 percent said it was a serious matter to oppose a child's marriage with a Black compared to 58 percent for someone of Maghreb background (Commission nationale 2008: 320-21).

Islam evoked a positive connotation in only 28 percent of the national sample compared to 38 percent for Protestantism, 39 percent for Judaism, 50 percent for Catholicism, and 71 percent for secularism (Commission nationale 2008: 322-23). Forty-eight percent said Muslims form a community apart—twice as high as for Blacks. Only 69 percent agreed that French Muslims are French like everyone else (Commission nationale 2008: 311).

There are different rationales for why sections of French society want to distance themselves from Islam. In a typology of hostility towards Islam, the largest group is informed by a traditional ethnocentrism that rejects different cultures and groups. These people are the most intolerant, are situated on the right of the political spectrum, and are often themselves disadvantaged. Religious identity defines a second group. It embraces Catholicism and its values and distances itself from Muslims. Finally, a third small group is found on the left. Even though it displays little ethnocentrism and is averse to discriminatory practices, it rejects Islam in the public sphere and wishes to limit its practice to private life (Mayer, Michelat, and Tiberj 2008: 119, 123).

These findings generally substantiate the proposition that French Islamophobia is driven by a dislike of the Islamic faith that has become politically salient over the past decade or two. Social constructions of the migrant and foreigner are inspired by the conviction that Islam is a religion alien to France and followers of it are alien, too. Because it is a religion, Islam and its adherents are viewed as foreign to France and its *laicité*. Only secondarily is Islam repudiated because it is not Catholicism.

To be sure, efforts are being made to de-stigmatize religiosity of all kinds. In 2007 President Nicolas Sarkozy gave a keynote speech in the

Lateran Palace of the Vatican outlining his idea of a positive *laïcité*. He boasted, unjustifiably, that no one challenges *laïcité* today because it has proved successful: "it is a liberty: the liberty to believe or not, to practice a religion or change it…, the liberty to not be discriminated against by the state because of one's belief" (Discours 2007). The French President stated that it was time for his country to openly recognize its Christian origins. Such a positive *laïcité* is "one which, while protecting the right to think freely and to believe or not, regards religions not as a danger but strength." Such new thinking would encourage dialogue between France's great religions while promoting—rather than constraining—their spiritual growth.

Positive *laïcité* can defuse the secular versus religious divide which is represented in France, in practice, by lapsed Christians juxtaposed with practicing Muslims (though these two categories involve a degree of essentialising). The insertion of this concept into official discourse on the place of religion in the country is itself recognition that dogmatic secularism can be counterproductive.

Antipathy towards Orthodoxy in Poland

As one of Europe's most religious nations, Poles are unlikely to hold unfavourable attitudes towards minorities and migrants on the grounds that these groups do not embrace secularism. On the contrary, any group in Poland that is not Roman Catholic may be the object of othering, of being viewed as "not Polish."

In mapping European cultures, French philosopher Étienne Balibar drew a system of concentric circles that led from the "true" Europe (the advanced Western states) to an "outer" one seeking to be Europeanised (the eastern part) (Balibar 2004: 169). The notion of an outer Europe seems particularly applicable to Poland governed by twin brothers Lech and Jarosław Kaczyński, who held the posts of President and prime minister simultaneously in 2006-07. Respected Polish intellectual Adam Michnik—a vigorous critic of the communist regime—mocked his country's nationalist turn under the twins: "During a dry summer, a group of coalition legislators called upon the Parliament to pray for rain. A similar group proposed that the Parliament vote to declare Jesus Christ the King of Poland"(Michnik 2007). For Michnik, the Kaczyńskis employed "a peculiar mix of the conservative rhetoric of George W. Bush and the political practice of Vladimir Putin." If anything qualifies as a characteristic of an outer—and paranoid—Europe, this combination does.

Other political developments, however, reflect more on the nature of Polish Catholic conservatism than on right-wing political elites. When Poland became an EU member in 2004, it was assumed that the country could opt out of any EU treaties or annexes that could interfere with its Christian moral principles, including the protection of the unborn and the prohibition on gay marriage. Conservative religious Poles had strong feelings on these issues. In 2005 a physical altercation took place in the European Parliament between right-wing Polish MEPs, who had put up a graphic anti-abortion exhibit, and western European MEPs. Juxtaposing photos of aborted foetuses with photos of Nazi concentration camp victims was especially objectionable for parliamentarians from old Europe. It was symbolic of "an incipient culture war in the heart of Europe, a clash of values that has intensified since countries from Central and Eastern Europe that are experiencing an increase in the influence of the Roman Catholic Church joined the European Union." One MEP from Britain, Michael Cashman, described how "New groups have come in from Poland, the Czech Republic, Latvia, and Catholicism is certainly becoming a very angry voice against what it sees as a liberal E.U" (Bowley 2005).

Poland's Catholic conservatism—inspired loosely, at best, by John Paul II's ecumenical papacy—also received attention during the drafting of the European constitution in 2003. Initially supported by Spain and several other Western Catholic nations, the Polish government argued for inclusion of a preamble to the constitution that would acknowledge Europe's Christian heritage. This was squarely at odds with the EU's secular ideology and Poland's effort failed.

The country is ethnically and religiously homogeneous: around 95 percent of the population is ethnically Polish and Roman Catholic. This was a consequence of territorial changes agreed upon by the major powers after World War II under which many minority peoples were deported from Poland or scattered across the country. According to the 2002 national census, the largest minorities include Germans (approximately 350,000, of which 175,000 consider themselves Silesians; however some estimates place the German minority at half a million); Ukrainians (30,000, though the figure could be as high as 250,000); and Belarusians (50,000, though a high estimate is 200,000). The census lists 6,000 self-declared Russians and 1,000 self-declared Jews, though the real size of these minorities may be about 15,000 each. The Gypsy (Roma) population is estimated at 25,000, while Polish-speaking Muslim Tatars number 5,000. The largest of the "new minorities" that emerged as a result of the highly controlled immigration policy of the communist era are Vietnamese (upwards of 50,000).

The 2002 census recorded Poland's immigrant population at the conservative figure of 34,000. It came from Ukraine (22 percent), Germany (13 percent), Russia (6 percent), Belarus (6 percent), the United States (5 percent), Armenia (4 percent), and Britain and France (3 percent each). Migrants from the West consisted primarily of "managerial migrants" as well as returning Poles.

The number of illegal migrants—mostly from former Soviet republics—was thought to be two or three times as large as the number of legal ones. In the 1990s a booming border trade across Poland's eastern frontiers resulted in the Polish labour market being expanded with the influx of small-scale merchants and seasonal workers from the east—overwhelmingly Ukrainians and Belarusians, with some Lithuanians and Russians. When Poland joined the EU, many of these dealers and labourers opted for long term or permanent residence in the country. One scholar summed up Poland's immigration phenomenon this way:

> One can observe during the 1990s the slow transformation of Poland from one of the biggest sending countries in Central and Eastern Europe into a country of net immigration and transit. Completely new and exotic for this part of Europe are such groups of foreigners as Vietnamese, Chinese and Armenians. Their arrival takes all forms of inflow, from illegal entry, temporary stay and arranged marriages through to the setting-up a business and permanent settlement. This is a beginning of processes of a 'new' ethnic diversity and also the creation of new ethnic consciousness (Iglicka 2005).

Research on discrimination against old and new ethnic minorities and migrants is of relatively recent vintage. We are interested in discovering whether average Poles were becoming xenophobic as in-migration increased. To do this, let us consider a time series analysis of survey results indicating significant trends in Poles' national likes and dislikes. One finding is of the "Europeanisation" of Polish biases. While in 1993 Americans were in the top three of Poles' favourite nationalities (together with Italians and French), by 2008 eight EU cohorts headed by Italians ranked higher than Americans.

In terms of rank order, Poles' least preferred nationalities changed little over this period, though overall levels of dislike were uniformly lower. In 1993 Romanians were the least favourite (a -57 percent net difference between those saying they liked and those saying they disliked them). But when Roma were added to the survey the next year they immediately overtook Romanians (-69 percent net rating for 1994). Three largely Orthodox nations, Ukrainians (-53 percent), Serbs (-45 percent) and Russians (-39 percent) ranked just after the majority Orthodox Romanian nation. Overwhelmingly Orthodox Belarusians did not fare well either (-28 percent), though they were well ahead of Germans (-53 percent) and Jews (-36 percent).

At the end of 2008 Poles' least favourite "nations" (neither was really a nation) were Roma (-30%) followed by Arabs (-28%), Romanians (-15%). Russians (-11%), and Turks (-9 percent). Mean scores showed that attitudes towards Ukrainians, Serbs, Armenians, Jews, Chinese, and Vietnamese were split just about down the middle (Centrum Badania 2008c).

What inferences can we draw from Polish respondents' ranking of preferred and disliked nations? The marked dislike of Arabs and Turks suggests possible Islamophobia. The interpretation offered by the Polish public opinion report is that Poles' attitudes are shaped by the stereotype of the affluent civilized "West" and the poor culturally backward "East." But this explanation is unconvincing and evidence points to the cleavage being centred on racial and religious factors. Thus in terms of mean scores Poles' fourteen favourite nations in 2008 were European, all of which were predominantly Catholic or Protestant. Conversely, not one of the eight nations with negative mean scores was a European Catholic or Protestant nation. Most Orthodox nations (Romanians, Russians, Serbs, and Ukrainians) ranked low. An antipathy towards Eastern Orthodoxy, defined by Samuel Huntington as a distinct civilization in *The Clash of Civilizations,* was discernable in Polish attitudes (Huntington 1998).

More evidence about Polish attitudes towards other religions comes from a 2007 survey which measured Poles' "social distance" from other nationalities and religious groups. Respondents were asked the classic question about approval of a spouse for one's child: Would you be opposed to your son or daughter marrying someone who was Jewish, Russian, or Chinese? One-third of Polish respondents said that they would oppose their child's marriage to someone who was Jewish or Chinese, and somewhat fewer—one-quarter— said they would oppose their child's intermarriage with a Russian.

Poles voiced stronger opposition, however, to interdenominational marriages: 55 percent opposed a son or daughter's marriage with a Muslim, 47 percent with a Jew. An Eastern Orthodox son-in-law or daughter-in-law evinced the disapproval of 38 percent of respondents. Marrying a Protestant was less critically perceived (31 percent). Someone of the same nationality and religion were two of the most important traits respondents looked for in a spouse, or even friend. Educational level, occupation, and political views were less influential factors (Centrum Badania 2007).

The clearest illustration of xenophobia targeting a foreign country rather than an ethnic minority or migrant community is Poland's russophobia. Many Poles associate Russians with an imperial nation that historically oppressed Poles as well as other peoples. Predictably, a 2008 survey conducted shortly after the Russian-Georgian war found that 40 percent of Polish respondents sided with the Georgians and just three percent with the Russians (Centrum Badania 2008b). While there may be an atavistic dislike of Russians on the part of many Poles, it cannot be understood without reference to a thousand years of history between the two countries.

Orthodoxophobia may, then, be a contrived explanation for interpreting Poles' historic grievances against Russia. We have not found a strong case for asserting its existence, though neither are we able to dismiss the salience of Orthodoxophobia out of hand. In 2001 Pope John Paul II, a Pole especially conscious of the history of difficult relations between the Roman and Byzantine churches, prayed for God's forgiveness for sins committed by Roman Catholics against "their Orthodox brothers and sisters," which included the plunder of Constantinople by Crusaders in 1204. He categorized the estrangement between the world's one billion Catholics and 200 million Orthodox Christians as nothing less than "a sin before God and a scandal before the world" (*Los Angeles Times* 2001). Poles' long-held view of constituting an easternmost *antemurale christianitatis* (a bulwark of Christianity) is an implicit acknowledgement that Eastern Orthodoxy is considered a peripheral, even non European form of Christianity.

Polish xenophobia appears to be profoundly shaped by a religious perspective. The first five years of EU membership did not advance the cause of secularism in Poland. For example, in 2008 two-thirds of Poles stated they wanted religion to be taught in school (Centrum Badania 2008a). Many continue to believe that being a member of the secular EU club threatens the country's Catholic identity. But, for Poles, so do non-Catholic nations to the east and in the Balkans.

The Religious Basis of Russian Xenophobia

The Russian Federation covers a vast area stretching from the Baltic to the Pacific. It includes over a hundred minorities of different ethnic and religious backgrounds. Islam, Buddhism, and even Shamanism are practiced in the country. The lower Volga and the north Caucasus are particularly diverse ethnic archipelagos. Recent violent conflicts in the Federation have pitted Russian forces against rebellious Muslim nationalities such as Chechens and Ingushetians. By contrast the Federation's largest minority, the Tatars (about five million Federation citizens speak Tatar as their first language) has its own autonomous territory—once referred to as the world's northernmost Islamic state—and it has remained a peaceful part of Russia.

Examining Russians' relations with their minorities is an enormous undertaking (Bremmer and Taras 1997). In contrast, studying immigration is problematic since Russia has welcomed few migrants since 1992; these have consisted primarily of Western managerial migrants, returning Russians who had been living in former Soviet republics, and Chinese border traders in the Far East. Instead of studying the religious prism through which Russians view migrants and minorities, then, let us consider Russian attitudes towards "missionary migrants" from other countries.

Just after he had been inaugurated in the Kremlin in 2000 as Russian President, Vladimir Putin walked over to the nearby Cathedral of the Annunciation for a thanksgiving service presided over by Patriarch Aleksii II. The Russian Orthodox leader—reputed to have collaborated with the KGB—prayed that President Putin would "help us to disclose the soul of the nation" (Anderson 2007).

Exactly a decade earlier, the Russian Duma had adopted a law governing freedom of conscience. Under it "existing religious communities enjoyed a certain institutional revitalization, and newer domestic- and foreign-based groups were able to operate freely." But the free marketplace of religious competition disadvantaged the Orthodox Church, which had been stifled during most of the Soviet period, to the benefit of mostly affluent Western-based religious groups. What became known as "the invasion of the sects" had begun. In response, the Orthodox Church began to lobby for special status.

The result was the 1997 Freedom of Conscience Law whose intent was to manage religious pluralism. "Traditional" Russian religious communities—Orthodox, Muslim, Jewish, Buddhist—secured rights that were now denied other less desirable religions, in particular, Roman Catholicism (which had 200,000 to 300,000 faithful). But U.S.-based "sects" seemed as much the target of the 1997 law—Pentecostals, Adventists, Baptists, Methodists, Evangelicals, Jehovah's Witnesses.

Under Putin's leadership, the Russian Orthodox Church has attained the status of *de facto* state religion. In a 2008 poll 71 percent of respondents identified themselves as Russian Orthodox and about that many want Orthodoxy to become the official religion of the state. In various regions of Russia public school children are required to take an Orthodox religion course. These schools often set aside a classroom for displaying traditional icons and portraits of Jesus Christ, Saints Cyril and Methodius, and other Orthodox religious imagery.

The ascendancy of the Orthodox Church was captured by Metropolitan Kiril of Smolensk and Kaliningrad, chairman of the Department for External Church Relations of the Moscow Patriarchate: *Rossia-pravoslavnaia, a ne mnogokonfessionalnaia strana*: "Russia is Orthodox, not a multiconfessional country" (Metropol Kiril 2002). Upon Alexii's death in 2009, Kiril became the sixteenth patriarch of Moscow and all Russia. He announced that he would increase dialogue with "sister churches" in the other former Soviet republics, such as the Ukrainian Orthodox church. As one of a handful of Russian Orthodox to have met Pope Benedict, Patriarch Kiril also made clear his desire to improve relations with Rome.

But no change seemed afoot on the prohibition ban on proselytizing by primarily American-based Protestant denominations. Protestant churches are required to register with state authorities if they plan on organizing any religious event other than holding a simple prayer service. The harassment of Protestant communities—they have about two million adherents out of the total population of 142 million—operating in Russia (especially in the southwest) by state and Orthodox authorities grew in tandem with Putin's increasingly hostile discourse about the United States. Putin's clinching argument was that never before had western Europe and the U.S. held such an openly hostile attitude toward Russia as in the early years of the new century. The governor of a region outside Moscow even accused U.S. military intelligence of using Protestant sects to infiltrate Russia (*New York Times* 2008). Many ordinary Russians needed little convincing that this was indeed the case. The Putin administration felt that it was time to confront Western russophobia—the concept of Orthodoxophobia was not invoked.

The Orthodox world is composed of Armenia, Belarus, Bulgaria, Cyprus, Georgia, Greece, Macedonia, Moldova, Montenegro, Romania, Russia, Serbia, and Ukraine. In Huntington's controversial *The Clash of Civilizations,* Russia is named as the core state of Orthodox civilization. It supposedly differs from Western Christianity by not having experienced the Renaissance, Reformation, Enlightenment, and overseas colonialism (Huntington 1998). Public opinion polling in Russia suggests a limited degree of Orthodox solidarity: when asked in 2004 what countries were Russia's friends, 22 percent of respondents named Belarus and Ukraine along with the former Soviet republic of Kazakhstan (where one third of the population is Russian). But this result ranked well behind Russia's perceived friends in Western Europe: forty percent named Western European countries, especially Germany, France, and Italy. Just eight percent listed the U.S, seven percent China, and only six percent various East European countries like Poland, the Czech and Slovak Republics, the Balts, and Hungary (FOM 2004).

In a 2006 survey of public opinion, Belarus topped the list of perceived best friends of Russia: one quarter of respondents saying that Russia had friendly international states singled out its western Slavic neighbour. Germany (13 percent), China and Kazakhstan (each ten percent), and France (nine percent) followed. Worsening relations with Ukraine's pro-Western government relegated that country to sixth place, tied with the U.S. (five percent) (FOM 2006). These results suggested that a civilisational bloc of Orthodox states had little bearing on which states were perceived to be Russia's friends.

The majority of what Huntington termed civilisational *fault line conflicts within states* (the two other types of civilisational conflicts encompassed *core-state conflicts*—the dominant states of rival civilizations—and f*ault-line conflicts between states*—states on civilisational borders) has, in the case of former Soviet bloc nations, involved an Orthodox society as one of the parties. Examples include Azerbaijan (the Armenians) and Bosnia and Kosovo (in both cases the Serbs). The 2008 Georgia-South Ossetia conflict involved two Orthodox nations, though the Georgian church is autocephalous while the Ossetian one maintains close ties with Russian Orthodoxy (Fox 2002: 434a, 434b). Generally Western powers have sided with the ethnic group—including Muslim Kosovars and Muslim Bosniaks—opposing the Orthodox nation that has closest ties to Russia. Kremlin leaders have drawn the appropriate inferences.

One incidental consequence of the Orthodox-versus-Western cleavage is that Islamophobic attitudes are not as marked in Russia as in France or Poland (noted above). The influence of a Eurasian ideology, elaborated most forcefully by Alexander Dugin, which calls for an alliance of Orthodox and Islamic civilizations, has been significant, if not decisive. For many Russians Islam is not viewed as a missionary religion nor as one claiming to be the one and only correct universal teleological faith. These characteristics have instead been attributed to American Protestant churches. In short, American missionaries have become, improbably, a principal target of Russian xenophobia.

Hostility towards Protestant missionaries would, we might assume, be separate from hostility towards Western secularism. But in the assault in today's Russia on Western cosmologies, missionaries and secularism have both become associated with the West. As a leading theoretician of Russian Orthodoxy, Patriarch Kiril has embraced a perspective which counterposes Russian clerical ethnonationalism to a secularized Occident built on liberal ideals. At one point he claimed that hostile forces had infiltrated Russia seeking to promote a secular society (Verkhovski 2006: 11, 14). Foreign Protestant sects are among these forces.

Secularism as Source and Subject of Xenophobia

Is godless secularism responsible for Western Europe's antipathy towards Muslim migrants and its conflicts with Catholic and Orthodox societies in Eastern Europe? Should we agree with Catholic theologian

George Weigel's assertion?—"European high culture is largely Christophobic, and Europeans describe their cultures and societies as post-Christian" (Weigel 2006: 42). It is not just high culture that is lukewarm about religion. Only 21 percent of Europeans say religion is very important to them and only 41 percent say they believe in a personal God; an additional 33 percent believe in a life force (*Christian Science Monitor* 2005).

The rise of post-secular modernity in Western Europe may be a plausible explanation for the spread of xenophobia (Breschi 2007). In debating European secularism versus European Christianity, Weigel asked: "Which culture, I wondered, would better protect human rights? Which culture would more firmly secure the moral foundations of democracy?" (Weigel 2006: 31). Which of the two, we might ask, better promotes the interests of migrants and minorities?

The conclusion Weigel reached was categorical. "Christianity establishes a transcendent understanding of human dignity, a clear affirmation of human responsibility, and the elaboration of a moral order that makes civilization possible. In committing itself to the path of radical secularism, Europe is setting the stage for its own destruction" (Weigel 2006: 177).

The argument against EU secularism can be taken one step further. It can act in an intolerant and exclusionary way towards nonsecular groups. As a result, it may camouflage its prejudice against religious practices of many kinds—Muslim, Orthodox, Catholic. The targets identified become both migrants—Muslims—from outside Europe, and "the other" from outer Europe—devout Lithuanian and Polish Catholics, as well as Russian, Romanian, Serb, and Ukrainian Orthodox. In recent years outer Europe has sent more than a million migrants of such religious backgrounds to the West. The politically-salient cleavage may best be described as not that between "Europeans" and migrants—from outside and from outer Europe—but between "Europeans" and, on the other hand, Muslims, Orthodox, and Catholics.

This Chapter suggests that societies defined by Catholicism or Orthodoxy are not free of antipathy towards "foreigners." Minorities, migrants, and missionaries espousing different religious beliefs regularly face hostility in countries such as Poland and Russia. But proposing secularism as the antidote is facile, for a secular godless Europe is equally capable of becoming one of fear, intolerance, and hatred of the stranger.

Works Cited

Anderson, John. 2007. Putin and the Russian Orthodox church: Asymmetric symphonia. *Journal of International Affairs*. Available online at: http://findarticles.com/p/articles/mi_hb6705/is_200710/ai_n32252029/

Balibar, Étienne. 2004. *We, the people of Europe? Reflections on transnational citizenship*. Princeton: Princeton University Press.

Bauman, Zygmunt. 1991. *Modernity and ambivalence*. Ithaca: Cornell University Press.

—. 1997. *Postmodernity and its discontents*. Cambridge: Blackwell.

—. 2004. *Wasted lives: Modernity and its outcasts*. New York: John Wiley.

Bilefsky, Dan, and Ian Fisher. 2006. Across Europe, worries on Islam spread to centre. *New York Times*, October 11.

Blanchard, Pascal, and Nicolas Bancel. 1998. *De l'indigène à l'immigré*. Paris: Gallimard.

Commission nationale consultative des droits de l'homme. 2008. *La lutte contre le racisme, l'antisémitisme, et la xénophobie: année 2007*. Paris: La documentation française.

Bowley, Graham. 2005. Poles on ramparts of EU culture war. *International Herald Tribune*, November 24.

Bremmer, Ian, and Ray Taras, eds. 1997. *New states, new politics: building the post-Soviet nations*. Cambridge: Cambridge University Press.

Breschi, Danielo. 2007. A new humanism in Europe: Between secularism and the return of religion. *Telos*Scope. Available online at: http://www.telospress.com/main/index.php?main_page=news_article&article_id=195

Centrum Badania Opinii Społecznej. 2007. Przejawy dystansu społecznego wobec innych narodów i religii. Warsaw: CBOS.

—. 2008a. Religia w systemie edukacji. Warsaw: CBOS.

—. 2008b. Stosunki polsko-rosyjskie i sytuacja na Kaukazie. Warsaw: CBOS.

—. 2008c. Stosunek polaków do innych narodów. Warsaw: CBOS.

Christian Science Monitor. 2005. What place for God in Europe? February 22.

Declerck, Patrick. 2004a. Je hais l'islam, entre autres. *Le Monde,* August 11.

—. 2004b. *Garantie sans moraline*. Paris: Flammarion.

European Commission against Racism and Intolerance. 2006. *Annual report on ECRI'S activities covering the period from 1 January to 31 December 2005, CRI(2006)32*. Available online at: http://www.coe.int/t/e/human_rights/ecri/1-ECRI/1-Presentation_of_ECRI/4-Annual_Report_2005/Annual_Report_2005.asp#TopOfPage

Presidence de la Republique. 2007. *Discours de Nicolas Sarkozy au Palais du Latran, 20 décembre*. Available online at: http://www.elysee.fr/documents/index.php?mode=cview&cat_id=7 & press_id=819

European Convention on Human Rights. 1950. Available online at: http://www.hri.org/docs/ECHR50.html

FOM Public Opinion Foundation. 2004. *Russia and the "outside world": Who is friend and who is foe, 7 October*. Available online at: http://bd.english.fom.ru/report/cat/frontier/rossiya_i_stran_mira/vragy/ed044027

FOM Public Opinion Foundation. 2006. *Russia's friends and foes, 5 October*. Available online at: http://bd.english.fom.ru/report/cat/frontier/international_relations/ed063915

Fox, Jonathan. 2002. *Ethnic minorities and the clash of civilizations: A quantitative analysis of Huntington's thesis. British Journal of Political Science* 32: 415-34.

Geisser, Vincent. 2003. *La nouvelle islamophobie.* Paris: Éditions La Découverte.

Huntington, Samuel. 1998. *The clash of civilizations and the remaking of world order.* New York: Simon and Schuster.

Iglicka, Krystyna. 2005. *Active civic participation of immigrants in Poland.* Country Report prepared for the European research project POLITIS, Oldenburg. Available online at: www.uni-oldenburg.de/politis-europe

Kastoryano, Riva. 1999. Transnational networks and political participation: The place of immigrants in the European Union. In *Europe without borders: Remapping territory, citizenship, and identity in a transnational age*, ed. Mabel Berezin and Martin Schain, 64-88. Baltimore: Johns Hopkins University Press.

Lahav, Gallya. 2004. *Immigration and politics in the new Europe: Reinventing borders.* Cambridge: Cambridge University Press.

Laqueur, Walter. 2007. *The last days of Europe: Epitaph for an old continent.* New York: Thomas Dunne Books.

Le Figaro. 2008. 80% des Français se déclarent catholiques. July 18.

Los Angeles Times. 2001. Pope apologizes for anti-Orthodox past. May 5.

Mayer, Nonna, Guy Michelat, and Vincent Tiberj. 2008. Étranger, immigré, musulman: les representations de 'l'autre' dans la société française. *La lutte contre le racisme, l'antisémitisme, et la xénophobie: année 2007, Commission nationale consultative des droits de l'homme*. Paris: La documentation française.

Messina, Anthony. 2007. *Logics and politics of post-WWII migration to Western Europe*. Cambridge: Cambridge University Press.

Metropol Kiril. 2002. Rossia – pravoslavnaia, a ne mnogokonfessionalnaia strana. *Radonej* 8.

Michnik, Adam. 2007. Waiting for freedom, messing it up. *New York Times*, March 25.

Mudde, Cas. 2007. *Populist radical right parties in Europe*. Cambridge: Cambridge University Press.

New York Times. 2008. At expense of all others, Putin picks a church. April 24.

Norris, Pippa. 2005. *Radical right: Voters and parties in the electoral market*. Cambridge: Cambridge University Press.

Renan, Ernest. 2003. *L'Islam et la science*. Montpellier: Éditions L'Archange Minotaure.

Roemer, John E., Woojin Lee, and Karine Van der Straeten. 2007. *Racism, xenophobia, and distribution: Multi-issue politics in advanced democracies*. Cambridge, MA: Harvard University Press.

Saideman, Stephen M. and R. William Ayres. 2008. *For kin or country: Xenophobia, nationalism, and war*. New York: Columbia University Press.

Simmel, Georg. 1950. The stranger. In *The Sociology of Georg Simmel*. New York: Free Press.

Taras, Ray. 2009. *Europe old and new: Transnationalism, belonging, xenophobia*. Lanham, MD: Rowman and Littlefield.

Verkhovski, Alexandre. 2006. Religion et l'idée nationale dans la Russie de Poutine. *Les Cahiers Russie* 3.

Weigel, George. 2006. *The cube and the cathedral: Europe, America, and politics without God*. New York: Basic Books.

Yegenoglu, Meyda. 2005. From guest worker to hybrid immigrant: Changing themes of German-Turkish literature. In *Migrant cartographies: New cultural and literary spaces in post-colonial Europe*, ed. Sandra Ponzanesi and Daniela Merolla. Lanham, MD: Lexington Books.

CHAPTER SEVEN

THE POLITICIZATION OF RELIGION IN THE WEST: ASSESSING THE EFFECTS OF POLICY LEGACIES AND GOVERNMENT CONSTRUCTION ON A EUROPEAN ISLAM

KATHRYN L. GARDNER

According to some media reports and scholarly accounts, a significant religious cleavage has emerged as a consequence of Muslim mass immigrant settlement in the West, unsettling in the process the historic relationship between religion and the state. As a result of the irreconcilability of Muslim religiosity and Western secular, liberal values, religion, which once was widely presumed to have been consigned to the margins of European politics, has assumed centre stage. A greater attention to religious difference has precipitated in turn various Muslim incorporation policies, policies that seek to manage the issues that arise from the new ethnic and/or religious diversity of European societies in light of Muslim immigrants and communities. Although the challenge of Muslim incorporation has emerged as a major issue in contemporary European politics, Muslim immigrants have not been identified primarily by their religion for most of the post-World War II period.

In demonstrating when religion emerged as a salient division within Europe, this chapter will address a significant thesis that pre-existing church-state relations have determined the level and degree of accommodation of Muslim needs at present (Fetzer and Soper 2005; Aluffi Beck-Peccoz and Zincone 2004). I argue that the church-state thesis needs revision to account for changes in how the government has viewed their domestic Muslim population and "problem" over time. This chapter will trace the history of policy toward Muslims in two cases, Great Britain and

France, and provide evidence for the thesis that policies changed over time and religion was not the primary focus of governments. Muslims were not defined initially or primarily by their religious characteristics – they were foreign, non-European, and different. It was not until the late 1980s and early 1990s that the category of "Muslim" gained a high level of resonance both as an identity marker for the population and as a political category. Moreover, this chapter will provide evidence to demonstrate that although church-state legacies may be important after the problem was framed as "religious," there were also important continuations of policies from the 1970s and 1980s. Indeed, my analysis demonstrates that church-state relations influenced the parameters of policy construction only after religion was politicized in the 1990s. And, more to the point, church-state legacies did not exert a similar level of influence across cases; in France, church-state relationships were predominant, particularly the concept of *laïcité*, while in Great Britain, the Labour government modelled its policy response after its race relations framework.

Institutional Theories of Muslim Incorporation

In seeking to explain how Western states have developed policy toward the accommodation of Muslims, domestic variables have played a prominent role. Several competing theories regarding Western European immigrant incorporation strategies, and especially those directed to the Muslim minority, vie to explain the role of pre-existing state institutions and policy legacies such as church-state institutions (Fetzer and Soper 2005), colonial policies (Bleich 2005), and, more generally, national philosophies regarding citizenship and integration (Brubaker 1992; Favell 1998). What all these theories have in common is the emphasis on how existing domestic structures and policies influence the rules of the game through policy legacies and power resources, constraining the range of policy options available to decision-makers. The focus is on the role of institutional arrangements such as standard operating procedures that either constrain or facilitate certain policy alternatives. State policy choices are thus shaped, mediated, and channelled by institutional arrangements.

A prominent position put forth by Fetzer and Soper (2005) and others (Minkenberg 2002; Aluffi-Beck and Peccoz 2004; Roy 2005; Foner and Alba 2008) suggests that the Muslim community in the West is constructed through its permanent interaction with the wider Western society, and, most importantly, those patterns established by or for other

Western religions.[1] Scholars of Western Europe have pointed to diverging church-state institutional environments as providing "opportunity structures" for religious interests within the political process. In contrast to the United States, the institutionalization of religion in Europe, regardless of the specific church-state structure, is highly regulated, privileging some historical confessions, and with various limitations on religious organization and the public exercise of religion. Thus, differences in the constitutional and legal status of religion in each country, along with the historical context through which the institutions of church and state have been related, influence policy outcomes by providing opportunities, in the form of pre-existing pluralistic commitments, as well as constraints, for example, in channelling demands through policy channels that may narrow acceptable options.

This is an important contribution by showing how church-state structures are important to the story of Muslim accommodation in Europe. Most accounts have looked to how Muslims are adapting and adjusting, focusing on Islam to understand the problem, rather than institutional determinants of policy. This account, while offering a clarion call to scholars to pay attention to the constructive aspects of religious institutions in contemporary Europe, is nonetheless incomplete. First, this argument does not account for the evolution in how the Muslim population was initially viewed and when and how religion rose to the forefront as *the* salient characteristic for Muslim communities.[2] National identities largely

---

[1] For example, in their book *Muslims and the State in Great Britain, France, and Germany* (2005), Fetzer and Soper demonstrate that different church-state structures account for important cross-national divergences in whether and how states recognize and accommodate Muslim religious practices in three cases. Great Britain has been the most accommodating across the three policy domains of interest (religious education, funding for religious schools, and mosque construction); France has been the least accommodating, if not hostile; and Germany falls between these two cases.

[2] While their account purports to address the entire history of Muslim accommodation in their three cases, the book's research focuses on the 1990s forward and the accounts seem to support the argument that there was a change in the problem definition among policy-makers. This is most clear in the British case study in which the authors focus on British race relations framework. Thus, the authors note that in the 1970s "race shaped the politics of immigration control" which, consequently, shaped how Muslims constructed their demands to the British state. Muslims tried to work with the Commission for Racial Equality (CRE), the institutional structure mandated to carry out the provisions of the Race Relations legislation, as well as through the court system. As Fetzer and Soper

trumped religious identities as markers of difference for most of the World War II period. What is more, accounts which focus on church-state structures often contain an implicit assumption that the purported religious cleavage in Western European politics was organic rather than a result of a *political* process. Indeed, there is not a sufficient account of how religion has been politicized and why Islam in particular became a problem and had to be made compatible with democracy. This last question addresses the construction of Islam as illiberal, undemocratic, and violent.

This chapter traces the policy trajectories of Great Britain and France to provide an historically-based account of the "turn to religion," demonstrating when, how, and why religion came to the fore with regard to the Muslim communities in these two states. Across many important indicators, Great Britain and France represent "most different" cases with what is commonly portrayed as opposite approaches to citizenship and integration regimes: France has pursued a civic-assimilationist citizenship model while Britain has developed a multicultural framework for integrating her immigrants (Koopmans *et al* 2005). What is more, these two countries have had substantially different colonial histories and, thus, historical relationships with their former colonial immigrants. And, importantly for this analysis, the two countries have very different church-state relationships. According to Fetzer and Soper's typology, Great Britain is an example a state church type which is characterized by a close relationship between state power and church existence and France is an example of strict separation. These differences explain why Great Britain is more inclusive and France is more restrictive toward accommodating their Muslim populations.

Despite these differences, however, an important cross-national and cross-temporal trend emerges: the government management and channelling of "difference" into acceptable avenues.[3] Western European

---

note, "[f]or Muslims, the government's unwillingness to include religious discrimination in race relations policy denied them their distinctive religious identity, and failed to provide the same protection that the government afford ethnic minorities" and that "Muslims groups have consistently expressed concern that the CRE...is insensitive to the issues of religious discrimination" (2005: 31). By their own account, Muslims have tried to work with the *secular* race relations institutions.

[3] Moreover, in addition to these policy actions across time, two other policy characteristics demonstrate a continuation of racial (and ethnic) policies that will not receive extensive treatment in this chapter. First, the British and French

governments were not passive participants, instead actively pursuing policies to construct acceptable civic racial/ethnic and, later, religious identities. Three main governmental actions can be identified across the cases. First, governments sought to manage and channel difference through the creation of institutions and institutional processes. Second, the government provided funding to particular civil society organizations that it deemed supportable and commissioned research which reflected governmental priorities and, ultimately, how it framed the problem and solutions. And, third, governments set about legitimating certain identities over others through the recognition of particular actors as acceptable mediators and/or leaders of a particular community, often through the above actions.

Rise of Immigrant and Racial Frames: From Immigrant to Racial/Ethnic Minorities

While Muslims in Europe are not a recent phenomenon, the start of the contemporary situation is the end of World War II when large numbers of Muslim males migrated to the European continent in search of jobs and, less frequently, permanent settlement for political, economic, or religious reasons. This initial context of immigration and its (often unintended) consequences in the following decades is crucial for understanding the development of Western policies toward their domestic Muslim communities. Established domestic Muslim communities, and new ethnic minorities more generally, were a direct consequence of state immigration policies and would result in ethnicity (and later, religion) becoming a salient political and social cleavage in Europe (Bleich 2004; Messina 1992; Messina 2007; Modood 2004; Modood et al. 2005). Irrespective of the specific national histories, a common trajectory can be ascertained. During the three decades following the end of WWII, Western European governments either actively recruited or benignly facilitated the migration of young foreign males to fuel their post-war booming economies, creating the first wave of immigration to post-WWII Europe. As temporary guests, these migrants were not a primary concern of domestic institutions. A combination of domestic factors and international economic conditions around the 1970s spurred the reexamination

governments undertook policies in the 1990s and 2000s as a response to concerns of social order much like the responses of the governments in the 1960s and 1970s. What is more, British and French governments in the contemporary period have adopted both restrictive and inclusive measures to manage their new problem.

of immigration policies, resulting in restrictionist immigration measures. These measures effectively halted primary labour migration but had the unintended consequence of ushering a second wave of immigration. This second wave of immigration was largely a period of family reunification, bringing women and children as well as extended families to Europe.

Permanent settlement brought new racial or ethnic and, importantly for our analysis, religious minorities to relatively homogenous cultures which would lay the foundation for the "second tier of ethnic conflict in Western Europe" and, subsequently, would bring about profound changes to the European political and societal landscape (Messina 2007: 2). Several of these changes will be important for our analysis of the politicization of religion. Permanent settlement marks an important turning point in state-Muslim relations as it placed pressure for state accommodation and the need to fashion policies for a domestic population. During this time period, race and ethnicity trumped religion as the predominant frame and relevant difference. These frames would then become important for the development of domestic policies for these populations.

These policies were adopted within a context of rising social tensions over the perceived difference of these minority populations. Indeed, during the 1970s and 1980s, we see the rise of anti-immigrant groups who, to varying degrees, successfully utilized societal anxieties over these tensions and, in many circumstances, shaped these tensions to their political and electoral advantage.

Another development bears mentioning. In the late 1970s and early 1980s, there was a noticeable shift to a discourse of ethnicity rather than the racial or colour discourse of the previous decades. This shift is notable as societal movements across all cases embraced a politics of difference discourse. Rather than reluctantly identifying with race or colour as a key feature of identity and fighting the adverse consequences of this noted difference (namely in the form of racial discrimination), the "right of difference" movements in the 1980s embraced this difference, at times even constructing a new difference, as a right and a source of strength and solidarity. This shift to a "difference discourse" would lay the groundwork for a Muslim identity to emerge across the West in the 1990s.

The Case of Great Britain

It is the new immigrant population from the New Commonwealth (non-white population) that prompted political debate over larger British Commonwealth policy and, specifically, immigration controls. Erik Bleich contends that this new population "ultimately induced Britain to develop domestic race frames" (2003: 38). Anwar and his colleagues take a similar view, arguing that immigration legislation was the defining feature during this period, in which immigration restrictions were passed to "stem mainly the tide of black and Asian immigration to Britain as a prerequisite to the maintenance of social order...Black immigration was a problem to be controlled; its effects were regarded as potentially destabilizing to notions of Britishness and the effective operation of British society" (2000: vii-viii). As race and/or ethnicity became important components of the immigration debate, they would then become important components of the developing domestic policies to deal with the new minority population.

During the 1940s and into the 1950s, this influx of immigration did not generate strong government or societal reaction as Britain was experiencing a post-war economic boom with an increased need for workers. Beginning in the mid-1950s, however, the British context was increasingly anti-immigrant, and this anti-immigrant sentiment was strongly tied to racial frames. It was not merely a matter of the growing immigrant presence, causing housing shortages and other adjustments; riots between the new populations and whites pointed to social control problems. Events in the late 1950s and early 1960s such as the 1958 "race riots" in Nottingham and London firmly placed race on the agenda in Britain. The riots conjured up the American example and its problem with the African American population, leading policy-makers to view the problem as one of social order and violence. After the riots, the government announced its intention to legislate against racial discrimination, an agenda espoused by the Labour government over the next several years. The government first responded in the area of immigration policy with the passage of the 1962 Commonwealth Immigration Act.

The passage of race relations legislation in conjunction with immigration controls demonstrates how race became the important frame for dealing with minority population in Britain at the time. In 1965, the Labour government introduced and passed the first of three landmark Race Relations acts. Within three years of the first Race Relations Act, Parliament passed a significant amendment to extend the scope of coverage. A third race relations act passed in 1976, significantly enhancing the enforcement measures of the previous legislation. The 1968 and 1976 acts were intended to strengthen the foundation laid by the first piece of legislation, addressing inadequacies that were apparent in the areas of implementation and enforcement. Indeed, the 1965 Act, which covered acts of threatening, abusive, or insulting written or spoken expressions with intent to stir up hatred against others on the grounds of colour, race, or ethnic or national origins, was quickly deemed insufficient to deal with the problems of racism and social order within Britain. Importantly, its definition of the domestic problem, that of colour and race modelled on the U.S. experience, was not questioned in subsequent policy debates and legislation (Bleich 2003). The 1968 Act's most important contribution was the creation of race bureaucracies that would institutionalize race relations through advocating additional legislation and funding initiatives.

The 1965 Race Relations Act would create several institutions, including the Race Relations Board (RRB), the National Committee for Commonwealth Immigrants (NCCI) and local institutions initially called Community Relations Commissions (CRCs). These institutions arose out of the apparent need to manage the newly established race relations legislation. Bleich argues that these institutions were a "small revolution within the British context" and did not "fit naturally within existing British institutions" (2003: 60).

With the passage of the 1976 Race Relations legislation, the government established the Commission for Racial Equality (CRE) to take the place of these institutions in order to create a more centralized system, to enforce the key provisions of the Race Relations Act and, more generally, to promote harmonious race relations (Messina 1989; Bleich 2003). The act also authorized the CRE to perform "race-relations audits," permitting the Commission to formally investigate an entity for instances of discrimination and the enforcement of its findings through the court system (Bleich 2003). The 1976 Race Relations Act, then, followed in the footsteps of previous legislation giving race institutions stronger mandates and wider leverage in deciding which acts of discrimination to privilege. Importantly, the issue of religious discrimination was explicitly ruled out by the race bureaucracies, furthering strengthening race as the only frame for minorities and effectively ruling out government recognition of religious or Muslim discrimination at this time (Bleich 2003: 81).

Race relations legislation and race institutions had an important channelling effect on British Muslims at this time. For example, an important outcome of race relations legislation in Great Britain, although not mandated in the 1976 legislation, was the introduction of ethnic monitoring by local authorities. With the introduction of ethnic monitoring, labels and classifications took centre stage. People had to be (self-)classified and counted. As Tariq Modood notes, "Arguments about which labels are authentic have become a common feature of certain political discourses" as a result of group labels (2006: 39). This evolution of race legislation shows how the government, in creating institutions with specific preferences, privileged race as the problem. This frame of reference would have implications. As Tariq Modood notes in his research, the racist frames that have been used in Britain have marginalized the experience of Asians and/or Muslims through the privileging of racial frames, and specifically, the black-white distinction, as well as ignoring other cultural characteristics that could be the basis for discrimination, for example religion.

While in a generally supportive environment due to the government's commitment to multiculturalism, the Muslim community was, nevertheless, required to organize as an ethnic community. The community was labelled "Asian" in official reports and documents. Religious needs were considered cultural needs of the Asian community and met, in varying degrees, through this frame. Muslims worked through the existing race relations institutions for funding; recognition was predicated on their ethnic or cultural minority status. Before the Rushdie Affair promoted a unified "Muslim" identity, Muslims were riven along political, linguistic, national and religious sectarian lines, rendering the "Asian identity" one of the only available overarching identities for authorities. The recognition of ethnic particularities within the British system served to reinforce the divisions within the British Muslim community.

The Case of France

The French state, unlike the British, actively recruited foreign labour in the post-WWII period in order to fulfil her economic needs. For roughly 30 years after the end of World War II, the French state, in conjunction with the private sector, turned to her former colonial holdings, especially those in the Maghreb, as a significant source of manual labour for the *metropole* in addition to experiencing spontaneous migration. It is during this period that immigrants arrived from predominantly Muslim countries of Algeria, Morocco, Tunisia, and Turkey in unprecedented numbers and over a relatively short period of time (Fetzer and Soper 2005; Laurence and Vaisse 2006). The favourable economic context under which these migrants came to France, then, would mean that immigration was a welcome feature.

The French state also sought to recruit a certain type of worker, one that was more easily assimilated, and this was based on ethnic and/or cultural criteria. State recruitment centres favoured those immigrants from within the European Community (the Italians, Spanish, and Portuguese) over immigrants of Muslim origin from Turkey and North Africa, suggesting a cultural preference in favour of European immigration that was maintained through the newly created Ministry of Public Health and Population (MSPP). Vincent Viet (1998) offers evidence that these selective practices were based, in part, on the notion that European populations were more culturally assimilable than non-European populations, and specifically, those populations from the Maghreb.

Over a decade after Britain passed its first restrictionist immigration act, the French government took steps to reduce immigration and tighten requirements for citizenship. As with the introduction of immigration restrictions in Britain, restrictionist policies had the effect of encouraging permanent settlement by the workers and their families. During this period, the government attempted various strategies to reduce both immigration and permanent settlement. The issue of immigration would eventually lead to a debate over citizenship, republican values, and universal nationhood, leading politicians to take up efforts to narrow citizenship as well as channel this new minority's activities to those which were commensurable to the state.

The concern with immigration and colour found in the Britain, however, unfolded differently in France due to the French Republic's national philosophy of integration and notion of the citizen. In the Republican notion of citizenship, stemming from the 1789 French Revolution, the individual is recognized as the only legitimate holder of rights by the state — ethnic, regional, and religious categorizations are ignored. At the official level, French politicians have been reluctant to adopt policies designed to recognize and target racial, ethnic, or religious minorities as officials fear that granting legal status based on group identity perpetuates the very boundaries that undermine a national sense of community (for a more detailed comparison between the Anglo-American and French racial policymaking models and the significant changes over the past decade, see Gehring, this volume). The issue of "nationhood" and French citizenship reached the national agenda during the mid-1970s. Within France, an intense debate over immigration and integration, utilizing grand themes of republicanism and *citoyenneté*, became "arguably the most visible and salient issue in French politics" in the mid-1980s to early 1990s, bringing forward "the big symbolic questions of 'belonging' and the cultural integrity of France" (Favell 1998: 40, 48).

During the 1980s, there emerged a nationalist politics of citizenship in France in response to the visibility of post-colonial migrants. The national debate which resulted demonstrated an important tension in the France over the dilemma of a Republican notion of citizenship versus ethnicity, a recurring dilemma in French history according to Bertossi (2007). France's post-colonial heritage was reassessed, largely with respect to its relationship with Algeria, leading to a reappraisal of national identity as a condition for citizenship. The far right espoused an ethnocultural notion of French citizenship as a key electoral issue and arguments for an ethnocultural citizenship gathered support during this period.

Although on the surface a seemingly difficult case to argue that the government managed and channelled difference because of its official refusal to acknowledge difference based on its assimilationist model, France would promote an ethnic civic identity in the 1980s. Support for this identity was predicated upon the associational and leadership capacities of the *beur* partners to produce results through the maintenance of public order and support of Republican ideals. Thus, the government largely responded to issues of social control. Difference, in terms of ethnicity and later religion, were considered acceptable by the French state if it did not challenge, but rather supported, the grand philosophies of the Republic: republican values, universal French nationhood, and, importantly for our purposes, *laïcité*.

In 1981, under Francois Mitterrand, the government passed a law that permitted the creation of ethnic associations, hitherto banned under a 1938 law which forbade the formation of associations by non-citizens. This marked a tentative institutionalization by public powers and the political class of an ethnic and communitarian collective expression in a laic and republican space (Withol de Wenden and Leveau 2001: 9-10). The 1981 law along with the 1983 *Marche des Beurs* opened a new era in the associationalism movement and its relationship with the French state, the

Beur movement (Withol de Wenden and Leveau 2001; Silverstein 2004; Laurence and Vaisse 2006). With a more permissive environment, hundreds of second-generation associations formed in the early 1980s, focusing on social and cultural issues.

The French government sought to actively manage *beur* associationalism, which would lead in part to the crisis of the movement in the late 1980s, through the promotion of "ethnic" associations, first, by granting legitimacy to these associations (for example, in the passage of the 1981 law of associations), and second, by the provision of public funding. Funding, provided for organizations through the Deixonne decentralization program and Social Action Funds, supported *beur* associations that furthered the state's agenda of integration. State support for the *Beur* Movement was strictly confined to the cultural and social sphere. By limiting its support to the cultural and social spheres, the French state was channelling beur activism away from collective action and communalist politics that the state deemed threatening. Thus, cultural activities were funded while any attempts at community organization were denied support; an example of which is the 1983 government-sponsored Georges Pompidou Centre exposition and live performances of *beur* artists. Another common tactic was official campaigns that highlighted *Beur* athletes and singers as icons of a multiracial France (Silverstein 2004: 167). The French state sought to "purchase" Beur leaders, creating what were derogatively referred to as "house Beurs" (*beurs de service*) (Wihtol de Wenden and Leveau 2001; Silverstein 2004). The majority of the associations created after 1981 were financed by government (either largely or moderately) and this is why some earned controversial reputations, in particular SOS-Racisme and MRAP (*associations "lucratives sans but"*, *associations-machines electorales*, *associations "faux nez" de l'Administration*) (Wihtol de Wenden and Leveau 2001: 12). Most of the organizations were funded by the *Fonds d'action social* (FAS), which played a determining role in the kind of projects the associations undertook, their strategies, and the stakes they faced (Wihtol de Wenden and Leveau 2001).

By taking public money, the associations were entering into a partnership with the government in which they understood their role to be a mediator, but, in receiving public money, this role was circumscribed by the goals of the government. This led the organizations to stress an ethnicity or identity that the state found acceptable in order to obtain funding for their projects. Leaders and their associations were expected to deliver certain goods to the government. These associations were viewed as promoting a model based on citizenship and thus were seen as loyal to the Republic.

By the 1990s, the hegemony of the racial or ethnic discourse — in Britain, the black discourse and, in France, the *beur* movement — was challenged by an emerging Muslim identity and religious frames which came to have significant, if not, primary, resonance. During this time, a younger generation of Muslims came of age in the West, often with citizenship of the Western nation in which they resided and not having a significant experience of their parent's country of origin, and were heirs to the disappointing results of the right of difference movements of the 1980s. However, while the black power movement in Great Britain and the *Beur* movement in France did not provide tangible advances in terms of equality, these movements did have at least one important legacy: they provided a platform for the (Muslim) religious identity to emerge. By providing a foretaste of activism, the younger generation asserted itself.

The Politicization of Religion and Policy Legacies

Around the 1990s, transnational events such as the Rushdie Affair in Great Britain and the *affaire du foulard* in France altered the political context in these two countries. First, these events provided a higher profile to Muslim community to citizens that were unaware or indifferent, increasing the salience of the issue among the general public. For the first time, one heard references within the media and government to "Muslim" activism, previously unrecognized and defined under the collective colour and ethnic discourse of previous decades. With the Rushdie Affair and headscarf controversies, the first formal recognition of domestic Muslims and the presence of Islam was a highly politicized one and became a visible focal point for politicians and society with respect to broader connections with violence and political Islam in the Muslim world. And, through these events, the threat posed to Western liberal and progressive values was highlighted. Subsequent events, including the 1995 Algerian terrorist bombings in France and the July 2005 bombings in Great Britain, furthered reinforced the concern over Islam's place in European society.

Religion, connected to larger international events and trends, became a target of societal anxiety. For example, public opinion polls have demonstrated is that there is significant negative perception among the general public regarding the rise of religious identities among the Western

Muslim population and the role of religion in public life. Indeed, when asked whether an increase in the Islamic identity of Western Muslims was a good or bad thing, 59% of respondents in Great Britain, 82% of respondents in Spain, 83% of respondents in Germany, and 87% of respondents in France considered it a bad thing (Pew 2006a: 9-10). The negative opinions held by Western publics have been linked to several concerns: a belief that a religious identity conflicts with Western values and contributes to a lack of integration, a loss of community cohesion (often associated with critiques of multiculturalism in general), and a fear of radicalization and violence.

International events increased the salience of religion and the Muslim community in the political/electoral realm as well, providing those among the Left concerned with illiberal religion and those on the Right with immigration, social order, and national identity issues with evidence of a problem — rendering *religion* a problem. And, here it is important that religion was targeted, thereby providing European publics the opportunity to deny second- and third-generation Muslims a European identity on the basis, as Ray Taras describes in his chapter, that a European identity is a modern, secular one and that a religious identity is anachronistic and a challenge for full integration (Taras this volume). Thus, the origin and subsequent development of Muslim incorporation policies resulted from changes in how the problem was defined among relevant actors within the policy-making sphere and larger society. These events provided "windows of opportunity" or catalysts for the political construction of Islam as illiberal.

When the security situation resulted in a focus on problems within the Muslim community, particularly those problems associated with an illiberal version of Islam, religion was addressed as a variable to be managed by the government, to be channelled away from negative aspects, particularly in its connection with radicalization and transnational loyalties, and to be formed into what would variously be termed liberal, moderate, mainstream, and/or European — that is, *secular* — Islam (Taras this volume). Across cases, Western governments differentiated among Muslim organizations and activities, seeking to legitimize those considered supportive of liberalism and democracy. This section will take a closer look at the different government initiatives to manage and channel a particular type of Islam within the Western state, focusing on how the British and French governments created new institutions and emphasized funding and research strands to legitimize certain actors and institutions.

New Labour Government's Institutionalization of Faith

In Great Britain, religion became a matter of public policy concern as a result of two separate, albeit connected, pathways which prompted the British government to undertake different policies that both dealt with faith as "a part of the problem" and faith as "part of the solution." In the first — and primary — path, the British government responded to specific security events that implicated religion in matters of social control. Religion was constructed as a problem and became an object of public policy concern.

Security events implicated the Muslim community as a "problem community" and faith as a part of the problem, particularly after the Oldham and Burnley riots in 2001 and the London bombings by British-born Muslims in July 2005. A series of riots between the Pakistani and white youths in the old northern industrial towns of England in the summer of 2001, much like the race riots in the 1950s, highlighted what the government would eventually frame as a lack of community cohesion. After the release of the Cantle Report looking into the causes of the disturbances, the New Labour Government initiated several different policy responses to address the problem of divided communities, collectively referred to as the community cohesion agenda. This agenda was largely merged with race relations in an overarching equality frame.

Faith was implicated in concerns over parallel communities. After the riots, and accelerating after the 7/7 bombings, there was an increased focus on the domestic Muslim community and its lack of integration. The Muslim community became the primary, if not the sole, reference point in debates over shared values and multiculturalism. Just as the "black-white" frame had gained hegemony in 1970s, the Muslim frame quickly became the predominant one with regard to government-faith partnerships, leading to the situation in which "faith communities" became shorthand for the Muslim community. At this time, government and private sector research found that the Muslim community was the most deprived minority across public policy indicators and contributing to the construction of the Muslim community as the most problematic of British minority communities.

In turn, the exclusive focus on the Muslim community further implicated problems within the Muslim community: the imam and mosque problem, youth radicalization, lack of compatible values, and the transnational nature of the community. This, in some ways, had the effect of framing religion or faith as a characteristic specific to the Muslim community, reinforcing its "outsider" position within British society. This is reflected in public opinion polls taken during this time that provide evidence of a significant negative perception among the general public regarding the rise of religious identities among the Muslim population and the role of religion in public life.[4]

This first path is perhaps not surprising in a post-9/11 context. However, to understand the particular form of the policies undertaken by the British government — that is how the religious values within the Muslim community became important components in the solution — it is important to understand a second path which placed religion on the government agenda. In this second path, religion was viewed as an asset — rather than an object — of policy and a facilitator of governmental objectives.[5] In this second path, the Blair government sought out partnerships with the faith sector in urban regeneration and community cohesion as a part of its larger policy commitment to privatization and greater efficiency in government service provision.

Similar to the racial buffers created in the 1970s, the Blair government created formal bureaucratic institutions to deal with faith and the Muslim

---

[4] For example, in a 2006 Pew Forum survey, when asked whether an increase in the Islamic identity of Western Muslims was a good or bad thing, 59% of respondents in Great Britain considered it a bad thing (Pew 2006a: 9-10). The negative opinions held by the British public is linked to several concerns, perhaps paramount being a belief that a religious identity conflicts with Western values and contributes to a lack of integration with 64% of British respondents in subsequent Pew survey believing that Muslims do not want to adopt customs of their country (Pew 2006b: 8).

[5] There were two camps in the British government that viewed religion as an asset. In the first camp, religion was viewed as a variable similar to other socioeconomic indicators, as a utilitarian resource but not of intrinsic value for policy. In particular, this approach viewed faith organizations as important resources in the form of infrastructure and personnel as well as access for government policy. This position was most commonly held by government officials in the race relations regime and by members within the Labour Party with a more secular outlook. In the second camp, religion was valued as an important component of an individual's identity, as a valuable resource beyond pragmatic considerations of the first camp. Religion was an important container of societal values and an important motivator of civic engagement. This approach focused on the unique resources religious organizations and communities contain and can mobilize. During this time, Prime Minister Blair was the staunchest supporter of this position as well as the bureaucrats within the newly created religious buffer institutions.

community, or "religious buffers." Much like the racial buffer institutions, faith-related issues became the responsibility of bureaucrats rather than politicians in an effort to take religion out of politics, allowing the government to manage faith while also maintaining, at least ostensibly, that the government was not interfering with the internal workings of Islam. The most important of these religious buffers was the Faith and Cohesion Unit and the Preventing Extremism Unit of the Department for Communities and Local Government (DCLG). These institutions were created to take charge of the Labour government's policy commitment to faith communities (Faith and Cohesion Unit) and the Muslim community (Preventing Extremism Unit).

The creation of these institutions served two primary purposes. The first was a pragmatic policy consideration: as the Blair government's faith policy shifted to working with more faith organizations, through the wider community cohesion framework and in its preventing extremism agenda, the government needed to create institutions that could effectively manage the new partnerships. The bulk of the work in supporting faith organization public service delivery was coordinated through these institutions, including the management of new funding streams. The different funding schemes set up by the Blair government sought to shape what was "acceptable" through funding objectives (for example, funding those faith organizations which delivered services to individuals outside of their faith) and stipulations, particularly those that supported the community activities of a faith organization or required interfaith interaction in order to receive funding.

After the 7/7 bombings, the British government shifted its funding priorities. First, the government allocated more funding toward faith initiatives. Second, the additional funding overwhelmingly benefited Muslim organizations and interfaith forums. Third, the funding priorities required faith organizations to demonstrate how their programs reduced the risk of extremism. One of the primary funding streams is the Preventing Extremism Pathfinder Funds, launched by the DCLG in October of 2006; for the 2007-2008 funding cycle, the DCLG allocated £6 million to support over 200 grassroots projects. Specific priorities include a focus on "empowering mainstream voices", promoting "dialogue," supporting theological teaching, and capacity building to "recognize and challenge violent extremism" (DCLG 2007b).

The religious buffer institutions also produced and disseminated important research. With the increasing recognition that faith was a major component in British citizens' lives, particularly for minority communities, the British government sought to understand the role of religion in relation to its major policy objectives. This resulted in a significant research agenda that both sought to assess and understand the relevance and salience of religion for individuals and communities as well as how faith could be utilized in the political and public domains. Since 1997, the Department for Communities and Government (DCLG) (and its predecessors, including the Faith and Cohesion Unit and Preventing Extremism Unit) produced upwards of 20 publications focusing on faith issues.

The second, and most important, purpose of religious buffer institutions was to depoliticize the Labour government's faith policy. By creating a bureaucratic institution, the government was able to manoeuvre more widely as many of the decisions and outcomes were out of the scrutiny of the public eye, an insulation for both the government and the Muslim organizations receiving support from the government. This insulation was particularly important after the July 2005 bombings. At this time, the Labour government began to critically access its relationship with faith, no longer viewing faith involvement within government or civil society as uncritically "good." Now there was a need to separate out "good religion" from "bad religion," as now there was a general view held both within society and among policy-makers that religion was also an illiberal force. At this time, Blair's Labour government dramatically overhauled its faith policy, still viewing faith organizations and leaders as vital partners but, crucially, differentiating among faith organizations, seeking to legitimize those with particular characteristics.

The Blair government initiated the "winning hearts and minds" strategy, the cornerstone of which was an engagement of the Muslim community toward promoting shared values (DCLG 2007a; DCLG 2007b). The new government strategy includes what the government calls a fundamental "rebalancing" of its engagement with the Muslim community to support those who are a providing "proactive leadership," and, to support those groups who have been marginalized (DCLG 2007a: 9). What is more, the new government policy explicitly sought to support "moderate" and "mainstream" Muslim organizations. This would have important implications for the evolution of Islam within Britain. The effect was that the Blair government privileged those actors with a liberal Islamic viewpoint. Particularly, in "rebalancing," the Labour government shifted away from national "representative" bodies such as the Muslim

Council of Britain to support "moderate" and "liberal" faith organizations, particularly focusing on women, youth, and interfaith bodies as key partners. Thus, my argument extends Peres' observation in this volume that the move from multiculturalism to the community cohesion framework resulted in a change in public policy priorities (Peres, this volume).

Let us take a closer look at how the British government has shifted its focus to Muslim women. In identifying Muslim women as key repositories of peace and moderation within the Muslim community, the British government sought to support what it viewed as forces for moderation and liberal reform within Islam. The government described its support as unlocking the potential of Muslim women, an untapped resource, viewing Muslim women as being "uniquely" placed to challenge extremist and radicalization within the community and as positive, peaceful forces.[6] In order to harness the positive influence of Muslim women, the government has undertaken two general policy initiatives. Through various Preventing Extremism program funding schemes, the government has prioritized Muslim women's organizations and those organizations with programs that serve Muslim women.[7] In rebalancing of its engagement with the Muslim community, the Labour government has increased its partnerships with women's organizations. What is more, beyond a specific priority laid out after the PET working groups, the shift to smaller, local bodies has benefited women's organizations and issues.

---

[6] The Cohesion and Faiths Unit publication, "Empowering Muslim Women," stated that women "have a unique viewpoint on the challenges faced by the communities they live in -- whether that is the threat of violent extremism, anti-social behaviour, or young people feeling isolated and disengaged. They are also uniquely placed to solve these problems, challenging unacceptable behaviour and supporting those in need" (DCLG, 2008, 2). They, according the publication, "play a positive and important role in society and represent an untapped potential in the part they can play in preventing violent extremism in communities" (DCLG 2008: 6).

[7] The government has sought to provide support to Muslim women through the Preventing Extremism Unit's Pathfinder Funds as well as the Faith Communities Capacity Building Fund (FCCBF), the fund supporting the Improving Opportunity and Strengthening Society initiative with a central priority, in addition to a support of interfaith activities, of bolstering faith organization capacity-building. Through these two funds, women's organizations have access to more than £6.5 million in resources with an individual grant of the FCCB Fund reaching £30,000 for the 2007-2008 funding year.

France's Lukewarm Embrace of Religion

France also experienced a "turn to religion"—that is to say, faith increasingly infused the political discourse in France and became a matter of politicization within the political space—during this time period, evident in different state initiatives in the area of legislative policy, organizational change, and research and funding. Religion became a matter of public policy concern as a "problem" for the French state through a politically-constructed "religious cleavage," driven by a successful far right and divided political left. The process resulted in a contradictory policy regime of restrictive and inclusive measures both seeking to depoliticize religion—that is, to take religion out of the public debate and/or political process—but resulted in a further politicization of religion and greater—rather than lesser—state involvement in religion.

The French state's "turn to religion" unleashed a national process to redefine several principles. This was most clearly demonstrated in the significant religious cleavage that re-emerged over this time period over the proper place of religion in the public sphere carried out through identity politics described by Tomen (this volume). During the headscarf affairs, Islam was constructed as an illiberal religion along two primary dimensions: as a religion that did not separate the political from the religious, i.e. did not abide by the Western conception of secularism, and as a theological and cultural system oppressive to women. The first illiberal characteristic threatened the sacred French notion of laïcité while the second threatened the French principle of gender equality. The headscarf affairs pitted those who desired a "neutral" public space, free of religious connotations, from those who argued for the need, if not to embrace, at least to enable religion to enter the public space (for a more detailed discussion, see Tomen, this volume).

By the end of this process, public rhetoric and state action placed up front the French commitment to an aggressive version of laïcité, "reinvented" as the very core of the Republican identity, and intimately connected to the principle of gender equality (Bertossi 2007). Indeed, the law of 1905, the law governing church-state relations, was the starting-, and end-, point for the official public narrative.[8] Government and private

---

[8] The law of 1905 contains two separate clauses governing the French state's relationship with religion. The first article provides for freedom of conscience for individuals, guaranteeing "freedom of conscience and the free exercise of organized religions." The second article is the disestablishment clause which

reports during the 1990s and 2000s on issues concerning the Muslim headscarf, Islam in the Republic, and even those reports focused on immigration and integration began with a section on the principle of laïcité. And, all of these reports concluded that laïcité was under threat and reach a consensus that the French state must intervene to strengthen laïcité.

Above all, French policy throughout this period was driven by a concern for public order, justifying restrictions on the individual right to freedom of religion because of "threats" to security and public order, culminating in the 2004 ban against headscarves and other "conspicuous" religious symbols in the public school. This concern for public order also prompted, since the early 1990s, successive Interior Ministers on both the political right and left to establish a "representative body" for the Muslim religion, seeking a single interlocutor to not only effectively manage the religious issues arising from Islam in France. The French government, in a more nationalized, top-down policy, has attempted to make Islam more "French" through the government's institutionalization of Islam in the creation, first of the Council of Reflection on Islam in France in 1990 (*Conseil de Reflexion sur l'Islam de France*, CORIF), and, in 2003, the French Council for Muslim Religion (*Conseil Français du Culte Musulman*, CFCM). The issue of creating a transparent Gallic Islam motivated then-Interior Minister Nicolas Sarkozy to assert in 2002 that the French state should encourage a more public form of Islam, stating "What we should be afraid of is Islam gone astray…'garage Islam'…'basement Islam'…'underground Islam.' It is not the Islam of the mosques, open to the light of day." (in US State Department, http://www.state.gov/g/drl/rls/Irf/2007/90175.htm).

The French Council of the Muslim Faith (CFCM), established May 4, 2003 under the auspices of Nicolas Sarkozy as Interior Minister, was intended to bring Islamic practices into the open, thereby affording more input from the French government and less dependence on foreign

---

states that the government shall do nothing to privilege or promote a particular religion, proclaiming the state "neither recognizes, nor pays the salaries of, nor subsidizes any religion." The 1905 law allows religious bodies to organize as private religious associations. Thus, the state does not recognize religion as such but it does recognize religious organizations. The law of 1905 created very strict conditions for an association to organize as a religious body: first, it must have as its sole (rather than, say, primary) purpose to organize religious worship; and, second, it must not disrupt the public order. France makes a clear distinction between religious activities and all other activities.

influence. If Republican principles of laïcité were evoked to support a ban against the wearing of the headscarf, Republican principles of equality were utilized by Interior Ministers to justify creating a national Muslim interlocutor. Once again, the debate over laïcité and Islam's place in the Republic took place through domestic references and principles. Throughout the process, the Interior Ministers justified their actions by referring to how the other major religions had representative bodies when dealing with the state. While an important signal of continuity with French tradition, the Interior Ministers found themselves having to defend their actions against the French principle of laïcité, particularly assuring that the law of 1905 was not to be touched. Sarkozy, in particular, was criticized for his role in the creation of the CFCM, particularly on the grounds of violating laïcité. Consequently, throughout the almost 15 years to establish a representative Muslim body, the French state insisted on how it was a representative body for the Muslim religion rather than a political interlocutor for a religious community.

Beyond concerns of equality and integration, however, French state action should be interpreted as ensuring Islam conforms to the French notion of religion. That is, government officials have defined, regulated, and observed through the CFCM in order to ensure that Islam, like other religions in France, is

> "organized, bounded, orderly, contained in its buildings and defined by worship practices in those buildings. If is strays into the street, selling tracts or proselytizing, it is out of bounds, and even when it is tolerated it is no longer protected by the French constitution and can easily be quashed in the name of protecting order" (Bowen 2007: 18).

The resulting composition of the CFCM demonstrates the active hand of the French Republic to influence the composition of the institution and steer debates within it.[9] This activist hand belies the government assertion that it is not interfering with the internal affairs of religion. Indeed, throughout the process, there has been a concern that radicals — while

---

[9] The December 2002 agreement provided that the top three positions would be allocated to the Paris Mosque, the UOIF, and FNMF. As more than 50% of Muslims were not members of major national Muslim organizations, six independent mosques were chosen to be represented as well. These mosques were: Evry Mosque, Mantes la Joli mosque, Grand Mosque of Lyon, Ad Dawa of Paris Mosque, Grand mosque of Saint Denis de la Reunion, Islah mosque (neo-Islamiste).

having to be included for the sake of establishing a "representative" institution — do not dominate; this was be done primarily through the propping up of moderates.

The French government has sought to legitimize moderate and liberal partners over a concern for "representativeness" during the institutionalization process. A rather conspicuous example concerns how Sarkozy negotiated the terms through which "moderate" Muslim figures were assured leadership positions. Fearing the influence of the UOIF (*Union de Organisations Islamique de France*) and the FNMF (*Federation National de Musulmans Français*), then newly-appointed Minister of the Interior, Nicolas Sarkozy, negotiated a political compromise that guaranteed the post of president-spokesman of the CFCM to Dalil Boubakeur, the director of the Paris Mosque, and the other two executive positions to representatives of the UOIF and FNMF. Insisting on Boubakeur as the first president illustrates how the government sought to privilege "moderate" Islam as the interlocutor and maintain the unofficial policy of working with the Algerian government to regulate Muslim affairs in France (Laurence and Vaisse 2006; Bowen 2007). The manager of the GMP, Dalil Boubakeur, was well-known among Parisian elites and well-liked, particularly as he has advocated a version of Islam that adopts Western values (Laurence and Vaisse 2006: 102). His liberal, moderate credentials were further instantiated when he supported the headscarf ban in 2004.[10]

Moreover, the final structure reflects additional government intervention, demonstrating a desire by the government to ensure that the Council maintains a particular ideological bent. Officially, representatives are chosen in a democratic process with representation based on the size of the mosque. In attempts to marginalize the bad from the good, the government's policy toward the CFCM has oscillated, according to Alexandria Caeiro, "between including the diversity of Muslims and favouring specific tendencies has shaped the state organization of Islam" (Caeiro, 2005, 73). Thus, the Framework Agreement of 2001 stipulated that the "designation of the representatives will be based on a transparent and democratic procedure"; but, in contrast, the French Interior Minister,

---

[10] In fact, Dalil Boubakeur warned to the members of the Stasi Commission during his testimony that emphasizing religious identity in public would "open the door to demands for a separate religious status, and to communalism, something the Republic rejects because it integrates individuals and does not recognize communities" (Bowen 2007: 159-160).

Daniel Vaillant, co-opted the institution at the outset by stretching the limits of laïcité through the provision of several government appointed personalities instead of "elected" members who would sit on the administrative council of the future Muslim body. This was done in order to ensure moderate Muslims as well as minorities such as women sat on the national body.[11]

The French state further legitimized the Paris Mosque as its "moderate" and preferred partner in 2008 with the creation of the imam training program. The Paris Mosque was chosen to provide the necessary theological training to complement the secular education provided by the Catholic Institute of Paris. Thus, once again, the French state provided the Paris Mosque with a privileged position.

The institutionalization of Islam in France, thus, is an effort to organize and regulate Islam within the French Republic. The main driving force in the process has been the secular state: the process has been initiated and directed by the French government, specifically by the Ministers of Interior, who have initiated the first meetings, participated in how to define the procedures of election to the Council, drew up criteria for participation (and, to a certain extent, to ensure broad representation of all Muslim perspectives), and provided the organizational support for the elections (Laurence and Vaisse 2006; Laurence 2006; Bowen 2007).

Assessing Policy Legacies Across Cases and Across Time in Western Europe

Across time and across cases, the European governments sought to channel what they framed as different into acceptable avenues, particularly activities and development of identities that were turned toward the liberal democratic state, that is, civic-minded, oriented to "opting in" to prevailing societal values. Western governments were responding largely to problems of social control, with domestic and international events pointing to the minority community as a "problem community," first in terms of colour or ethnicity and then in terms of religion. The

[11] In a speech given on October 21, 2002, Sarkozy publicly declared his support for placing women and other minority (in this case, theological, ideological, etc) representation, arguing that it was essential that minorities were represented in the CFCM, particularly noting that women have an equal representation as men in qualified persons category (Billon, 2005).

contemporary situation in which Western governments and societies question the compatibility of Islam and democracy, thus, is a continuation of rather than a departure from the debate over whether the racial minority population was compatible.

As religion rose to the forefront of public policy concern, particularly a concern with an illiberal version of Islam, Western governments sought to channel this through new institutions, such as national Muslim councils, which would at times follow established church-state institutional patterns, but would also reflect a continuation of policies from the previous decades to manage and co-opt racial and ethnic difference. Church-state relations would emerge as important predictors of public policy response only *after* religion was implicated and sometimes not even then. For example, the British government's "turn to faith," a shift to considering religion as a public policy concern, would be channelled in a similar manner to the British race relations regime. In the case of France, government efforts to find a Muslim interlocutor would ostensibly fit into church-state relations, in that the French state sought a national council along the lines of previously established religious councils, namely the Protestant Federation of France (*Federation Protestante de France*) and the Jewish Central Consistory of France (*Consistoire Central de France*).

Works Cited

Al Sayyad, Nezar and Manuel Castells, eds. 2002. *Muslim Europe or Euroislam: Politics, culture and citizenship in the age of globalisation (transnational perspectives)*. Lanham, MD: Lexington Books.

Alba, Richard. 2005. Bright vs. blurred boundaries: Second-generation assimilation and exclusion in France, Germany, and the United States. *Ethnic and Racial Studies* 28(1): 20-49.

Allievi, Stefano and Jorgen S. Nielsen, eds. 2003. *Muslim networks and transnational communities in and across Europe*. Leiden and Boston: Brill.

Aluffi Beck-Peccoz, Roberta and Giovanna Zincone, eds. 2004. *The legal treatment of Islamic minorities in Europe*. Leuven: Peeters.

Banton, Michael. 2000. Strategic vision in combating racial discrimination. In *From legislation to integration? Race relations in Britain*, ed. Muhammed Anwar, Patrick Roach, and Ranjit Sondhi, 158-77. New York: St. Martin's Press.

Bertossi, Christophe. 2007. Distant neighbours: Understanding how the French deal with ethnic and religious diversity. *Runnymede Perspectives Series.* London: Runnymede Trust.

Bleich, Erik. 2005a. The legacies of history? Colonialisation and immigrant integration in Britain and France. *Theory and Society* 34: 171-95.

—. 2005b. Religion, violence, and the state in 21st Century Europe. Paper presented at the Migration, Religion, and Secularism – a Comparative Approach (Europe and North America) Conference, June 17-18, in Paris, France.

Bowen, John R 2007. *Why the French don't like headscarves: Islam, the state, and public space*. Princeton: Princeton University Press.

Brubaker, Rogers. 1992. *Citizenship and nationhood in France and Germany*. Cambridge, MA: Harvard University Press.

Caeiro, Alexandre. 2005. Religious authorities or political actors? The Muslim leaders of the French representative body of Islam. In *European Muslims and the Secular State*, ed. Jocelyn Cesari and Sean McLoughlin. London: Ashgate.

Cesari, Jocelyne. 2004. *When Islam and democracy meet: Muslims in Europe and in the United States*. New York: Palgrave.

Cesari, Jocelyne and Sean McLoughlin, eds. 2005. *European Muslims and the secular state*. London: Ashgate.

Department for Communities and Local Government. 2007a. *Preventing violent extremism pathfinder fund 2007/2008: Case studies*. London: Department for Communities and Local Government.

—. 2007b. *Preventing violent extremism pathfinder fund 2007/2008: Case studies*. London: Department for Communities and Local Government.

European Monitoring System on Racism and Xenophobia. 2002. *Islamophobia in the EU after 11th September 2001*. Budapest: Open Society Institute.

—. 2002. *Monitoring minority protection in EU Member States*. Budapest: Open Society Institute.

Faith and Cohesion Unit. 2008. *Empowering Muslim women*. London: Department for Communities and Local Government.

Favell, Adrian. 1998. *Philosophies of integration: Immigration and the idea of citizenship in France and Britain*. London: Macmillan.

Fekete, Liz. 2004. Anti-Muslim racism and the European security state, race and class. *Race and Class* 46(1): 3-29.

Fernando, Mayanthi L. 2004. The avowal and disavowal of difference France. *Anthropological Quarterly* 77(4): 835-43.

Fetzer, Joel S. and Christopher Soper. 2005. *Muslims and the state in Britain, France, and Germany.* Cambridge: Cambridge University Press.

Gehring, Jacqueline. 2010. Riots and rights: Comparing racial policy making in France and the United States. In *Migrants and minorities: The European response*, ed. Adam Luedtke. Newcastle upon Tyne: Cambridge Scholars Publishing.

Grillo, Ralph D. 2004. Islam and transnationalism. *Journal of Ethnic and Migration Studies* 30(5): 861-78.

Guiraudon, Virginie and Christian Joppke, eds. 2001. *Controlling a new migration world.* London: Routledge.

Joppke, Christian. 2007. Beyond national models: Civic integration policies for immigrants in Western Europe. *West European Politics* 30(1): 1-22.

Kepel, Gilles. 2004. *The war for Muslim minds: Islam and the West.* Cambridge, MA: Harvard University Press.

—. 2002. *Jihad: The trail of political Islam.* Cambridge, MA: Harvard University Press.

Klausen, Jytte. 2005a. *The Islamic challenge: Politics and religion in Western Europe*. Oxford: Oxford University Press.

Klausen, Jytte. 2005b. The re-politicization of religion in Europe: The next ten years. *Perspectives on Politics* 3: 554-7.

Koopmans, Ruud, Paul Statham, Marco Guigno, and Florence Passy. 2005. *Contested citizenship: Immigration and cultural diversity in Europe*. Minneapolis: University of Minnesota Press.

Laurence, Jonathan. 2006. Managing transnational Islam: Muslims and the state in Western Europe. In *Immigration and the Transformation of Europe*, ed. Craig Parsons and Timothy M. Smeeding, 251-73. New York: Cambridge University Press.

Laurence, Jonathan and Justin Vaisse. 2006. *Integrating Islam: Political and religious challenges in contemporary France*. Washington, D.C.: Brookings Institution Press.

Lester, Anthony. 2000. The politics of the Race Relations Act 1976. In *From legislation to integration? Race relations in Britain*, ed. Muhammed Anwar, Patrick Roach, and Ranjit Sondhi, 24-39. New York: St. Martin's Press.

Messina, Anthony M. 1989. *Race and party competition in Britain.* Oxford: Oxford University Press.

—. 2007. *The logics and politics of post-WWII migration to Western Europe*. Cambridge: Cambridge University Press.

Minkenberg, Michael. 2002. Religion and public policy: Institutional, cultural, and political impact on the shaping of abortion policies in Western democracies. *Comparative Political Studies* 35(2): 221-47.

Modood, Tariq. 2006. British Muslims and multiculturalism. In *Multiculturalism, Muslims, and citizenship: A European approach*, ed. Tariq Modood, Anna Triandafyllidou, and Ricard Zapata-Barrero, 37-56. New York: Routledge.

Modood, Tariq, Anna Triandafyllidou, and Ricard Zapata-Barrero, eds. 2006. *Multiculturalism, Muslims, and citizenship: A European approach*. New York: Routledge.

Modood, Tariq. 2005. *Multicultural politics: Racism, ethnicity, and Muslims in Britain*. Minneapolis: University of Minnesota Press.

Peres, Hubert. 2010. Towards the end of national models for the integration of immigrants in Europe? Britain, France and Spain in comparative perspective. In *Migrants and minorities: The European response*, ed. Adam Luedtke. Newcastle upon Tyne: Cambridge Scholars Publishing.

Pew Forum Global Attitudes Project. 2006a. The great divide: How Westerners and Muslims view each other; Europe's Muslims more moderate. Washington, D.C.: Pew.

—. 2006b. Muslims in Europe: Economic worries top concerns about religious and cultural identity. Washington, D.C.: Pew.

Ramadan, Tariq. 1998. *To be a European Muslim*. Leicester: The Islamic Foundation.

—. 2003. *Western Muslims and the future of Islam*. Oxford: Oxford University Press.

Rath, Jan and Shamit Saggar. 1992. Ethnicity as a political tool in Britain and the Netherlands. In *Ethnic and racial minorities in advanced industrial democracies*, ed. Anthony M. Messina, Luis R. Fraga, Laurie A. Rhodebeck, and Frederick D. Wright, 201-21. New York: Greenwood Press.

Roy, Olivier. 2004. *Globalized Islam: The search for the new Ummah*. New York: Columbia University Press.

Silverstein, Paul A. 2004. *Algeria in France: Transpolitics, race, and nation*. Bloomington: Indiana University Press.

Taras, Ray. 2010. Secular and religious groundings of European xenophobia: Distinguishing French, Polish, and Russian prejudices. In *Migrants and minorities: The European response*, ed. Adam Luedtke. Newcastle upon Tyne: Cambridge Scholars Publishing.

Tomen, Bihter. 2010. A clash of identities? The challenge of minority integration in France. In *Migrants and minorities: The European response*, ed. Adam Luedtke. Newcastle upon Tyne: Cambridge Scholars Publishing.

Viet, Vincent. 1998. *La France immigrée, construction d'une politique 1914-1997.* Paris: Fayard.

Warner, Carolyn and Manfred Wenner. 2006. Religion and political organization in Europe. *Perspectives on Politics* 4(3): 457-79.

Wihtol de Wenden, Catherine and Remy Leveau. 2001. *La beurgeoisie: Les trois ages de la vie associative issue de l'immigration.* Paris: CNRS Editions.

CHAPTER EIGHT

MUSLIMS AND MULTICULTURALISM IN THE EUROPEAN UNION: PUTTING DIVERSITY, ACCEPTANCE AND EQUALITY TO THE TEST

ALESSANDRA BEASLEY VON BURG

An American Beginning

Barack Hussein Obama was elected President of the United States in 2008. His historic victory is a reminder of how long it took a divided nation to reconcile with its own racial tensions and its still troubled relationship among people of different ethnicities, religions, races. Obama is unique not only because of the colour of his skin. He is the son of a white woman from Kansas, who had him as a teenager, and a black man from Kenya, who was Muslim. The world rejoiced when Obama won because many took his triumph as a signal of the end of the anti-intellectual, anti-cosmopolitan, anti-deliberation years of George W Bush. Obama's own exotic family, with siblings scattered around various continents and his own experience living abroad, appeals to millions across the world. Global citizens 'voted' almost unanimously for Obama (Cheers from the Rest of the World) for what he represented and for the hope he promised to bring to the US and the rest of the world. However, even with Obama's great accomplishments, there was one unanswered issue.

His middle name and his Muslim father were enough to convince many voters that he is a practicing Muslim. For those unrelenting and sceptical citizens, his faith and background were not considered private matters during the campaign, rather sure signs of danger and a threat to American ideals, even after he directly and frequently stated his beliefs and even faced a controversy linked to his Christian pastor. The problem laid in the mere possibility that he was a Muslim and the answer denying those "rumours" came quickly, but an answer to the larger problem never came. Obama tacitly distanced himself from all things Muslim and his campaign even made sure a couple of veiled women would be removed from the background that was to frame the candidate during a rally, surely connecting him to the dangerous faith of Islam (Lee 2008). While Obama tried to appear sympathetic to Muslims, he walked a fine line to distance himself from those who many still associate with nothing but terrorism, violence and hate. The question he never dared to answer is: what is wrong with being a Muslim? What if he were a Muslim? Why could he not just openly defend his own faith while standing up for those who, like his father, are Muslims?

Politically, asking this question publicly would have been disastrous and potentially detrimental to his historic election. Only towards the end of his long campaign, Colin Powell, while endorsing Obama, reminded us that being a Muslim ought not to be considered a crime or, hard to believe, a reason not to be elected. Obama's non-Muslim status, however, is an important reminder of the situation many Muslims still face daily, in the US and in the rest of the world. Even after the elections, young Muslims who supported Obama kept to themselves as they celebrated the new president and reflected back on their semi-forced isolation from the campaign craze. What if they had gone out in public to support Obama? Would other voters be ready to welcome the candidate many Muslims endorsed?

The question about what is 'wrong' with being Muslim is one that is particularly salient now in the European Union, as the land where approximately 16 to 20 million Muslims reside, compared to the mere 3 to 5 million in the US (Pan 2005, Kuper 2007). The recent events in the US, however, are a forceful reminder of the constant, pervasive and almost taken-for granted discrimination against Muslims. Obama's struggle, even as he successfully balanced his background of 'difference' and 'otherness' with his message of sameness, may remain an untold story for those who are relieved he dodged that bullet. But what does that mean for those who are Muslims? If the President of the United States made it to the White House by reassuring voters he is not one of 'them,' what message does he send to those across the world who are not only ready to embrace their religion and way of life, but would like others to accept them for who they are?

The 'problem' of being a Muslim dates back before the tragic events of September 11, 2001, and even the consequent headlines from the bombings in Madrid in 2004, in London in 2005, the Parisian riots later that year, the brutal murder of Theo Van Gogh in 2004 and the uproar over cartoons published in Denmark in 2006, inter alia. Many events remind us of the difference between Muslims and everyone else. Often, the dramatic events that grab the world's attention focus on the few terrorists who want to be recognized for their hatred of the 'West' and everything that the 'infidels' believe. But what about the millions of Muslims who live, work, pray peacefully and respectfully? For those, Obama may represent the eventual acceptance of what is different as normal, what has traditionally been 'them' as 'us' and what has been considered dangerous as familiar. The very fact that he was elected despite the rumour that he was a Muslim may start a new discussion on what the world can do to accept those who really are Muslims, one Obama initiated in his speech to the Muslim world in Cairo in June 2009, so that being one is not automatically considered a problem because of a perceived sense of 'otherness.'

As of now, however, being a Muslim *is* still considered a problem in many parts of the world, especially in the European Union, because of race, religion, immigrant status, and even the perceived inability to be effective members of liberal, secular Western democracies (see Gardner, this volume). I focus on the European Union because of the size of the Muslim population and because of the difficulties that Muslims face in their efforts to either assimilate or maintain their religion and culture and still be respected as equals. Most importantly, I focus on the European Union for their self-proclaimed goals of equality and respect of difference, captured by the motto 'united in diversity,' and for the unique possibility of addressing the perceived 'otherness' of Muslims at the supra-national or inter-national level. Too often scholarship about the Muslim population, especially in Europe, seems to be searching for the answer to the problem of being a Muslim, the reasons why Muslims cannot simply assimilate or, especially after September 11, the reasons why Muslims want to destroy those who don't agree with them (Franz 2007, Shore 2006). Instead, I suggest a way of understanding the Muslim population in the EU, and possibly elsewhere, for what they already do and believe and for the possibilities of action towards a solution, not a bigger problem.

This is not an attempt to erase differences or to promote sameness. Rather, I propose a theoretical framework that prevents us from looking for the 'otherness' associated with being a Muslim in an attempt to bridge the chasm between perceived differences. In an almost paradoxical move, I follow the work of Hannah Arendt, a Jewish philosopher and writer who knew what it meant to be considered a problem. In an intentional move to connect what seems different as inherently similar, I propose the problem of Muslims in the European Union can be analyzed through their roles in the private and the public spheres and the understanding of tradition and permanence. I promote a mode of multiculturalism that opposes multiplicity as the idea of many as different, separate pieces or people unable to connect. The task is to bring centrifugal forces back to what is common among people, religions, and ideas. In this conception, multiplicity is a force that brings us together while stopping us from falling on each other (Arendt 1958), a reminder that only when we treat each others as equals we can truly shine for our differences.

In the next three sections, first, I describe why the EU is uniquely positioned to contribute to the understanding and possibly a solution of the Muslim 'problem,' on the backdrop of their vision of unity, equality and respect of difference and for the several institutional efforts to reach out to the Muslim population. Second, I separate the spheres of understanding the Muslim population in their private and public space, positioning religion as an individual matter that needs not be hidden but used as motivation to reach out to others and recognize what is common. I also address the need for both spheres to create opportunities for the permanence and continuity of culture and religion. Finally, I conclude with a redefinition of multiculturalism as multiplicity of people and ideas, so that they may come together for their commonalities rather than differences, to recognize that what appears different is often not, so that EU institutions, the member states, their citizens and others around the world listen to the multiple Muslim voices and do not silence what it is often misrepresented as one uniform group.

Acceptance: The European Union and its Muslims

In the European Union, member states have a unique opportunity to address the Muslim problem and lead the way in dealing with their Muslim population because of their very promise of inclusion, summarized in the motto 'United in Diversity' and for the several institutional efforts to reach out to the Muslim population. Ever since 1957, with the founding Treaty of Rome, European member states have declared a commitment to an 'ever closer union' that would work together economically, politically and socially to guarantee a stable, prosperous and peaceful place to live for all their citizens. Along with union, however, comes division, so that from the very beginning, the European Coal and Steel Community, then the European Economic Community and eventually what we now call the European Union, were founded by a process of inclusion that would bring nations, especially those that had been bitter enemies, closer together, while excluding others. The process of strengthening unity via division dates back to the very beginning of the idea and name of the continent, in ancient Greece.

When Hesiod was still referring to Europe as a creature, Isocrates shaped its political meaning in "obstinate opposition" (de Romilly 1992, 3) to Persia and Asia. As he encouraged citizens to fight for Europe, he recognized the differences in culture and interpreted it as a matter of superiority for Europe, because while Persia was ruled by a King, Greece was for Isocrates "the country of freedom" (de Romilly 1992, 4). What would become the pride of Western society for political freedom, democracy, and human rights, were ideals in their embryonic stage, and Isocrates believed that what gave birth to the concord that made Europe (Greece) powerful was "the real union" among the city states. Europe established then its credibility in matters of union with people like Helen of Troy and Agamemnon, who created concord (*homonoia*) and good will and sympathy (*eunoia*) among people otherwise divided and hostile to one another. Even war, Isocrates argued, produced the unity he believed to be a political ideal, later known as panhellenism. The term paneuropean and then European followed, used to refer to efforts "made toward creating Europe" (de Romilly 1992, 9-10).[1]

From the beginning, this dilemma between inclusion and exclusion became apparent when dealing with immigration and the acceptance of non-Europeans, particularly Muslims, as well as citizens of other European nations, who had come to work in the member states where labour was needed. When the founding documents came together in the Rome Treaties,[2] the six founding nations were "determined to lay the

[1] Isocrates, according to de Romilly, used the word 'Europe' fifteen times in numerous passages, including the Paneg, the Philippus, and the Panath. In all of his uses, Isocrates says Europe when he means Greece (de Romilly 1992, 3).

[2] The Rome Treaties include the historical signing into existence of the European Economic Community and the European Atomic Energy Community (Euratom). The signatories of the agreements were Christian Pineau of France, Joseph Luns from the Netherlands, Paul Henri Spaak from Belgium, Joseph Bech from

foundations of an ever closer union among the peoples of Europe," so that the Community could work to "eliminate the barriers which divide Europe" and make more efforts toward "the constant improvements of the living and working conditions" of the people (Treaty of Rome). The Treaty tackled the idea of unity "to ensure the harmonious development" of the Community "by reducing the differences existing between the various regions and the backwardness of the less favoured regions." The member states called upon "the other peoples of Europe who share their ideal to join in their efforts." Integration was one of the main goals, with an emphasis on "the abolition of any discrimination based on nationality between workers" (title III, chapter 1, article 48).

As progress toward more integration among member states trickled down to their citizens, the apparent efforts to unite Europeans, or at least the citizens of the six founding members, revealed the struggle between unifying some and distancing others. This apparent contradiction between unity and division would become more apparent as the EU developed the concept of EU citizenship, which would question notions of inclusion and exclusion, of rights and freedoms, of status and practice, in the context of the promises of 'Europe 1992.' In 1992, the Treaty on European Union, also known as the Treaty of Maastricht, was signed as an amendment to the Treaty establishing the European Economic Community, but remained based on the European ideals of unity, freedom, equality and justice, stressing the need for political integration. As an important building block of the EU, the Treaty posed the issue of immigration and dealing with 'others' as one impossible to ignore by institutions that basked in the glory of equality and respect for diversity. Only in 1997, however, the Treaty of Amsterdam finally expanded the notions of unity, equality, and diversity that the EU had already appropriated to include others who might have not been nationals of a Member State. While people from third countries had resided and lived on European soil long before the Treaties acknowledged their presence, the Amsterdam Treaty documented the effort to balance freedom of movement among EU and non-EU residents (see Chou, this volume). The commitment to respecting fundamental and social rights already agreed upon in Turin and Paris in the 60s was renewed as the Community realized they could not discriminate against some of the residents who were responding to the invitation to live, work and move freely across the EU. Limitations and restrictions remained, and still are in

---

Luxembourg, Antonio Segni from Italy, and Konrad Adenauer from the Federal Republic of Germany.

place, but the language of the Treaty of Amsterdam at least began to reflect a commitment and concern for citizens and non-citizens alike.

In 2001, the Treaty of Nice became an additional reminder of the "historic importance of the ending of the division of the European continent." As the leaders declared, they desired "to complete the process started by the Treaty of Amsterdam" to prepare the Community to function as "an enlarged Community."[3] As the member states prepared to share a single currency and unite with some of their eastern neighbours, the Treaty reinforced a commitment to citizens' rights proclaiming the Charter of Fundamental Rights of the European Union.[4] The importance of this Charter came from the themes of the opening articles, which included "human dignity, the right to life, the integrity of the person" and solidarity.

The Treaty solidified respect for human rights and fundamental freedoms (Title XXI, Article 181a) and recalled the themes previously addresses by all the other Community treaties. But the Nice Treaty also continued to hint at the impossibility to differentiate among EU and non-EU citizens when proposing human rights and freedoms. The Draft Treaty establishing a Constitution for Europe also addressed these issues, but after the French and Dutch rejection in May and the Parisian riots of November 2005, France became just an example of how ideals clash with reality. After those set-backs, the ideals of freedom, equality, and brotherhood were mocked by the American online magazine Slate as "Liberté, Egalité, Stupidité" (Kobrzynski and Watson-Boles 2005). As mostly Muslim immigrants (many of them third country nationals who are long-term residents) torched cars and attacked law enforcement, the past as violence, not as a unity, came to mind. The more recent attempts to resuscitate the Constitution as the Lisbon Treaty in 2007 were once again stopped by the Irish NO in June 2008, so that the vision of a united Europe with common goals was once again challenged, even after the Irish finally accepted the Treaty.

---

[3] This resonates with Kant's language, urging to think with "an enlarged mentality" (cited in Arendt).

[4] The Charter was drawn up by a Convention composed of members of the national and European parliaments, representatives of the national governments and a member of the Commission. Under six headings - Dignity, Freedoms, Equality, Solidarity, Citizens' rights and Justice - its 54 articles spell out the European Union's fundamental values and the civil, political, economic and social rights of the EU citizen. *(A citizens' Europe)*

The issues of immigration and difference, the problem of accepting others, and in theory, placing nationals and non-nationals on almost equal terms, are then a reminder of the difficulties the EU's lofty goals meet when facing the real division and at times even xenophobia across EU territory. The very promise of the EU clashes with the legal and practical differences between EU and non-EU citizens, in debates over the status and rights of immigrants. EU institutions are then caught in a dilemma between promoting equal rights and well-being for all and guaranteeing them only for EU citizens. This problem is even more complex with dealing with issues of diversity with Muslims, since the Muslim population in the EU includes both EU citizens who have long resided in EU member states like Germany, France, and Britain and are thus full-fledged legal citizens; and non-EU citizens, immigrants from northern Africa and the Middle East who come to work and live, legally and illegally, in the European Union (see Gardner, this volume). This distinction, however, while extremely important for access to political rights, legal protection and economic opportunities, dissipates in the light of the massive discrimination that people of Muslim descent face.

In the last decade, the EU has addressed the 'Muslim problem' directly with numerous conferences, publications and efforts to close the chasm often perceived between the diverse Muslim population living in the EU and those who treat them as a single threat. As Silvestri writes, "at the popular level, Islam and Muslims are often still perceived, both in cultural and in political terms, as a threat to European identity and cohesiveness, as well as to the integration process of the EU" (Silvestri 2005, 385). The magnitude of the Muslim problem is described by some as the very end of Europe, as conservative authors such as Novak write that "Europe is becoming Eurabia" (Novak 2006, 36). He focuses on what he perceives as the 'otherness' of what he clumps as one unified Muslim people, warning his audiences that Islamic thought "does not separate religion from politics, either analytically or in practice, exactly as Westerners do," so that for 'them,' "the religion of Islam is not really distinguishable from the one, united, universal Islamic caliphate and its military vanguard" and, according to Novak, "this singular Islam has been at war with 'infidels,' since its origin" (Novak 2006, 37). He condescendingly derides those who believe that multiculturalism places all cultures as equal "in their moral and political preferences," and he rejects universal principles and rights, placing his own Christian faith above all as the only moral compass that can truly save people and nations. Novak continues to scare his readers by reminding them that "the long term dangers of radical, alienated European

Muslims feeding the leadership of worldwide terrorism are already being felt" (Novak 2006, 38) and he warns us to be aware and prepared to deal with the "intense hatred for and violent opposition to democracy of a small but intense faction of extremists who claim to be Islamists, for whom an adequate and accurate name seems to be Islamofascists" (Novak 2008, 38).

Novak's open and intentional call to resist what he perceives as dangerous Muslim principles are as extreme as those very beliefs he is calling us to fight. He assumes most Muslims think and act alike and leaves no room for acceptance and tolerance, or even acknowledgment, of the majority of Muslims living in Europe without the goal of turning it in 'Eurabia.' On the other end of the political spectrum, authors like Younge admit what everyone, even Muslims, agrees upon: "There *are* a handful of nihilistic young Muslims keen to bomb and destroy and a far larger number sufficiently disaffected that they are prepared to riot." But he also reminds us that there are numerous "Europeans keen to see equality and meaningful integration, defending civil liberties and opposing wars against predominantly Muslim lands" (Younge 2008, 10).

Muslims, however, still face discrimination and resentment. Younge tells stories of common citizens urging each other to have babies quickly, because "The Muslims are breeding. Soon, they'll have the whole of Europe." Others come together to stop the building of mosques in their communities, even when Muslims react by planting a Christmas tree at the site "as a good-will gesture." This clash of civilizations happened in a small Italian town, where locals responded to the attempt at reconciliation by pelting Muslims with sausages and by dumping "a severed pig's head at the site," defacing the place with their call for a Christian Hill, not a mosque (Younge 2008, 10). Younge also reports that British novelist Martin Amis argued that,

> There's a definite urge—don't you have it?—to say, 'the Muslim community will have to suffer until it gets its house in order.' What sort of suffering? Not letting them travel, Deportation—further down the road. Curtailing of freedoms, strip-searching people who look like they're from the Middle East or from Pakistan.... Discriminatory stuff, until it hurts the whole community and they start getting tough with their children (Amis cited in Younge 2008, 10).

These individual instances of hatred are backed by statistics that, even when data are not collected, not reported or at best under-reported by national governments, reveal a rise in violence and discrimination against Muslims. Younge concludes that Muslims face the problem of "Integrating into a society that won't employ you, educate you or house you," so that "participating in a political culture that scapegoats you is also tough" (Younge 2008, 10).

EU institutions realize that the Muslim population faces incredible challenges as they attempt to live, work, and pray peacefully, and they have responded with some efforts, reporting the range of discrimination they face in their daily lives and urging citizens, national governments and public institutions to prevent and stop those hurtful and unfair practices (*Perceptions of Discrimination and Islamophobia: Voices from members of Muslim communities in the European Union* 2006 and *Muslims in the European Union: Discrimination and Islamophobia* 2006). The European Union Agency for Fundamental Rights, an EU institution, has particularly been active reaching out to the Muslim community. They have recently reported limited success in local initiatives attempting to build community cohesion and address the needs of Muslim communities in the European Union (Agency for Fundamental Rights 2008).[5]

These are just examples of what Silvestri argues are numerous EU "informal practices as well as policies that have an impact on Islam and Muslims living in the Euro-Mediterranean zone." These include "initiatives in the sphere of immigration control, social affairs, and external relations." Additionally, the EU has sponsored "ad hoc activities (on intercultural and interfaith dialogue)" (Silvestri 2005, 387). The Treaty of Amsterdam and other EU documents address the issue of immigration and that is important because "the majority of the Muslim population of the EU tends to be composed of immigrants or descendants of immigrants" (Silvestri 2005, 388). Silvestri summarizes the many conferences and meetings held between EU representatives and the Muslim population, ranging from clerics to diplomats, and she particularly highlights religion as one of the many issues addressed in an effort to bring about acceptance of differences and respect of culture.

[5] Their report stresses that "diversity and equality can reinforce each other within one community cohesion policy vision." The cities that were the subject of this study "moved from a policy of integrating immigrants to a policy concept of addressing the needs of city residents," so that all residents were "seen as having rights and responsibilities and an important role to play in improving inter-community."

Silvestri reports examples of the tentative ways in which EU institutions balance their willingness to cooperate with the Muslim population with the risk of singling them out for their beliefs. One example is a 2003 conference that was "advertised as an 'interfaith' event" but really focused on Islam, so that "the Muslim representative, turned out to be the principal interlocutor, both of the ministers and of the media" (Silvestri 2005, 392). Another conference in 2004 also addressed Islam to discuss multiple political issues, demonstrating the willingness of the EU to engage in constructive dialogue about inter-faith, inter-cultural issues, thus "extending its hands," toward the Muslim population in an effort to encourage them to participate in public life. Silvestri argues that the numerous positive moves toward inter-faith dialogue demonstrate an interest in interacting with the Muslim population as equals, in order to improve relations not only with the Muslims in Europe but also those in the rest of the world. Silvestri concludes that a belief "in the dialogue of cultures, religions and civilizations means nourishing the hope that political, economic and social tensions can be resolved through a dialogic relation based on shared values, sense of responsibility and reciprocal desire to come into contact with and make space for new cultures and traditions" (Silvestri 2005, 399). However, she also recognizes that the EU initiatives can be nothing more than publicity stunts that mask the real discrimination Muslims face under the banner of unity and equality. Particularly when the 'Muslim problem' is far from being solved, a real commitment to an overhauling of the perceptions of Muslims as others and their position in society as immigrants or second-class citizens is necessary. As of now, none of these well-intentioned initiatives have "produced any immediate results or clear guidelines on how to improve relations, in practical terms" and there is definitely not an "illuminating solution" (Silvestri 2005, 400) to the Muslim problem.

Writing again in 2007, Silvestri notes that "concentrating solely on Muslims could pose a double risk," because efforts to reach Muslims could single them out as a problem and because more than just a minority of Muslims needs to feel like they have the ability to participate as part of a well orchestrated, unified solution, not just an isolated problem. Silvestri encourages EU institutions to be "faithful" to what they claim is the goal "to bring about change and promote trust between individuals and communities as well as institutions" (Silvestri 2007). The solution to the Muslim problem resides then in EU and national institutions that provide a space for participation and action for Muslim people who have the right to participate and, most importantly, feel they have a legitimate claim to living well in a society that accepts them and respects them. The EU has taken some important first steps toward what surely will be a difficult process of reconciliation. The founding treaties and consequent documents that solemnly state the EU commitment to equality and diversity remind both EU and non-EU citizens, Muslims and non-Muslims, people who consider themselves the same or different, that who they are and what they practice is neither a matter to be left completely alone in the private sphere, nor is a matter that can be left out of the public sphere. Especially since religion is considered such an instrumental part of Muslim life and, unfortunately, the perceived threat of an Islamic rebellion against the West, in the next section I trace the roots of the important distinction between the private and the public sphere to argue that the Muslim problem needs to be addressed holistically, as we all exist in both.

Diversity: Where Can One Be Different?

The relationship of Muslims with religion is intrinsically connected with political participation. The 'Muslim problem' emerges often because their status as 'others' is based on their religion, not strictly limited to what they may believe, but on the perception that their Islamic faith motivates and guides them to act in ways 'different' than other citizens. Most dramatically, Islam is associated with extremism and rejection of all Western principles, so that in the EU and the rest of the world, non-Muslims think that Muslims cannot or will never willingly participate in the public sphere as contributing members of political, civil, social and economic life. Unfortunately, this becomes a self-fulfilling prophecy as Muslims are denied access to opportunities based on what many believe is the irreconcilable relationship of their faith with public life.

Hellyer dispels that erroneous assumption, addressing the misconceptions on Islamic law and the roles Muslims can and should play in public life. He revisits traditional Islamic texts particularly focusing on Sharia law and the position of Muslims as guests in non-Muslim nations. After historically contextualizing the possibilities of participation and summarizing conflicting views, Hellyer considers the situation of Muslims in the European Union, where Muslims are a minority both because the host countries are non-Muslim and because many reside there on a temporary basis, as immigrants. Often, however, Muslims are citizens and, Hellyer argues, start to consider themselves "as belonging to their state of citizenship" so that some ask what role Islamic law should play in their 'new' life. Regardless of their status, Hellyer, following another Islamic scholar, Ramadan, believes Muslims should stop thinking in temporary terms and do "away with ideas of 'return' while still wishing to remain committed to Islam" (Hellyer 2007, 9).

The myth of return to Muslim nations or to a state of perfect harmony with their religion is a problem both for those Muslims who fail to embrace their religion for what it teaches them to do and for the non-Muslims that use religion as an excuse to exclude them from public life as if they were unable to participate. For Hellyer, however, this myth of return has been abandoned by many Muslims and he argues that is essential to political participation because as long as Muslims perceive themselves as a temporary, politically non-influential minority, the 'Muslim problem' remains an "exceptional situation" that cannot be part of "normal life" (Hellyer 2007, 102). Hellyer adds that participating in public life and remaining consistent with religious principles go hand-in hand, so that Muslims need not alienate themselves. "On the contrary," Hellyer writes, "engagement with the mainstream" is necessary, but only when there exists "an understanding of their own situation as Muslims (i.e. adhering to Sharia), a position that Ramadan notes as agreed upon within the Muslim community." He posits that "any answer to a query on political life for Muslim minorities would be 'more in harmony with the comprehensive principles of Islamic jurisprudence' if it were resolved in a manner that focuses on the 'logic of duty and positiveness' rather than a logic of 'negative license,'" typical of people who only see themselves as guests rather than part of the community where they live (Hellyer 2007, 95).

Hellyer admits that the concept of citizenship in a non-Muslim nation can be innovative, but he concludes that it is actually the Muslims' duty, in accordance with Sharia law, to participate in their country and to feel the responsibilities to others living with them. Instead of being sceptical of secular countries, according to him, Muslims need to recognize that it is that very "secularism that has allowed pluralism to come into existence in Europe," where freedom of religion is one of the founding principles (Ramadan cited in Hellyer 2007, 97). Hellyer concludes that "Muslims should remain Muslims, but, as long as that is safeguarded, it is far more preferable for them to view contact with the majority as the norm, and separation or distinctiveness from the majority as the exception, and not the reverse" (Hellyer 2007, 98). Following Ramadan, he encourages Muslims in Europe to take the responsibility to become "Muslims of Europe," remaining committed to their faith. For Hellyer, "Islam is a religion that can exist anywhere, and demands that contributions be made to the wider society as a matter of course, so that Muslims may assist in creating a better society for the benefit of all" (Hellyer 2007, 104).

Assimilation and participation in the public sphere are then, or at least can be, in accordance with both Islam and Sharia law. The diversity that the EU encourages and supports is supposedly welcome in the political realm, at least for full-fledged citizens, but the discrimination and marginalization that Muslim minorities often face, according to Crowley, reflect "identity processes embedded in patterns of structural inequality and intentional prejudice" that cannot be reduced to a mere invitation to join the mainstream political culture (Crowley 2001, 100). Especially when Muslims are perceived as a problem, the risk of entering an unwelcoming public sphere leads to both isolation and, as we more often hear about, extremism.

This separation of the public and private spheres is then not constructive at all if it produces division, not unity. The public sphere is not intended as the Habermasian space for deliberation and consensus-building, where Muslims could engage others about personal issues. Nor is the private sphere the place for isolation and, for Muslims, religion. Arendt's model of the public and the private spheres stresses that we exist in both and until the Muslim problem stops being perceived as such, multiculturalism is only another tool to mask acceptance of diversity as an excuse not to recognize what we have in common. Permanence and tradition are also particularly important for Arendt, so that humans of all religions and backgrounds can remember, maintain and perpetuate their ideas. Therefore, I follow Arendt not to create a European public sphere where Muslims can deliberate à la Habermas or to advocate a retreat in the private sphere, but to understand how we live in both, as humans. My aim is to develop the distinction of the private and public sphere to connect action and inaction, equality and diversity, unity and division in the realm of humanity, where Muslims and non-Muslims exist together. This is not a naive separation of what is public and what is private (Salvatore 2004). I address the need for both, not to erase differences and force consent as the ultimate goal (Young 1990), but to allow a space where, as supposedly equals, participants can shine for their differences as they build traditions not only for themselves but for others. This, I believe, is not naive, but based on the idea that what we have in common is more than what tears us apart.

Muslims as Part of the Human Condition

Arendt sees the human condition of plurality as the foundation on which the public realm is built, and as the element necessary for the *vita activa* to be the "proper place for human Excellence" (Arendt 1959, 49). Arendt believes that the only place where one can be fully human is the *vita activa,* the public realm, to which she opposes the quiet life of inactive contemplation typical of the private realm. Arendt argues that in the past, as well as in the future, "a man who lived only a private life, was not fully human" (Arendt 1958, 38) and only in the public sphere one can succeed in the journey through time, as part of the world. Arendt would like to separate the two realms, but she also understands that human beings are formed in between and need both for a life in which people are simultaneously affecting each other and moulding the human condition, that is their ability to act.

Muslims who are citizens of any EU member states have access to what Arendt calls the public sphere, even if many who are permanent or temporary residents do not. Their ability to act is not limited to political life, but often the inability to participate as equals leads to feeling 'not fully human,' because the v*ita activa* is the necessary prerequisite for humans to encounter everything in the world as part of the human condition. Arendt sees the condition of plurality as essential to action and she mentions the example of the Romans who defined the term "to live" as *inter homines esse* (Arendt 1957, 7) to emphasize the importance of life among others. It is here that people gather as equals to express their uniqueness. This is important for Muslims, who are not considered equal even when legally so and rarely have the opportunity to express openly what makes them unique and different, even when living and working among others.

Arendt sees *vita activa* as the only place for freedom and choice. Action has its home in this realm because it is only here that people, through words and deeds, are able to come in contact with others to express themselves. However, the freedom to express themselves is often limited for Muslims in the EU, most notably in France, where in the spirit of *laïcité* headscarves are banned in the public realm (see Tomen this volume). The public sphere is then the space where Muslims could have opportunities to be equal, but as of now their ability to act, in order to address issues common to all, is often restricted by the perception of them as a problem, as different, second-class citizens who confine themselves to the private sphere or, in countries like the United Kingdom, to their separate courts (Pious, Loyal and Unhappy).

To the togetherness typical of the *vita activa,* Arendt opposes the isolation of the *vita contemplativa* as essential to prepare one for the *vita activa.* She compares the harsh "light and illumination" of the public sphere to the "warmth of intimacy" (Arendt 1983, 30) of the private realm. In the private, the warmth protects one from the space of appearances and tacitly shelters one within the walls of intimacy, contributing to the development of the courage necessary to enter the public sphere, where actions and words have to be in the cool and sober spotlight. Arendt recognizes that the private realm is where one finds, grows, and masters the abilities necessary to stand in the spotlight through public discourse. However, Arendt seems to fear the alienation of people in the private realm, which would interfere with the process of becoming human typical of the public sphere. This is particularly relevant to the Muslim population in the EU, where often their religion and culture separate them from others because of different beliefs. Those private matters, however, for Arendt, ought not to be forgotten in the public sphere nor promoted to everyone else. They become guidelines for action and thoughts to be used for the good of all.

Arendt's own past, which forced her to leave her homeland because of the Nazi persecution of Jews, has left her with a fearful suspicion for people's refuge into the *vita contemplativa* to escape the brutality of the *vita activa.* She discusses how people, especially during times of despair, persecution, and monstrosities, namely "dark times," can be guided by "their hope of preserving some minimum of humanity in a world grown inhuman" (Arendt 1983, 17) and consequently run the risk of doing so in their isolation, rather than in the togetherness necessary for the world. What Arendt is referring to is her Jewish heritage, particularly the group of Jews who escaped Germany because of the Nazi terror. Her personal example, however, has to be interpreted on a much larger scale, one that magnifies the experience of one group of persecuted people to the whole of humanity. The instance Arendt discusses is what was known as "inner emigration," that is "the withdrawing to an interior realm, into the invisibility of thinking and feeling" (Arendt 1983, 19) by people who, far from being found only in Nazi Germany, cannot resist the temptation to escape the reality of the public world, its harsh light, to the isolation of "an imaginary world as it ought to be or as it once upon a time had been," (Arendt 1983, 19) in the comfortable intimacy of the private sphere.

Arendt's interpretation of the world and her fear of the alienation and marginalization of Jewish people, paradoxically, are similar to the reasons why Muslims in Europe ought not to be isolated as a problem or, even worse, be ignored. Arendt's emphasis on the *vita activa* as the proper place for freedom achievable only through action and speech is reinforced by her notions of permanence, durability, and memory. Arendt emphasizes the importance of the others to create a togetherness that sets the stage for humanity. As she interprets it, "the public realm, as the common world, gathers us together and yet prevents our falling over each other" (Arendt 1958, 52). As in ancient Greece, the common world has to be public for one to express his or her uniqueness and transcend it into permanence. Arendt wants the public realm to make it through time and that is why people cannot lose the notion of immortality and eternity by egoistically keeping, or being forced to keep, common concerns in the private sphere. Their role as participants in the *vita activa* is to "transcend the life-span of mortal men" through the existence of a public sphere, which is a place where the actors can transmit a sense of continuity by influencing others, keeping its tradition alive.[6]

Arendt reinforces her position on the non-actuality of a person who lives only isolated in the private life, by stressing the deficiency and irrelevancy that such a person would embody for the others. Using Marx's words, Arendt fears that the refugee into the private realm would eventually cause the "withering away" (Arendt 1958, 55) of the public sphere because of its lack of new actors who contribute to the permanence through time. Issues like women's rights and marriage law are then not only private matters for Muslims just because they are dealt with 'at home.' Because private matters have public consequences, even personal issues, particularly related to the interpretation of Islam, ought not to be relegated to the private sphere when they have a potential impact on

---

[6] This becomes problematic for religions that reward mortality with an afterlife where immortality is granted to those who sacrifice for 'higher causes.' Arendt's public sphere, however, addresses the dilemma with a focus on those involved in the public sphere and, therefore, active in *this* world. The most common 'ultimate' sacrifice of suicide bombers who leave this world with the promise of absolution and eternal bliss for their martyrdom is then not an act for the public sphere, according to Arendt's theory. The act circumnavigates the actions and words typical of the public sphere and it leaves behind a tradition of fear and violence that does not contribute to the amelioration of life for other Muslims. Namely, the image left is one that does contribute to a more active and engaged public life, nor does it follow the private principles of a religion against self-induced violence.

others. This does not translate to a license to be intrusive and mind Muslims' business or to refuse to intervene when human rights violations, such as honour killings, occur. The private sphere is where Muslims protect their rights to be different in their practices, not as a refuge away from others or a substitute for the public sphere, but as the space that prepares them for public life.

Arendt shows the risks of a life lived only in the private sphere, but she also recognizes the benefits of the *vita contemplativa* as opposed to the *vita activa*. She writes that, "private life too can retain a by no means insignificant reality, even though it remains impotent" (Arendt 1983, 22). In the instance of "inner emigration," Arendt adds that at times this kind of attitude is justified and necessary, but one still has to wonder "to what extent do we remain obligated to the world even when we have been expelled from it or have withdrawn from it?" (Arendt 1983, 22). Arendt reinforces the importance of the world's reality in that, even when escaped, it cannot be ignored, but must always be acknowledged.

Freedom can never be found in the private sphere alone, and no matter how significant the experiences and activities in this realm can be, they can never replace the public world. Arendt places freedom in the public sphere when she writes that, "the raison d'être of politics is freedom, and its field of experience is action" (Arendt 1968, 146). Freedom, expressed through action and words, happens in the presence of others, where one can cultivate thoughts that could never grow "without a politically guaranteed public realm" (Arendt 1968, 149). As of now, Muslims appear often in the public sphere as problems, not as free actors working with others for common purposes. Access to political life as equal and free actors in the EU could encourage Muslims to leave the private sphere, where concerns brewing in isolation could become common issues at both the national and European level.

This may sound unrealistic or even idealistic, but Arendt believes that in the public sphere one is free because one is a beginning and has the power and the capacity to perform miracles. The notion of miracle is important for Arendt because she interprets the evolution of human kind on earth, against nature and all the improbabilities of life, as a miracle that should never stop surprising people. The improbable becomes probable through one's initiative, through one's *initium*, a beginning made possible by freedom and action, consequently creating the reality of the human condition (Arendt 1968, 169-71). Politics depend for "continued existence upon acting men," (Arendt 1968, 153) who maintain the public sphere alive by persuading each other. Persuasion, for Arendt, is only possible among equals, where actors possess the same authority and influence over one another and are able to work through a process of argumentation. Arendt stresses how only in equality one can express one's uniqueness and this is exactly what happens in the space of the public realm. But in order to perform in front of others in the *vita activa,* one requires courage and strength to be able not only to excel through words and deeds, but also to persuade the other actors to take action.

In the EU, Muslims seldom are in a position of equality and, thus, seldom have the possibility to persuade others. Their marginalization and exclusion from various opportunities do not allow them the opportunity to persuade others, and that is at times the reason why Muslims, especially young ones, feel silenced and oppressed and, according to Franz (2007), resort to violence, hatred and extremism against those who refuse to treat them as equals. Their voices are silenced by the actors, and Arendt would interpret this unidirectional performance as coercion. What she calls persuasion among equals becomes coercion among un-equals. The inability of those outside of the public sphere to respond to the action taken in the public realm makes action coercive, because they are restricting the range of possibilities by delineating the options for what needs to be done, or simply by showing them what to do and think. Arendt connects the masking of facts as truth to coercion, because when something is pronounced true in the public sphere, it becomes beyond agreement and dispute, so that others cannot do anything but witness the manufacturing of words and deeds.

Thus, the facts presented as true possess "an infuriating stubbornness," (Arendt 1968, 241) that according to Arendt, can only be supported by the actors' ability to persuade others. The equality and freedom which allow the manufacturing of facts as true in the public sphere through discursive actions are communicated by means of coercion to those who cannot participate, who are neither free nor equal to the actors. The real or perceived isolation of Muslims and their inability to influence others as equals often leads to mistrust in the institutions that supposedly guarantee them access, so that what comes from the public sphere is interpreted as lies and excluded minorities see themselves as 'truth-tellers.' While Arendt argues that, in politics, the truth-teller has a very hard task to accomplish in making people see that what has been accepted as true is merely a fabrication in the public realm, self-proclaimed 'truth-tellers' can be dangerous as outsiders looking in, silenced by a public sphere that becomes then the object of resentment. This is at times the case for extremists who feel that EU nations and their governments tell them what to do without listening and preach their righteousness while judging what is different as dangerous. While I am certainly not condoning these extreme and often violent views, Arendt's model reminds us of the importance of granting access to all as equals, so that everyone has a chance to enter the public sphere and contribute through actions.

The possibility of organized liars has very much to do with what Arendt has referred to as "dark times," during which one's alienation into the isolation of the *vita contemplativa* can strengthen rather than oppose the manufacturing of words and actions by the actors in the *vita activa*. The truth-teller can then represent the necessary step to be taken in the direction of whatever action is necessary and he has the opportunity to "start toward changing the world" (Arendt 1968, 251). Since the action becomes meaningful only when it occurs in the public sphere, the truth-teller must become the actor. This emphasizes the potential to participate in public life, and the necessity to do so. The potentiality to transform those who cannot yet participate in the future is of great importance for posterity because there is where the successors of the public sphere are to continue the actions that guarantee freedom by maintaining it through time. For Arendt permanence, continuity, and durability are essential characteristics of the *vita activa*, because they ensure its existence.

The continuity and permanence of the public sphere does not always have to generate actors, but it must continue the tradition of action achieved through the freedom of being with others. Arendt sees tradition as the essential element that allows the survival of both the *vita activa* and the *vita contemplativa*. She writes,

> without tradition, which selects and names, which hands down and preserves, which indicates where the treasures are and what their worth is, there seems to be no willed continuity in time and hence, humanly speaking, neither past nor future. (Arendt 1968, 5)

Tradition needs remembrance, memory, namely thinking about what happened and being able to tell others the importance of the events, not just in the private sphere, but especially in the public sphere. In the EU, Muslims often feel their traditions are threatened by those in power, as nations promote assimilation as a way to invite them as equals, but not on their own terms. Access to political life and meaningful participation in the public sphere, following Arendt, could empower Muslims as equal actors who can then maintain their own tradition through others, not against them. Permanence, durability, and continuity transmit a tradition so that, in their plurality, people can act together in the creation of what is common to them all, their human condition.

Thinking about what is possible and working toward common goals, for Arendt, happens in the *vita activa*. Thinking is not only the activity that connects, creates, and encourages growth, but also the very beginning of the potential transformation of non-actors into actors. Arendt stresses the two conditions essential for thinking: political freedom and presence of others. She believes that one has to be free in order to think and during "dark times" the process of thinking is the most vulnerable, because of the risk of isolation into the private realm, as opposed to the togetherness of the public sphere. Often minorities and marginalized groups like Muslims in Europe do their thinking in isolation and even protect it from the public sphere in the fear of losing their beliefs and traditions. Arendt, instead, would encourage thinking to happen with others who can then work together to address issues common to all. This is particularly important because often thinkers become leaders and that is dangerous in the coercion of the public sphere, where instead of thinking together, some may tell others *what* to think, not as an action but a mere reaction.

Loss of thinking translates then to loss of power and authority, even at times when authority is necessary to address issues common to all. Arendt seems deeply distressed by the modern world's loss of authority and she reminds people that "authority is whatever makes people obey," (Arendt 1968, 103) and she does not believe this would restrain in any way one's ability to excel. Namely, "authority implies an obedience in which men retain their freedom" (Arendt 1968, 106), and if force is used, than authority has failed. What Arendt wants from authority is to provide a sense of guidance and orientation that looks at the past to point to the future, in order to create a sense of continuity, permanence, and durability that is necessary for actions and words to happen in the public sphere. In regard to this, she writes,

> The loss of world permanence and reliability-which politically is identical with the loss of authority-does not entail, at least not necessarily, the loss of human capacity for building and preserving, and caring for the world that can survive us and remain a place fit to live for those who come after us. (Arendt 1968, 95)

Therefore, Arendt believes in "men's growth toward the past," (Arendt 1968, 123) as the Romans did, to use authority in its meaning that generates from *augere*, to augment, from which the word *auctoritas* derives (Arendt 1968, 121). "Auctor" is the author, the one who can add to the public sphere through actions and speech, not through power. Authority is necessary to augment the impact of the actor and to lead the way into remembrance. For progress, more thoughts and ideas have to be generated in both the public and the private spheres, in order for thinking to provide a beginning that connects people to their past through memory (Arendt 1968, 126).[7] Permanence has its roots in tradition, so that remembrance of the past leads actors towards the future. Arendt returns to the gift of freedom and action that men are given as 'beginners' to explore the ways in which humans can take the initiative to establish their human condition. She interprets man as "the artist in the world and in history, who does not "do" like a human being, but "creates"...though in appearance only" (Arendt 1993, 161). It is in the public realm that people come together in their freedom to encounter the "plurality of men" (1951, 437) who simultaneously affect each other and mould the human condition through their ability to act.

Following Arendt's theories, minorities and marginalized groups like the Muslims in Europe have the possibility to connect their past and unique traditions to the a common future when they reconcile their life in the private sphere with opportunities to participate as free and equal actors in the public sphere. Arendt argues that,

> Our feeling for reality depends utterly upon appearance and therefore upon the existence of a public realm into which things can appear out of the darkness of sheltered existence, even the twilight which illuminates our private and intimate lives is ultimately derived from the harsher light of the public realm. (Arendt 1968, 51)

Once again, Arendt reinforces her position that makes action and speech possible only in the presence of others. This otherness is the common denominator of authority, freedom, permanence and continuity into history, and thought. The 'Muslim problem' is then one both for the private and the public sphere, both needed for humans, not just Muslims, to develop as different but also as equals, to feel protected and respected in the isolation of the private sphere, but welcome in the plurality of the

---

[7] Augustine's "Sedis animi est in memoria."

public sphere. Only as humans, not as a problem, Muslims have the ability and responsibility to live, work, pray peacefully and respectfully.

Conclusion: Equality Multiculturalism as Unity, not Division

The private and the public spheres form the backdrop as we learn to live with each other, without trumping freedoms or constraining what is unique about us. Multiculturalism becomes then a mode of understanding differences and collecting people and ideas not to erase them, as assimilation requires, or to accept them all without questions, especially when human rights are violated, or not even to fear what is different and scapegoat some to excuse the marginalization of all. Aggestam and Hill (2008) summarize these three models of multiculturalism and argue that the EU has been struggling to grant immigrants equal rights, including legal, economic, social and cultural, without asking minorities like the Muslim population to give up their "cultural distinctiveness" (Aggestam and Hill 2008, 99). They believe that in the EU, "the multicultural idea of 'unity in diversity' rests on a 'constructive ambiguity" that has to be both "acceptable to everyone" and workable at the national and EU level, but also at the individual and community level. These tensions test the limits of tolerance and understanding daily, for Muslims and non-Muslims alike.

Therefore, as long as citizens and institutions treat Muslims as a problem and tip-toe around delicate issues like religion, culture, tradition, political participation, like a bull in a China shop, tensions are bound to intensify and even well-intentioned EU initiatives directed at the Muslim population risk heightening differences, rather than smoothing relationships. Instead, I argue that multiculturalism can be redefined as a mode of multiplicity where all that is different is gathered back together, bringing people out of the private sphere, yet respecting their right to have one, and collecting all in the public sphere, accepting minorities as free and equal actors. This is not a mode that simply supplements "traditional human rights with minority rights" or merely explains how they co-exist, as Kymlicka has argued. Namely, he defines multiculturalism as what "arises from national and ethnic differences" and argues that a state is multicultural when "its members either belong to different nations…or have emigrated from different nations, and this fact is an important aspect of personal identity and political life" (Kymlicka 1995, 18). The EU, as a collection of nations, is definitely multicultural, but as much as its vision is based on unity of differences, the marginalization of minorities like the

Muslim population is bound to prevent them from actually participating in the process of making, inventing and even changing what the EU and the member states embody and represent.

Equality for all is then acceptance of multiplicity, commitment to what Arendt claims is 'the right to have rights' for the multiple minorities like Muslims, and the real possibility of participation and influence in political life. Only as humans who live both in the private and public spheres, Muslims have the opportunity and right to "belong to some kind of organized community" (Arendt 1976, 297) and until the EU institutions, member states and their citizens actually invite and accept them as equal participants in political life and respect them in their private life, the Muslims will remain a problem. This is not an either-or option between integration and assimilation and does not force Muslims to commit to a life in either the private or public sphere (see Tomen and Gardner, this volume), nor does it mean that multiplicity erases what is similar. Muslims ought to be able to choose to be individuals so that, like others, they are characterized and defined by all the aspects that make them who they are, so that they are neither only a Muslim, nor unlike other non-Muslims, and equality balances multiculturalism with individualism (Salih 2004).

Multiculturalism also has the potential to provide Muslims with their own voice, not as a group, but as individuals who agree, disagree, debate and discuss issues important to them, from religion to political participation, as active interlocutors who use what Arendt calls words and deeds in the public sphere. The public agency they would have as interlocutors is essential both for internal debates as a community and to initiate a dialogue with the EU institutions and member states, as EU leaders struggle to 'speak' to the Muslim community and learn that neither imams nor extremists represent all Muslims. As the Economist reports about Britain, "Among those who claim to speak for disadvantaged Muslims and articulate their grievances, there has been an outpouring of indignation over the government's stated aim of "preventing violent extremism" by making Muslim communities more "resilient" and better at dealing with hotheads" (How the Government Lost the Plot). Many complain this only adds to the stigmatization of all Muslims, while a multicultural voice for Muslims would allow various answers, numerous responses and multiple opportunities to be an individual who is an agent, an actor, a member of both the public and the private sphere and, most importantly, an audience willing to listen to others, be it EU institutions, national governments or fellow citizens, not just other Muslims. A space in what the Economist calls the "European square" necessitates compromises between Muslim and other traditions so that "talk of civilisational war in Europe's cobblestoned streets" do not undermine "the ability of democratic politics, especially local politics, to adapt to new social phenomena" (When Town Halls Turn to Mecca). The ability to accept, respect and listen to multicultural voices and to acknowledge the ability of young and old Muslims, as well as other Europeans, to persuade each other and to be persuaded to have a stake in the community where they live is essential for both the public and the private spheres. This continuity between the two allows a multicultural dialogue that, as the Economist reminds us, takes time. The author argues that,

> Historically, multi-ethnic societies have worked in many different ways. In some, each individual's freedom was limited by the taboos and hierarchies of his or her community. But at best, cities have been places of liberation where people of all faiths and cultures can interact and make their own choices. Today, Europe's Islamisising towns lie somewhere between those two poles—and every politician in Europe, whether national or local, should think about how to discourage restriction and encourage freedom. (A Case for Vigilance, not Despair)

In 1967, Frantz Fanon wrote passionately and eloquently about being considered a problem in a racist and segregated United States and wished he could be acknowledged for what he did as a doctor, not for being the "Negro doctor." He was troubled not just by the extreme sense of isolation, but also by all the observant eyes that almost eagerly waited for him to make a mistake. Unlike others, a mistake for him would have been "the end of him and all those who came after him" (Fanon 1967, 65). As spectators, many watched Obama with similar eagerness and, maybe not intentionally or even consciously, both hoped and feared a mistake, because like Fanon, that would have closed the curtain not only on his dream of being a president, but on the dream of many more African-Americans who know too well what it means to be isolated as a problem. Maybe this heavy burden justifies Obama's handling of only one difference at the time. Especially as a non-Muslim, it may not be fair to ask him to answer why being Muslim ought not to be a problem.

This problem and perceived 'otherness' must be confronted based on the assumption of equality, not difference, so that we can embrace multiplicity of beliefs, cultures, ideas, religions and practices as those of free and equal actors who truly have the possibility to engage each other meaningfully in public life and influence what happens in the private sphere. I have argued that EU institutions, member states and their citizens are uniquely positioned to welcome their Muslim population as equals and really put their motto to the test, not just to declare solemnly that they believe what they have been writing for more than half a century, but to recognize equality as a fundamental right that still needs work.[8] Moreover, the EU already has and continues to implement several initiatives to reach out to the Muslim population and has the structural framework to invite them as active members of the public sphere, while respecting their commitment to their private life. The marginalization and discrimination Muslims face across the EU territory, however, give us reasons to fear there won't be a happy ending to the Muslim 'problem.' But Arendt reminds us that, unfortunately, the Muslims are not the first and sadly will not be the last minority to be the scapegoat for all our fears. It has happened before and it will happen again, but we have the responsibility to move toward progress now.[9]

Works Cited

Aggestam, Lisbeth and Christopher Hill. 2008. The challenge of multiculturalism in European foreign policy. *International Affairs* 84(1): 97–114.

Arendt, Hannah. 1968. *Between past and future.* New York: The Viking Press.

—. 1972. *Crises of the republic.* New York: Harcourt Brace Jovanovich.

—. 1993. *Essays in understanding.* New York: Harcourt Brace & Company.

—. 1958. *The human condition.* Chicago: University of Chicago Press.

—. 1976. *The origins of totalitarianism.* Orlando: Harcourt Books.

[8] The June 2009 EU and national elections and the after-math of the Iranian elections, also in June 2009, demonstrate the malleability of people in both the West and the Muslim world, as EU citizens (or at least the 43% who voted) move to the political right and speak up against 'difference' and people in Iran fight for democratic practices, feeling robbed of their role in the public sphere (The Endless Election Round; Demanding to be Counted).

[9] I certainly don't claim to represent or speak for the Muslim population and I surely do not believe I have summarized their problems. The Muslim population in the European Union and everywhere else in the world is very diverse and the risk of clumping them as one homogenous group is one I am sure I have taken in this essay. However, I argue that multiculturalism as multiplicity leaves room for this kind of mistakes and provides the theoretical framework to address differences respectfully and appropriately.

—. 1983. *Men in dark times*. Orlando: Harcourt Brace & Company.
—. 1951. *The burden of our time*. London: Secker & Warburg.
Chou, Meng-Hsuan. 2010. The free movement of sex workers in the European Union: Excluding the excluded. In *Migrants and minorities: The European response*, ed. Adam Luedtke. Newcastle upon Tyne: Cambridge Scholars Publishing.
Crowley, John. 2001. The political participation of ethnic minorities. *International Political Science Review* 22(1): 99-121.
The Economist. 2009. Pious, loyal and unhappy, May 7. Available online at: http://www.economist.com/world/britain/displaystory.cfm?story_id=13612116&CFID=59378866&CFTOKEN=71745937
The Economist. 2009. How the Government lost the plot, February 26. Available online at: http://www.economist.com/world/britain/displaystory.cfm?story_id=13186100
The Economist. 2009. Demanding to be counted, June 18. Available online at: http://www.economist.com/world/mideast-africa/displaystory.cfm?story_id=13856232
The Economist. 2009. The endless election round, June 11. Available online at: http://www.economist.com/world/europe/displaystory.cfm?story_id=13825164
The Economist. 2008. A case for vigilance not despair, December 4. Available online at: http://www.economist.com/opinion/displaystory.cfm?story_id=12724930&CFID=59378866&CFTOKEN=71745937
The Economist. 2008. Cheers from the rest of the world, November 8, 23.
The Economist. 2008. When town halls turn to Mecca, December 4. Available online at: http://www.economist.com/world/international/displaystory.cfm?story_id=12724966&CFID=59378866&CFTOKEN=71745937
European Monitoring Centre on Racism and Xenophobia. 2006. *Perceptions of discrimination and Islamophobia: Voices from members of Muslim communities in the European Union*. Brussels: EUMC.
—. 2006. *Muslims in the European Union: Discrimination and Islamophobia*. Brussels: EUMC.
European Union Agency for Fundamental Rights. 2008. *Community cohesion at local level: Addressing the needs of Muslim communities. Examples of local initiatives*. Brussels: FRA.

Fanon, Frantz. 2006. The fact of blackness. In *Identities: Race, class, gender and nationality*, ed. Edoardo Mendieta and Linda Alcoff. Malden, MA: Blackwell Publishing.

Franz, Barbara. 2007. Europe's Muslim youth: An inquiry into the politics of discrimination, relative deprivation, and identity formation. *Mediterranean Quarterly* 18(1): 89-111.

Gardner, Kathryn. 2010. The politicization of religion in the West: Assessing the effects of policy legacies and government construction on a European Islam. In *Migrants and minorities: The European response*, ed. Adam Luedtke. Newcastle upon Tyne: Cambridge Scholars Publishing.

Hellyer, Hisham. 2007. Minorities, Muslims and Sharia: Some reflections on Islamic law and Muslims without political power *Islam and Christian–Muslim Relations* 18(1): 85–109.

Kuper, Simon. 2007. EU Muslims: Seeking Jihad or democracy? *Financial Times*, August 23.

Kymlicka, Will. 1995. *Multicultural citizenship: A liberal theory of minority rights*. Oxford: Oxford University Press.

Lee, Jennifer. 2008. Among Muslims, support for Obama but reluctance to show it. *New York Time*s, November 8. Available online at: http://cityroom.blogs.nytimes.com/2008/11/07/among-muslims-support-for-obama-but-reluctance-to-show-it/?scp=2&sq=muslims&st=cse

Novak, Michael. 2006. Troubled continent: A crisis of demography—and of the spirit. *The National Review,* February 13, 36-8.

Salih, Ruba. 2004. The backward and the new: National, transnational and post-national Islam in Europe. *Journal of Ethnic and Migration Studies* 30(5): 995-1011.

Salvatore, Armando. 2004. Making public space: Opportunities and limits of collective action among Muslims in Europe. *Journal of Ethnic and Migration Studies* 30(5): 1013-31.

Shore, Zachary. 2006. *Breeding Bin Ladens: America, Islam and the future of Europe*. Baltimore: Johns Hopkins University Press.

Silvestri, Sara. 2005. EU relations with Islam in the context of the EMP's cultural dialogue. *Mediterranean Politics* 10(3): 385–405.

—. 2007. *Islam and the EU: The merits and risks of inter-cultural dialogue*. Policy Brief. Brussels: European Policy Centre.

The Treaty of Amsterdam. 1997. Available online at: http://eur-lex.europa.eu/en/treaties/dat/11997D/htm/11997D.html.

The Treaty on the European Union. 1992. Available online at: http://europa.eu.int/en/record/mt/top.html.

The Treaty of Nice. 2001. Available online at: http://europa.eu.int/eur-lex/en/treaties/dat/nice_treaty_en.pdf.

The Treaty of Rome. 1957. Available online at: http://europa.eu.int/eur-lex/en/treaties/dat/EC_consol.html.

Tomen, Bihter. 2010. A clash of identities?: The challenge of minority integration in France. In *Migrants and minorities: The European response*, ed. Adam Luedtke. Newcastle upon Tyne: Cambridge Scholars Publishing.

Young, Iris Marion. 1990. *Justice and the politics of difference*. Princeton: Princeton University Press.

Younge, Gary. 2007. In Europe, where's the hate? *The Nation*, January 7, 10.

CHAPTER NINE

A CLASH OF IDENTITIES? THE CHALLENGE OF MINORITY INTEGRATION IN FRANCE

BIHTER TOMEN

Introduction

In recent years, it is often argued that France has witnessed a rise of discrimination and marginalization of its minority groups, along with riots and protests where minorities have voiced their claim for difference (Watts, 2002; Guenif-Souilamas, 2006; Giry, 2006; Chapman & Frader, 2004; Laurence & Vaisse, 2006). On the other hand, the French official discourse argues that French identity is under threat (Guenif-Souilamas, 2006; Giry, 2006). This study addresses the question of identity. In recent years, identity politics has come to the forefront in political debates on immigration, settlement and integration of minorities in Europe and North America. This chapter will argue that the problem of integration in France is a problem of identity. The chapter will first conceptualize the notion of identity, because the concept of identity is often used carelessly in the literature, and it needs a clear definition. It will then discuss the emergence and significance of national identity. The relationship between French national identity, Jacobinism and secularism will be analysed in detail as to demonstrate how they limit the cultural practices of minorities. I will briefly discuss the rise of Jacobinism in historical context and how its influence is still intact in modern France. The chapter will then explore the limits of cultural pluralism within the French education system and in society. Lastly, this chapter will point out how definitions of integration and assimilation are used interchangeably and why this disposition is closely linked to the Jacobin Republican political culture.

With mass non-European migration in 1950s and 1960s, France witnessed a social transformation and this transformation challenged the existing understanding of what it means to be French, how to accommodate diversity and how to maintain the French national identity. High volumes of immigration for three decades consequently made an impact on the social profile of the country. The notion of national unity through cultural assimilation is ultimately challenged as cultural diversity has grown in society. This chapter asserts that the consequences of this transformation for migrants were not always positive. It attempts to discuss how the deeply embedded Jacobin political culture has led to the marginalization of ethnic minorities in France in recent years.

A Discussion on National Identity

Issues of identity are difficult to address because they are complex and multifaceted. Identity itself is multi-dimensional. In a culturally diverse society like France, minority groups constantly mediate between their ethnic identities and their French national identity, while the state makes efforts to maintain its civic national identity (Barber, 2001). These efforts can lead to social exclusion for minority groups in France.

Before we analyze the effects of national identity construction, however, it is important first to define what identity means. A crucial point in understanding the significance of identity is its process of separating and categorizing different groups of people or what we refer to as "other-ing". Edward Said (1994) argues that "the development and maintenance of every culture require the existence of another, different and competing *alter ego*. The construction of identity involves the construction of opposites and "others" whose actuality is always subject to the continuous interpretation of their differences from 'us'" (p. 331-332). Accordingly, identity is an attempt to differentiate oneself from the other.

Benjamin R. Barber (2001) suggests three models of identity: civic, ethnic and commercial. Civic identity refers to democratic citizenship based on secularism, civil liberties, and legal and political rights (p.57). In this view, French national identity is argued to be based on civic identity (Schor, 2001, p.220). Barber asserts that civic identity, as the basis of a free, civil society, is threatened by the emergence of ethnic and consumerist identities. According to this argument, ethnic identity relies on "blood brotherhood" and "tribalism" implicitly expressed in the recent Jihadist movements (Barber, 2001, p.58). On the other hand, commercial identity reduces the citizen to a passive consumer. Because the consumer exists in a private economic sphere, namely the market, he/she is deprived of his/her rights as a citizen to influence social change. The shift from public to private sphere signals a shift from active to passive citizenry where the person does not have an impact on political decision-making anymore (Barber, 2001, p.58; see also Beasley Von Burg, this volume). Barber (2001) praises civic identity by associating it with liberty, democracy and civil society. He argues that the only way a citizen can make a social impact is by attaining a civic identity and becoming an active member in the public sphere. Arguably, one of the problems of identity in France emerges from immigrants' and ethnic minorities' lack of full participation in the public sphere while negotiating between their ethnic, civic and commercial identities. This is evident in lack of minority participation in the French political life: out of 321 senators in 2004, only 2 were minorities: there was no minority representation among 577 parliamentary deputies (Laurence et al. 2006). By 2006 there were only 11 total minority members of the 577-member National Assembly, despite the fact that 10 percent (6 million) of France's 60 million residents are estimated to be of Arab or African descent (Anderson, 2006).

It could be argued that lack of minority representation in France is a consequence of the construction of a limited definition of national identity and an issue of who is entitled to this definition of identity. In other words, construction of national identity defines membership to a nation. It is achieved through "intellectual, political and cultural activity, including the public discourses structured by political leaders and the narratives and sentiments fostered by state institutions like the schools, the army and broadcast authorities" (Norman, 2004, p.88). National identity is not a given; rather, it is a socially constructed notion that has to be continuously produced and re-produced through public narratives by politicians and institutions. As mentioned above, the significance of national identity is its implication of "membership" in a particular nation. One may, in fact, believe that the membership in a nation is through blood and descent. This is called *ethnic national identity* (Norman, 2004, p.95, see also Smith, 1986). Ethnic identity reflects membership by descent. On the other hand, *civic national identity* draws attention to the membership in the state and acceptance of its universal values, such as human rights. Civic identity is about the relationship between the citizen and the state based on mutual rights and responsibilities. Lack of minority participation in French politics could be a sign of a weak implementation of civic national identity.

Origins of any national identity, according to Anthony D. Smith (1986, 1991), is based on ethnicity. Although every nation is composed of a combination of civic and ethnic elements, each nation primarily requires some pre-modern ethnic ties, whether they are mythical or primordial (p.40-41). Smith (1991) defines an ethnic group as "a type of cultural collectivity, one that emphasizes the role of myths of descent and historical memories, and that is recognized by one or more cultural differences like religion, customs, language and institution" (p.50). While ethnicity is historical, the notion of nation and nationalism are modern concepts. For instance, Turks in Anatolia were not self-aware of a distinct Turkish identity until the beginning of the twentieth century. Instead, they were attached to a religious, local or regional identity because they did not have national conscious (Smith, 1991). Furthermore, Smith argues that nations are initially formed around a dominant ethnic group. Through the economic, cultural and social revolutions of the 18th Century in Europe, ethnic identity evolved to national identity. This transformation was possible by the emergence of an upper-middle class, namely the bourgeoisie and intellectuals (Smith, 1991, p.60-61). However, the cultural roots of the nation go back further to the culture of aristocrats and religious scholars "for though it was, in a sense, *their* culture and heritage that was being diffused by the state, the result was a marginalization of aristocrats and clergy; their heritage and culture had become, in principle, everyone's" (Smith, 1991, p.68).

Roger Brubaker (1996) opposes the notion of "nation" as a natural grouping. Nations as real, collective, enduring entities are accepted by theorists like Smith. However, he argues that posing the question "what is a nation?" readily presupposes the existence of a nation as a group (p.16). Instead, Brubaker understands the nation as an institutionalized political and cultural form. Nations are constructed by the political institutions of the country. Therefore, nationalism emerges because of the policies of a country. More importantly, he looks at a nation *not* as an idea that develops in time, as argued by prominent scholars like Benedict Anderson (1983), Ernest Gellner (1983) and Anthony Smith (1992), but rather as "something that *happens*" (Brubaker, 1996, p.19). This means that we need to focus on the events that result in nationhood. Brubaker gives the example of Croatia which engaged in a process of "nationalization" of society after the collapse of Yugoslavia. The significance of Brubaker's argument is that he understands collective action giving rise to identity and not vice versa. In this view, the French revolution, as a collective action, gave rise to a certain civic national identity that had never existed in France before.

Luedtke (2005) suggests that national identities precede citizens of a nation-state and thus construct the identities of citizens. If national awareness is indeed a prerequisite for the nation-state, then it lies at the *core* of the modern state. We argue that this argument holds true for the French nation-state. French national identity is so deeply embedded in the culture, language and history of the state that it even *makes* citizens and constitutes the public opinion. Any perceived threat to the national consciousness is thus confronted with hostility.

Language is one of the most fundamental cultural elements, which is utilized to unify a nation and diffuse national consciousness. William Safran (1991) discusses the importance of language in nation-building in France. He argues that the state utilizes language to construct a certain socio-political consciousness and unity. Benedict Anderson, one of the prominent modernist theorists of nationalism, explains language as the unifying force for every community. As discussed below, it is no wonder that the "integration contract" in France places such a big emphasis on language instruction. However, the recent incident of a Moroccan Muslim woman who was denied French citizenship because she was perceived as "unable to assimilate into French society because of her faith"1 clearly indicates systemic discrimination on other grounds, since the woman had been living in France since 2000, speaks perfect French and has three French-born children who are French citizens (CBC News, 2008; Guardian, 2008). This is also an indication of the system's "other-ing" in hostility towards other cultural practices based on religion or ethnicity.

Construction of one's identity necessitates the existence of the "other" to juxtapose with. It is an effort of separating oneself as distinct and different. This is how the state constructs and represents the nation's and its citizens' identity. Therefore, the process of "other-ing" is also an attempt to constantly legitimize and perpetuate the existing status quo. In an opinion poll in 2003, French respondents who think the numbers of Muslims in the country are too many (40 percent) give reasons such as the threat to French identity (30 percent), unemployment (28 percent),

---

[1] The council said it refused citizenship to the woman because she had "adopted, in the name of a radical practice of her religion, social behaviour that is incompatible with the basic values of French society, particularly the equality of the sexes." The main offense seems to have been wearing a *burqa* to administrative meetings.

insecurity (22 percent) and social cohesion (22 percent) respectively (Laurence et al. 2006, p.60). Here we can witness the other-ing of Muslim minorities and also understand the significance of French identity as an issue more important to the French than aspects of basic economic security, such as employment.

French National Identity and Jacobinism

French national identity is based on the notion of Jacobinism which is the idea that the *state* produces a nation (Safran, 1991, p.219). Jacobinism emerged in France with the political Jacobin Clubs (*Clubs des Jacobins*) which played an important role in the Revolution of 1789 (Safran, 2003, p.438). In this view, the state has the role of unifying the nation politically and legitimizing its existence. Safran (1991) argues that Jacobin ideology explains Frenchness after the Revolution as a "voluntary commitment to common political values" which contains common consent and willingness to live together (p.220). In other words, it is a social contract that people sign up to after the French Revolution. The state has the role of maintaining that social contract. During the French revolution the requirements for membership in the national community were commitment to the revolution, the Enlightenment and the rights of man (Safran 1991).

According to Jacobinism, the state represents the general will of people and any prior loyalty to a local community or minority group divides the will of people (Safran, 2003, p.439). This means that the state creates and seeks the support of citizens as *individuals* for its legitimate existence. Accordingly, Jacobin ideology rejects the idea of cultural pluralism. According to this ideology, the state designs policies to achieve a sense of unity and a common identity. Therefore, Safran (1991) suggests that French national identity is equated with supporting a centralized and secular republic (p.221). Jacobinism explains membership in the nation as a social and cultural act, instead of a matter of ancestry. Hence, national identity is constructed on the basis of homogenizing minority groups by politically de-legitimizing them:

> Since the Revolution, the nation has been a matter not of heredity but of political and cultural identities, loyalties, rights, and duties. The nation was defined, created, or recreated by the state, which meant that sub-nations and sub-national identities were deprived of political legitimacy and integrated into the nation-state. The nation, thus redefined, was to be composed, not of communities, but of individuals. (Safran, 1991, p.221)

Here it is important to note that Jacobinism has fallen short of fulfilling these universal notions of democracy, freedom and equality in the context of the non-white immigration of recent decades. Mechanisms of modernization, urbanization, immigration and European integration have posed important challenges to French national identity. Safran (1991) asserts that national identity is threatened by the supranational institutions of the European Union, globalization and US cultural hegemony (p.225). Nevertheless, the question "What does it mean to be French?" posed in an opinion poll in 1987, shows that French identity is still based on the Enlightenment ideas of freedom, sovereignty and democracy: 51 percent of the respondents said being French is defending freedoms; 42 percent said it means defending the country; 35 percent said it means having the right to vote. Furthermore, 24 percent of the respondents said being French means speaking French (Safran, 1991, p.227). This information indicates that despite the increasing cultural pluralism in France, the majority of the society still elaborates national identity in relation to secular republican values.

An important consequence of the French Revolution is the rise of secularism, which lies at the heart of the French nation-state. The 1905 Act states that France is a "secular Republic which does not recognize any religion" (Basdevant-Gaudemet, 2004, p.64-65). Until 2003, France did not grant any public funding for the construction of religious buildings such as mosques. Then-Interior Minister, Nicolas Sarkozy, created the *Conseil Français du Culte Musulman (*French Council of the Muslim Religion, or CFCM*)* even though many argue that its aim is to create a *French* version of Islam while reducing the influence of Muslim countries on the issues of training Imams and funding mosques (Laurence et al. 2006, p.138; see also Gardner, this volume).

French National Identity and Secularism

Historically, the Jacobin ideology in France, which is associated with state-centrism and secularism, also required a linguistic unity through education. At the time of the French Revolution, only 20 percent of the society could speak French frequently, and 40 percent did not speak a word of French (Safran, 1992, p.399). As part of the nation-building project in France, a centralized, republican and secular school system was established with French as the only language of instruction under the Third Republic. Hence, other regional languages such as Breton, Alsatian and Basque were marginalized (Safran, 1992, p.397-398). Freedman (2004) argues that the same assimilationist attitudes are now in place in the French secular education system for the non-European minorities (p.5).

The institution of education in France is the main channel to deploy and maintain the notion of secularism and national identity (Freedman, 2004, p.6). The intention to maintain the secular system was evident in the law that banned the wearing of religious symbols in public schools, which was passed on 10 February 2004 by the National Assembly (Freedman, 2004, p.19). The headscarf ban is an interesting case in French political history. In 1989, three Muslim girls were expelled from school in Creil when they insisted on wearing their headscarves in the classroom. The decision to expel students was made on the basis of *laïcité* (secularism), the separation of religious institutions from the state (Akan, 2003, p.22). The Muslim headscarf was targeted as an "ostentatious sign" in 1992, which was considered as a symbol of proselytism by Francois Bayrou, former Minister of Education, despite the *Conseil d`Etat*, the highest administrative court in France, deciding that it was not incompatible with secularism (Todd, 2003, p.118). Even though such incidents began taking place in 1989, the headscarf ban did not come until 2004. In 1993, the Interior Minister, Charles Pasqua, claimed that wearing the headscarf to school had the potential of spreading racist and xenophobic sentiments. It has also been argued that religious expressions are a threat to the security and stability of the French nation-state (Freedman, 2004, p.15). The French emphasis on secularism is crucial since France perceives ethnic and religious characteristics and their practice in society as divisive (Giry, 2006, p.2) In this view, only a secular system, which removes religious practices from the public sphere, could be acceptable for a socially stable country. If we look at the number of Muslim students who have worn the headscarf, the issue will be put in perspective: according to the Ministry of the Interior, in 1994, there were 2,000 Muslim girls wearing headscarves in schools, while in 2003, it dropped to 1,254. (Laurence & Vaisse, 2006, p.165) These numbers are insignificant in comparison to the minority population (of which a large portion is Muslim) and they are not sufficient to threaten the stability of a social system. Ahmet Kuru (2007) argues that French "assertive secularism" caused the ban. The aim of this social policy is to construct one singular French identity through public school education, not to maintain stability. The legislation clearly deprives minority students of their religious/cultural symbols, which are part of their cultural identities. Assumptions to create stability construct a paradox: forbidding expressions of cultural symbols in the public sphere to prevent racism and instability has the potential to become the source of instability itself within society, because it creates resentment, frustration and political mobilization among marginalized groups. In fact, the ban of the headscarf was initially a recommendation of the Stasi Commission, which was appointed by President Jacques Chirac in 2003 in order to examine the situation of secularism in France (Freedman, 2004, p.18; see also Gardner, this volume). The ban on wearing the headscarf, along with other religious symbols in public schools, was understood by the Commission as "furthering of *integration* through an affirmation of common values" (Freedman, 2004, p.18). The state strongly argues that policies like these help create harmony and unity within society and thus help integrate minorities. Therefore, we argue that the French definition of integration is indeed a re-affirmation of its secular and assimilationist attitudes. The French state believes that citizenship is built on common cultural values and therefore, immigrants who want to become French should embrace French values and culture (Freedman, 2004, p.20). But the enduring paradox in the social structure is that even those minorities who embrace French values and norms are faced with discrimination in France.

Franz Fanon (1963), in his famous book, *The Wretched of the Earth*, stresses that the racial minorities (even intellectuals like himself) who voluntarily embraced French values still got marginalized in post-colonial France. According to a poll in 2005, majority of Muslims indicated their confidence in France despite the widespread discrimination and racism. (Laurence and Vaisse, 2006, p.47) Indeed, minorities in France consciously feel this discrimination, as a 2006 Eurobarometer special survey indicates. In the survey, 71 percent of the participants state that being a person of visible minority is a disadvantage in France, in comparison to the EU average of 62 percent. Also, 80 percent of the participants indicate that discrimination on the basis of ethnic origin is widespread in France, compared with a 64 percent EU average. Participants also mentioned that discrimination against religion/belief is more widespread in France than other categories, such as ethnic origin, gender, sexual orientation or disability (Eurobarometer, 2007).

Cultural Pluralism in France

We need to have some historical context to understand the contemporary social situation in France. France found itself in the middle of an "identity crisis" after the Second World War. Even though France has long been a country of immigration, since the Italian and Portuguese immigration in the 19th century, it has been socially challenged by the flow of non-European immigrants. The government's decision to bring immigrants into the country after the war was a consequence of economic reconstruction. In return, high volumes of immigrants entering the country altered the cultural homogeneity of society. This raises the question of belonging to the nation. In other words, the government's decision to bring immigrants into the workforce has created unintended consequences which undermined the national identity (Safran, 1991, p.223). High volumes of immigration flows began right after World War II, when the decolonization process unfolded around the world. In the immediate post-World War II period, France was in need of labour to boost its industrial economy. This era of immigration was initiated when France began to receive immigrant workers from Algeria, Morocco, Turkey, Tunisia and Yugoslavia (Adler, 1977, p.90).

Ultimately, immigrant workers helped build industry in Western Europe, starting in 1945 and continuing steadily until the 1973 oil shock (Hollifield, 1990, p.64). In the immediate post-World War II period, France was the only country in Europe to encourage permanent immigration without a quota system (Guiraudon, 2002). Between 1945 and 1974, the National Immigration Office (ONI) regulated the flow of immigrants into France. Within this period, the highest levels of labour migration were actually received from Algeria and countries that signed bi-lateral agreements with France: Spain, Portugal, Morocco, Turkey, Tunisia and Yugoslavia (Hollifield, 1990, p.90). These two groups of immigrants were required to arrange their own recruitment, the arrival of their families, getting a work and residence permit and receiving professional training by ONI. At the time, there was a flow of large numbers of Algerian immigrants into France due to the lack of immigration quotas. There was a trend of employers recruiting workers illegally and then legalizing their status while working (Adler, 1977, p.92). Workers also tended to enter France with visitor visas and then change their status to workers. Between 1968 and 1973, the average immigration rate per year was 341,000 (Watts, 2002, p.44). These trends indicate the easy entry of immigrants into France in this period, when the state was in desperate need of labour. The oil crisis in 1973, combined with slower economic growth and high levels of unemployment, led to the suspension of foreign workers' entry into France. The entry of workers was officially banned in 1974 when immigrant workers and their families already made up 6.54 percent of the French population (Watts, 2002, p.47). After this date, immigration continued with family reunifications, asylum seekers and illegal immigration. Changing immigration trends after 1974 began forcing immigrants to assimilate into the French society and culture. Before the official ban of immigration, it was not clear to the French state whether or not the immigrant workers would remain permanently in the country (Laurence et al. 2006). Therefore, there was no clear integration/assimilation plan in process until the mid-1970s.

The flow of immigrants had an impact on the societal profile of France as much as its economy. In January 2005, the population of France was estimated as 62.5 million (INED, 2006). The latest French census, published in March 1999, shows that there are 3,258,000 foreigners residing in France, born in France or born abroad, which make up 5.6 percent of the total population. The estimated total number of all immigrants residing in France in 2006, including foreigners born abroad and naturalized persons, is 4,306,094, which make up 6.8 percent of the population (INED, 2006). It is important to note that according to the data on the National Institute of Demographic Studies website, the number of naturalized persons and foreigners born abroad are collected in the same category and named under "total number of immigrants". Here, there is an indication that French official discourse mirrors the public perception conflating naturalized individuals and immigrants. The census does not provide details on the total number of ethnic minorities in France as the French state forbids the collection of information based on race or ethnicity, which would include many second-generation citizens born to immigrant parents. Today, roughly 10 percent of the French population are minorities, the majority of whom are Muslims (Kesselman, Krieger & Allen, 2002, p. 299; Laurence et al. 2006, p. 15).

Despite some efforts of de-centralization and institutional pluralism in France, resistance to cultural pluralism still strongly persists (see Gardner, this volume). Lawrence Kritzman (1995) attributes this type of resistance to embedded relations of power:

> (…) all social systems owe their existence to relations of power, and that they embody the inclination of various sectors of society to dominate and exclude other sectors. If the idea of the modern nation seeks to represent itself according to certain aspects of Enlightenment thought, one must never forget that its universal ideal necessitates the exclusion of any excess (the non-homogeneous) so that the autonomy of the universal may be affirmed. (p.13)

In order for any political power structure to legitimate itself and perpetuate its existence, it has to exclude other social sectors which challenge its core ideals, norms and values. In France, ethno-cultural pluralism, especially in the case of Islamic culture, is considered incompatible with universalism. In 1991, Kofi Yamgnane, then-Secretary of State for Social Affairs and Integration, said in an interview with *Le Monde*, “Islam must accept the Republican pact. That is to say, accept the separation of Church and State; renounce polygamy, the low status of women and the wearing of headscarves in schools” (Markus, 1995, p.89). It is evident from this interview that official discourse does not allow the acceptance of the open co-existence of different cultural practices in the country. Resistance to pluralism comes from both ends of the political spectrum, unlike in many European countries: right-wing Gaullists believe that cultural pluralism could lead to separatism on the part of ethnic minorities, whereas left-wing Jacobins claim that pluralism contradicts with the statist political structure which relies on the individual relationship of the citizen with the state (Safran, 1991, p.226). The French state still focuses on the assimilation of its immigrant populations because difference is seen as a threat to the harmony of the state. Safran (2003) claims that in France, “tolerance toward a multiplicity of *origins* has not yet comfortably translated into a tolerance toward multiple *identities*” (p.463). Although, there have been some social transformations which challenge the universalist notions of national identity, such as political de-centralization, funding of Muslim religious spaces and recognition of holidays, the state remains intact in protecting and perpetuating a narrow definition of “Frenchness”.

Integration- Assimilation Dilemma

As mentioned earlier, the process of integration began in the mid-1970s with the immigration ban. Integration can be defined as “the enjoyment of a common citizenship in conjunction with the maintenance of diverse practices in private life, or national unity without cultural conformity” (Wayland, 1995, p.129). The French state, however, also demands the cultural conformity of its citizens as evident from the integration contract (discussed below) and the ban of the headscarf in public schools. Moreover, this definition seems to emphasize the liberty to practice cultural and religious practices in the private sphere while conforming to national values in public (see Beasley Von Burg, this volume). In spite of the frequent use of the word “integration” in the French context, the policies are, in fact, policies of assimilation. The establishment of *Haut Conseil a l’Intégration* (High Council of Integration) in 1989 and the introduction of an “integration contract” in

2003, which new immigrants have to sign if they want to get a ten-year residency, are part of the process of the French state's drive towards cultural assimilation.

The High Council of Integration defines integration as the effective participation of the whole of the people called to live in France with the construction of a community gathered in respect of shared principles (freedom of conscience and thought, equality between man and woman) such that they are expressed in equal rights and common duties (*Haut Conseil a l'Intégration*, 2007). On the other hand, the Council offers a complementary definition of assimilation which clearly locates the French understanding between "integration" and "assimilation", referring to a: "supposed or awaited result of a process of integration of the immigrant such that the immigrant does not offer any more cultural characteristics distinct from those which are the majority of the members of the community" (*Haut Conseil a l'Intégration*, 2007). By this definition, the Council understands and defines assimilation as the end result of a process of integration. The French version of integration constitutes the framework for social policy-making and it sheds light on the assimilationist approach in France. Hubert Peres (this volume) argues that French assimilationism should be understood from a sociological point of view, rather than a political one, as a gradual decline of cultural differences in the host country. As discussed above, European immigrants in the 19th and 20th centuries were successfully assimilated into the society but non-European immigration after 1945 is a different story. Arguments assuming the possibility of one-way assimilation do not shed light on the contemporary issues of ghettoisation and the spatial segregation of minorities, poor relations between minority communities and the authorities, and widespread ethnic discrimination in hiring and education. Clearly, France has thus far failed to live up to its ideals in integrating and/or assimilating its ethnic minorities. Even former Prime Minister Pierre Messmer declared in an interview in 1973: "France, as a historic nation, is at risk of dying because of the plethora of immigrants that it cannot assimilate or even integrate" (Laurence et al. 2006, p.52).

The Council of the European Union defines integration as a "two-way" process where both the immigrants and the receiving society have to take on certain responsibilities (Joppke, 2007, p.3). On one hand, the receiving country is required to create economic and social opportunities for immigrants. On the other hand, the immigrants are required to respect basic political values of the EU such as liberty, democracy, rule of law and human rights.

Assimilation is an absolute negation and intolerance of otherness (Joppke, 2007). In fact, a politics of assimilation strives to "eradicate the culture of the *Other* and to absorb it. It is not a matter of excluding the *Other*, but of including it to the extent that one renders it like oneself" (Joppke, 2007). This marginalization can take place in two ways: As Fanon talks about, the decolonization process led to French subjects being seen as non-French even when they embraced the values of the country (Fanon, 1963). Exclusion also takes place when diverse cultures resist or oppose assimilation while trying to maintain their cultural identities. This approach is evident in the education system, where French identity is prioritized while other expressions of minority cultures are marginalized.

The integration contract details "willingness to integrate" and "respect for fundamental values of the Republic" (Freedman, 2004, p.20). The secular policies prevent policy-makers from developing special programs, research or statistics to understand the ethnic diversity in France, despite the fact that France has the largest Muslim minority population in Europe (Giry, 2006, p.1). The secular policies help construct a strict separation between the public and private sphere where the public sphere is not informed by the ethnic and cultural diversity of its citizens (Beasley Von Burg, this volume). In return, this prevents minorities from fulfilling their active citizenry where they could have an impact on political decision-making in French society. A more representative democracy could be achieved by including diversity into the public sphere.

The civic integration courses, which were voluntary, half-day instructions, were initially introduced by the Socialist Jospin government in France in 1998 (Giry, 2006). In 2003, the obligatory "integration contract" was introduced by the conservative Raffarin government and is composed of a one-day "civics instruction" and 500 hours of French language courses (Giry, 2006). The contract details "willingness to integrate" and "respect for fundamental values of the Republic" (Freedman, 2004, p.20).

The former Interior Minister and current French President, Nicolas Sarkozy, introduced a new law in 2003 which restricts the easy integration of immigrants by restricting access to permanent residency, and by granting family members only a temporary one-year residency card which they can extend up to two years before they can apply for a ten-year residency card (Joppke, 2007, p.10) Receiving permanent residency depends on the successful integration of the immigrant in the society, which is explicitly defined in this law as "the knowledge of the French language and principles that govern the French Republic" (Joppke, 2007). In 2006, the second *Sarkozy Law* was designed to target high-skilled immigrants by changing the conditions for post-graduation and entry of foreign students. The law created a three year renewable residence card for high-skilled immigrants who would foster economic development. Sarkozy defended the new law by explaining how it is intended to make the shift from "unwanted to chosen immigration" (Joppke, 2007, p.11) By "unwanted immigration", Sarkozy implies asylum, illegal migration, and most importantly family re-unifications through marriage between second-generation French citizens and foreigners which tripled between 1997 and 2004. Accordingly, France limited family re-unification by increasing the wait time to apply for a ten-year residence card from two to three years. The time to become a French citizen has been doubled from two to four years, and the foreign spouses of French citizens are also obliged to sign an integration contract upon arrival to France (Joppke, 2007). The Sarkozy laws made the integration contract tougher. The laws now oblige anyone above 16 years old to sign the contract and fulfil its requirements before renewing their residency permits and/or receiving permanent residence rights (Joppke, 2007). It is evident from the strict requirements of this contract that integration is forced upon immigrants. It is even getting tougher with stricter rules on family reunifications. This is an indication that supposedly economically-driven migration debates are really about culture. The integration contract is far from being a voluntary social contract between the newcomers and the state.

The new immigration measures drafted after the riots of minorities in the Parisian suburbs in October-November 2005 introduced further restrictions to France's immigration policies. These restrictions would only help to further exclude immigrants who are from different cultural backgrounds. The measures include stricter law enforcement measures in the suburbs such as the law that says any group of 5 of more can be stopped by the police, screening inter-racial marriages between a French citizen and a foreigner, and screening international students before they are admitted to a French university (CBC News, 2005).

Marginalisation of Minorities

The systemic racism and discrimination have intensified with major contemporary societal changes in France. Firstly, the shift from an industrial to a service society marked the end of full employment for low-skilled workers, many of whom were immigrants (Guenif-Souilamas, 2006, p.24) As heavy industry moved out of the countries of Western Europe, the service sector gained importance, which consequently reduced the demand for low-skilled workers. With globalization, industrial companies have begun investing in developing countries where the labour is much cheaper. The service sector, on the other hand, often requires educated and skilled employees. This situation, combined with the implementation of restrictive immigration policies, led immigrants to seek illegal employment opportunities in underground economies. Globalization also increased the high demand of employers for undocumented workers because of evolving labour practices, such as part-time flexible work, non-union jobs and sub-contracting. Today, the underground economy is estimated to constitute 14% of France's GDP (Samers, 2003, p.570). Thus, employers prefer flexible labour for the service sector.

> (...) Industrial restructuring from 1975 to 1990 eliminated 40 percent of the unskilled and semi-skilled industrial jobs occupied by immigrants, including in those sectors which traditionally absorbed large numbers of foreigners: the automobile industry and the building and public works. By 2000, only 22 percent of foreign workers held an industrial job, and 57 percent were concentrated in services. These jobs have increasingly involved temporary or fixed term contracts. (Samers, 2003, p.570)

As traditionally immigrant-populated jobs moved to other parts of the world, immigrants have begun taking less stable jobs which make them more visible and vulnerable in society. Second-generation minorities experience unemployment, discrimination in hiring, as well as having less job security and stability in flexible part-time positions (Guenif-Souilamas, 2006, p.24-29). There is a two-tier economy in France, where highly protected "insiders" are rarely in danger of losing jobs, but vulnerable "outsiders" work on temporary contracts or in the inflexible economy. The latter tier tends to be immigrant-heavy, which helps to account for the youth unemployment rate in the banlieues which is twice as high as the French unemployment rate. Another social chance has been the rise of extreme-right French ethno-nationalism. This rise of radical nationalism was caused by the economic recession of the 1990s and resulted in an increase in discrimination. The ethno-nationalists stigmatize the Muslim population as responsible for the country's economic and social ills. Lastly, there is a resistance to social change within France despite increasing cultural diversity. The resistance manifests itself in terms of stereotyping minorities, demonizing the suburban youth and fighting against the Islamic "veil" as a religious symbol, as well as perpetuating images of ethnic minorities as "uncivilized", "inclined to violence", "sexist", "rapist" and "veiler" (Guenif-Souilamas, 2006, p.26). All of these labels clearly illustrate the French psyche for portraying the minorities as non-French, or as not one of them. Stereotypes are put in place to justify the resistance to social change. More importantly, however, the unwillingness of the state to address broader social and political questions of equality creates a space in which such stereotypes can persist. The failure of integration in France is blamed on the inability of the minorities to adjust to the culture rather than on the role of systemic discrimination. Stereotypes only help to stigmatize the minorities and keep the public from analyzing deeper and complex questions of social integration and equality. Despite official "colour-blindness", any person who does not fit into the universalist definition of what a French citizen is de facto categorized, labelled and marginalized:

> "Through a rhetoric system that claims to be universalist, an entire generation of French people suffers from a particular and illegitimate status limited to their specific origin, class, or gender, thereby (…) denied equal access to citizenship" (Guenif-Souilamas, 2006, p.24).

In fact, as mentioned earlier, second-generation minorities are considered to be "the children of immigrants", even though they are born in France. Therefore, an immigrant will always be an immigrant in the eyes of the state and/or the society regardless of the years s/he lives in the country and whether or not s/he is granted French citizenship by naturalization. There is a societal distinction between an immigrant and a citizen even after immigrants make the transition to become French citizens.

Furthermore, minorities experience economic alienation in France. The unemployment rate in France, at over 9.6 percent in 2004, is high by OECD standards. The immigrant populations are deeply affected by the rising unemployment levels since they are a more vulnerable group compared to other French citizens. Poverty and unemployment rates are higher among minority groups in comparison to the national percentage. It is believed that 30 percent of Algerian and Moroccan-origin French citizens are unemployed compared with 9.6 percent of the whole population (Giry, 2006, p.90). Lack of successful integration is evident in numbers: the unemployment rate in Paris suburbs is 10 percent higher than the national rates. The household income in these suburbs is 40 percent lower than the national income in France. The country's immigrant populations have often been settled by the state in poor neighbourhoods just outside Paris, such as *Savigny-sur-Orge* and *Raincy*, forming large minority-heavy communities (CBC News, 2005).

The October-November 2005 riots were a sign of a serious social unrest among minorities who are isolated, marginalized and criminalized under the current immigration and integration policies. The importance of this socio-economic problem was made clear after the riots in Parisian suburbs. These riots broke out when two French citizens of African descent were accidentally electrocuted while running from the police. Riots quickly spread to many other suburbs populated by immigrants and their children. In three weeks, 8,500 vehicles were burned, 100 public buildings were harmed, and 3,400 people were arrested (CBC News, 2005). In a sign of rage against decades of discrimination tolerated by the French state, rioters specifically targeted government buildings and vehicles. Perhaps not surprisingly, the CFCM created by Sarkozy, "played no role in tampering down violence during the riots" (Laurence et al. 2006, p.157). The riots also helped perpetuate the negative image of immigrants, Arabs and Muslim. According to a public poll, people who consider themselves racist increased from 25 percent in 2004 to 33 percent in November 2005. There was also a 10 percent increase –from 45 to 55 percent- in the number of people who think there are too many immigrants in France (CNCDH, 2005).

This chapter argued that the state-centric Jacobin approach in French political culture resists the social changes that have begun with flows of non-European immigration after the Second World War. Therefore, it is argued that the French political structure does not accommodate cultural pluralism; on the contrary, it seeks to assimilate it through established institutions such as the education system. However, universal claims to equality can only try to camouflage the power struggle and privilege of dominant groups in France (Solorzan & Yosso, 2001). This universal, colour-blind Jacobin approach does not eliminate but only create, maintain and perpetuate the existing inequalities between minorities and the rest of the population.

Works Cited

Adler, Stephen. 1977. *International migration and dependence.* Farnborough: Saxon House.

Akan, Murat. 2003. Contextualizing multiculturalism. *Studies in comparative international development,* 38(2): 57-75.

Alba, Richard. 2005. Bright vs. blurred boundaries: Second-generation assimilation and exclusion in France, Germany, and the United States. *Ethnic and Racial Studies* 28: 20-49.

Anderson, John W. 2006. A multi-hued national team thrills racially uneasy France. *The Washington Post*, July 7.

Audard, Catherine. 2001. The French republic and the claims of diversity. In *Cultural Identity and the Nation-State*, ed. Carol C. Gould and Pasquale Pasquino, 85-109. Devon: Rowman and Littlefield.

Basdevant-Gaudemet, Brigitte. 2004. *Islam in France*. Turin: Peters.

CBC News. 2005. France tightens immigration rules in wake of rioting. Available online at: http://www.cbc.ca/cp/world/051129/w112984.html.

—. 2005. French violence eases as curbs extended. Available online at: http://www.cbc.ca/world/story/2005/11/17/france-law051117.html.

—. 2008. Opposition mounts to French ruling against Muslim woman. Available online at: http://www.cbc.ca/world/story/2008/07/16/france-ruling.html

Eurobarometer Special Surveys. 2007. Discrimination in the European Union. *European Commission Public Opinion Analysis.* Available online at: http://ec.europe.eu/public_opinion/archives/eb_special_en.htm#263

Freedman, Jane. 2004. Secularism as a barrier to integration? The French dilemma. *International Migration* 42: 5-25.

Giry, Stephanie. 2006. France and its Muslims: The politics of assimilation. *Foreign Affairs* 85, 87-96.

Guenif-Souilamas, Nacira. 2006. The other French exception, virtuous racism and the war of the sexes in postcolonial France. *French Politics, Culture & Society* 24: 23-41.

Guiraudon, Virginie. 2002. Immigration policy in France: U.S.-France analysis, *The Brookings Institution.* Washington, DC. Available online at: www.brook.edu/rios/data/sources/view/f88b4294e083ff3b7fffe6750a1415cb.xml.

Haut Conseil a l'Intégration. 2007. *Words of integration.* Available online at:

http://64.233.179.104/translate_c?hl=en&u=http://www.hci.gouv.fr/rubrique.php3%3Fid_rubrique%3D19&prev=/search%3Fq%3Dhaut%2Bconseil%2Ba%2Bl%2527integration%26hl%3Den%26rls%3Dcom.microsoft:en-us%26sa%3DX

Hollifield, James. 1990. Immigration and the French state. *Comparative Political Studies* 23: 56-79.

Institut National D'etudes Demographiques. 2006. *Immigration or foreign population since 1982*. Available online at: http://www.ined.fr/en/pop_figures/france/immigrants_foreigners/immigrants_foreigners_1982.

Joppke, Christian. 2007. Beyond national models: Civic integration policies for immigrants in Western Europe. *West European Politics* 30: 1-22.

Kesselman, Mark, Joel Krieger and Christopher S. Allen. 2002. Chapter IV: France. *European Politics*. Boston: Houghton Mifflin.

Kuru, Ahmet T. 2007. Passive and assertive secularism: Historical conditions, ideological struggles, and state policies toward religion. *World Politics* 59(4): 568-94.

Kritzman, Lawrence D. 1995. Identity crisis: France, culture and the idea of the nation. *SubStance* 24: 5-20.

Laurence, Jonathan and Justin Vaisse. 2006. *Integrating Islam: Political and religious challenges in contemporary France.* Washington, D.C: The Brookings Institute.

Luedtke, Adam. 2005. European integration, public opinion and immigration policy: Testing the impact of national identity. *European Union Politics* 6(1): 83-112.

Marcus, Jonathan. 1995. *The National Front and French politics*. New York: New York University Press.

Safran, William. 1991. State, nation, national identity, and citizenship: France as a test case. *International Political Science Review* 12: 219-38.

—. 2003. Pluralism and multiculturalism in France: Post-Jacobin transformations. *Science Quarterly* 18, 437-65.

Said, Edward. 1994. *Orientalism.* New York: Vintage.

Samers, Michael. 2003. Invisible capitalism: Political economy and the regulation of undocumented immigration in France. *Economy and Society* 32: 555-83.

Schor, Naomi. 2001. The crisis of French universalism. *Yale French Studies* 100, 43-64.

Smith, Anthony D. 1986. *The ethnic origins of nations.* Oxford: Blackwell.

—. 1991. *National identity*. Reno: University of Nevada Press.
Solorzano, Daniel G. and Tara J. Yosso. 2001. From racial stereotyping and deficit discourse toward a critical race theory. *Multicultural Education* 9(1).
The Guardian. 2008. France rejects Muslim woman over radical practice of Islam. Available online at: http://www.guardian.co.uk/world/2008/jul/12/france.islam
Todd, Jean Marie. 2003. *Affirmative exclusion: Cultural pluralism and the rule of custom in France*. Ithaca: Cornell University Press.
Watts, Julie. 2002. *Immigration policy and the challenge of globalization*. Ithaca: Cornell, University Press.
Wayland, Sarah V. 1995. Immigrants into citizens: Political mobilization in France and Canada. PhD diss., University of Michigan.

CHAPTER TEN

CITIZENSHIP AND IMMIGRANT INTEGRATION IN THE NETHERLANDS

WILLEM MAAS

> The European Union must ensure fair treatment of third country nationals who reside legally on the territory of its Member States. A more vigorous integration policy should aim at granting them rights and obligations comparable to those of EU citizens.
> —European Council

Within the panoply of national citizenship and integration policies, the Netherlands was long among the most tolerant and open states. Recently, however, Dutch policy has become decidedly more restrictionist. The 1990s witnessed a debate about whether the granting of citizenship should be seen as a means of encouraging integration or rather as the statement of its successful conclusion. Political parties on the left tended to promote the former view; those on the right the latter, arguing that naturalization should be seen as the "crowning moment" at which a completely integrated person finally achieved complete legal equality. Those on the right argued that giving citizenship too easily would place in question the recipients' loyalty, while those on the left argued that naturalization inherently provided a source of loyalty. Between 1992 and 1997, the view of the parties of the left held sway. The complete toleration of dual nationality that resulted caused large-scale naturalizations, peaking at over 80,000 in 1996. The openness towards dual nationality then waned, and policies once again became more restrictionist. By 2009, naturalization was more difficult, dual nationality had become more restricted, and new laws even made it possible to strip individuals of their Dutch citizenship for engaging in activities such as terrorism. This chapter considers this seemingly complete reversal in citizenship law, situating it within the broader field of changes in Dutch immigrant integration policies.

Western liberal democracies grappling with the challenges of immigration often turn to citizenship laws and policies. The politics of citizenship are intricately related to broader questions surrounding immigration. The granting of citizenship—denoting an individual's full legal status in a sovereign state—has long been used as a tool of political integration, both of established populations and of newcomers. The long history of political accommodation in the Netherlands (Lijphart 1968), coupled with the apparent rapidity of social and political change over the past few decades, make the Netherlands a key case study for a range of questions related to explaining change and continuity in citizenship laws and policies.

Do changes in naturalization requirements, openness towards dual nationality, strategies for incorporating immigrants, and related policies and attitudes flow from transformations in cultural preferences, structural factors, institutions, or some combination—or are contingent political events the main, and therefore somewhat random and unpredictable, cause? What is the relationship between changes in migration patterns and the politics of citizenship? Or perhaps citizenship laws and policies are resistant to change and what is required is a theory explaining such "stickiness" in the face of societal changes. Answering such broad questions is clearly beyond the scope of a single chapter, but examining the Dutch case may help us to better conceptualize them. Indeed, investigating developments in the Netherlands offers more than simple conceptual clarification. By focusing on a society that has undergone rapid and dramatic shifts in citizenship laws and policies, we can shed light on the relative weight of the causes of these transformations.[1]

By the 1990s, the Netherlands had become famous as one of the few countries whose public policies reflected a genuine commitment to multiculturalism. Postcolonial immigrants from Indonesia, Surinam, and the Netherlands Antilles had been joined by growing immigration from new sources, particularly Turkey and Morocco, and refugees and asylum seekers from elsewhere. Naturalization was made easier and dual nationality supported. The legacy of pillarisation – the social phenomenon known as *verzuiling* in Dutch, meaning the vertical segregation of society into distinct, usually denominational, social pillars each with its own

---

[1] See also the Money chapter in this volume for an attempt to develop a general theory of citizenship change, the Vink chapter in this volume for more on the value of Dutch citizenship policy as a focal case study, and the Peres chapter in this volume for a discussion of the end of national models of immigrant integration.

social, cultural, and political institutions – resulted in publicly-funded Muslim and Hindu denominational schools and broadcasting facilities. The welfare state provided high benefits and low unemployment while promoting cultural diversity. Then, within the space of a few years: terrorist attacks and war in Afghanistan and Iraq, an anti-immigrant politician assassinated and his upstart political party posthumously becoming the second largest in parliament, a filmmaker murdered gruesomely, repressive policies causing asylum applications to plummet and the best-educated non-western immigrants to leave the Netherlands.

For a long time, the Netherlands was widely perceived as one of the few clear examples of multiculturalism. As a leading Dutch scholar of immigrant integration noted only a few years ago: "Wake up any expert on immigrant integration in the middle of the night and ask that person to name a country known for its multiculturalism. Ten to one that answer will be Canada, Australia, or the Netherlands" (Entzinger 2003: 59). Today, the picture is decidedly different as Dutch society has undergone significant recent shocks. But perhaps both the earlier perception of the Netherlands as a multicultural paradise and the current conception of it as stuck in an illiberal and nativist nightmare are overly simplistic. It is necessary to reevaluate the Dutch case.

Recent years have witnessed an impressive number of studies of how Western liberal democracies are responding or should respond to non-Western, particularly Islamic, immigration and the demographic diversity that accompanies it. Much of the nonacademic writing (and even some of the academic literature) has been strident, even alarmist. But there is a long history of studies of immigrant integration strategies that focus on the wide variation of policy responses to immigration. Within this literature, the Netherlands was usually cast as one of the most liberal regimes, possessing a unique form of multicultural accommodation that developed from its pluralist, consociational institutions (Entzinger 2002, Kymlicka and Banting 2006).

In parallel with the burgeoning attention to the relationship between diversity—especially diversity caused by immigration—and politics, there has been renewed attention to citizenship because citizenship promises to capture contemporary transformations in political relations while also retaining the essential link between individuals and states (Kymlicka and Norman 1994, 2000, Benhabib 2002, 2004, Maas 2007). Such studies sometimes refer to earlier ones about the relationship between state-building and citizenship (Bendix 1977, Weber 1976) but more often are silent about the political use of citizenship in plural societies.

There is a need to both revise an earlier view of the Netherlands as an idyllic multicultural society governed by extreme tolerance and deep, pluralist consociationalism and a current view of the "extreme" and hardline Dutch response to the terrorist attacks in the United States, Europe, and elsewhere; Pim Fortuyn; and the murder of Theo van Gogh. The real political development of Dutch citizenship and integration policies does not appear to fit either caricature.

Citizenship and Nationality

Political elites have often promoted citizenship as a tool to create a shared sense of community, but the precise ways in which public authorities do or should respond to ethnic and other diversity is a key question of political science. Modern states are expected to incorporate their people as individual citizens (Marshall 1950), but the use of citizenship as a means to achieve political integration has a long history (see for e.g. (Maas 2007, 2001, Lemke 1997, Noiriel and Offerlé 1997, Ireland 2004, Nicolet 1976). Rights usually emerge with the appearance of new social groups (Hanagan and Tilly 1999) but can also be created as a result of elite bargaining (Maas 2005). Because of the wide variation in national development, citizenship rights differ dramatically even within Europe (Hansen and Weil 2001, 2002, Preuss, et al. 2003). Some have posited that national citizenship has lost its importance as supranational and transnational rights have become more pronounced (Jacobson 1996, Jacobson and Ruffer 2006, Soysal 1994). But unless individuals possess citizenship, social rights can be withdrawn (Jones Correa 2002). National welfare states, rather than supranational sources of human rights, continue to provide the basic guarantees of rights (Maas forthcoming).

Within the panoply of citizenship policies in Europe, the Netherlands was situated at one end of the spectrum. For example, a 1998 study of foreigners' rights in France, Germany, and the Netherlands found that the Netherlands had gone furthest, because foreigners could vote in local elections and their cultural rights were guaranteed under the minorities policy (Guiraudon 1998: 274).

The 1990s witnessed a debate about whether the granting of citizenship should be seen as a means of encouraging integration or rather as the statement of its successful conclusion. Political parties on the left tended to promote the former view; those on the right the latter, arguing that naturalization should be seen as the "crowning moment" at which a completely integrated person finally achieved complete legal equality. Those on the right argued that that giving citizenship too easily would place in question the recipients' loyalty, while others argued that naturalization inherently provided a source of loyalty (Groenendijk 2005: 194).

Between 1992 and 1997, the view of the parties of the left held sway: "Nationality is an expression of connection, not of indivisible loyalty. Because that connection can be of many kinds, it is possible for an individual to have connections to more than one country. Nationality should therefore no longer be seen as an exclusive link with a single country; dual nationality not a phenomenon that should automatically be opposed" (Driouichi 2007: 123) my translation). The complete toleration of dual nationality that resulted from this kind of argument resulted in large-scale naturalizations (Vink 2007: 341), peaking at over 80,000 acquisitions of Dutch nationality in 1996:

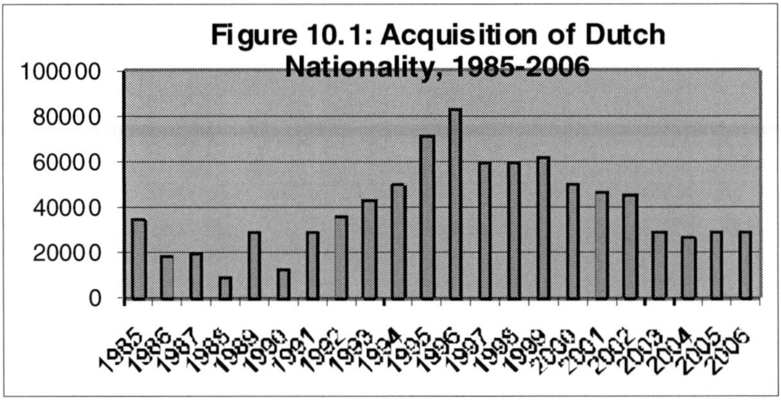

Compiled from Centraal Bureau voor de Statistiek data. Numbers include Dutch nationality acquired by adoption (averaging between 500 and 1100 cases annually) and that acquired by "option" (a form of simplified naturalization) such as that granted to stateless persons or to individuals who have reached the age of majority and were born in and have resided continuously since birth in the Netherlands, the Netherlands Antilles, or Aruba.

Subsequently, however, the openness towards dual nationality waned, and policies once again became more restrictionist (Penninx 2005). By 2007, the far right politician Geert Wilders was proposing that dual citizens could not be cabinet ministers, a jab at two new cabinet members, one Dutch-Turkish and the other Dutch-Moroccan. His proposal was defeated, but the government did propose making it harder for those who naturalize at the age of 18 to retain their other nationality, and new laws make it easier to strip individuals of their Dutch citizenship for engaging in activities such as terrorism.

The constantly changing rules and policies concerning the conditions for admission to citizenship are a fascinating subject in many states, not just the Netherlands. The exact relationship between levels and sources of immigration, the scale of naturalization, and the nature of debates about citizenship laws and policies deserve closer scrutiny. There are many good earlier studies of the relationship between immigration and ideas of citizenship (see e.g. (Favell 1998, Fermin 1999, de Hart 2005, Heijs 1995, Kastoryano 2002) but no book about the Dutch case (see (Driouichi 2007) for a good start, though the actual treatment of citizenship and nationality rules is brief). It is clear, however, that citizenship always privileges certain public identities over alternatives (Yashar 2005), meaning that issues of citizenship cannot be divorced from those of identity.

Diversity and Multiculturalism

Questions surrounding the political accommodation of ethnic and other forms of diversity within liberal democracies continue to grow in importance and are particularly relevant for culturally-segmented states. Many such states are federal, but even unitary states like the Netherlands can possess remarkable diversity. Federalism and rights often have a mutually reinforcing impact (Lenaerts 1996), but the same could be said of other institutional ways of accommodating diversity. In the Netherlands, citizenship was for a very long time quite decentralized, with provinces and even cities taking primary responsibility for safeguarding rights (Prak 1999). The unitary Dutch state that has evolved since the departure of Napoleon's troops in 1813, however, gradually concentrated authority. The resulting centralization of responsibility for citizenship in the Netherlands can be compared to analogous processes in other states.

Unlike citizenship, immigration is an area of policy where the will of the national government and the desires of the municipalities and other devolved authorities tasked with executing it do not always coincide. Consider the case of asylum. In the decade between 1992 and 2001, the Netherlands was the third largest recipient of asylum applications in Europe, behind Germany and the United Kingdom. Per capita, this made the Netherlands (along with Switzerland and Sweden) one of the most popular destinations in the world, at 2.27 applications per thousand inhabitants. (By comparison the rate for the United States was 0.45 and Canada's was 0.94.) By the end of the decade, however, asylum policy had become decidedly less welcoming (Van Selm 2000, Maas 2004).

At least some of this change can be attributed to a former sociology professor who styled himself as the Dutch Samuel Huntington in reference to the "clash of civilizations" thesis, Pim Fortuyn. In his book *Against the Islamicisation of our Culture*, first published in 1997, Fortuyn warned that Muslims living in the Netherlands threaten traditional Dutch values: "Because of their advanced individualization, Dutch people are not aware of their own cultural identity and the rights they have gained: the separation of church and state, the position of women and of homosexuals. Their indifference makes the Dutch an easy and vulnerable prey" (Fortuyn 2002) my translation).

At first dismissed, then vilified, Fortuyn could no longer be ignored after his party won the Rotterdam municipal elections. Nine days before the 2002 national elections, he was assassinated by an ethnically Dutch environmental activist. The elections rank fourth among all West European general elections in the period 1900-2002 on the Pedersen index of electoral volatility (after Italy 1994, Germany 1920, and France 1906), leading commentators to argue: "after many years of stability and predictability, it is more important than ever to understand the nature of the increasing volatility of the Dutch electorate and the sudden changes in the Dutch political landscape" (van Holsteyn and Irwin 2003).

Demographic developments, debates about integration (Prins 2004, Rutgers and Molier 2004), and projections for the future of the Dutch state (Lucassen and de Ruijter 2002) combined to test the limits of Dutch tolerance (Duyvendak and Veldboer 2001, Erp 1994, Koopmans, et al. 2005, Sniderman and Hagendoorn 2007). Classic debates about multiculturalism (e.g. (Taylor and Gutmann 1994, Young 1990) seemed outdated as Dutch citizenship and integration policy shifted. One observer now notes that "the supposedly difference-friendly, multicultural Netherlands is currently urging migrants to accept 'Dutch norms and values' in the context of a policy of civic integration that is only an inch (but still an inch!) away from the cultural assimilation that had once been attributed to the French" (Joppke 2007: 2).

Yet it would be a mistake to portray the change as a seismic shift. There were earlier examples of restrictionist policies and current examples of more open ones. For example, in mid 2007, the government granted amnesty to thousands of individuals who had been living in the Netherlands without authorization, and many mayors and town councils asked organizations working with illegal migrants to forward only those applicants who fulfil the requirements to apply for a residence permit, thereby tolerating the continued presence of unauthorized residents.

Pluralism and Consociationalism

Political scientists have traditionally regarded the Netherlands—along with Switzerland, Belgium, and perhaps Canada—as a paradigmatic example of consociationalism, in which institutional arrangements safeguard the integration of societal groups united by a shared citizenship but divided by ethnicity, language, religion, or some other cleavage (Lijphart 1968). This reflects the institutional legacy of pillarisation (see e.g. (Bakvis 1981) which created a segmented society: a Catholic baby would typically be born in a Catholic hospital, attend Catholic schools, watch Catholic television, listen to Catholic radio, play in Catholic sports leagues, read a Catholic newspaper, join a Catholic union, and vote for a Catholic political party, all of which would be publicly funded.

The traditional pillars started to dissolve in the 1960s and faded rapidly in the 1970s due to secularization, but their institutional legacies continued in such areas as denominational schools and in access to broadcasting networks. Most salient is the hypothesis that consociationalism encourages appeals to a sectarian base rather than the construction of cross-communal alliances, so that existing groups are reified and communal competition for votes is encouraged yet, at the level of elites, the necessity of having to work together leads to increased pragmatism and practical cooperation (McGarry and O'Leary 2004). Despite the disappearance of the old pillars, it is relevant to ask whether the pragmatism that they engendered continues today (de Haan 1993).

The Dutch electoral system is peculiar—the entire country constitutes a single electoral district and elections are purely proportional, with no threshold. This feature places the Netherlands at one extreme of electoral systems and makes it possible to ask whether it is in spite of its electoral system that the Netherlands can be qualified as a "consensus democracy" (Lijphart 1999). It appears somewhat remarkable that a country with around one million Muslim citizens out of a total population of around sixteen million, and a purely proportional electoral system with a 0.67% (or 1/150 seats in the lower house) threshold, has not given rise to a Muslim party; particularly when the electoral system allows such odd groups as the *Partij voor de Dieren* (Party for the Animals) to be elected.[2] The role of citizens of non-EU countries is changing across Europe (Maas 2008), but most Muslims in the Netherlands have acquired Dutch citizenship as a result of earlier liberal naturalization policies. Given the number of Muslims and the ease with which the proportional electoral system translates votes into seats, those who view Muslims as a single demographic bloc have difficulty explaining why there is no Muslim or Islamic political party. Perhaps one indicator that the "politics of accommodation" (Lijphart 1968) continue to operate in the Netherlands is that there are Muslim members of parliament in several longstanding political parties. Still, the classic theory of pillarisation would predict the emergence of a Muslim pillar, thus it is worth studying why this has not occurred in the way that the theory envisages.

Demography

Contrary to the perceived "restrictive turn in Dutch citizenship policy" (Van Oers 2008: 40) the demographic data paint a more nuanced picture.

[2] The party was formed in 2002 to highlight animal welfare and in the November 2006 parliamentary elections won 179,988 votes, enough for two out of the 150 seats in the lower house. The Party for the Animals thereby became the world's first animal welfare party to be elected to parliamentary office. In those same elections, the *Staatkundig Gereformeerde Partij* (Political Reformed Party), a Calvinist party that is the oldest political party in the Netherlands, won 153,266 votes, also enough for two seats. In the March 2007 elections for the upper house, the Party for the Animals won one of the 75 seats and would have gotten two seats had a GreenLeft member of the North Holland provincial council not made a mistake in voting.

Figure 10.2: Dutch population by citizenship status

	Total population (000s)	Dutch nationality only (000s)		Dutch and other nationality (000s)		Non-Dutch nationality (000s)	
1995	15,424	14,263	92.5%	402	2.6%	749	4.9%
1996	15,494	14,295	92.3%	472	3.0%	719	4.6%
1997	15,567	14,333	92.1%	552	3.5%	675	4.3%
1998	15,654	14,366	91.8%	608	3.9%	674	4.3%
1999	15,760	14,420	91.5%	676	4.3%	656	4.2%
2000	15,864	14,477	91.3%	736	4.6%	645	4.1%
2001	15,987	14,529	90.9%	790	4.9%	660	4.1%
2002	16,105	14,574	90.5%	841	5.2%	683	4.2%
2003	16,193	14,599	90.2%	893	5.5%	692	4.3%
2004	16,258	14,617	89.9%	938	5.8%	694	4.3%
2005	16,306	14,629	89.7%	977	6.0%	693	4.3%
2006	16,334	14,629	89.6%	1,013	6.2%	687	4.2%
2007	16,358	14,629	89.4%	1,047	6.4%	678	4.1%

Calculated from Centraal Bureau voor de Statistiek data. Includes only legally resident individuals. Numbers may not add to 100% because of rounding and because of a residual category which includes stateless individuals and a small number of individuals who have Dutch nationality and three or more foreign nationalities.

As shown in Figure 2, the proportion of the Dutch population with a nationality other than Dutch has been growing while the proportion of the population with only Dutch nationality has been declining. Even numerically, the number of individuals who hold only Dutch nationality has stabilized and will presumably start to decline.

The striking phenomenon is the growth of dual and multiple citizenship. The number of individuals resident in the Netherlands holding both Dutch and one more other nationalities increased from 402,088 (2.6% of the total Dutch population) in 1995 to 1,047,165 (6.4% of the total population) in 2007. (Most of these individuals hold Dutch and one other nationality; in 2007, a total of 14,371 individuals held Dutch and two other nationalities.)

At the same time, both the number and proportion of residents of the Netherlands who do not hold Dutch nationality has been declining, from 749,061 individuals (4.9% of total population) in 1995 to 677,795 individuals (4.1% of total population) in 2007.

Table 10.3: Nationality of foreigners resident in the Netherlands. Number in 000s and proportion of total foreign population; twelve largest nationalities

1998			2003			2008		
Moroccan	135.7	20.0%	Turkish	100.3	14.3%	Turkish	93.7	13.6%
Turkish	114.7	16.9%	Moroccan	97.8	14.0%	Moroccan	74.9	10.9%
German	53.9	8.0%	German	56.1	8.0%	German	62.4	9.1%
British	39.2	5.8%	British	44.1	6.3%	British	40.2	5.8%
Belgian	24.4	3.6%	Belgian	26.3	3.8%	Belgian	26.2	3.8%
Italian	17.4	2.6%	Italian	18.7	2.7%	Polish	26.2	3.8%
Spanish	16.6	2.5%	Spanish	17.5	2.5%	Italian	19.0	2.8%
Bosnian	14.6	2.2%	American	15.4	2.2%	Spanish	16.5	2.4%
Somali	13.6	2.0%	French	14.5	2.1%	Chinese	16.2	2.4%
Iraqi	13.0	1.9%	Portuguese	11.3	1.6%	French	15.1	2.2%
American	13.0	1.9%	Chinese	11.2	1.6%	American	14.5	2.1%
Surinamese	11.8	1.7%	Indonesian	10.8	1.5%	Portuguese	12.9	1.9%

Calculated and compiled from Centraal Bureau voor de Statistiek data. Individuals who hold two or more foreign nationalities are attributed to one nationality based on a hierarchy: other EU state, other European state, non-European state.

Table 1 shows the twelve largest nationalities of the residents of the Netherlands who do not hold Dutch nationality. The most striking change is the decline in the number of citizens of Morocco and Turkey, from over 250,000 (approximately 37% of all foreigners) in 1998 to under 170,000 (under 25% of all foreigners) ten years later. This change is presumably largely due to the naturalization of Turkish and Moroccan individuals, so that they no longer appear in these statistics. The contrast with the numbers of citizens of EU member states is stark: with some fluctuations, the numbers (and hence also the proportion) of citizens of Germany, the United Kingdom, Belgium, Italy, Spain, France, Portugal, and so forth are stable or increasing gradually. (Noteworthy here is the rise in the number of citizens of Poland resident in the Netherlands. These statistics include only legally resident individuals, and anecdotal evidence suggests that 26,200 is a significant undercount.)

Conclusion: The politics of Citizenship and Integration in the Netherlands

For immigrants, acquiring Dutch citizenship has clearly become more difficult over the past few years, as demonstrated by the data (presented above in figure 1) on the acquisition of Dutch nationality. But the increase in the numbers of residents of the Netherlands who hold both Dutch nationality and one or more foreign nationalities is significant: from barely four hundred thousand (2.6% of the total population) to over one million (6.4% of the total population) in the space of twelve years. Because only Dutch citizens can vote, and assuming the age structure of the dual/multiple citizen population resembles that of the Dutch-nationality-only population, this means that roughly 6.7% of the Dutch electorate now holds more than one nationality. At least partially because of the extreme proportionality of the Dutch electoral system, issues relating to citizenship and nationality can be expected to remain sensitive.

One wider point is that attempts to explain change and continuity in citizenship laws and policies should pay attention to electoral institutions as much as other factors such as cultural preferences, structural factors, or contingent political events. The relationship between changes in migration patterns and the politics of citizenship remains fertile ground for academic inquiry.

Works Cited

Bakvis, Herman. 1981. *Catholic power in the Netherlands*. Kingston: McGill-Queen's University Press.

Bendix, Reinhard. 1977. *Nation-building and citizenship: Studies of our changing social order*. Berkeley: University of California Press.

Benhabib, Seyla. 2002. *The claims of culture: Equality and diversity in the global era*. Princeton: Princeton University Press.

—. 2004. *The rights of others: Aliens, residents and citizens*. Cambridge: Cambridge University Press.

de Haan, Ido. 1993. *Zelfbestuur en staatsbeheer: Het politieke debat over burgerschap en rechtsstaat in de twintigste eeuw*. Amsterdam: Amsterdam University Press.

de Hart, Betty. 2005. Het probleem van dubbele nationaliteit: Politieke en mediadebatten na de moord op Theo van Gogh. *Migrantenstudies* 21(4): 224-38.

Driouichi, Fouzia. 2007. *De casus inburgering en nationaliteitswetgeving: iconen van nationale identiteit: Een juridische analyse*. Amsterdam: Wetenschappelijke Raad voor het Regeringsbeleid.

Duyvendak, Jan Willem, and Lex Veldboer. 2001. *Meeting point Nederland: Over samenlevingsopbouw, multiculturaliteit en sociale cohesie*. Amsterdam: Boom.

Entzinger, Han (2002) *Voorbij de multiculturele samenleving*. Assen: Van Gorcum.

—. 2003. The rise and fall of multiculturalism: The case of the Netherlands. In *Toward assimilation and citizenship: Immigrants in liberal nation-states*, ed. Christian Joppke and Ewa Morawska, 59-86. New York: Palgrave Macmillan.

van Erp, Herman. 1994. *Het politiek belang: Over de politieke orde in een pluralistische samenleving*. Amsterdam: Boom.

Favell, Adrian. 1998. *Philosophies of integration: Immigration and the idea of citizenship in France and Britain*. New York: St. Martin's Press.

Fermin, Alfons. 1999. Inburgeringsbeleid en burgerschap. *Migrantenstudies* 15(2): 96-112.

Fortuyn, Pim. 2002. *De islamisering van onze cultuur: Nederlandse identiteit als fundament*. rev. ed. Uithoorn: Karakter.

Groenendijk, Kees A. 2005. Het desintegratiebeleid van de kabinetten Balkenende. *Migrantenrecht*.

Guiraudon, Virginie. 1998. Citizenship rights for non-citizens: France, Germany, and the Netherlands. In *Challenge to the nation-state:*

Immigration in Western Europe and the United States, ed. Christian Joppke, 272-319. Oxford: Oxford University Press.

Hanagan, Michael, and Charles Tilly, ed. 1999. *Extending citizenship, reconfiguring states*. Lanham: Rowman & Littlefield.

Hansen, Randall, and Patrick Weil, ed. 2001. *Towards a European nationality: Citizenship, immigration, and nationality law in the EU*. New York: Palgrave.

—. ed. 2002. *Dual nationality, social rights, and federal citizenship in the U.S. and Europe: The reinvention of citizenship*. New York: Berghahn Books.

Heijs, Eric. 1995. *Van vreemdeling tot Nederlander: De verlening van het Nederlanderschap aan vreemdelingen 1813-1992*. Amsterdam: Het Spinhuis.

Ireland, Patrick R. 2004. *Becoming Europe: Immigration, integration, and the welfare state*. Pittsburgh: University of Pittsburgh Press.

Jacobson, David. 1996. *Rights across borders: Immigration and the decline of citizenship*. Baltimore: Johns Hopkins University Press.

Jacobson, David, and Galya Benarieh Ruffer. 2006. Social relations on a global scale: The implications for human rights and for democracy. In *Dialogues on migration policy*. ed. Marco Giugni and Florence Passy, 25-44. Lanham: Lexington Books.

Jones Correa, Michael. 2002. Seeking shelter: Immigrants and the divergence of social rights and citizenship in the United States. In *Dual nationality, social rights and federal citizenship in the U.S. and Europe: The reinvention of citizenship*, ed. Randall Hansen and Patrick Weil. New York: Berghahn.

Joppke, Christian. 2007. Beyond national models: Civic integration policies for immigrants in Western Europe. *West European Politics* 30(1): 1-22.

Kastoryano, Riva. 2002. *Negotiating identities: States and immigrants in France and Germany*. Princeton: Princeton University Press.

Koopmans, Ruud, Paul Statham, Marco Giugni, and Florence Passy. 2005. *Contested citizenship: Immigration and cultural diversity in Europe*. Minneapolis: University of Minnesota Press.

Kymlicka, Will, and Keith G. Banting, ed. 2006. *Multiculturalism and the welfare state: Recognition and redistribution in contemporary democracies*. Oxford: Oxford University Press.

Kymlicka, Will, and Wayne Norman. 1994. Return of the citizen: A survey of recent work on citizenship theory. *Ethics* 104: 352-81.

—. ed. 2000. *Citizenship in diverse societies*. Oxford: Oxford University Press.

Lemke, Christiane. 1997. Crossing borders and building barriers: Migration, citizenship, and state building in Germany. In *European Integration in Social and Historical Perspective*, ed. Jytte Klausen and Louise Tilly. Lanham: Rowman & Littlefield.

Lenaerts, Koen. 1996. Federalism and rights in the European Community. In *Federalism and Rights*, ed. Ellis Katz and G. Alan Tarr, 139-72. Lanham: Rowman & Littlefield.

Lijphart, Arend. 1968. *The politics of accommodation: Pluralism and democracy in the Netherlands.* Berkeley: University of California Press.

—. 1999. *Patterns of democracy: Government forms and performance in thirty-six countries.* New Haven: Yale University Press.

Lucassen, Jan, and Arie de Ruijter. 2002. *Nederland multicultureel en pluriform?: Een aantal conceptuele studies, NWO-reeks sociale cohesie.* Amsterdam: Aksant.

Maas, Willem. 2001. Grotius on citizenship and political community. *Grotiana* 21: 163-78.

—. 2004. Asylum policy in the Netherlands. Resolving the European Asylum Crisis workshop, New School University, New York.

—. 2005. The genesis of European rights. *Journal of Common Market Studies* 43(5): 1009-25.

—. 2007. *Creating European citizens.* Lanham: Rowman & Littlefield.

—. 2008. Migrants, states, and EU citizenship's unfulfilled promise. *Citizenship Studies* 12(6): 583-95.

—. Forthcoming. Citizenship and social rights. In *Welfare state reform in the United States and the European Union*, ed. Joseph Cordes and Christian Toft.

Marshall, Thomas H. 1950. *Citizenship and social class and other essays.* Cambridge: Cambridge University Press.

McGarry, John, and Brendan O'Leary. 2004. *The Northern Ireland conflict: Consociational engagements.* Oxford: Oxford University Press.

Nicolet, Claude. 1976. *Le Métier de citoyen dans la Rome républicaine.* Paris: Gallimard.

Noiriel, Gérard, and Michel Offerlé. 1997. Citizenship and nationality in Nineteenth-Century France. In *European integration in social and historical perspective*, ed. Jytte Klausen and Louise Tilly. Lanham: Rowman & Littlefield.

Penninx, Rinus. 2005. *Dutch integration policies after the Van Gogh murder.* Expert Panel on Social Integration of Immigrants, House of Commons. Ottawa: Canada.

Prak, Maarten. 1999. Burghers into citizens: Urban and national citizenship in the Netherlands during the Revolutionary Era (c. 1800). In *Extending citizenship, reconfiguring states*, ed. Michael Hanagan and Charles Tilly. Lanham: Rowman & Littlefield.

Preuss, Ulrich K., Michelle Everson, Mathias Koenig-Archibugi, and Edwige Lefebvre. 2003. Traditions of citizenship in the European Union. *Citizenship Studies* 7(1): 3-14.

Prins, Baukje. 2004. *Voorbij de onschuld: Het debat over integratie in Nederland*. 2nd ed., *Kennis, openbare mening, politiek*. Amsterdam: Van Gennep.

Rutgers, Rob, and Gelijn Molier. 2004. *Het multiculturele debat: Integratie of assimilatie?*, *Criminaliteit, rechtshandhaving en veiligheid*. Den Haag: Boom.

Sniderman, Paul M., and Louk Hagendoorn. 2007. *When ways of life collide: Multiculturalism and its discontents in the Netherlands*. Princeton: Princeton University Press.

Soysal, Yasemin N. 1994. *Limits of citizenship: Migrants and postnational membership in Europe*. Chicago: University of Chicago Press.

Taylor, Charles, and Amy Gutmann. 1994. *Multiculturalism: Examining the politics of recognition*. Princeton: Princeton University Press.

van Holsteyn, Joop J.M., and Galen A. Irwin. 2003. Never a dull moment: Pim Fortuyn and the Dutch parliamentary election of 2002. *West European Politics* 26(2): 41-67.

Van Oers, Ricky. 2008. From liberal to restrictive citizenship policies: The case of the Netherlands. *International Journal on Multicultural Societies* 10(1): 40-59.

Van Selm, Joanne. 2000. Asylum in the Netherlands: A hazy shade of purple. *Journal of Refugee Studies* 13(1): 74-90.

Vink, Maarten P. 2007. Dutch "multiculturalism" beyond the pillarisation myth. *Political Studies Review* 5(3): 337-50.

Weber, Eugen Joseph. 1976. *Peasants into Frenchmen: The modernization of rural France, 1870-1914*. Stanford: Stanford University Press.

Yashar, Deborah J. 2005. *Contesting citizenship in Latin America: The rise of indigenous movements and the postliberal challenge*. Cambridge: Cambridge University Press.

Young, Iris Marion. 1990. *Justice and the politics of difference*. Princeton: Princeton University Press.

PART III

ISSUES IN COMPARATIVE INTEGRATION POLICY: CONCEPTS AND CASES

CHAPTER ELEVEN

THE CHALLENGE OF MEASURING IMMIGRANT ORIGIN AND ETHNICITY IN EUROPE

DIRK JACOBS, MARC SWYNGEDOUW, LAURIE HANQUINET, VÉRONIQUE VANDEZANDE, ROGER ANDERSSON, ANA PAULA BEJA HORTA, MARIA BERGER, MARIO DIANI, AMPARO GONZALEZ FERRER, MARCO GIUGNI, MIRUNA MORARIU, KATIA PILATI, PAUL STATHAM

Counting and classifying inhabitants of foreign origin and/or identifying them as being part of ethnic minorities is often a sensitive issue. Categorization of certain social and ethnic groups when monitoring the population is an important tool in developing adequate policy, among other things to be able to tackle discrimination and unequal opportunities. Although often meant to improve the situation of those being counted, census material and statistical data have at repeated times, however, been misused to single out "foreign" elements in order to contain, mistreat or even deport and – in the worst case scenario - to exterminate them (Seltzer & Anderson, 2001). As a result, discussions of the measurement of ethnicity or foreign background often provoke strong feelings.

Furthermore, although seemingly a technically neutral tool, statistics are often the product of a particular social and political context. In the context of ethnicity, they may reflect ad hoc dominant views on insider-outsider relations and thus become contested over time. Moreover, when used as a basis for affirmative action, specific demarcations can have important consequences for vested interests of particular groups.

There is no uniform European system for ethnic categorization. Different European nation-states use the most diverse statistical constructions of foreign origin or ethnic minority populations. Several countries traditionally even shun from producing such data. This makes international comparison a very difficult endeavour. Anyone wanting to perform comparative research on immigrants or (immigrant origin) ethnic minorities in Europe is unavoidably confronted with the most diverse types of national statistical data and has to opt for ad hoc solutions. Attempts at international comparison (of employment levels, educational attainment, political inclusion, etc.) can thus be very tricky due to data characteristics. It is important that researchers are aware of these problems and do not simply accept data (especially in comparisons) at face value.

In this contribution we embark on a comparative explorative study of the way in which immigrant background[1] and immigration related ethnicity[2] are taken stock of by national statistical institutes in a set of European nation-states. We restrict the scope of the chapter to an exploratory study of the existence (and non existence) of official definitions and related operationalisations. We are mainly interested in looking at potential applications of statistical data on foreign origin and (immigration related) ethnic background for academic research. We will then reflect on the question what kind of data we would need in the future.

Different Traditions across Europe

In all European states the classification and counting of nationals and foreigners are regarded to be a legitimate endeavour. When examining migration and international mobility, nationality is often the most readily available criterion for distinction. In the member states of the European Union the category of 'EU citizen' has recently become sort of an intermediary category in between the 'national citizen' on the one hand and the 'genuine foreigner' on the other hand (Jacobs & Rea, 2005). Indeed, in a growing number of policy matters the process of *Europeanisation* has lead to equal rights for residents from other EU member states, to which other foreigners are not necessarily entitled. As a

[1] When we refer to figures on immigrants in this paper, our focus is on nationals with an immigrant background and on foreigners with a legal residence status, but *not* on undocumented migrants.

[2] There is a vast literature on the exact definition of the concept of ethnicity. As a reference point for the purpose of this article we want to refer to the definition used by Conference of European Statisticians for the United Nations Economic Commission for Europe (2006): "*Ethnicity is based on a shared understanding of the history and territorial origins (regional, national) of an ethnic group or community as well as on particular cultural characteristics: language and/or religion and/or specific customs and ways of life*" (UNECE, 2006: 100). The current paper wants to take a more limited view on ethnicity in focusing on the importance of (post World War II) migration as a source of ethnic diversity.

result, in all kinds of official statistics increasingly the distinction is being made between "EU citizens" on the one hand and "third country nationals" (inhabitants who do not hold the nationality of one of the EU Member States) on the other hand. The latter are often presented as being more "foreign" than the EU-citizens. Take for instance Italy which distinguishes foreigners as being either EU-citizens or "*extracomunitari*" (non-EU-citizens). Tellingly, the first law focusing on working conditions of immigrants referred to *extracomunitari* to pinpoint workers of non-EU nationality[3], whereas the 1998 immigration law and its 2002 modification[4] identify "foreigners" as citizens of states who are not members of the EU and stateless people.

Most countries in Europe lack an official (legal) definition of people of foreign origin or of ethnic minorities (of foreign origin). They only use the distinction between nationals and non-nationals (or "foreigners"). As a side effect some forms of ethnic disadvantage and discrimination can often not be measured by making use of official population statistics since immigrants disappear as a specifically identifiable group once they have acquired state citizenship.

At first sight, the existence of uniform statistics on non-nationals does seem to offer some possibilities for comparative work between nation-states. The fact that all countries produce statistics distinguishing nationals and non-nationals within their population does, however, not guarantee us a reliable basis for international comparison. Nationality legislations apply conditions for nationality acquisition so differently, and the logics of *jus sanguinis* (blood links as the basis for nationality attribution) and of *jus soli* (residence as the basis for nationality attribution) in such varying manners, that one would be comparing apples and pears. It is much more likely for a person with a foreign background to have state citizenship in Belgium or the Netherlands than it is in Austria or Switzerland, to give but one example. This makes a correct comparison – for instance with regard to unemployment figures of immigrants - between these sets of countries very difficult. Across all EU member states important differences in the modes, requirements and procedures for the attribution and acquisition of citizenship persist (Cantisani & Greco, 2006a).

---

[3] Italian law 943/1986.

[4] Italian law 286/1998 and Italian law 189/2002.

Counting nationals and non-nationals has nothing controversial and few critical questions are raised with regard to the growing importance of distinguishing EU-citizens and third country nationals. Counting and classifying individuals on the basis of their ethnic origin or even 'race' is, however, to a far lesser degree seen to be acceptable in (western) continental Europe, while it is a standard operating procedure in the United States, the UK, Canada and Brazil. In the latter countries interethnic relations are judged to have as much importance and relevance as gender or class relations. Official statistics routinely distinguish races and this does not seem to provoke large scale criticism. Indeed, in recent years, the statistical construction of ethnic and racial groups in the US has mainly provoked a debate with the possible introduction of the category of a "mixed race" in the 2000 Census (Amaro et Zambrana, 2000; Krieger, 2000; Lee, 1993; Nobles, 2000; Riche, 1999; Sondik *et al.*, 2000; Waters, 2000; Williams et Jackson, 2000), without fundamentally questioning the whole *racialising* framework to start with (but see Kertzer & Arel, 2002).

In (Western) continental Europe, ethnic classifications often have no comparable institutional or statistical translation, although they are very currently being used in day to day life. One could argue in favour of such classifications as tools to measure ethnic and racial discrimination. Moreover, targeted groups might mobilise them in order to defend their interests in policies of redistribution of social goods (jobs, housing, etc.). However, the possibility of using such categorisations to tackle discrimination apparently does not provide sufficient justification for the construction of ethnic categories in official statistics. The misfit between the vastness of the debate, particularly in France, which is triggered by the mere possibility of constructing ethnic categories in statistics (see for an overview: Spire et Merllié, 1998; Blum, 2002) on the one hand and the limited number of studies pertaining to the actual possibilities of operationalisation of ethnicity on the other hand (Bulmer, 1996; Simon, 1997, 1998; Aspinall, 2002; Lie, 2002) attests to the strong political dimension of the matter. The political passions which feed the scientific debate strongly demonstrate that the definition of statistical categories on ethnicity and race is not merely a technical matter. The construction of these categories is influenced by ideologies, visions about nations and visions about interrelations between social groups. An additional element which further complicates the debate is that they are also performative: the use of ethnic categories reinforces the ethnicisation and racialisation of society. Once they are socially constructed, these categories gain their own life.

Although this is a rather crude classification and central and eastern European countries do not really fit straightforwardly into the picture, one can schematically distinguish two traditions related to 'ethnic statistics' in Europe[5]. In France and most southern European countries, the dominant statistical categorisations merely distinguish individuals on the basis of their nationality. It basically boils down to a limitation to two categories: the national and the foreigner. Often an additional distinction is made among the foreign population between those coming from other EU-member states and those who don't. With the introduction of the category 'immigrant population' – including all people born as a foreigner abroad (i.e. all people who were foreigners at the moment of birth, regardless of their current nationality status) - France has nevertheless tried to make the demographic contribution of immigration to its population a bit more visible without however distinguishing ethnic groups.

In contrast, most northern European countries have been producing data on the ethnic and/or foreign origin of their populations in a more detailed manner, albeit using different techniques. The UK has for instance a system of self-identification of ethnicity. Norway, in contrast, keeps track since 1994 of its 'immigrant population' by counting the number of persons who neither have parents nor grandparents born in Norway (Vassenden, 2005). National background is kept track of by looking at the person's own, their mother's or possibly their father's country of birth. Separate statistics are produced for different regions of origin[6]. Although in strict legal terms "foreigners" are non-nationals, Denmark also uses the term "foreigners" (*Udlaendinge*) as a statistical concept, regardless of citizenship, to refer to immigrants (people born outside of the country whose parents are either foreign citizens or both were born outside of Denmark) and descendants (people born in Denmark by parents of whom

---

[5] Simon (2007) tentatively distinguishes three traditions: a "state-centred type" one (EU-15 except the northern European countries) in which country of birth and citizenship variables are collected; a "mosaic type" in which variables on nationality/ethnicity and language are collected (Baltic countries, central and eastern Europe, Balkans) and a "post-migration multicultural type" (UK, Ireland, Netherlands and the Scandinavian countries) in which information on ethnic group, religion and/or parents' country of birth is gathered. Since our interest is focused on (post World War II) migration related ethnic diversity, we prefer to limit our attention to the "state-centred type" and the "post-migration multicultural type".

[6] For instance Nordic countries, Non-western countries (Asia including Turkey, Africa, South and Central America and Eastern Europe) and Third world countries (Asia including Turkey, Africa, South and Central America).

neither is Danish citizen born in Denmark). Specific numbers are produced for "lesser developed nations" (countries outside of Scandinavia, the EU and North America)[7]. Similarly, Sweden uses country of birth registration along with data on parents, which enables the identification of exact nationalities and of foreign background (*utländsk bakgrund*). As a result of a vivid debate on who was to be classified as an "immigrant" (*invandrare*), the definition of the latter was changed in the late 1990s. It used to be enough to have one foreign-born parent to be classified into the foreign background category; now only those born in Sweden having two foreign-born parents get this classification. It is however still possible for researchers to chose their own classification as detailed country of birth data is available at –and can be aggregated from– the individual level.[8] The Dutch equally try to count their population of foreign origin (regardless whether they hold Dutch nationality or not) since 1995 on the basis of country of birth of the parents of its residents. The Dutch have adopted the category of "allochthones" to label the ethnic or foreign origin of segments of its population and can make distinctions with regard to countries of origin.

Interestingly, Belgium is caught somewhere in between these two traditions (Jacobs & Rea, 2005) and finds itself in a stalemate position. The French-speaking part of Belgium tends to follow the French tradition of refusing ethnic categorisation, while the Flemish (the Dutch speaking part) try to copy the Dutch model in distinguishing "allochthones" and "autochthones". In Flanders, as in the Netherlands, the term "allochthone" is widely used in academic, political and institutional circles to refer to immigrant (mainly non-EU origin) inhabitants. This difference in conceptualisation within one and the same state has, however, not led the federal Belgian state – which is still in charge of population statistics – to produce any official data on the number of "allochthones" on the national level. Federal law stipulates that the national statistical office, *l'Institut*

---

[7] Statistical Yearbook of Foreigners in Denmark 2002. Annotated edition. (Danish Ministry of Refugee, Immigration and Integration Affairs).

[8] Statistics on Sweden's population are reported monthly, quarterly, biannually and annually. The Population Statistics are reported in three groupings:
1. Population by sex, age, civil status, citizenship and country of birth
2. Population change including, among other things, migration, births and death
3. Population projections (forecast).
More information is available in English at
http://www.scb.se/templates/Product____25799.asp

National de Statistique (INS), does not have the authorisation to produce any statistics relating to ethnic origin:

> "In no case whatsoever can the investigations and statistical studies of the national institute for statistics be related to the private life, the political, philosophical or religious opinions or activities, race or ethnic origin"[9].

The INS seems to follow this guideline in a strict manner and thus refrains from producing statistics on place of birth of parents and grand-parents (one of the criteria of the Flemish definition of "allochthone"). The result is that the Flemish administration has a detailed definition of "allochthones" but does, at the same time, not have the appropriate instruments to count how many there are (Jacobs & Rea, 2005).

European Efforts towards Harmonisation of Statistics

Is the deadlock situation in Belgium predictive of the way in which the issue will be handled on the European level? If Belgium up till now has failed to find a compromise between the two traditions in the matter, will Europe do better? The European Commission indeed hopes it will be able to push EU member states in the direction of a uniform statistical apparatus for counting immigrants by going beyond the criterion of nationality.

The Commission has recently (July 2007) adopted a regulation on community statistics on migration, attempting to harmonise data collection on this topic (COM 2005, 375 final)[10]. The regulation pushes the member states to produce annual statistics disaggregating the population according to country of birth[11]. It equally calls for (annual) statistics on the number of persons acquiring citizenship and formerly holding citizenship of another state (or being stateless). This does indeed already constitute an important step forward in facilitating transnational comparison.

---

[9] Article 24 quinquies of the law of 4 July 1962 with regard to public statistics, modified by the law of 1 August 1985.

[10] Regulation (EC) No 862/2007 of the European Parliament and of the Council of 11 July 2007.

[11] Preceding the drafting of the regulation, annual information on country of birth (combined with age and sex) was not available for the following EU member states: Czech republic, Germany, Estonia, Greece, Italy, Cyprus, Lithuania, Luxemburg, Hungary, Malta, Poland and Portugal (Cantisani & Poulain, 2006: 200-2001).

There are, however, still quite some technical issues to be resolved. Coverage of data on nationality acquisition currently varies significantly across countries – some counting all changes in nationality, others limiting themselves to certain procedures[12]. Tailoring will be necessary to allow for genuine comparability (Cantisani & Greco, 2006b). Even if technical matters are sorted out, the produced figures will still not be completely satisfactory for all research purposes (Cantisani & Poulain, 2006).

One of the fundamental problems will be that new acquisitions of citizenship can be counted but that the exact magnitude of the existing stock of foreign origin citizens will remain unknown if this kind of data is not available for earlier periods[13]. The so-called second and third generations, an intensively studied group in social sciences and the focus of quite some political debate and policy making, will furthermore still remain out of sight since they were born in the country to which their parents or grand-parents migrated. Moreover, in a number of countries (Belgium, France, Spain, the Netherlands, Germany, Ireland, Portugal and the UK) they have been attributed citizenship at birth, according to the place of birth of the parents or certain residence requirements (Cantisani & Greco, 2006a: 174) and thus will not be made visible in statistics on acquisition of citizenship. A classification based on country of birth of parents or self-identification, which would be able to resolve this problem, is not proposed in the Regulation.

The Dutch notion of "allochthone" (based on country of birth of parents) does allow for pinpointing this segment of the population. The question should, however, be raised to what extent that logic should be extended to the level of grandparents – which the Dutch are increasingly doing. Perhaps even more importantly, the issue should be resolved what to do with the 'offspring' of mixed couples in your classification system.

Some would argue a self-identification system is better, as it exists in the UK. Such a system is, however, equally not devoid of problems and

---

[12] Tricky issues are (a) incomplete registration mechanisms for semi-automatic types of acquisition and (b) inclusion (or exclusion) of atypical forms of acquisition (for instance naturalisation of people living abroad, acquisition through adoption, reacquisitions of citizenship by former citizens, etc.) (Cantisani & Greco, 2006b ; Perrin, 2006).

[13] In cases where the stock cannot be determined using information of population registers, an alternative ad hoc solution might be provided by a cohort approach using retrospective data from the census (Perrin, 2006).

pitfalls. Decisions have to be made on the categories among which respondents can choose (unless one opts for an open question). Members of visible minorities can furthermore deliberately choose to classify themselves as being part of the majority group. This would then, of course, be their legitimate choice but would at the same time frustrate correct analysis of discriminatory practices against so-called "visible minorities".

Comparing the situation of immigrant origin (ethnic minority) groups in different European countries might in our view profit from using data which does not remain limited to the current citizenship status of inhabitants. If all national institutes of statistics would gather data – and make them available - on indicators such as nationality at birth, place of birth, nationality of the parents, place of birth of the parents or nationality at birth of the parents, this would open up possibilities for comparisons which are not (or at least less) blurred by differences in nationality legislations.

Most European countries today, however, do generally not possess a lot of readily available data on these "alternative" indicators. Moreover, when state administrations do collect this kind of data, they are often not publicly accessible for research purposes and often not even available to the national statistical offices. Some countries have annual data, others only have (ten yearly) census data. Particular data might be collected for administrative purposes but this does not guarantee that they are available for statistical analysis – let alone that they would allow for international comparative work. Let us just address the situation in a selected number of countries to clarify this point.

In *Germany*, the national institute of statistics (*Bundesambt für Statistik*) has only data based on current nationality (annual data) and place of birth (census data). *Switzerland* has information on current nationality, nationality at birth and place of birth[14]. Information on nationality of the parents is present for children born out of wedlock and for offspring of mixed couples (in order to be able to apply particular regulations on *jus sanguinis*). In *Spain* current nationality and place of birth are equally available. Data on nationality of the parents and place of birth of the parents is only available for individuals who (still) live in the same household as their parents. In *Portugal* the National Statistics Institute

[14] This information being, however, presented as "born in Switzerland and nationality" and "born in a foreign country and nationality".

basically only has information on current nationality (annual data), although the Census equally delivers information on the place of birth. In *Italy* information is available on current citizenship (annual data) and place of birth (census). Information on citizenship at birth is limited to data deduced from the question whether one had Italian citizenship at birth or not (through a Census question). Technically speaking, data on nationality of the parents is available for people who were born and resident in Italy. *Belgium*, to give a last example, is technically capable of tracking place of birth, nationality of parents and place of birth of parents in its detailed Population Register but due to legal obstacles the National Institute for Statistics can only present information on current nationality. The National Institute for Statistics has data on nationality at birth for the 1991 Census but no longer for the 2001 Census (when that question was struck).

Table 1 provides an overview of available annual statistics in the (pre 2007) 25 EU member-states plus Norway and Switzerland. All countries have Census information on citizenship and country of birth[15], but not all countries can provide annual data. It should equally be stressed that the methods used to produce annual statistics are quite diverse. Some countries rely directly on population registers (Belgium, Denmark, Latvia, Finland, Sweden, the Netherlands, Spain, Austria, Norway), while other countries make estimates (mostly based on Census data and other information) (Cantisani & Poulain, 2006).

As a result of all this divergence in available data, international comparisons are doomed to stick to the lowest common denominator, which is in practice often the simple distinction between nationals and non-nationals. It is for this reason that the European Commission in its regulation wants to develop a new European wide system including data on country of birth.

As we have stated before, some countries in the EU have tried to conceptually classify their population according to (pseudo-) ethnic criteria by clearly moving beyond the simple distinction between nationals and foreigners and going further than country of birth. In the remainder of this article we will discuss the (proto-) typical cases of the Netherlands

---

[15] For France the data are estimates. No Census data exists on country of citizenship for the UK (Cantisani & Poulain, 2006). Estonia has Census data on the country of birth of the parents. Estonia equally has data on the self-indicated ethnic composition of its population, with an indicator of what they call "ethnic nationality".

(which has a similar approach as the Nordic countries) and the UK in more detail. We will first, however, take a closer look at the notion of "ethnic minorities".

Table 11.1. Annual statistics across the 25 EU-member states, Norway and Switzerland

	Population register	Annual statistics on citizenship (stock)	Annual statistics on country of birth (stock)	Annual statistics on country of birth of parents (stock)
Austria	Y	Y	Y	N
Belgium	Y	Y	N	N
Cyprus	Y	N	N	N
Czech Republic	Y	Y	N	N
Denmark	Y	Y	Y	Y
Estonia	Y	N	N	N
Finland	Y	Y	Y	N
France	N	Y*	Y*	N
Germany	Y	Y	N	N
Greece	N	N	N	N
Hungary	Y	Y	N	N
Ireland	N	Y*	Y*	N
Italy	Y	Y	N	N
Latvia	Y	Y	Y	N
Lithuania	Y	Y	Y	N
Luxembourg	Y	Y	N	N
Malta	N	N	N	N
Netherlands	Y	Y	Y	Y
Norway**	Y	Y	Y	Y
Poland	Y	N	N	N
Portugal	N	Y	N	N
Slovak Republic	Y	Y	Y	N
Slovenia	Y	Y	Y	N
Spain	Y	Y	Y	N
Sweden	Y	Y	Y	Y
Switzerland**	Y	Y	Y	N
United Kingdom	N	Y*	Y*	N

* as an estimate (based on survey) ** not an EU member state

Sources: own country investigations and Cantisani & Poulain, 2006

The Notion of "National Minorities" and "Ethnic Minorities"

Most countries lack a clear definition (and operationalisation) of ethnic minorities. If public authorities do use the notion of minorities it is often focused upon so-called national minorities, in most cases historical linguistic minorities, in line with the Framework convention on the protection of national minorities of the Council of Europe. In the EU only France, Belgium, Luxembourg and Greece have not signed or ratified this convention.[16]

The Baltic states have a particular statistical interest in keeping track of the ethnic composition of their populations. Estonia talks about "ethnic nationality" in this context and distinguishes the following groups: Estonian, Russian, Byelorussian, Finnish, Tatar, Latvian, Polish, Jewish, Lithuanian, German and other ethnic nationalities. The data on "ethnic nationalities" comes from the Census in which people are asked to self classify themselves. Parents determine the ethnic nationality of their children. If the child's mother and father were of different "ethnic nationalities" and the parents cannot agree on the ethnic nationality of their child, the ethnic nationality of the mother is preferred. Lithuania distinguishes as "ethnicities" Lithuanian, Russian, Polish, Belarusian, Ukrainian, Jewish, Latvian, Tatar, German, Romany and Other. The Baltic states are somewhat particular in this respect and their stance should be interpreted in the light of difficulties in dealing politically with (in particular) its Russophone minorities after independency from the Soviet Union. It is clear ethnic minorities in the context of the Baltic states does not refer to "classic" immigrant origin populations; some would indeed argue that Baltic Russians did not really migrate, but that a modification in state borders suddenly made them 'outsiders'.

Other former communist central and eastern European countries (such as Bulgaria, Croatia, Czech Republic, Hungary, Poland, Romania and Slovakia among the EU countries) equally have a tradition in monitoring the presence of 'national minorities' and 'language groups' through open

[16] Belgium is an interesting case in that it denies – mainly due to a Flemish veto - that there are 'national minorities' within its borders. Instead it claims there are only "national majorities" which enjoy sufficient protection through complex linguistic laws and a federal system of checks and balances (Jacobs & Swyngedouw, 2003).

or multiple choice Census questions. These data collection efforts did not originate out of a desire to track recent migration related ethnic diversity – in contrast to the situation in north-western European countries - but are rather aimed at keeping track of historical linguistic and diasporic ethnic minority groups. In the remainder of this article we wish to focus our attention on statistical efforts in keeping track of (recent) migration related ethnic diversity. As prototypical examples for this kind of measurement of "ethnic minorities", we will focus on the United Kingdom and the Netherlands.

Although the term "ethnic minority" is widely used both in official policy and in public discourse in the UK, it is not a recognised legal term. Instead, the UK Government defines a national ethnic minority as a "racial group", under the Race Relations Act 1976. A "racial group" is a group of people defined by race, colour, nationality and ethnic or national origins, and the Race Relations Act 1976 protects all racial groups from unlawful discrimination. The courts have explicitly recognised Romany Gypsies, Irish Travellers, Jews and Sikhs as constituting racial groups for the purposes of the RRA 1976 legislation. A more precise definition of "racial group", based on ethnic origins, was given by the House of Lords.[17] In 1983 the House of Lords emphasised that the word "ethnic" should be interpreted "relatively widely, in a broad, cultural/historic sense", but also observed that "the word 'ethnic' still retains a racial flavour". Tribunals and courts have ruled on the basis of this that the English, Scots and Welsh, among others, are not racial groups by virtue of distinct "ethnic origins". As we shall discuss in the specific section on the UK, "white" is considered to be a separate ethnic category.

One country, the Netherlands, does have a strong tradition of using the term of 'ethnic minority' in public policy discourse to refer to immigrant origin populations without using an explicit racial discourse. In 1983 the Dutch government launched a so-called "minorities policy" explicitly aimed at emancipation of officially defined categories of ethnic minorities, with the objective of elevating the "ethnicised" groups to equal social status with the indigenous groups in Dutch society, while at the same time propagating the ideal of a multicultural society. In the original Dutch governmental discourse it was stipulated that the ethnic minorities policy limited itself to those immigrants "for whom the presence is seen by the

[17] Mandla v Dowell-Lee, House of Lords, 1983 IRLR 209 H.L. 1983 2 A.C. 548, 1983 1 All E. R. 1062

authorities as being their special responsibility (due to the colonial past or because they have been recruited by the authorities) and who find themselves in a minority situation" (Minderhedennota, 1983: 12). The minorities policy thus concerns on the one hand the Surinamese, Antilleans, Arubans and Moluccans (and their offspring) and, on the other hand, the Moroccans, Turks and other guestworkers from the Mediterranean area (Italians, Spanish, Greeks and (ex-)Yugoslavs) and their offspring. A foreign origin group is only considered to be an ethnic minority group if one judges that the group is structurally trapped in a disadvantageous socio-economic position. As a result, gypsies and asylum seekers have equally become to be considered as part of the ethnic minorities, but other groups as foreigners coming from neighbouring countries (Belgium and Germany) have not been defined as such. It is interesting to note that the Chinese have for a long time equally not been recognized as being an ethnic minority (as a policy category). In sum, the category of ethnic minority was defined in a way cumulating both the social situation as criteria of foreignness.

The Notion of "Allochthones" in the Netherlands

Although the central terminology is still 'ethnic minorities' in policies targeted at foreign origin groups the category of "allochthones" has in the meantime gained importance through extensive use. The notion was introduced in the policy domain by the report *Allochtonenbeleid* (WRR, 1989) of the academic advisory body for the government (*Wetenschappelijke Raad voor Regeringsbeleid*, in short: WRR). In this document "allochthones" were defined as:

> "Allochthones are, generally speaking, all persons who come from elsewhere and have durably settled in the Netherlands, including their descendants until the third generation, in as far as the latter want to consider themselves as allochthones. Minorities are allochthonous groups which find themselves in a disfavoured position: it has to be assessed periodically which groups have to be considered to be minorities" (WRR, 1989: 10).

It was also in this report that a plea was held to install a system of ethnic registration which goes further than the distinction between nationals and non-nationals. The report preferred a system of self-registration. In its reaction to the report, the Dutch government, however, stated it preferred to stick to the notion of ethnic minorities and it did not go into the matter of ethnic registration. Although the notion of "allochthone" was starting to be routinely used in policy documents, it only got an operational basis in 1995, following the introduction of a new population administration system at the municipal level (*Gemeentelijke Basisadministratie*, GBA). It was the national statistical office, the *Centraal Bureau voor de Statistiek* (CBS), which *de facto* defined and constructed the new category of "allochthone" in a semi autonomous manner, using information coming from the GBA.

It is the definition of the national statistical office which would become hegemonic and is still the reference today. Since 1999 the CBS defines allochthones as:

> "every person living in the Netherlands of which at least one of the parents was born abroad"

Note that the definition does not in itself suggest any racial or cultural connotation.[18] The criterion is place of birth of the parents. Place of birth of the parents is used as a proxy for foreign origin. It is 'imprecise' as an ethnic category in the sense that it for instance equally includes children of Dutch expatriates.

Before 1999, the CBS already used the category of "allochthone": the allochthonous population was systematically counted on the basis of municipal data since 1995.[19] However, during the period 1995-1999, there were two definitions in use: an enlarged one and a restricted one. According to the enlarged definition, the allochthones were all persons who lived in the Netherlands and were either not born in the Netherlands or were born in the Netherlands but had at least one parent which was not born in the Netherlands. In a more limited definition, the CBS only took account of people born abroad of whom at least one parent was equally born abroad and of people who were born in the Netherlands but who had two parents born abroad. In the year 1998, the CBS had the habit of privileging the restricted definition in its publications. Due to insistence by the government, the CBS in 1999 however once again preferred to use the enlarged definition before finally opting for the new definition which is still in use in 2007.

---

[18] It can equally be noted that, according to this definition, most members of the Dutch royal family can be considered to be "allochthones".

[19] Figures are available on the basis of estimations since 1972 and on the basis of data from the municipal administrations since 1995 (following the introduction of the *Gemeentelijke Basisadministratie* in 1994).

y, the nationality laws associated with Britain's former coloni
too complex for nationality to be a useful variable on its own.
nsus question on ethnic group records each person's perceiv
roup and cultural background. The wording of the 2001 Englan
es Census question[24] on ethnic group was the following:

c *Group*. 'What is your ethnic group? Chose ONE section from A to
en tick the appropriate box to indicate your cultural background.

ite. Tick box options of: British; Irish or Any other White background
e write in).

xed. Tick box options of: White and Black Caribbean; White and
African; White and Asian or any other Mixed background (please
in).

ian or Asian British. Tick box options of: Indian; Pakistani;
adeshi; Any other Asian background (please write in).

ck or Black British. Tick box options of: Caribbean; African; Any
Black background (please write in).

nese or other ethnic group. Tick box options of: Chinese; Any other
write in).

ic classification question is in other words a self-classification
ut one in which one has to choose among pre-established
s. Of course, these pre-established categories -just as the wording
estion- can provoke criticism. Tellingly, the ethnic classification
or Scotland was under review by the Scottish Executive in 2005,
e was concern about the categories that were used in the 1991
Censuses to classify the population along ethnic lines, and
sought to establish categories that were acceptable both to data
and data users. Questions were piloted in 2006 and a broad
on with stakeholders was organized. In July 2008 a new official
lassification was determined and a set of recommendations were

stion was similar to the one asked in 1991, but with changes in some
for example, people could tick 'mixed' for the first time. Further
on the 2001 England and Wales Census questions on ethnicity and
vailable online at:
statistics.gov.uk/census2001/profiles/commentaries/ethnicity.asp.

The most recent definition of "allochthones" thus entails all people of the restricted definition, while adding all persons born in the Netherlands of whom at least one parent was not born in the Netherlands. The difference with the older enlarged definition is that it no longer includes people who were born abroad out of two parents born in the Netherlands. In the 1999 annual report regarding the minorities policy, the government stipulated it preferred to keep the children from "mixed" couples in the new definition (as opposed to the old restricted definition). The (odd) argumentation was as follows:

> "The mixed group is interesting because they seem to succeed better than the group of whom the two parents are born abroad."[20]

Following the operationalisation by the national statistics office, the category of "allochthone" was increasingly used in policy documents, academia, public debate and the media. As a result, it was eventually even adopted in ordinary language. Not surprisingly, in the process the notion of "allochthone" underwent a change of meaning and became increasingly used in ways differing substantially from its original administrative definition. It began to be widely used to pinpoint people of Turkish, Moroccan, Surinamese and Antillean origin – the largest official "ethnic minorities" - and for refugees from Africa, Asia and Latin America. It was gradually bestowed with a connotation of the "non-white non-European Other". Originally constructed as a mere descriptive statistical category by CBS, the diffusion of the term in ordinary speech acts led to a transformation into a racial-culturalist category. It was now targeted toward everyone who was supposed not to have a "western" origin. European immigrants and their offspring tended not to be included in the semantic field of the notion, in contrast to its official definition.

The pressure towards a racialising content was reflected in the statistical distinction which the CBS itself introduced in 1999 when distinguishing western allochthones and non-western allochthones.[21] This distinction is mainly used for statistical purposes in the field of education (given the established fact that non-western allochthones on average do worse than western allochthones), although it has not remained limited to that policy domain.

[20] Our translation. Second Chamber, 1999-2000, document 26815, p.5, note 2.
[21] Since 1999, statistical data on this distinction were produced, starting with data for the year 1996.

Part of the category of western allochthones according to the CBS are: "the allochthones of European origin (with the exception of Turkey), of North-American origin, of Oceanic origin, of Indonesian origin and of Japanese origin". Part of the category of non-western allochthones according to the CBS are: "people originating from Turkish, African, Latin-American and Asian immigration, except for people of Japanese and Indonesian origin". The subdivision within the generic category of allochthones has thus more than an ethnic dimension. In the words of the national statistics office CBS the Japanese and Indonesians have to be excluded from the category of non-western allochthones because of "their socio-economic and cultural position" (http://statline.cbs.nl). The classification thus links up with two ideal typical contents of the 'immigrant' in popular discourse: ethnic origin and inferior social origin (Jacobs & Rea, 2005). We can note that people of Indonesian origin are excluded from the category since a lot of (descendants of) Dutch colonizers 'returned' to Europe after the independence of Indonesia. In the definition of non-western allochthones the 'impreciseness' of the proxy of country of birth of parents was thus 'corrected' for a particular group of colonial expatriates (while at the same time introducing a new bias with regard to people of Indonesian origin without a genealogical link with white Dutch colonizers).

The third generation of foreign origin is automatically considered to be 'autochthonous' by the definition of the CBS. The category of "allochthone" hence does not function as an eternal racial category. Nevertheless, in ordinary life this limitation of the definition of "allochthone" is not as strictly respected. Interestingly, although the CBS scrupulously avoids to use the term "allochthone" to designate the third generation, the national statistical office has tried to keep track of this third generation. Indeed, since 2000 the CBS offers figures related to the "non-western third generation", in which it classifies everyone who has at least one grandparents who was born abroad in a 'non-western' country (following the earlier distinction between 'western' and 'non-western'). The data is produced in quite some detail, allowing to distinguish those who have respectively 1, 2, 3 or all 4 grandparents of non-western origin. Specific data is provided for groups of Moroccan, Turkish, Surinamese and Antillean origin. It should be noted that comparable figures are not made available for the "western third generation".

A number of problems are evident when one uses the country of birth of parents or grandparents as a proxy for foreign origin or ethnicity. How

many generations (two, three?) based on asce continue to distinguish? What rule should be with mixed origins in one or the other cate justification for making culturalist distinctions western groups? Not to mention the fact that as being "allochthones" (in the Netherlands), " even "foreigners" (in Denmark), regardless o not like this at all. One way out would be themselves as is done in the UK.

Self-Identification of Ethni

In the UK, the main criterion used w ethnicity is ethnic group, although the Office also collects data on place of birth[22] (and reli Census (and in the major household surve statistics on ethnicity are collected and repo Statistics, using Census data (from 1991 o ethnicity was first included in the Census specific areas by key government departm Deputy Prime Minister), the labour marke Pensions), health (Department of Health) Education and Skills) and criminal justice a Statistics on ethnicity are collected separat the responsibility of the Scottish Executi where they are published by the governme and Research Agency.

Unlike in most EU countries, citizensh recorded in UK Censuses. The UK does population register nor a linked system allows precise measurement of where peo censuses. The approach of using nationali not been taken in UK, since firstly, from a do not cease to be minorities once they ha

[22] There is also some information available c Though not collected by the census, data has b (for England and Wales since 1970) and by the
[23] A question on religion was present in the 20

The most recent definition of "allochthones" thus entails all people of the restricted definition, while adding all persons born in the Netherlands of whom at least one parent was not born in the Netherlands. The difference with the older enlarged definition is that it no longer includes people who were born abroad out of two parents born in the Netherlands. In the 1999 annual report regarding the minorities policy, the government stipulated it preferred to keep the children from "mixed" couples in the new definition (as opposed to the old restricted definition). The (odd) argumentation was as follows:

> "The mixed group is interesting because they seem to succeed better than the group of whom the two parents are born abroad."[20]

Following the operationalisation by the national statistics office, the category of "allochthone" was increasingly used in policy documents, academia, public debate and the media. As a result, it was eventually even adopted in ordinary language. Not surprisingly, in the process the notion of "allochthone" underwent a change of meaning and became increasingly used in ways differing substantially from its original administrative definition. It began to be widely used to pinpoint people of Turkish, Moroccan, Surinamese and Antillean origin – the largest official "ethnic minorities" - and for refugees from Africa, Asia and Latin America. It was gradually bestowed with a connotation of the "non-white non-European Other". Originally constructed as a mere descriptive statistical category by CBS, the diffusion of the term in ordinary speech acts led to a transformation into a racial-culturalist category. It was now targeted toward everyone who was supposed not to have a "western" origin. European immigrants and their offspring tended not to be included in the semantic field of the notion, in contrast to its official definition.

The pressure towards a racialising content was reflected in the statistical distinction which the CBS itself introduced in 1999 when distinguishing western allochthones and non-western allochthones.[21] This distinction is mainly used for statistical purposes in the field of education (given the established fact that non-western allochthones on average do worse than western allochthones), although it has not remained limited to that policy domain.

---

[20] Our translation. Second Chamber, 1999-2000, document 26815, p.5, note 2.

[21] Since 1999, statistical data on this distinction were produced, starting with data for the year 1996.

Part of the category of western allochthones according to the CBS are: "the allochthones of European origin (with the exception of Turkey), of North-American origin, of Oceanic origin, of Indonesian origin and of Japanese origin". Part of the category of non-western allochthones according to the CBS are: "people originating from Turkish, African, Latin-American and Asian immigration, except for people of Japanese and Indonesian origin". The subdivision within the generic category of allochthones has thus more than an ethnic dimension. In the words of the national statistics office CBS the Japanese and Indonesians have to be excluded from the category of non-western allochthones because of "their socio-economic and cultural position" (http://statline.cbs.nl). The classification thus links up with two ideal typical contents of the 'immigrant' in popular discourse: ethnic origin and inferior social origin (Jacobs & Rea, 2005). We can note that people of Indonesian origin are excluded from the category since a lot of (descendants of) Dutch colonizers 'returned' to Europe after the independence of Indonesia. In the definition of non-western allochthones the 'impreciseness' of the proxy of country of birth of parents was thus 'corrected' for a particular group of colonial expatriates (while at the same time introducing a new bias with regard to people of Indonesian origin without a genealogical link with white Dutch colonizers).

The third generation of foreign origin is automatically considered to be 'autochthonous' by the definition of the CBS. The category of "allochthone" hence does not function as an eternal racial category. Nevertheless, in ordinary life this limitation of the definition of "allochthone" is not as strictly respected. Interestingly, although the CBS scrupulously avoids to use the term "allochthone" to designate the third generation, the national statistical office has tried to keep track of this third generation. Indeed, since 2000 the CBS offers figures related to the "non-western third generation", in which it classifies everyone who has at least one grandparents who was born abroad in a 'non-western' country (following the earlier distinction between 'western' and 'non-western'). The data is produced in quite some detail, allowing to distinguish those who have respectively 1, 2, 3 or all 4 grandparents of non-western origin. Specific data is provided for groups of Moroccan, Turkish, Surinamese and Antillean origin. It should be noted that comparable figures are not made available for the "western third generation".

A number of problems are evident when one uses the country of birth of parents or grandparents as a proxy for foreign origin or ethnicity. How many generations (two, three?) based on ascendance can and should one continue to distinguish? What rule should be applied to classify people with mixed origins in one or the other category? What is the precise justification for making culturalist distinctions between western and non-western groups? Not to mention the fact that quite some people classified as being "allochthones" (in the Netherlands), "immigrants" (in Norway) or even "foreigners" (in Denmark), regardless of their citizenship status, do not like this at all. One way out would be to allow people to classify themselves as is done in the UK.

Self-Identification of Ethnicity in the UK

In the UK, the main criterion used when producing statistics on ethnicity is ethnic group, although the Office of National Statistics (ONS) also collects data on place of birth[22] (and religion[23]) through the 10-yearly Census (and in the major household surveys). For England and Wales, statistics on ethnicity are collected and reported by the Office of National Statistics, using Census data (from 1991 onwards, when a question on ethnicity was first included in the Census), and also on the following specific areas by key government departments: housing (Office of the Deputy Prime Minister), the labour market (Department for Work and Pensions), health (Department of Health), education (Department for Education and Skills) and criminal justice and citizenship (Home Office). Statistics on ethnicity are collected separately for Scotland, where this is the responsibility of the Scottish Executive, and for Northern Ireland, where they are published by the governmental Northern Ireland Statistics and Research Agency.

Unlike in most EU countries, citizenship and nationality data are not recorded in UK Censuses. The UK does furthermore not have a single population register nor a linked system of administrative sources that allows precise measurement of where people are in the country between censuses. The approach of using nationality as the principal criterion has not been taken in UK, since firstly, from a UK-policy perspective migrants do not cease to be minorities once they have taken British citizenship, and

[22] There is also some information available on the place of birth of the parents. Though not collected by the census, data has been collected via the British Register (for England and Wales since 1970) and by the General Household Survey.
[23] A question on religion was present in the 2001 Census.

secondly, the nationality laws associated with Britain's former colonies are deemed too complex for nationality to be a useful variable on its own.
The Census question on ethnic group records each person's perceived ethnic group and cultural background. The wording of the 2001 England and Wales Census question[24] on ethnic group was the following:

> *Ethnic Group.* 'What is your ethnic group? Chose ONE section from A to E, then tick the appropriate box to indicate your cultural background.
>
> *A White.* Tick box options of: British; Irish or Any other White background (please write in).
>
> *B Mixed.* Tick box options of: White and Black Caribbean; White and Black African; White and Asian or any other Mixed background (please write in).
>
> *C Asian or Asian British.* Tick box options of: Indian; Pakistani; Bangladeshi; Any other Asian background (please write in).
>
> *D Black or Black British.* Tick box options of: Caribbean; African; Any other Black background (please write in).
>
> *E Chinese or other ethnic group.* Tick box options of: Chinese; Any other (please write in).

The ethnic classification question is in other words a self-classification system but one in which one has to choose among pre-established categories. Of course, these pre-established categories -just as the wording of the question- can provoke criticism. Tellingly, the ethnic classification question for Scotland was under review by the Scottish Executive in 2005, since there was concern about the categories that were used in the 1991 and 2001 Censuses to classify the population along ethnic lines, and ministers sought to establish categories that were acceptable both to data providers and data users. Questions were piloted in 2006 and a broad consultation with stakeholders was organized. In July 2008 a new official ethnicity classification was determined and a set of recommendations were

---

[24] This question was similar to the one asked in 1991, but with changes in some categories; for example, people could tick 'mixed' for the first time. Further information on the 2001 England and Wales Census questions on ethnicity and religion is available online at:
http://www.statistics.gov.uk/census2001/profiles/commentaries/ethnicity.asp.

formulated in view of the 2011 Census (Scottish Government 2008)[25]. The new Scottish classification is as follows:

> 'What is your ethnic group? Chose ONE section from A to E, then tick ONE box which best describes your ethnic group or background.
>
> *A White.* Scottish; English; Welsh; Northern Irish; British; Irish; Gypsy/Traveller ; Polish ; Any other white ethnic group, please write in.
>
> *B Mixed or multiple ethnic groups.* Any mixed or multiple ethnic groups; please write in.
>
> *C Asian, Asian Scottish or Asian British.* Pakistani, Pakistani Scottish or Pakistani British; Indian, Indian Scottish or Indian British; Bangladeshi, Bangladeshi Scottish or Bangladeshi British; Chinese, Chinese Scottish or Chinese British; Other, please write in.
>
> *D African, Caribbean or Black.* African, African Scottish or African British; Caribbean, Caribbean Scottish or Caribbean British; Black, Black Scottish or Black British; Other, please write in.
>
> *E Other ethnic group.* Arab; Other, please write in.

Without going into a detailed discussion of this new Scottish classification, let us just note that it reflects a number of concerns resulting from Scottish nationalist sensitivities and that it is made possible by the process of devolution. Indeed, the urge was felt to explicitly mention the possibility of a 'Scottish' national identity, to offer it as the first answering category for those self-identifying as 'white' and to include it as a hyphenated identity for non-white groups.

National Statistics of the UK acknowledged that collecting data on ethnicity is difficult because of the subjective, multi-faceted and changing nature of ethnic identification and the lack of consensus on what is an "ethnic group":

> "Membership of any ethnic group is something that is subjectively meaningful to the person concerned and the terminology used to describe ethnic groups has changed over time. As a result, ethnic groups, however defined and measured, will tend to evolve depending upon social and political attitudes or developments. Therefore we do not believe that basing

[25] The report can be consulted on-line: http://cci.scot.nhs.uk/Publications/2008/03/13131959/0

ethnic identification upon an objective and rigid classification of ethnic groups is practicable" (National Statistics, 2003: 7).

This might be true, but the self identification in the UK system does imply a choice between pre-established categories. These pre-established categories are piloted and pre-tested, but it does in the end boil down to a forced choice and the offered categories do still largely reflect the dominant discourse (and legislative framework) of the state. Furthermore, there is the particular difficulty of self identification for people with mixed ascendance (although the "mixed" option, which was introduced in the 2001 Census, does provide some kind of a solution to this problem).

Conclusion and Debate

Data on immigrants and ethnic minorities of different European countries are today hardly comparable. A number of countries can produce very detailed distinctions with regard to the foreign origin and composition of their population, while other countries feel the production of such data is inappropriate and dangerous. As a result, we have data on apples and pears and proper comparative social scientific work is being frustrated. If we want to do serious (quantitative) comparative work with regard to foreign origin groups across Europe, we need comparable operationalisation systems which go beyond the simple distinction between nationals and non-nationals. The latter system is biased given the important variation in nationality legislations across Europe. The Regulation on harmonised statistics proposed by the European Commission is a step forward but does not resolve the issue of identifying and quantifying second generation immigrants and longer established ethnic minority groups.

In the Netherlands and Nordic countries a formalized criterion (birth place of parents) has been introduced in the 1990s to pinpoint ethnic minority and foreign origin groups. It has proven to be a useful instrument in documenting discriminatory practices and social exclusion of ethnic groups. At the same time, however, the differentiation between western allochthones/immigrants and non-western allochthones/immigrants, has added to the process of racialisation of society. Even worse, in public discourse these statistical notions sometimes function as (dis)qualifying social categories. As a result, the categories have incited quite some resistance among those being classified against their will. One way out would be to allow people to classify themselves as is done in the UK.

From a methodological point of view there are equally problems. Country of birth of parents (or grandparents) can only function as a proxy for immigrant background and ethnicity for a limited time span, especially because people with mixed origins are difficult to classify in a coherent and sensible manner. Furthermore, there is no "objectively" fixed transition point - like being of the third or firth generation of immigrants - between being part of an ethnic minority group and no longer being part of ethnic minority group. Self identification shifts the burden of this problem to the people we want to classify. That does not entirely resolve a number of fundamental challenges. People might legitimately want to classify themselves as part of the dominant ethnic group or as part of no ethnic group at all but still be faced with discrimination (or ethnic disadvantage) if they are judged to be part of a visible minority or negatively racialised group. When we confront the ethnic self-categorisation questions with the theoretical framework on ethnic groups, we notice that these do not overlap; also opinions and behaviours of *others* are crucial in the formation of ethnic groups (Jenkins, 1994; 1997). Furthermore, objective approaches, as well as self-categorisation questions threaten to erase the necessary logical connection between categorization by others and disadvantageous treatment. A person is not discriminated because he or she *is* black, but because other people *believe* this person is black (Sabbagh en Morning 2004: 50). Therefore -for conceptual as well as for policy reasons- it might be useful to let people classify themselves in the way they belief most other people perceive them. When ethnic group membership is operationalised in this manner, it comes close to the Canadian concept of visible minorities, in which visibility (in terms of skin colour) has a central place.[26]

In the end every system of ethnic categorisation holds the risk of essentialism: it reifies ethnic groups. Furthermore, ethnic categorisations reflect (dominant) opinions about who is 'in' and who is 'out', which are embedded in a specific time and place. Scientific classifications, and their statistical formalisation, - even if informed by self classification - are not immune to this. They are equally subordinate to the societal context and power relations as other social products. We agree with Bourdieu when he writes:

> "every science which pretends to propose criteria which are in the best way anchored in reality should not forget that it does not do anything else than

---

[26] Although the concept is operationalised in a very different way by *Statistics Canada*; namely by means of a self-categorization question

> registering a particular *state* of the struggle of classification, that is to say, a particular state of material and symbolic relations of power between those who have an interest in this or that particular way of classifying and who, just as itself, call upon scientific authority to establish in reality and in reason an arbitrary division which it hopes to impose" (Bourdieu, 1980: 66).

The double hermeneutics which are inherent to social scientific activity do not allow us to imagine the constitution of scientific categories which are truly autonomous. Products of a social and political context, they are not immutable.[27] They can be redefined when the context changes or they can lose their relevance when they have been instrumentally used – for instance when being used more as means of declassification than as means of classification. Categories which want to distinguish social groups and individuals should thus be treated with prudence and large reservations.

Nevertheless, one should equally be able to name problems in order to resolve them and to identify particular groups in order to be able to study them. Simon has nicely formulated this dilemma with which researchers and policy makers are confronted:

> "(…) is it preferable to defend the invisibilisation of ethnic differences in the observational apparatus, while at the same time risking to allow hidden discriminatory practices to prosper, or should one construct categories which, by their simple existence, can potentially reinforce a stigmatising designation of particular populations?" (Simon, 1997: 9).

Social scientists (and policy makers) need analytical categories that allow to count and classify people according to their foreign origin or ethnic background in order to be able to examine their integration into mainstream society. We need reliable data to measure racial discrimination or processes of social exclusion of which visible minorities are victim. General public support to such registration is rather high: In 2006, 75% of the EU25 population said to be in favour to providing information about their ethnic origin if that could help to combat discrimination in their country (Special Eurobarometer 263, 2007: 169). However, we should be

---

[27] This can be exemplified by the various manners in which self-classification questions in the US, UK and Canada are posed. Ethnicity, race, skin colour, cultural background, ancestry and geographical areas or countries are used as operationalisations in various forms and in various combinations, across as well as within countries.

conscious (and remain vigilant) with regard to the performative effects of ethnic categorisations, especially in their statistical form. As Keith puts it:

> "empirical academic studies potentially reify minority presence through ascribed ethnicities that are monitored, counted, and measured in terms of demographic penetration of political systems, employment profiles, and attempts to promote equal opportunities. Such measurement may be pragmatically progressive and politically defensible but inevitably it highlights the 'border problems' of definitions of demographic fixity that reveal the absurdity of racial languages enshrined in politics of affirmative action and census monitoring" (Keith, 2005: 258-259).

The classification of ethnic groups in our view, however, constitutes a necessary evil in the construction of an efficient policy aiming at equal opportunities and in the struggle against racism. Furthermore, if we want to promote the quality of international comparative work on the issue, it is essential that classification systems of foreign origin and ethnic background are as similar as possible. For the time being this is not (often) the case. Researchers should bare this in mind and reflect on the consequences. Policy makers want to know whether their immigrant integration policies are effective and in a European context increasingly seek to compare the outcomes of their policy choices to those of other national models (for instance assimilationism versus multiculturalism). Academics are urged to provide answers on questions like what the best model for immigrant inclusion might look like and some colleagues (Koopmans, 2008) are trying to do so even though they have to rely on limited amounts of genuinely comparable data. Immigrant integration policy is high on the political agenda of quite a number of European Union member states. The debate on what the best immigrant inclusion policy might be, is at the political centre stage in several countries. The media and policy makers expect that academics working in the field of ethnic and migration studies help and come up with some reliable analyses on which these evaluations can be based. Even in perfect circumstances this is a risky business, but a lack of qualified comparable data to base claims on, makes things even worse.

We cannot propose a "perfect" system for classification here. We do, however, think that comparative research will profit from the availability of reliable data on country of birth of parents of the population across Europe to be able to investigate recent immigrant groups of first and second generation. Possibly, a two speed Europe could develop, in which those countries that today already have a good registration system, agree on some basic definitions so that at least these countries produce comparable data in a short time frame. Later, other countries may adjust their definitions and data collection methods. In the long term, and for those countries which have already long established ethnic minority groups, such a formalised classification system should in our opinion be combined with a self identification procedure. It is not a matter of one or the other system being better. For (comparative) research on immigrant origin groups and ethnic minority groups both strategies have their advantages and disadvantages. External classification (with proxies as country of birth of parents) is better suited for statistical comparative work on people linked to recent immigration waves. Self identification allows to (somewhat) remediate imposition effects and is better equipped to deal with "historic" ethnic minority groups, but is more difficult to organize and more difficult to compare across countries.

Works Cited

Hortensia Amaro and Ruth E. Zambrana. 2000. Criollo, Mestizo, Mulato, LatiNegro, Indigena, White or Black? The US Hispanic/Latino population and multiple responses in the 2000 Census. *American Journal of Public Health* 90(11): 1724-27.

Aspinall, Peter J. 2002. Collective terminology to describe the minority ethnic population: The persistence of confusion and ambiguity in usage. *Sociology* 36 (4): 803-16.

Balibar, Etienne. 1992. *Les Frontières de la Démocratie*. Paris: La Découverte.

Blum, Alain. 2002. Resistance to identity categorisation in France. In *Census and ethnicity: The politics of race, ethnicity and language in national censuses*, ed. David Kertzer and Dominique Arel, 121-47. Cambridge: Cambridge University Press.

Bulmer, Martin. 1996. The ethnic group question in the 1991 Census of Population. In *Ethnicity in the 1991 Census, Volume One: Demographic characteristics of the ethnic, minority populations*, ed. David Coleman and John Salt, 33-62. London: HMSO.

Cantisani, Giambattista and Valeria Greco. 2006a. Registration of acquisition of citizenship. In *Thesim: Towards harmonised European statistics on international migration*, ed. Michel Poulain, Nicolas Perrin and Ann Singleton, 167-78. Louvain: Presses Universitaires de Louvain.

Cantisani, Giambattista and Valeria Greco. 2006b. Statistics on acquisition of citizenship. In *THESIM. Towards harmonised European statistics on international migration*, ed. Michel Poulain, Nicolas Perrin and Ann Singleton, 261-270. Louvain: Presses Universitaires de Louvain.

Cantisani, Giambattista and Michel Poulain. 2006. Statistics on population with usual residence. In *THESIM. Towards harmonised European statistics on international migration*, ed. Michel Poulain, Nicolas Perrin and Ann Singleton, 181-201. Louvain: Presses Universitaires de Louvain.

Institut National de Statistique. 1986. *Loi du 4 Juillet 1962 relative à la statistique publique, modifiée par la loi du 1er Août 1985*. Brussels: Ministère des affaires économiques.

Jacobs, Dirk and Andrea Rea. 2005. Construction et importation des classements ethniques: Allochthones et immigrés aux Pays-Bas et en Belgique. *Revue Européenne des Migrations Internationales* 21(2): 35-59.

Jacobs, Dirk and Marc Swyngedouw. 2003. Territorial and non-territorial federalism: Reform of the Brussels Capital Region, 2001. *Regional and Federal Studies* 13(2): 127-39.

Jenkins, Richard. 1994. Rethinking ethnicity: Identity, categorization and power. *Ethnic and Racial Studies* 17(2): 197-223.

—. 1997. *Rethinking ethnicity: Arguments and explorations*. London: Sage.

Keith, Michael. 2005. Racialisation and the public spaces of the multicultural city. In *Racialisation: Studies in theory and practice*, ed. Karim Murji and John Solomos, 249-70. Oxford: Oxford University Press, 2005.

Kertzer, David and Dominique Arel. 2002. Censuses, identity formation and the struggle for political power. In *Census and ethnicity: The politics of race, ethnicity and language in national censuses*, ed. David Kertzer and Dominique Arel, D., 1-42. Cambridge: Cambridge University Press.

Koopmans, Ruud. 2008. *Tradeoffs between equality and difference: Immigrant integration, multiculturalism, and the welfare state in cross-national perspective.* Discussion Paper. Berlin: Wissenschaftszentrum Berlin für Sozialforschung.

Krieger, Nancy. 2000. Counting accountably: Implications of the new approaches to classifying race/ethnicity in the 2000 Census. *American Journal of Public Health* 90(11): 1687-9.

Lee, Sharon N. 1993. Racial classifications in the US Census: 1890-1990. *Ethnic and Racial Studies* 16(1): 75-94.

Lie, Einar. 2002. Numbering the nationalities: Ethnic minorities in Norwegian population censuses 1845-1930. *Ethnic and Racial Studies* 25(5): 802-22.

Minderhedennota. 1983. *Tweede Kamer, zitting 1982-1983.* 16102(21). Den Haag.

National Statistics. 2003. *Ethnic group statistics: A guide for the collection and classification of ethnic data.* London: National Statistics.

Nobles, Melissa. 2000. History counts: A comparative analysis of racial/colour categorization in US and Brazilian Censuses. *American Journal of Public Health* 90(11): 1738-45.

Perrin Nicolas. 2006. A cohort approach to acquisition of citizenship statistics. In *THESIM: Towards harmonised European statistics on international migration*, ed. Michel Poulain, Nicolas Perrin and Ann Singleton, 321-66. Louvain: Presses Universitaires de Louvain.

Riche, Martha F. 1999. Cultural and political dimensions of the US Census: Past and present. *American Behavioural Scientist* 42(6): 933-45.

Sabbagh, Daniel and Ann Morning. 2004. *Comparative Study on the collection of data to measure the extent and impact of discrimination in a selection of countries - Medis Project – Final report on The United States*. Brussels: European Commission.

Scottish Government and the General Register Office for Scotland. 2008. *Scotland's new official Ethnicity Classification. For Scottish Official Statistics and recommended for Scotland's 2011 Census.* July 2008. Edinburgh: Scottish Government.

Seltzer, William and Margo Anderson. 2001. The dark side of numbers: The role of population data systems in human rights abuses. *Social Research* 68(2): 481-513.

Simon, Patrick. 1997. La représentation statistique de l'immigration: Peut-on comptabiliser l'ethnicité? In *Old and new minorities/Anciennes et nouvelles minorités*, ed. Jean-Louis Rallu, Youssef Courbage and Victor Piché, 1-30. Paris: INED.

—. 1998. Nationalité et origine dans la statistique française. Les catégories ambiguës. *Population* 3: 541-68.

—. 2007. *"Ethnic" statistics and data protection in the Council of Europe countries: Study report.* Strasbourg: Council of Europe.

Sondik, Edward J., Jacqueline W. Lucas, Jennifer H. Madans and Sandra S. Smith. 2000. Race/ethnicity and the 2000 Census: Implications for public health. *American Journal of Public Health* 90(11): 1709-13.

Special Eurobarometer 263. 2007. *Discrimination in the European Union.* European Commission. Available online at: http://ec.europa.eu/public_opinion/archives/ebs/ebs_263_en.pdf

Spire, Alexis and Dominique Merllié. 1998. La question des origines dans les statistiques en France: Les enjeux d'une controverse. *Le Mouvement Social* 188: 119-29.

United Nations Economic Commission for Europe. 2006. *Conference of European Statisticians recommendations for the 2010 Censuses of Population and Housing.* New York & Geneva: United Nations.

Vassenden, Kaare. 2005. Statistical definitions of persons with immigrant background: New developments and international comparison. Paper presented at the Nordic Demographic Symposium, April 26, in Aalborg, Denmark.

Waters, Mary C. 2000. Immigration, intermarriage, and the challenges of measuring racial/ethnic identities. *American Journal of Public Health* 90(11): 1735-7.

Williams, David R. and James S. Jackson. 2000. Race/ethnicity and the 2000 Census: Recommendations for African Americans and other black populations in the United States. *American Journal of Public Health* 90(11): 1728-30.

CHAPTER TWELVE

TOWARDS THE END OF NATIONAL MODELS FOR THE INTEGRATION OF IMMIGRANTS IN EUROPE? BRITAIN, FRANCE AND SPAIN IN COMPARATIVE PERSPECTIVE

HUBERT PERES

The existence of national models about the integration of immigrants has long been a commonplace for many scholars although there is no general agreement on the classification itself (Schnapper 1991; Brubaker 1992; Todd 1994; Hollifield 1997; Castles and Miller 1998; Blanco 2000; Favell 2001; Bleich 2003). However, others have been sceptical about the effectiveness of such models for just as long. Indeed, these models do not seem relevant to show the effective social integration of immigrants in countries that supposedly adopt different frameworks of public policies. As Patrick Weil and John Crowley argued, as far as France and Britain are concerned, the processes (or more precisely the difficulties) of integration can be much more similar than expected. The gap between "integration in theory" and "integration in practice" can be largely accounted for by the fact that the "greater part of the process of integration takes place beyond the reach of state policy, at the levels of social and economic structure and of individual action" (Weil and Crowley 1994: 120). Even to consider "national models" as coherent and distinctive sets of public actions that could appear as "idiosyncratic general styles and approaches to making public policy" (Freeman 2006: 227) can be disappointing. The comparison between concrete policies in different European countries can lead to the conclusion that there are more similarities than differences and that policies are eventually guided by pragmatism rather by ideology (Wihtol de Wenden 1999: 121-156).

For others, whatever substance these models once had, they are now condemned by global or regional trends that constrain nation-states policy-making. From this perspective, some insist on the role of international human rights norms (Soysal 1994) while many others point to the effect of European integration. Although there has been no real common policy for immigrants' integration so far, supra-national legislation can challenge national traditions (Geddes 2002). From another point of view, the notion of national models has lost its substance, given the widespread "de facto multiculturalism" in liberal states (including the European ones) (Joppke and Morawska 2003). More recently, by observing that this "de facto multiculturalism" now co-exists with a common will among European countries to implement "illiberal civic integration policies", Christian Joppke abruptly concludes that the "notion of national models no longer makes sense, if it ever did" (Joppke 2007: 2). But, by examining the process of setting up citizenship courses and tests across Europe, Dirk Jacobs and Andrea Rea come to the opposite conclusion: "There is indeed some convergence in policy towards newcomers, but there is still sufficient divergence in integration policies (and related dominant political discourses) across nation-states to analytically distinguish national integration models." (Jacobs and Rea 2007: 281).

This debate owes much to the ambiguity of the notion. A "national model" is first of all a "model", that is to say a specific way of conceiving and implementing integration policies (as a matter of fact, it must be at the same time distinctive and coherent, and it cannot be truly distinctive if it is not coherent). Yet, meeting these conditions is hard. Coherence alone would require that, first, there be no gap between the framework and the policies and, second, all policies related to the whole process of integration have the same rationale. Yet the field of integration policies is broad (education, housing, anti-discrimination, nationality rules, religious matters, etc…), and it is easy to find contradictions between these different elements. Hans Mahning and Andreas Wimmer give a key explanation of the controversies between scholars either defending or questioning the existence of national models: "the contradicting conclusions may well be explained by the different aspects of immigrant policies they examine. Whereas some analyses highlight the politics of citizenship and nationhood, others compare civil and social rights granted to migrants or antidiscrimination legislation. Because modern governments comprise relatively independent policy sectors with often divergent principles of operation (..), it is not surprising that cross-national comparisons of different domains of immigrant policy produce different results" (Mahnig and Wimmer 2000 : 179).

But when discussing "national models", one must also focus on the "national" dimension. First, we could point to some kind of connection between the dominant conceptions of national identity and the framework of integration policies. That is what Rogers Brubaker meant when he wrote that the politics of citizenship in France and Germany (a founding element of the philosophies of integration in both countries) was "a politics of identity, not a politics of interest". The central question, he claims, is not "who gets what?" but rather "who is what?" (Brubaker 1997: 275). Then, the formation of national political communities (as long as they are democratic) implies the constitution of "spheres of dialogue and negotiation" (Schnapper 2002: 11) where the actors interplay in the political debate by using common concepts and historical references, setting a particular political agenda, in order to convince, mobilize and fight by peaceful means. In that sense, a "national" model of integration is also a common frame of reference for actors who share the same feeling of belonging to a single political community. Even if there are different interpretations, this common frame allows actors to agree on the terms of the debate. The representation of how to deal with immigrants (and their descendants) and how they can, or not, and in what way, become part of the national community, has become a relevant issue in many national public debates. That is another reason why national integration models are not mere tools for scientific discussion. They are elaborated, discussed, distorted, by political actors. What is generally the focus of public attention is not the set of policies as a whole, but the specificity of the framework that defines both the terms of the debate in politics and builds the "normative judgments about effective and acceptable policies" (Bleich 2003: 29).

In short, in the discussion about the persistence of national integration models, we must distinguish between the specificity of the frames, the range of policies involved, and the "national" feature. In this paper, I will insist, on the one hand, on the changing frameworks of ideas about integration (in other words, the policy paradigms (Hall 1993)) and, on the other hand, on their "national feature" with the dual meaning discussed above. In this perspective, does the convergence of paradigms of integration policies in Europe mean that they are less connected with the idiosyncratic nature of national identities and politics? In this study, I will focus on the cases of Britain, France and Spain. First, I will briefly review the different national models in these countries. Then I will outline the following paradox: there is both a convergence of paradigms and a resilience of national idiosyncrasies and identities, a phenomenon which seems to limit the consequences of rhetorical changes on policies and demands.

A Brief Review of Integration Models in France, Britain and Spain

Much has been written about the French and the British models which are generally considered as two prominent opposite models and much comparative research on these countries has been carried out. (Weil and Crowley 1994; Favell 2001; Bleich 2003; Geddes and Guiraudon 2004; Garbaye 2005). Yet it is necessary to clarify a few points about these two cases as well as explain why the Spanish case must also be taken into consideration.

Ambiguities of the "French Republican Model"

France has a special status in the classifications of "national models": it might be the only case in which the political elites largely see themselves as they are seen by both French and non-French academics. For nearly twenty five years, there has been a common view on a so-called "French Republican Model of Integration". Adrian Favell has perfectly described the main components of this "republican" model and underlined that it only appeared as a consistent framework in the late 1980s (Favell 2001). However, it is necessary to emphasize that there are two interpretations of this model in the present literature. In France, the model is generally described as the transformation from "immigrants into citizens" (Costa-Lascoux 1989), that is to say the political integration of individuals who obtain the same legal rights as any other French citizen without any consideration of colour, origin, culture or religion. These peculiarities are supposed to belong to the "private sphere" and play no role in the "public sphere". Outside France, it is common to consider that the "French Republican model" combines this opening to "colour-blind" citizenship with the obligation for immigrants "to adopt the national culture" (Castles and Miller 1998: 43). From this standpoint, the French model is not only "republican" but "assimilationist", in the sense that there is "no room for cultural diversity or for the formation of ethnic communities" (Castles 2000: 138). These interpretations are debatable.

The idea of a separation between a private sphere, where specificities of any kind may flourish, and a public sphere, where we only know abstract citizens, very popular among French political actors and intellectuals, is a source of misunderstandings. In itself, this idea is vague and confusing because no one in France is able to define precisely where the public sphere begins and the private sphere ends. When a Catholic mass is said for the state funeral of an ex-president, are we in the public or the private sphere? When public authorities attend the annual meeting of a Jewish community body or a leading Muslim association, are we in the public or the private sphere? When the state-owned television company broadcasts religious programmes every Sunday morning, is it a public or a private matter? We could find a lot of similar examples. To understand what is really at stake in the theory of the "two spheres", we must consider what is usually deemed as a violation of the principle of "indifference to differences" in the public sphere: other sources of differentiation than strictly social, economic or territorial, are neither relevant (1) to inform public authorities and conceive public policies nor (2) should not be used by collective actors as means to legitimize their claims. Consequently, any apparently "private" matter (as for example wearing a headscarf or a court decision on a divorce case) can be considered as a transgression of the "republican model" if it is politicized as a contradiction of the principle (1) and claims from the civil society must be not presented as motivated by specific requirements other than social, economic or territorial to comply with the principle (2). The 2000 "parity reform" (Baudino 2003) which established gender quotas to improve women's representation in elected assemblies clearly illustrates this point. To make this claim conform with "republican universalism", the leaders of collective action argued successfully that "women are not a category" because gender is a "universal difference" affecting all human groups (Bereni and Lépinard 2004).

Eminent scholars have concluded that this "indifference to differences" is above all rhetorical, especially if one considers the national and local levels of public action (Schain 1999; Safran 2004). In fact, French integration public policies have taken into account the cultural diversity of immigrants for a very long time; and more generally, in a large number of areas, public action has adjusted, at different levels and according to varied procedures, to the differentiation of the population as a consequence of immigration. But, this mode of intervention has long co-existed with the regular restatement of the dogma of "republican integration", because it is at the same time sectional, local and not admitted as such. Sectional, insofar as these trends can influence at various levels housing, education or cultural policies without appearing in the public debate as a coherent set of ideas. Local, insofar as, on the one hand, these sectional interventions often only affect some parts of the national territory and, on the other hand, are carried out under the immediate responsibility of infra-governmental authorities. Not admitted as such, because one can generalize Gwénaële Calvès's assessment of urban development policies: "Although officially refusing to take into account the origins of individuals, the French policies of territorial positive discrimination –that is a secret for no one- allow members of groups which, in other countries, would be labelled as ethnic or racial groups, to be reached –but without naming them explicitly or, above all, exclusively." (Calvès 2004 : 113). The rhetorical aspect of the French "republican model", sometimes hiding the reality or the complexity of public action, should be understood less as a weakness of the model than as a central part of it, in accordance with a political culture that highly values ideological discourses and abstract ideas.

On the other side, the word "assimilation" which is used by many foreign observers of the French case is also ambiguous. First, because it introduces a confusion between a sociological process and a political project. From a sociological perspective, if the word assimilation is used to describe the progressive decline of cultural and ethnic differences in a host country (Alba and Nee 1999: 137-160), it points accurately to one central feature of the long social history of immigration in France (Noiriel 1988; Tribalat 1995; Tribalat, Simon et al. 1996) but it doesn't really distinguish France from other old immigration countries such as the United States. Nevertheless, it would be hard to prove that French society has become more homogeneous than others. In terms of variety of religions, clothing, cooking, music, arts, popular idioms, etc.., France is no less multicultural than others, and its presumed "national culture" is actually a very composite one with a great deal of cultural diversity which is largely the consequence of successive waves of immigration.

If describing the French model as "assimilationist" only implies that the traditional and explicit "philosophy of integration" (in Favell's terms) requires the immigrants and their descendants to give up their cultural roots, it doesn't fit either. In public discourses, "assimilation" has for a long time become a 'taboo' word epitomizing the quest for an ethnic conception of national identity, in opposition to the republican conception (Lochak 2006). In one of his earliest reports, the "Haut Conseil à l'Intégration", officially in charge of the formulation of the framework of integration policies since its creation in December 1989, considered that the integration process implied that the persistence of cultural specificities is accepted even if we emphasize the "similarities and convergences in equal rights and duties with a view to maintaining the cohesion of our social fabric" (Haut conseil à l'intégration 1993: 8). More recently, the same public body underlined that "it seems necessary to distinguish integration from assimilation" because "the notion of assimilation is a form a cultural violence" (Haut conseil à l'intégration 2006: 24).

One could argue that this quasi-official rejection of an assimilation goal for integration policies is immediately denied in practice, but, again, it is not easy to find serious evidence of such deception. Of course, immigrants have always been required to use French in public services and to send their children to French-speaking schools. But this is not dissimilar from what happens in many other western immigration countries. A thorough study of languages used at school in five European countries found very few differences between France and Britain that both insist that immigrants should learn the national language (Vermeulen 1997). Trica Danielle Keaton has recently argued that a "common culture" is imposed by French schools to the second or third generation of immigrants by the means of teaching a vision of history that ignores some critical periods (such as colonization) and offering a narrow range of French literature. But she acknowledges that "clearly France is not alone in this construction of history. The treatment of Reconstruction and the Vietnam War in textbooks in the United States are obvious examples" (Keaton 2006: 126). It is obvious that French textbooks do not abide by multiculturalist standards, but if "assimilationist" only meant that schools do not promote multiculturalist versions of national history and cultures, many countries, including Britain, should be considered as "assimilationist". This could justify the fact that Stephen Castles and Mark Miller put France and Britain in the same "assimilationist" category (Castles and Miller 1998: 245-248).

A British Model Not So Easy to Identify

Unlike Castles and Miller, most observers now distinguish France and Britain on the basis of their attitude towards cultural diversity and consider them as opposite cases rather than as belonging to the same category. As Bhikhu Parekh puts it, if France and Britain are both multicultural societies, only Britain is "multiculturalist" while France is characterized by its "monoculturalist" response (Parekh 2000: 1-11). But the case is more complex that it seems.

The characterization of the British model is much less consensual than the French one. In the British case, there "have been no policy reflections as centrally powerful" as in France "and certainly no comparably influential public intellectuals" (Favell 2001: 96). Therefore, there is no label as widely accepted and reiterated as the French "republican model". Adrian Favell uses the expression "Multicultural Race Relations" in order to define the British philosophy of integration he compares with the French republican philosophy (Favell 2001: 94-149). But this compound formulation, which adds a "multiculturalist" definition to the ancient "race relations" framework, is not widely used. Some prominent scholars hardly ever use the world "multiculturalism" in their books on immigration and integration policies in the UK (see (Hansen 2000; Solomos 2003). Many academic works as well as official documents merely mention the centrality of the "race relations policy" developed since the 1960s, which was designed as a set of measures against discriminations and resulted in a series of legal texts, the Race Relations Acts, officially aiming to tackle the negative effects of the so-called "racial" differences and to promote equal opportunities. The very fact of using such a framework, inspired by the American experience, contrasts with the "French aversion to race consciousness" (Bleich 2003: 181). This race relations policy collides with the requisites of the French model that does not recognize racial differences as relevant to public policies, and leads to ethnic and racial classifications, included in the British official census (since 1991), that French political actors and experts would be very reluctant to adopt because of philosophical and historical (memory of the Vichy period) reasons.

The more recent but now very popular "multiculturalist" presentation of the British model is also much more evasive than the "race relations" approach and has never been clearly formulated as a comprehensive framework at the state level. In his famous and often-quoted speech in 1966, the then Home Secretary Roy Jenkins, defined integration, not as an assimilation process, but as the combination of the respect of cultural diversity, equality of opportunities and mutual tolerance[1], but the word "multiculturalism" was of course not used. In 1985, the first chapter of the

---

[1] " ..I define integration (…) not as a flattening process of uniformity, but cultural diversity, coupled with equality of opportunity in an atmosphere of mutual tolerance" (Roy Jenkins, Speech on 23 May 1966 to the National Committee for Commonwealth Immigrants)

"Swann Report" presented a conception of a multicultural society where ethnic minority groups must be assisted in maintaining their specific identities (Swann, Great Britain. Department of Education and Science. et al. 1985: 3-8), but the report only dealt with education and was never consensually approved. It has been argued that the concept of "multiculturalism" has above all justified the promotion of ethnic cultures by local government, mainly in councils run by left-wing Labour politicians in their conflict with the Thatcher governments (Joppke 1999, (Hewitt 2005). Local politics, with the help of institutional factors (electoral system) encourages the claims and the political representation of ethnic minorities activists with the commitment to foster cultural differences (Vertovec 1996; Garbaye 2005). But many of these initiatives led to violent criticisms from the conservative press for lacking any "common sense" (Hewitt 2005: 32). Even in the eyes of traditional anti-racist activists, the "efflorescence of race relations programmes at local levels (…) reflects not a genuine multiculturalism" but a "trend towards different and separate provision" (Rex 1997: 211) that does not comply with egalitarian principles.

The main reason for the shift of focus from "race relations" to "multiculturalism" is the emergence of the "Muslim" question triggered by the Rushdie affair. Muslim political activists and supporters criticized the anti-racist framework and legislation for ignoring religious diversity and failing to protect Muslim identity. According to them, religion is the base of culture, not race. Eventually, the influential "Parekh Report" provided a kind of synthesis between the two conceptions with the idea of "racism*s*", meaning "hostility which uses skin colour and physical appearance as markers of supposed difference does not represent the whole picture. There is also hostility using markers connected with culture, language and religion." (Parekh and Runnymede Trust. Commission on the Future of Multi-Ethnic Britain. 2000: 59). In order to fight these racisms it is important to define Britain not only in terms of "racial divisions" but of cultural pluralism. The decisive move towards philosophical multiculturalism is achieved when the authors consider that, along with popular prejudices and stereotypes, the "lack of recognition" of the "cultural identity of some groups" is "damaging to people's self-esteem" (ibid.: 48). As a consequence, Britain must be "understood as a community of communities and a community of citizens, not a place of oppressive uniformity based on a single substantive culture." (ibid.: 56).

The "Parekh report", followed by further theoretical developments by its main author (Parekh 2000), can be seen as the most coherent attempt to define "British multiculturalism". But it has never been as overwhelmingly adopted by British political and intellectual elites as the "Republican model" was in France. Tony Blair was able to declare: "I never know, although I use the term myself occasionally, quite what people mean when they talk about multiculturalism." (Blair 2005). In France, no senior political figure could say that he doesn't know what the expression "republican integration" means! The uncertainty about the meaning of "multiculturalism" and its importance in the British public debate on integration plays the same kind of role as the flexibility of the notion of the "separation of the public and private sphere" in France. It provides space for political debate and dissent within the same loose framework. But we must keep in mind that this vagueness is much more prevalent in the British case than in the French one.

Spain: Looking for a Model

Unlike Britain and France, Spain does not appear in academic classifications. The explanation is simple: Spain is a very recent host country, it has shifted very quickly from an emigration country to an immigration country. The figures are impressive. Among many indicators, we could point to the percentage of foreigners, as part of the whole population, who have registered in municipal census (that include a large number of irregular immigrants), that has risen from 1.6% in 1998 to 11.3% in 2008[2]. Immigration flows have begun to be significant only a few years after Franco's death (1975) and the setting up of a democratic system. Since the late 1990s, Spain has become the favourite destination of immigrants from South America and North Africa. Nowadays, Spain is the European country with the highest influx of immigrants and immigration is a major topic in the public debate and one of the main concerns of citizens, as measured by opinion polls.

One of the logical consequences of such a sudden upsurge in immigrants' flows is the initial absence of any "national model" of integration. Spanish authorities, political and academic circles have had to build their own conception and set of policies without any tradition to preserve or to modify. Most of these recent immigrants are legally

---

[2] Figures from the Instituto Nacional de Estadística (Institute of National Statistics).

considered as “foreigners”, and their integration has been considered mainly as a socio-economic problem (employment, housing, their children’s education. In government documents and academic works, the word “integration” has most of the time been combined with the adjective “social”. In the 1990s, the main obstacle to “social integration” was defined in terms of social exclusion and of xenophobic hostility against immigrants from Africa (mostly Morocco). The prevailing image of the immigrant, presented by public figures and organizations in charge of immigration problems, was that of a “victim” of intolerance on the part of local people. Social sciences have taken an active part in the construction of this image, along with support groups for immigrants, by carrying out an increasing number of surveys meant to assess the expression and intensity of racism and xenophobia as well as their evolution in Spanish society (Cea D'Ancona 2004).

In their quest for a comprehensive framework of integration, some scholars explicitly refer to the French and British models as two opposite poles between which Spain has to find its own place. Progressively, integration has come to be mainly defined as a “two way process” which means a “dynamic process of mutual adaptation (Gobierno Vasco 2004: 63) between immigrants and native Spaniards. The cultural dimension of this process requires “interculturality”, which has become a recurrent theme in academic literature (Birsl, Solé et al. 2004) as well as in the numerous official plans for the integration of immigrants which are produced both by central government, Autonomous Communities and local government (at municipal and provincial levels). The notion of “interculturality” is widely used to draw attention on the acknowledgement and respect of differences while encouraging communication between people from different cultural backgrounds so that they can interact and share essential common values. In these plans, public authorities aim, on the one hand, to promote economic and social equality and, on the other hand, encourage better understanding of cultural and religious differences by native people –differences that academic circles have no problem to label as “ethnic”. The educational system, which has been particularly disturbed by the massive arrival of immigrants’ children, is a sector where the paradigm of interculturality can be most effectively brought into play thanks to many initiatives aiming at developing “intercultural mediation” as a means to resolve conflicts, and “intercultural education” as a means to foster mutual understanding and acceptance between native people and immigrants’ children (Checa, Soriano et al. 1999).

Paradigmatic Convergences

In the last few years, the integration paradigms in France and the UK have converged and are now closer to the EU common views on integration that have been explicitly adopted in Spain.

From Universality to "Diversity"

In December 2004 France established an equal opportunities and anti-discrimination commission, the *Halde* (Haute Autorité de Lutte contre les Discriminations et pour l'Égalité) as an independent statutory authority. It is competent to deal with all forms of discrimination, whether direct or indirect, prohibited by law or by an international agreement signed by France. In the speech he delivered when he officially launched the commission on 23 June 2005, the French President of the Republic, Jacques Chirac, used the word 'diversity' eleven times and presented the duty "to encourage diversity, which enriches our nation" as one of the major components not only of "the refoundation of integration policies" but also of public action against all forms of discrimination. Neither this emphasis nor its context were fortuitous. As early as 2004, the perspective of diversity and the focus on the fight against discriminations were already part of the presentation of this "refoundation" by the High Council for Integration (Haut conseil à l'intégration 2004). In the last few years, this new representation that we could call the "paradigm of diversity" has taken a major place in the public sphere. There have been numerous references to "diversity", most of the time qualified, without much concern for notional accurateness, by the adjective "cultural", in official reports, political speeches, literature of French think tanks such as the *Institut Montaigne,* or among senior researchers, largely responsible for producing and legitimizing norms on such matters.

This description of French society as a "diverse society", supposed to inform public action, is closely linked, in most of these interventions, to the imperative task of fighting against discriminations whose identification, as well as the way to tackle them, has become a major issue in public debates and on the political agenda since the late 1990s (Bleich 2003). But, what has really appeared in the last few years, is a combination of the discourse on diversity and of anti-discrimination policies that tends to shift these policies away from the traditional framework of the relationship between the Republic and (its) foreigners which was still emphasized in the 1999 Belorgey report dedicated to the fight against discrimination. The report claimed that the word “discrimination” was a means “to characterize all, or part of, the difficulties in the relationships between foreigners and French economic agents, public services and people” (Belorgey 1999: 12). This strict definition now tends to loosen. Under this new “paradigm of diversity”, the specific way immigration is dealt with disappears behind the more general problem raised by the challenges of pluralism in a society in which immigrants and their descendants have become a component among others. The status of “immigrant” as such has become less important than the much more long-term, even permanent, features due to physical types. Senior public figures now acknowledge the existence of a “visible immigration” (Begag 2004), even “visible minorities” (Bébéar 2004) in a French society that is no longer only composed of individuals undifferentiated within a universalistic Republic. The emphasis put on the discriminations affecting people who are the target of stigmatization means that it is possible to make a link between “overseas French people” and immigrants or their descendants, as the latter share with the former physical traits which can handicap them socially.

As soon as individuals affected by discrimination are identified by characteristics which they share with only a few others in the national community, the very dogma of a public space “indifferent to differences” is put into question. It is acknowledged, at least implicitly, that the transformation of “ immigrant into citizen”, which epitomizes the traditional journey into the so-called “republican” integration, does not in itself ensure the egalitarian coexistence of individuals who bear differences, whether they have come to terms with them or have been forced to accept them. Logically, the controversy about the granting of the French nationality, a volatile issue in the 1980s, has now almost disappeared from public debates insofar as the criterion of nationality is no longer relevant to determine who can be a victim of discrimination. It is indeed because one acknowledges that French people might experience differences in the way they are treated socially that the actual differences between French people now prevail over the limits fixed by legal status. As a consequence, the identification of individuals by collective standards has not only become legitimate but also indispensable to inform anti-discrimination public policies. While, in the early 1990s, the efforts of some social scientists to conceive categories which would go beyond the difference between French and foreigners” used to lead to extremely hostile reactions, there is now an increasing number of surveys and reports which take into account the “origin” of immigrants as a research variable, particularly thanks to studies ordered by central government (Peres 2004; Wihtol de Wenden and Bertossi 2005). And the objective of reflecting the diversity of the population "has been taken up in the last few years by political parties, television channels, large corporations, and higher education establishments" (Calvès 2005: 165). Here are a few examples: in 2004 an official report on "Diversity in the public service", pointed to the weak representation of French people of immigrant origin in public services; in 2005 the High Council for Integration published the report "Cultural diversity and common culture in audiovisual communication" stressing how "cultural" diversity (in fact, physical diversity) did not appear on French television; in 2006, the Higher Audiovisual Authority (Conseil Supérieur de l'Audiovisuel) was endowed by law with the new responsibility to promote social cohesion and fight discrimination in the field of audiovisual communication. In particular, it was supposed to ensure that radio and television service providers broadcast programmes that reflect the diversity of French society. Soon after, it published a report entitled "The representation of diversity of origins and cultures on the radio and television"; in January 2007 an agreement was signed between French trade unions and employers about "Diversity in companies" which aims to promote the diversity of recruitment[3]. Several big companies had already used the alleged diversity of their staff as an advertising argument. In April 2007, just before the presidential election, the UMP party that had won the legislative elections of 2002 and 2007, published a document on: "Diversity, an enrichment for French identity", in which it proposed to encourage the so-called "candidates of diversity" to stand for elections.

So, many important aspects of the "French model" have been shaken up by the new paradigm which seems to have seriously reduced the gap between France and Britain. One can draw a parallel between the way these ideas developed and anti-discrimination policies were implemented in Britain in the mid-1960s and the current situation in France. First, the emphasis was put on integration at a time when mainstream political parties agreed on a strict control of immigration; second, the issue of citizenship, in its legal sense, became less important than the visible differences between British citizens because "immigrants" from the former British Empire were full-fledged citizens and the discriminations resulting from these differences collided with the idea of real equality. When analyzing the present situation, one may think of John Crowley's foresight when, a few years ago, he asked the following question: "Being twenty

[3] This initiative was followed up in Germany.

years behind the United Kingdom as far as the management of migration flows are concerned, will France reproduce, with the same time lag, the British evolution in racial relations policies?" (Crowley 1992:109)

From "Multiculturalism" to "Community Cohesion"

"Following the election of the Labour government in 1997, multiculturalism (which was never defined) became a fashionable term in the UK. Cabinet members used it frequently, the Home Office commissioned reports on and organized conferences around the topic (..). By 2007, the term had almost become a dirty word." (Hansen 2007: 4). This harsh statement reveals the major shift that has occurred in the government discourse and in the political debate in the last few years. Besides, many newspapers have denounced the negative effects of multiculturalism.

In fact, change began in the early 2000s, when the riots which took place in Bradford, Oldham and Burnley in 2001 fuelled an intense debate (McGhee 2005). This led the government to reinforce anti-discrimination provision and to qualify the defence of cultural diversity with a concern for "Community Cohesion" as the title of the "Cantle Report" put it (Cantle, Community Cohesion Review Team. et al. 2001). "The independent Community Cohesion Review Team", chaired by Ted Cantle, reported at the end of 2001, some six months after the riots. Their main conclusion was that the roots of the riots were "separate lives". The word "multiculturalism" is never used in the report that insists on: "Separate educational arrangements, community and voluntary bodies, employment, places of worship, language, social and cultural networks, means that many communities operate on the basis of a series of parallel lives. These lives often do not seem to touch at any point, let alone overlap and promote any meaningful interchanges." (ibid.: 9). In order to avoid this, the report emphasizes the importance of "community cohesion", which is "about helping micro-communities to gel or mesh into an integrated whole. These divided communities would need to develop common goals and a shared vision." (ibid.: 70). The Government responded favourably to this report and produced a ministerial document ("The Denham Report") that follows the same approach: "Our central recommendation is the need to make community cohesion a central aim of Government, and to ensure that the design and delivery of all Government policy reflects this." (Great Britain. Ministerial Group on Public Order and Community Cohesion 2001: 2). These initiatives met with the approval of leading policy makers, such as Trevor Phillips, chairman of the Commission for Racial Equality, who has multiplied his condemnations of multiculturalism. Significantly, the 2004 annual report of the CRE contains a chapter entitled "from multiculturalism to integration" (Great Britain. Commission for Racial Equality. 2005: 10-15) in which the notion of "community cohesion" is vigorously promoted. Ted Cantle himself promoted "community cohesion" as a "new framework for race and diversity" (Cantle 2005).

Indeed, the notion of "community cohesion" has become a central element of the government policy framework after the London bombings of July 2005. A few months later the government set up a "Commission on Integration and Cohesion", as an independent advisory body to explore communities' relations in England and possible solutions to "bring people together". The chair of the commission, Darra Singh, declared, at the launch of the Commission's Interim Statement in February 2007: "We don't use the term multiculturalism. It's a word that in our views is struggling under the weight of the conflicting meanings placed upon it (..) It belongs in 1967 and not 2007"[4]. The Commission produced its final report 'Our Shared Future' in June 2007 which states that "focusing on diversity and difference has the potential to divide communities" (Commission on Integration and Cohesion 2007: 41). The members of the Commission argued that, in the course of their inquiry, they had heard "concern about how the multiculturalism of the past at times placed an emphasis on the different routes that brought people into local communities in the UK, rather than keeping sight of the shared concerns that matter to everyone –no matter what group they are from, no matter how they have ended up in the places they live" (ibid.: 46). This shift of emphasis has led to organizational changes in the government. On June 2007 Parmjit Dhanda was appointed Parliamentary Under Secretary of State (Department for Communities and Local Government) in charge of "community cohesion" and, consequently, is known in the media as 'cohesion minister'. The Conservatives, whose leader declared that "the doctrine of multiculturalism has undermined our nation's sense of cohesion"[5] have backed this move and now have a Shadow Minister for Community Cohesion and Social Action (Sayeeda Warsi, of Pakistani origin).

---

[4] Speech by Darra Singh Chair of the Commission on Integration and Cohesion, http://www.integrationandcohesion.org.uk/news/Speech_by_Darra_Singh_at_the_launch_of_the_Commissions_Interim_Statement.aspx).

[5] The Observer, 28 January 2007.

These attacks on multiculturalism resulted in a change in the definition of public policies priorities in three major areas considered as essential by multiculturalist activists: language, public funding of ethnic groups, schools. Following the recommendation of the final report of the Commission of Integration and Cohesion, which was to give priority to the teaching of English, the Secretary of State John Denham has recently announced that public funding for English language teaching should be targeted where it can best encourage the integration of immigrants with a long-term commitment to Britain[6]. Indeed, the chairman of the Specialist Schools and Academies Trust claims that the fact that parents do not speak English at home is the main reason for the failure of some schools[7]. Another proposal of the Commission is for funding bodies to adopt a policy of single Group Funding as the exception and not the rule (Commission on Integration and Cohesion 2007), stating that single group funding means funding "awarded on the basis of a particular identity, such as ethnic, religious or cultural" (ibid.: 160). The government has followed this recommendation as all bids for government grants from ethnic and faith groups should be tested to assess whether they will promote community cohesion. As regards the school system, the Education and Inspections Act 2006 has made the governing body of maintained schools in England responsible for the promotion of community cohesion. One of the practical aspects of this idea is to reinforce citizenship classes which became part of the school curriculum in 2002. This emphasis on citizenship in education is part of a more general trend to promote citizenship as "our common bond" (Lord Goldsmith QC and Review 2008) which has led, for instance, to organizing citizenship tests and ceremonies for applicants to British citizenship.

Another aspect of the weakening of the notion of multiculturalism, in the name of "community cohesion" and citizenship, is the creation of a new Commission on Equality and Human Rights (CEHR) that replaces the former CRE (Commission for Racial Equality) and other anti-discrimination bodies. The new commission explicitly no longer puts the emphasis on racial differences. In this sense, the "CEHR can be described as a parallel 'integration with diversity' strategy in which the dignity of difference is to be upheld through the creation of a culture of respect for

---

[6] Steve Hook, Speaking up for Esol, 11 January 2008 *Times Educational Supplement.*

[7] Julie Henry Speak English at home, schools adviser tells Muslim mothers , 14 January 2007 *The Sunday Telegraph.*

human rights that once again promotes a meta-allegiance to an ideal of British national citizenship through attempting to displace what are presented as micro-allegiances" (McGhee 2008: 107).

A case for EU homogenization?

In the Spanish case, the reference to Europe is constant. Since immigration became a priority on the political agenda, it has been obvious for most participants to the debate that Europe should be the reference, both as a representation of the nature of the problems and as a norm upon which to found public action. For instance, in the first state-wide "plan for the integration of immigrants" published in 1994, the end of the introduction reads as follows: "The government considers that the immigration policy is part of the far-reaching action programmes which must be implemented within the framework of the Treaties of the European Union and of Schengen, adjusting to our national context the recommendations and orientations of the European Commission, Parliament and Council of Europe"[8]. Thus, in the last governmental integration plan, the definition of integration as a two-way process derives explicitly from EU literature and was adopted in November 2004 by the European council as a "common basic principle"[9]. Infra-national authorities have the same approach as central government when they establish their own "integration plans". It is significant that an autonomous government such as the Basque government, having conflictual relationships with Madrid, keeps presenting itself as the blameless champion of European principles and sets its own lines of action according to standards which put the "international" and "European" frameworks at the top. In a sense, the Spanish case could exemplify the emergence of "post-national models" defined by European standards, including some aspects of older national models that converge to combine "unity with diversity", a motto cherished by European rhetoric. We will see later that it is not that simple, but, at this point of our discussion, the hypothesis of a weakening of national models under the influence of the European Union also seems to be confirmed by the French and British cases.

The convergences between the French and British paradigms occurred under the aegis of the European construction. In France, the creation of the

---

[8] Plan para la integraci□n de los inmigrantes, Ministerio de Asuntos Sociales, 1994 : 7.

[9] Plan Estratégico de Ciudadanía e Integración 2007-2010 : 26 (http://www.mtas.es/migraciones/Integracion/PlanEstrategico/Docs/160207pecitextocompleto.pdf).

High Authority against Discriminations and for Equality (Halde) was a direct consequence of EU policies as "the directive on racial equality requires a specialized organization to be appointed in each state so as to promote equality of treatment and to fight discrimination founded on racial or ethnic origin." (Commission Européenne 2004: 8). This is an example of the achievements of the emerging anti-discrimination European policy (Guiraudon 2004) that has relied on a representation of the social fabric founded on the plurality of cultures, and that goes as far as mentioning diversity in terms of ethnic and racial differentiation. EU initiatives to fight discrimination had multiplied even before the treaty of Amsterdam established EU competences in this area. These initiatives led to the two 2000 directives (2000/43/CE and 2000/78/CE) on racial equality and equality at work. Then, in 2003 an EU campaign was launched : "For diversity, against discriminations". Besides, the theme of diversity prevailed in the failed project of the Constitution for Europe, claiming that Europe should be "United in its diversity". It is hardly surprising that the French move in the direction of the British model is coherent with the EU paradigm that is influenced by multiculturalist ideas, put forward in particular by European lobbies, such as the Starting Line Group founded by British and Dutch NGOs (Chopin and Niessen 2001).

However, in the last few years, the EU paradigm has also developed along the lines of the French conception of integration based on republican values and citizenship. The "common basic principles" adopted by the European Council in November 2004 were restated en 2007. On the one hand the "Council and the Representatives of the Governments of the Member States emphasize the need to continue to strengthen the integration policies of Member States with a view to managing diverse societies, counteracting all forms of discrimination and intolerance, maintaining social cohesion and ensuring that immigrants are able to reach their full potential and are able to participate to the fullest extent possible in the social, economic, cultural and civic life of the relevant Member State". But on the other hand, as integration is considered as a "dynamic two-way process involving both immigrants and the host society" (the formulation we literally find in the Spanish public plans), long-term immigrants are required to "make a deliberate effort to integrate, in particular learning the language of their host society, and understanding the basic values of the European Union"[10].

[10] PRESS RELEASE 2807th Council meeting Justice and Home Affairs Luxembourg, 12-13 June 2007 Council conclusions, 24.

These requirements, that are traditional for the defender of the French model, are also in tune with the new British principles of "community cohesion", even if the wording is usually milder. These convergences between the EU policies and language and the paradigmatic changes in France and Britain should not yet be analyzed too quickly as the triumph of supra-national frames over old national models. The current emphasis of the EU discourse on the duties of immigrants towards host countries can, on the contrary, be considered as a consequence of changes that occurred in the national polities (Joppke 2007). In our case, just as in that of Alexander Caviedes' study on high skilled labour migration (Caviedes, "this volume"), it is not the European paradigm that is imposed on the nation states, but the convergences between the nation states that allow the formulation of an EU paradigm. This is another reason why, as Maarten P. Vink warns us, we should not overestimate "the significance of the European factor" (Vink, "this volume").

Integration paradigms, national idiosyncrasies and identities

When they discuss integration, public authorities tend to do so from a wider perspective than the mere problem of dealing with immigrants: for instance, the place of religion in society or the way the composition of the population is described. All these elements play an enduring part in the representation of the national community and can therefore limit the scope of the changes in integration paradigms.

Changes in paradigms and national interpretations

In France, when applying the EU directives on discrimination, Parliament has avoided as much as possible to adopt and legitimize "race" or "ethnicity" as categories that could inform public action. (Calvès 2002). The Halde reports reflect this persistent reluctance: "The law prohibits discrimination on the grounds of origin, gender, family marital status, physical appearance, surname, state of health, disability, genetic characteristics, lifestyle, sexual orientation, age, political opinions, religious beliefs, union activities, and real or supposed membership or non-membership of an ethnic group, nation or « race »." (HALDE 2007: 1). This list refers to a potentially unlimited range of differences. The diversity of what "diversity" means can be claimed to reduce the importance of ethnic differences. The words "ethnic" and "race" appear at the bottom of the list, between brackets. Moreover, the expression "supposed membership and non membership" put the emphasis on the fact that these categories are based on a subjective assessment of reality and are not as clear-cut and obvious as the other causes of discrimination. Generally, the successful new paradigm of diversity has been strictly constrained by the restatement of a typical French way of dealing with visible or cultural differences. One of the major limits lies in the enduring prohibition of "ethnic statistics". Traditionally, the "French gather statistics on the basis of gender, not on the basis of race. They therefore refused to accept statistics as the legal basis to prove indirect racial discrimination in the courts" (Geddes and Guiraudon 2004: 348). In a recent decision about the new law on immigration control, integration and asylum in France, the Conseil Constitutionnel invalidated part of a law voted in October 2006 which made the production and use of statistics on racial and ethnic origins possible. The decision was founded on the article 1 of the Constitution which admits no exception to the principle of nondiscrimination.

By contrast the description of Britain's objectives in the field of integration still relies on ethnic and religious categories. Here is a striking illustration. We have seen that in the formulation of the "community cohesion" paradigm, schools are supposed to play a major role in promoting this concept. Yet, the much publicized report of the independent review for the former Department for Education and Skills (DfES) stated that : "through the school curriculum, pupils should • explore the origins of the UK and how different cultures have created the United Kingdom • explore the representations of different racial, ethnic, cultural and religious groups in the UK and the world • explore the consequences of racial and religious intolerance and discrimination • develop critical literacy (understanding of how language constructs reality) which allows them to reflect on their own cultural traditions and those of others" (DfES 2007: 23). In Britain, hardly anyone is thinking of doing away with ethnic categories and ethnic monitoring while, in France, they are deemed to encourage disunity and even discrimination.

In the same way, the representation of the place of religion in the construction of "community cohesion" would be unthinkable in France. The emergence of the new paradigm occurred at the same time as the development of political support for Muslim faith schools and their integration in the state system (Flint 2007). Despite the fact that "mono-cultural" schools were identified in the "Cantle report" as a cause of the creation of segregated communities, the report considered that "as faith based Christian schools were already supported, fairness demanded that the same facility should be available to the Muslim and other communities" (Cantle, Community Cohesion Review Team. et al. 2001: 34). This contradiction between the importance of faith issues, and faith schools in particular, in public life and their potential threat to community cohesion became even stronger after the London bombings as some mosques and Islamic institutions were suspected of fuelling extremism and fostering support for terrorism. Nonetheless, in June 2007, the Commission of Integration and Cohesion recognized the "contribution of faith to integration and cohesion" and claimed it was "clearly in the interests of government to encourage faith groups (though not their proselytizing activities) and where these groups indicate that their existence is threatened by public policies, local and national, that should be taken seriously" (Billings, Holden et al. 2007: 10). In order to avoid the negative effects of mono-cultural education, the report pleaded for "interfaith" activities and an effort from the Muslim community "to produce fresh theological expressions of how one can be both British and Muslim" (ibid.: 19). As a matter of fact, a few weeks later, a joint document signed by the Government and leaders of Britain's main faith communities reasserted the importance of faith in education and society and stated that the "Government will work with local authorities (..) and with faith organizations to remove unnecessary barriers to the creation of new faith schools" (Department for children 2007, 18). Of course, such a conception of the cohesion of the community based upon particular faiths sharply contrasts with the French conviction that an integrated collectivity needs transcending religious allegiances rather than reinforcing them. This conviction has been recently reasserted in the context of the development of a fear of Islam which could be described, as Raymond Taras does in this volume, as "French islamophobia" (Taras "this volume").

Another element of continuity between the old multiculturalist model and the new "community cohesion" is the centrality of local communities and local government's responsibility for dealing with integration (Brighton 2007: 5). In general, in the expression "community cohesion", the word "community" refers to local communities. In the foreword to the final report of the Commission, Darah Singh defines clearly what is at stake : "It is at a local level that leaders can understand in detail the profile of the population, the changes that are taking place, the impact of these changes on the local economy and services. And most importantly it is only at this level where specific initiatives can be crafted and delivered to build better integration and cohesion" (Commission on Integration and

Cohesion 2007: 4). The idea that local councils are responsible for "community cohesion" is reflected by the fact that the government structure in charge of this issue is the Department for Communities and Local Government. Again, there is a great difference with the French "paradigm of diversity" that doesn't question in anyway the traditional role of the state and of law regulation as the only guarantee of social cohesion.

The limitation of change due to national idiosyncrasies about ethnic classifications, the place of religion, relations between national and local communities, allows the presentation of new paradigms not as entirely new concepts, but as a re-formulation of the old ones.

Jacques Chirac, in his speech, already quoted, for the launch of the Halde, claimed that this new institution "is rooted in the deepest of Republican values". In the introduction of the first report, the Halde chair wrote: " The influence and prosperity of our country, the happiness of its inhabitants are founded on the successful implementation of a republican model of integration that ensures stringent compliance with human rights, embraces the diversity of people and cultures, and implements true secularism." (HALDE 2006: 4) And he repeatedly insists on the same objective of "successful implementation of a republican model of integration" in the forewords to the two following reports. Major academic experts also understand the new paradigm as a reformulation of the Republican model, not as a form of protest against it. More precisely, by emphasizing the discriminations which affect people with a difference, the paradigm of diversity is supposed to help implement a republican model so far only virtually exemplary. "Each time the Republic is confronted to its diversity, it is in fact a policy of equality which is deemed as the best response. Equality has been a core Republican value since the Revolution; the principle is not itself devoid of hypocrisy and its formality sometimes conceals an ethnocentric reluctance to accept diversity, but it provides precious resources for action and helps reduce the gap between our values and our practice" (Weil 2005: 11). From the same perspective, Jacqueline Costa-Lascoux claims that France has always been characterized by its cultural diversity, and nonetheless "The Republic "one and indivisible" is on a permanent quest for the cohesion of a polymorphous society" (Costa-Lascoux 2005: 5). Far from paving the way for the recognition of a multiculturalist polity, the paradigm of diversity is much more often used in France as an alternative to multiculturalism.

The same process has happened in Britain. The institute of community cohesion indicates that the notion “can be seen as a development of the concept of multiculturalism, in which the emphasis on separateness and differences is counterbalanced by the creation of interaction and commonalities”[11] Ted Cantle himself presents the concept as a “new multiculturalism”[12]. Community cohesion is seen as the fostering of interaction between people from different origins and not a means to make people forget their differences. In a Home office handbook designed to assist people helping immigrants to integrate and immigrants taking citizenship tests, one can read that “integration is very important but does not mean complete assimilation” (Great Britain. "Life in the United Kingdom" Advisory Group, Crick et al. 2004: 14). In order to emphasize this point, reference is made to the historical formation of the UK: “Assimilation to such a degree has not, after all, happened for most people in Wales and Scotland, nor historically for Irish and Jewish immigrant communities, nor for smaller communities such as the Poles who once fled from persecution. There is no reason why loss of a distinctive identity within a wider British identity should occur to immigrants from the new Commonwealth or from elsewhere” (ibid.: 15).

One of the origins of this effort of reconsidering the new paradigms as a reformulation of the old ones is the need to respond to criticisms voiced in the public sphere. In France, some influential intellectuals have denounced the public acknowledgement of diversity and the will to implement anti-discrimination policies as “a war machine against the Republican ideal” (Slama 2004: 140-141) or as “a revenge of the principle of identity or tribal belonging” (Taguieff 2005: 271). In Britain, some political actors and academics have criticized this “New Labour’s idea of community cohesion” as “a case of blaming the victim” that encourages islamophobia (Abbas 2005: 12). More generally, the national debates on these issues is shaped by actors who can have views very different from the new prevailing policy paradigms and who start political debates which could not occur in another national context. One extreme example of this is the suggestion made by the Archbishop of Canterbury, Rowan Williams, to include parts of the Sharia law into English law. This proposal, reminiscent of active multiculturalism, is not in tune with the new paradigmatic development in Britain and would be utterly unimaginable in France. According to Virginie Guiraudon and Andrew

---

[11] http://www.coventry.ac.uk/researchnet/icoco/a/2471

[12] www.slough.gov.uk/documents/migration-TedCantle.pdf

Geddes, in "the case of anti-discrimination, member states with divergent 'philosophies of integration' agreed to a new supranational system without much resistance or soul-searching. A key factor is that at the EU policy-making level, negotiations are largely sheltered from partisan politics and public scrutiny" (Geddes and Guiraudon 2004: 351). However, it is difficult to apply this kind of paradigm at the level of the nation where frames are more resistant in the public sphere than they might be among policy makers. National models prove resistant as they are deeply rooted in the conscience of the multiple actors who can participate in the public debate. The reference to national traditions is also an important resource in the political fight that one should not overlook, which is illustrated by the short-lived notion of "the right to be different" in the discourse of the French socialist left in the early 1980s. This slogan was quickly replaced by the usual republican creed in order to curb the rise of an extreme right-wing party, the *Front National*, that used the socialist emphasis on differences to promote its own ethnic conception of the nation (Brubaker 2001).

What occurred in Spain seems to confirm this analysis. In the long-term, the Spanish consensus about immigrant's integration did not withstand electoral fights and the recurrent opposition between the nationalistic projects of the centre and of the peripheries. The racist riots of El Ejido in February 2000, and other similar events on a lesser scale, which belie the high degree of tolerance towards foreigners appearing in opinion polls, have certainly played a major part in the strategic reorientation of the Popular Party. Indeed, while the party was still in office at the time, they suddenly decided to tighten the conditions of entry and stay in Spain for foreigners and –a radical U-turn, reminded the latter of their duty to adapt to Spanish society. Almost at the same time, the tone of the public debate has changed with the publication, especially in the conservative press, of opinions, so far unheard of. Anti-Muslim academic publications have appeared which denounce the "Al-Andalus myth" (Fanjul 2000) (that is to say the Muslim contribution to the national construction) and promote a largely Catholic interpretation of Spanish history. These two evolutions, at government and society levels, went in the same direction. In the wake of the publication of a book in which he means to deny the "racist" interpretation of El Ejido events (Azurmendi 2001), Mikel Azurmendi was appointed president of the very official "Forum for the social integration of immigrants"; and he has launched violent attacks against multiculturalism, claiming that it is "a social disease".

The declarations and the personality of this anthropologist, a former militant of ETA, threatened with death by the organization for leaving and criticizing it, make a link between the questioning of the hitherto prevailing paradigm on immigrants and the debate on territorial organization and nationalistic claims. In his view, multiculturalism applied to immigrants is of the same nature as the exclusive and ethnic nationalism which prevails in the Basque country.[13] But nationalist groups have also distanced themselves from the initial image of immigration as a factor of cultural diversity which would only be threatened by racist discriminations. They did so in Catalonia where the presence of immigrants is much more important, but not in the Basque country.

Some senior public figures, among whom Jordi Pujol, President of the Generalitat (Catalonia's government) since its creation (in 1980) to 2003, have expressed their concern about the effects of multiculturality on "Catalan identity" and put the teaching of Catalan at the top of their "intercultural" priorities. We can draw a parallel between this evolution and that occurring among pro-Spanish groups: immigrants (in fact those who come from Muslim countries) are now presented as a threat to national identity in antagonistic conceptions of the nationalist project. This is taking place at a time when there is increasing tension between these groups which are involved in a conflict which questions the compromise between the State and the autonomous authorities reached during the democratic transition.

The return of Socialists to state government and their victory in Catalonia has meant the return to the "intercultural" rhetoric, which shows that the formulation of paradigms is highly dependent on political events and the tone of the political debate. Finally, during the campaign for the general elections of March 2008 the Popular Party (PP) promised to force immigrants to sign an "integration contract" and forbid girls to wear Muslim headscarves in schools if they won the election. A survey showed

---

[13] "The Basque Country is a multicultural and multiculturalist society. They not only see Spain as different but also as the enemy. They have an ancient dispute with Spain, which cannot be solved except by separation from Spain. Put in even stronger terms, you would have to scare, terrorise or kill all those Basques who defend their choice to be Spanish citizens. In the Basque Country multiculturalism exists. There is the creation of a regime that favours certain people over others" (Azurmendi, M. (2002). Is multiculturalism helping or hindering integration in Spain? . *Immigration & the Labour Market - where now for the EU? Stockholm Network Conference.* Madrid.).

that a majority of people polled supported this proposal. The PP was defeated, and the integration contract rejected by the Socialists. However, because of the high degree of decentralization in Spain, the PP is able to implement this policy in the Autonomous Communities they run. It is happening in the Community of Valencia where a law on integration including an "integration contract" is being discussed.

Moreover, all these debates about integration reactivate the political construction of national identities.

Renewed Discussions on National Identities

In Britain, the promotion of "community cohesion" has largely contributed to put the question of "Britishness" at the centre of the political debate. The reflection on British identity and the concept of Britishness had of course begun before the change of integration paradigm. One could argue that New Labour, because of the issues raised by its programme of constitutional reform (devolution to Scotland and Wales), was particularly keen to promote a "new" definition of Britishness. But the discussion about devolution has become closely linked to the "debate about multiculturalism", as Gordon Brown puts it: "the question is essentially whether our national identity is defined by race and ethnicity (…). Or whether there are values which shape our national identity and which all citizens can share –thus separating citizenship from race – and which can find explicit expression so that they become a unifying and strengthening force" (Brown and Stevenson 2006: 7). As we said earlier, in the expression "community cohesion", "community" initially referred to "the local community". Stressing the idea of Britishness could therefore lead to a definition of what the British community is as a whole and foster a sense of national belonging among ethnic minorities. Of course, in the British context, the definition of a national identity can only refer to political values that are not specific to Britain but belong to the liberal-democratic creed in general. But what Britishness means is less important than the process of focusing on a common sense of belonging. The insistence on "Britishness" as the formulation of this supposed common bond has led to the proposal to create a "national day" (Lord Goldsmith QC and Review 2008), a classic ritual in the process of construction of national identities.

In France, paradoxically, in spite of the convergence of integration paradigms, there has been a restatement of the French national identity as a reaction to the British model. The new formulation of the Republican imperative, with priority given to anti-discrimination policies, is the positive outcome of a process whose negative outcome is the criticism of "communitarianism" –presented as an anti-model, which has been increasingly popular in the last few years. Indeed, the idea of communitarianism in France is closely linked to the so called "Anglo-Saxon model" and the British situation whereas neither the expression itself nor its French meaning (that is to say the promotion of the coexistence of separate communities) are commonly used in Britain. The headlines of the French press and the reactions of senior academics, in the wake of the terrorist attacks in London, in July 2005, are revealing: they considered the attacks as the demonstration of the failure of British "communitarianism". The existence of this anti-model reinforces the French feeling of being different. Therefore, the fantasy of "communitarianism" is a form of collective defence mechanism against an interpretation of the paradigm of diversity which would pave the way to "multiculturalism" as misunderstood in France, that is to say ignoring all the subtleties and contradictions of this trend of thought. It is largely because wearing the Muslim headscarf at school was eventually perceived as an outcome of communitarianism that the call for "laïcité" gained so much support. And that is why it was so politically easy to retain only the recommendations of the Stasi commission to ban outward religious signs and ignore its recommendations on allowing different religious celebrations.

In both countries a common means to reinforce a sense of national belonging is to ignore foreign influences, including the EU dimension. In France, the new paradigm of diversity has never been justified by European commitments, but has been seen as the logical development of the traditional French model. Public figures do not mention the fact that anti-discrimination policies and the setting up of the High Authority against Discriminations comply with a European directive. Foreign experiences are generally ignored or dismissed. The report of the Stasi Commission set up to reflect upon the implementation of the "laïcité" principle and which eventually led to the law banning Islamic headscarves and other visible religious symbols in state schools, shows how one can pretend to take the European dimension into account and, at the same time, minimize its influence or even reverse the terms of the exchange. In his presentation, Bernard Stasi mentions the visits of the members of the commission to other European countries as follows: "So, delegations of the Commission went to Germany, England, Belgium, Italy and the Netherlands, which enabled us to have very interesting exchanges and to realize that our European friends were very interested in the current debate in France, and I can say, in all modesty, that they are looking forward to seeing the proposals of the Commission and the decisions made by public authorities." (Commission de réflexion sur l'application du principe de laïcité dans la République 2003: 5). So, Europe expects more from France than France can learn from Europe. Besides, there is no reference to EU policies in the report. The only norm acknowledged as a constraining one is the much more general norm set by the European Convention for Human Rights.

We can find the same kind of attitude in the UK despite the fact that British forms did influence EU legislation on discrimination. As several major studies have underlined (Joppke 1999; (Favell 2001; (Geddes and Guiraudon 2004), the influence of British conceptions on the production of EU norms has not challenged the general view, shared by organizations from ethnic minorities, that the European level is not relevant to discuss such issues. When the EU dimension, or national situations within the European context, happen to be mentioned, it is usually to argue that the British model is far superior to the continental one. Since 1999 there has been no significant evolution of the situation described by Christian Joppke: "The negative attitude toward Europe is a good indicator of successful immigrant integration in Britain. If confronted with the other EU member states' lesser tolerance for minority identities and weaker anti-discrimination provisions, even hardened race activists switch to a triumphalist reading of the British race-relations framework" (Joppke 1999: 258). The most frequent attitude on this matter in Britain is simply not to mention what happens elsewhere in Europe or in Brussels as "the normative logic of the British philosophy resolutely refuses the introduction of any higher normative authority, such as the universal perspective of international law and human rights; it is even less internationalist than the already exceeding nationalist French position" (Favell 2001: 136). In Britain, with a few exceptions[14], most of the references to the EU, or more generally to foreign experiences, remain negative when they concern migrants' rights and integration.

Apparently, the Spanish case is very different. As far as border control is concerned, governments have first tried to justify their own policies by the need to fulfil duties deriving from the country's membership to the EU

[14] For instance, the Joint Council for the Welfare of Immigrants refers to Europe to defend asylum seekers' rights (cf. The Path to Citizenship Next steps in Reforming the Immigration System A Response to the Green Paper by JCWI – May 2008).

–duties which turn Spain into "Europe's sentinel" (Peres 1999). It is no longer the case today as, since the end of the 1990s, the need to curb migration flows has been accepted as a course of action by mainstream political forces. However, the European reference remains explicit when it comes to integration issues. But it would be wrong to jump to the conclusion that this omnipresent EU allegiance heralds the disappearance of a national identification. The Spanish relationship with Europe is much more ambivalent that what it seems at first sight. Generally, the way participants to the public debate project themselves in a European normative and philosophical space is in fact consubstantial with the emergence of post-Franquist Spanish democracy and is a fundamental element of the reconstruction of a distinctive political community. Even before Spain actually joined the European Community, belonging to Europe was deemed a fundamental dimension of the democratization process by all the main actors of the democratic transition. They recurrently referred to the prevailing European conceptions and values put forward by European institutions to justify their actions, set long-term political objectives and, finally, legitimize the persistence of the state structure common to both the proponents and the opponents of the former regime. The European dimension was established as the key element of a "national story" legitimizing not the dissolution but, on the contrary, the continuation of the State, although the type of political order which had been disqualified by Franquism was dismissed. European pledges made it easier to break away radically from the major tenets of Franquist ideology (the "exceptional destiny" of "eternal" Spain, concentration of authority, national-Catholicism) and to replace them by ideals understood as part of the democratic normality (doing away with national selfishness, pluralism and human rights, religious and ideological tolerance).

To cut a long story short, the reference to Europe has been used to rebuild a common Spanish identity which had been upset by the memories of the civil war and Franquist repression. And the European ideal of going beyond national peculiarities and the concrete process of the political weakening of States could, and still can, justify both the aims of the critics of "peripheral nationalisms" and the aims of those who attempted, in the name of these claims, to gain power over the Spanish state. Nothing is more revealing of this strategic use of the European idea for nationalist objectives than, on the one hand, the attempt of the Popular Party to stop the intended reform of the 1978 Constitution in 2002 by defending a conception of national identity founded on Habermas' theme of "constitutional patriotism" and, on the other hand, the strong European pledges of the Catalan and Basque governments controlled by supposedly moderate nationalist parties. Paradoxically, the idea of Europeanisation upon which the consensus about immigration is founded is but an illustration, among others, of a process of national definition –original but nonetheless constrained by the very specific context of Spanish democratization; it is in fact a definition of a political community which, thanks to its European belonging, could minimize, for a while, the effects of diverging views on the foundations of Spanish identity (a multinational state, a "nation of nations", a decentralized nation, etc...). The breach of consensus over the representation of the place of immigrants does not fundamentally put into question the general allegiance to the European paradigm. The different interpretations of this paradigm, made according to ideological vested interests, only put this allegiance into perspective. This process occurred because immigration has become a common political issue: a *Spanish* issue, to be understood in the context of the transformation of a particular democratic system characterized by identity conflicts.

Conclusion

In the debate about the end of national models, the study of these three cases tends to support the arguments of those who are sceptical about the scope of paradigmatic convergences. This conclusion echoes the predictions about citizenship, a major component of integration policies, stated here by Jeannette Money: "there will be continued variation in citizenship policy across Europe" (Money "this volume"). Our views are also consistent with a recent study on the German case. In Germany, "elite and media discourse are critically shaped by accepting the need to change basic provisions of national citizenship and basic provisions to downplay the categorically divisive character of national boundaries. Yet at the same time, and in stark contrast to the rational debate on the desirability of giving up sovereignty and changing patterns of immigration or naturalization, there remains a strong discourse on ethnic-cultural difference. (..) Although notions of national or even racial superiority are virtually non-existent, dominant ways of framing the relationship between German society and its immigrants are significantly shaped by narratives of national exclusiveness." (Schmidtke 2007: 104-107). As many scholars have pointed out, frames are flexible. This flexibility allows for change and convergence between integration models. France, Britain and, to a lesser extent but in a subtle way, Spain, have experienced significant changes in their own approaches to integration. But this flexibility has also allowed them to renew national interpretations of the place of immigrants in society in relation to specific representations of national identity.

A critical test of the balance between the effects of paradigmatic convergences and the resilience of national idiosyncrasies and identities can be the found in the form taken by claims-making and participation of immigrants' associations in the public sphere. Thorough comparative studies including France and Britain have shown that there are significant differences between these forms of participation in different national contexts. Even if we cannot eliminate the hypothesis that the diversified origins of immigrants in the different European host countries play a part, immigrants' claims and collective mobilization are very likely to be shaped by national features. "Since France invites migrants into the political community on the basis of equality, but to the exclusion of cultural difference, it could follow that migrant claims for multicultural rights are not nearly as important in this country as in Britain" (Koopmans and Statham 1999: 692). According to Tariq Modood, Muslim mobilization in Britain owes much more to British multiculturalism than to Islamic identity (Modood 2005, p. ix). Following the same path, Bhikhu Parekh argues that the activism of Muslim groups about the Rushdie affair can be explained by the peculiar opportunities offered to them by the British political culture and institutions that put restrictions on free speech on religious grounds (Parekh 2000: 312).

It will be interesting to see what happens to these differences in the future. For example, will the recognition of diversity in France eventually lead to ethnic mobilization along the British lines? The creation of a black movement, the CRAN (Conseil Représentatif des Associations Noires de France) in 2006 seems to confirm this possibility. But both the difficulty of the movement to rally people under the label "black" and its rhetorical emphasis on the defence of Republican values indicate that this hypothesis remains fragile.

Works Cited

Abbas, Tahir. 2005. British South Asian Muslims: Before and after September 11. In *Muslim Britain: Communities under pressure*, ed. Tahir Abbas, 3-17. London: Zed Books.

Alba, Richard and Victor Nee. 1999. Rethinking assimilation theory for a new era of immigration. In *The handbook of international migration:*

The American experience, ed. Hirschman, Charles, Philip Kasinitz and Joshua DeWind. 137-60. New York: Russell Sage Foundation.

Azurmendi, Mikel. 2001. *Estampas de el Ejido: Un reportaje sobre la integración del inmigrante*. Madrid: Taurus.

—. 2002. Is multiculturalism helping or hindering integration in Spain? Paper presented at the Stockholm Network conference, Immigration and the labour market: Where now for the EU?, in Madrid.

Baudino, Claudie. 2003. Parity reform in France: Promises and pitfalls. *Review of Policy Research* 20(3): 385-400.

Bébéar, Claude. 2004. Des entreprises aux couleurs de la France – minorités visibles: Relever le défi de l'accès à l'emploi et de l'intégration dans l'entreprise. Paris: La Documentation Française.

Begag, Azouz. 2004. La République à ciel ouvert. Rapport pour Monsieur le ministre de l'intérieur, de la sécurité et des libertés locales. Paris.

Belorgey, Jean-Michel. 1999. Lutter contre les discriminations: Rapport à Mme la ministre de l'emploi et de la solidarité. Paris.

Bereni, Laure and Eléonore Lépinard. 2004. Les femmes ne sont pas une catégorie: Les stratégies de légitimation de la parité en France. *Revue Française de Science Politique* 54(1): 71-98.

Billings, Alan and Andrew Holden. 2007. The contribution of faith to integration and cohesion and the threat posed by "enclavisation" in some northern towns. Wetherby: Commission on Integration and Cohesion.

Birsl, Ursula and Carlota Solé. 2004. *Migración e interculturalidad en Gran Bretaña, España y Alemania*. Barcelona: Anthropos.

Blair, Tony. 2005. PM's Press Conference - 5 August 2005. Available online at: http://www.number10.gov.uk/Page8041.

Blanco, Cristina. 2000. *Las migraciones contemporáneas*. Madrid: Alianza Editorial.

Bleich, Erik. 2003. Histoire des politiques françaises antidiscrimination: Du déni à la lutte. *Hommes et Migrations* 1245: 6-18.

—. 2003. *Race politics in Britain and France: Ideas and policymaking since the 1960s*. Cambridge: Cambridge University Press.

Brighton, Shane. 2007. British Muslims, multiculturalism and UK foreign policy: "Integration" and "cohesion" in and beyond the state. *International Affairs* 83(1): 1-17.

Brown, Gordon and Wilf Stevenson. 2006. *Moving Britain forward: Selected speeches, 1997-2006*. London: Bloomsbury.

Brubaker, Rogers. 1992. *Citizenship and nationhood in France and Germany*. Cambridge, MA: Harvard University Press.

—. 1997. *Citoyenneté et nationalité en France et en Allemagne*. Paris: Belin.

—. 2001. The return of assimilation? Changing perspectives on immigration and its sequels in France, Germany, and the United States. *Ethnic and Racial Studies* 24(4): 531-48.

Calvès, Gwénaële. 2002. "Il n'y a pas de race ici." Le modèle français à l'épreuve de l'intégration européenne. *Critique Internationale* 17: 173-86.

—. 2004. *La discrimination positive*. Paris: Presses Universitaires de France.

—. 2005. "Reflecting the diversity of the French population": Birth and development of a fuzzy concept. *International Social Science Journal* 183: 165-74.

Cantle, Ted. 2005. *Community cohesion: A new framework for race and diversity*. Basingstoke: Palgrave Macmillan.

—. 2001. *Community cohesion: A report of the Independent Review Team*. London: Home Office.

Castles, Stephen. 2000. *Ethnicity and globalisation: From migrant worker to transnational citizen*. London: Sage.

Caviedes, Alexander. 2010. Towards a European model for high-skilled labour migration? In *Migrants and minorities: The European response*, ed. Adam Luedtke. Newcastle upon Tyne: Cambridge Scholars Publishing.

Castles, Stephen and Mark J. Miller. 1998. *The age of migration: International population movements in the modern world*. Basingstoke: Palgrave.

Cea D'Ancona, María Ángeles. 2004. *La activación de la xenofobia en España: Qué miden las encuestas?* Madrid: Centro de Investigaciones Sociológicas.

Checa, Francisco, Encarna Soriano and Ángeles Arjona. 1999. *Inmigrantes entre nosotros: Trabajo, cultura y educación intercultural*. Barcelona: Icaria.

Chopin, Isabelle and Jan Niessen. 2001. *The Starting Line and the incorporation of the Racial Equality Directive into the national laws of the EU Member States and Accession States*. Brussels/London: Commission for Racial Equality and Migration Policy Group.

Commission de réflexion sur l'application du principe de laïcité dans la République. 2003. Rapport au président de la République. Paris.

Commission Européenne. 2004. Egalité et non-discrimination. Rapport annuel 2004. Luxembourg: Office des publications officielles des Communautés européennes.

Commission on Integration and Cohesion. 2007. Our shared future. Final report of the Commission on Integration and Cohesion.

Costa-Lascoux, Jacqueline. 1989. *De l'immigré au citoyen*. Paris: La Documentation française.

—. 2005. République et particularismes. *Problèmes Politiques et Sociaux* 909. Paris: La Documentation française.

Crowley, John. 1992. Consensus et conflits dans la politique de l'immigration et des relations raciales au Royaume-Uni. In *Logiques d'Etats et immigrations*, ed. Janine Costa-Lascoux and Patrick Weil, 73-118. Paris: Kimé.

Department for Children, Schools and Families. 2007. *Faith in the system: The role of schools with a religious character in English education and society*. Nottingham: Department for Children, Schools and Families.

Department for Education and Skills. 2007. *Curriculum review: Diversity and citizenship*. London: Department for Education and Skills.

Fanjul, Serafín. 2000. *Al-Andalus contra España: La forja del mito*. Madrid: Siglo XXI de España Editores.

Favell, Adrian. 2001. *Philosophies of integration: Immigration and the idea of citizenship in France and Britain*. New York: Palgrave.

Flint, John. 2007. Faith schools, multiculturalism and community cohesion: Muslim and Roman Catholic state schools in England and Scotland. *Policy & Politics* 35(2): 251-68.

Freeman, Gary P. 2006. National models, policy types, and the politics of immigration in liberal democracies. *West European Politics* 29(2): 227-47.

Garbaye, Romain. 2005. *Getting into local power: The politics of ethnic minorities in British and French cities*. Malden, MA: Blackwell.

Geddes, Andrew. 2002. *The politics of migration and immigration in Europe*. London, Sage.

Geddes, Andrew and Virginie Guiraudon. 2004. Britain, France, and EU anti-discrimination policy: The emergence of an EU policy paradigm. *West European Politics* 27(2): 334-53.

Gobierno Vasco. 2004. *Plan Vasco de Inmigrácion*. Vitoria-Gasteiz: Servicio Central de Publicaciones del Gobierno Vasco.

Great Britain. Life in the United Kingdom Advisory Group. 2004. *Life in the United Kingdom: A journey to citizenship*. London: Stationery Office.

Great Britain. Commission for Racial Equality. 2005. *2004 Annual report of the Commission for Racial Equality*. London: Stationery Office.

Great Britain. Ministerial Group on Public Order and Community Cohesion. 2001. *Building cohesive communities: A report of the*

Ministerial Group on Public Order and Community Cohesion. London: Home Office.

Guiraudon, Virginie. 2004. Construire une politique européenne de lutte contre les discriminations: L'histoire de la directive "race". *Sociétés Contemporaines* 53: 11-32.

HALDE. 2006. *Rapport annuel 2005*. Paris.

—. 2007. *Rapport annuel 2006*. Paris.

Hall, Peter A. 1993. Policy paradigms, social learning, and the state: The case of economic policymaking in Britain. *Comparative Politics* 25(3): 275-96.

Hansen, Randall. 2000. *Citizenship and immigration in Post-War Britain: The institutional origins of a multicultural nation.* Oxford: Oxford University Press.

—. 2007. United Kingdom. *Focus Migration Country Profile* 12.

Haut Conseil à l'Intégration. 1993. *L'intégration à la française*. Paris: UGE.

—. 2004. *Le contrat et l'intégration: Rapport à Monsieur le Premier Ministre*. Paris: La Documentation Française.

—. 2006. *Le bilan de la politique d'intégration 2002-2005*. Paris: La Documentation Française.

Hewitt, Roger. 2005. *White backlash and the politics of multiculturalism.* Cambridge: Cambridge University Press.

Hollifield, James F. 1997. *L'immigration et l'Etat-Nation: A la recherche d'un modèle national*. Paris: L'Harmattan.

Jacobs, Dirk and Andrea Rea. 2007. The end of national models? Integration courses and citizenship trajectories in Europe. *International Journal on Multicultural Societies* 9(2): 264-83.

Joppke, Christian. 1999. *Immigration and the nation-state: The United States, Germany and Great Britain*. Oxford: Clarendon Press.

—. 2007. Beyond national models: Civic integration policies for immigrants in Western Europe. *West European Politics* 30(1): 1-22.

Joppke, Christian and Ewa T. Morawska. 2003. Integrating immigrants in liberal nation-states: Policies and practices. In *Toward assimilation and citizenship: Immigrants in liberal nation-states*, ed. Christian Joppke and Ewa T. Morawska, 1-35. Basingstoke: Palgrave.

Keaton, Tricia D. 2006. *Muslim girls and the other France: Race, identity politics, and social exclusion.* Bloomington: Indiana University Press.

Koopmans, Ruud and Paul Statham. 1999. Challenging the liberal nation-state? Postnationalism, multiculturalism, and the collective claims making of migrants and ethnic minorities in Britain and Germany. *American Journal of Sociology* 105(3): 652-96.

Lochak, Danièle. 2006. L'intégration comme injonction: Enjeux idéologiques et politiques liés à l'immigration. *Cultures & Conflits* 64: 131-47.

Lord Goldsmith QC and Citizenship Review. 2008. *Citizenship: Our Common Bond*. London.

Mahnig, Hans and Andreas Wimmer. 2000. Country-specific or convergent? A typology of immigrant policies in Western Europe. *Journal of International Migration and Integration* 1(2): 177-204.

McGhee, Derek. 2005. *Intolerant Britain? Hate, citizenship and difference*. Maidenhead, NY: Open University Press.

—. 2008. *The end of multiculturalism? Terrorism, integration and human rights*. Maidenhead: Open University Press.

Modood, Tariq. 2005. Foreword. In *Muslim Britain: Communities under pressure*, ed. Tahir Abbas, viii-xii. London: Zed Books.

Money, Jeannette. 2010. Immigrants as fellow citizens? In *Migrants and minorities: The European response*, ed. Adam Luedtke. Newcastle upon Tyne: Cambridge Scholars Publishing.

Noiriel, Gérard. 1988. *Le creuset français: Histoire de l'immigration, XIXe-XXe siècles*. Paris: Seuil.

Parekh, Bhikhu C. 2000. *Rethinking multiculturalism: Cultural diversity and political theory*. Basingstoke: Macmillan.

Parekh, Bhikhu C. and Runnymede Trust. 2000. *The future of multi-ethnic Britain: Report of the Commission on the Future of Multi-Ethnic Britain*. London: Profile.

Peres, Hubert. 1999. L'Europe commence à Gibraltar: Le dilemme espagnol face à la découverte de l'immigration. *Pôle Sud* 11: 8-23.

—. 2004. L'accès aux fonction publiques des jeunes d'origine immigrée. *Migrations Etudes* 122.

Rex, John. 1997. The concept of a multicultural society. In *The ethnicity reader: Nationalism, multiculturalism, and migration*, ed. Montserrat Guibernau and John Rex, 205-220. Malden, MA: Polity Press.

Safran, William. 2004. Ethnoreligious politics in France: Jews and Muslims. *West European Politics* 27(3): 423-51.

Schain, Martin A. 1999. Minorities and immigrant incorporation in France: The state and the dynamics of multiculturalism. In *Multicultural Questions*, ed. Christian Joppke and Steven Lukes, 199-223. Oxford: Oxford University Press.

Schmidtke, Oliver. 2007. Borders in public perception: Renationalizing modes of inclusion and exclusion. In *Of states, rights, and social closure: Governing migration and citizenship*, ed. Oliver Schmidtke and Saime Ozcurumez, 91-110. New York: Palgrave Macmillan.

Schnapper, Dominique. 1991. *La France de l'intégration: Sociologie de la nation en 1990*. Paris: Gallimard.

—. 2002. Citizenship and national identity in Europe. *Nations and Nationalism* 8(1): 1-14.

Slama, Alain-Gérard. 2004. Contre la discrimination positive: La liberté insupportable. *Pouvoirs* 111: 133-43.

Solomos, John. 2003. *Race and racism in Britain*. New York: Palgrave Macmillan.

Soysal, Yasemin N. 1994. *Limits of citizenship: Migrants and postnational membership in Europe*. Chicago: University of Chicago Press.

Swann, Lord M. M. 1985. *Education for all: The report of the Committee of Inquiry into the Education of Children from Ethnic Minority Groups*. London: HMSO.

Taras, Raymond. 2010. Secular and religious groundings of European xenophobia: Distinguishing French, Polish, and Russian prejudices. In *Migrants and minorities: The European response*, ed. Adam Luedtke. Newcastle upon Tyne: Cambridge Scholars Publishing.

Taguieff, Pierre-André. 2005. *La république enlisée: Pluralisme, communautarisme et citoyenneté*. Paris: Syrtes.

Todd, Emmanuel. 1994. *Le Destin des immigrés: Assimilation et ségrégation dans les démocraties occidentales*. Paris: Seuil.

Tribalat, Michèle. 1995. *Faire France: Une grande enquête sur les immigrés et leurs enfants*. Paris: Editions La Découverte.

Tribalat, Michèle, Patrick Simon and Benoît Riandey. 1996. *De l'immigration à l'assimilation: Enquête sur les populations d'origine étrangère en France*. Paris: Editions La Découverte/INED.

Vermeulen, Hans. 1997. *Immigrant policy for a multicultural society: A comparative study of integration, language and religious policy in five Western European Countries*. Brussels: Migration Policy Group.

Vertovec, Steve. 1996. Multiculturalism, culturalism and public incorporation. *Ethnic & Racial Studies* 19(1): 49-69.

Vink, Maarten P. 2010. European integration and domestic immigration policies: Convergence, causality and counterfactuals? In *Migrants and Minorities: The European response*, ed. Adam Luedtke. Newcastle upon Tyne: Cambridge Scholars Press.

Weil, Patrick. 2005. *La république et sa diversité: Immigration, intégration, discrimination*. Paris: Seuil.

Weil, Patrick and John Crowley. 1994. Integration in theory and practice: A comparison of France and Britain. *West European Politics* 17(2): 110-26.

Wihtol de Wenden, Catherine. 1999. *L'immigration en Europe*. Paris: La Documentation Française.

Wihtol de Wenden, Catherine and Christophe Bertossi. 2005. Les militaires français issus de l'immigration. *Les Documents du C2SD* 78.

CHAPTER THIRTEEN

IMMIGRANTS AS FELLOW CITIZENS?

JEANNETTE MONEY

Introduction

In the last half century, Western Europe has become a continent with a significant permanent resident alien population. Figures range from two percent of the population (Finland) to over twenty percent of the population (Switzerland).[1] Of the "old" European Union fifteen, only two have foreign-born populations of less than five percent (Italy, Finland) and ten have foreign-born populations of more than ten percent. As these foreign-born populations have grown, the question of incorporation has become a pressing political issue.

There are many dimensions of immigrant incorporation (Freeman 2004), but the fullest measure of equal treatment is the acquisition of citizenship. Although citizenship laws of European countries were often generated by the process of nation-building in a specific historical context (Brubaker 1992), they are not immutable. Recent examples of change abound. After more than a decade of public debate, in 1999, Germany adopted legislation that granted German citizenship at birth to some children born in Germany to foreign parents, thus adopting the principle of conditional *jus soli* for the first time since the creation of the German

[1] Figures are available for the "foreign-born population" and the "foreign population." Usually, the foreign-born population is larger than the "foreign population," as some foreign-born become citizens; Luxembourg is an exception: 34.8 percent of the population is foreign-born whereas 41.6 percent of the population is foreign, indicating the presence of a significant second and third generation immigrant population that has not been incorporated through citizenship. Figures are from the OECD (2008).

state.[2] Thus, rather than remaining "foreign," a significant proportion of babies born annually to foreign parents in Germany have all the rights and responsibilities of citizenship previously obtained only through a difficult naturalization process, a step that many fail to undertake. In contrast, in 1993, France, which had previously provided automatic French citizenship at the age of 18 to children born in France to foreigners, adopted legislation that required these young adults to apply for French citizenship.[3] In this chapter, I examine the circumstances under which states change their citizenship laws to become more accommodating or more restrictive, relative to the immigrant population.[4]

Early work on citizenship in Europe tended to focus on the immutability of citizenship law, forged in the crucible of nation-building. More recently, scholarship on citizenship has acknowledged that citizenship law does change (for example, Bauböck et al. 2006; Hansen and Weil 2001). With this recognition have come efforts to theorize the sources of change. There are numerous works that focus on different explanatory frameworks. Because the debate on citizenship has often been a politically charged issue with a considerable amount of public debate, issues of identity and ideas about societal membership are often brought to the fore (Feldblum 1999, Favell 2001). Others have examined more closely the actual political process of legislative change and have referenced the political composition of the government (Joppke 2003) or the degree to which the policy debate is politicized (Howard 2007).[5]

These theorists have made significant advances but have not told the full story. When examining changes in citizenship laws, there is a

---

[2] *Jus soli* is the term describing the grant of citizenship by birth in the territory of the country; *jus sanguinis* is the term describing the grant of citizenship according to the citizenship of the parent(s). Until this legislation, German had only *jus sanguinis* citizenship laws, supplemented by onerous naturalization procedures. The *jus soli* citizenship is not unconditional, however; one parent must be legally resident in Germany for a minimum of eight years prior to the birth.

[3] That law was subsequently repealed in 1998.

[4] Citizenship laws cover the "native" population as well as the foreign population. As Joppke (2003) notes, citizenship laws governing the "native" population can become more or less restrictive as well. He labels the process of extending ties to the expatriate population "re-ethnicisation," as opposed to "de-ethnicisation" generated by extending ties to the foreign population. In this chapter, I focus only on the latter process.

[5] Outside of the European context, Seely (2007) has examined the level of resources of the country as one determinant of ease of naturalization.

tendency to overlook some of the variation by using measures that capture only the gross differences in citizenship regimes – as reflected in the dichotomous distinction between *jus soli* and *jus sanguinis* citizenship regimes. Moreover, the literature on Europe tends to focus on unidirectional change–toward greater ease of citizenship acquisition – even though several countries have moved in the opposite direction. And, although the "stickiness" of citizenship legislation is often recognized, the literature currently does not theorize the conditions under which the status quo will be maintained.

I focus more closely on the political incentives that politicians face as key to understanding changes in citizenship law, a focus that has been developed by Weil (2002), Sadiq (2009) and Howard (2007). In this article, I build on this work to lay out a more systematic theory of politicians' incentives. I focus on the rights and responsibilities of citizenship and the efforts of politicians to maximize the payoffs of citizenship laws. I hypothesize that where non-citizens have rights similar to those of citizens but few responsibilities, politicians will seek to increase returns by facilitating citizenship. Similarly, where non-citizens have responsibilities similar to those of citizens, but few rights, politicians will seek to increase returns (decrease costs) by making access to citizenship more difficult. Where rights and responsibilities are "matched," (few rights/few responsibilities; many rights/many responsibilities) politicians face few incentives for change in citizenship laws.

This focus on politicians' incentives can be seen as either competing with other explanations in the literature or complementary to other explanations. I argue that, although politicians' incentives are central to the process, other factors may well be at work.

The chapter first provides an overview of the literature on citizenship on which I build. I then lay out the theoretical framework and generate a series of hypotheses. In the third section, I examine the case of Germany, in light of my hypotheses and the broader literature. In the final section, I suggest a research agenda that includes recommendations for more quantitative analyses to sort among hypotheses, as well as a broader geographical research agenda, to determine if the processes present in Europe carry to other regions of the world.

An Overview of the Literature

Research on citizenship has tended to be descriptive and historical, with very little comparative theory generation. What work there is tends to focus on the "nation-states" of Western Europe. One of the early theoretical works is by Rogers Brubaker (1990, 1992). He compares the construction of citizenship law in France and Germany, pointing to the distinctive problems of nation-building that forged an emphasis in France on *jus soli* and in Germany in *jus sanguinis*. *Jus sanguinis* grants citizenship based on the citizenship of the parent(s) whereas *jus soli* grants citizenship based on birth in the territory of the state. Brubaker (1990, 1992) builds a compelling story of the pragmatism of politicians in crafting citizenship laws that best fit the needs of the state in constructing a nation – either ethnic or civic. I believe this is an essential insight into the process of citizenship construction. What Brubaker failed to acknowledge was the potential for change in citizenship policy. Moreover, despite the fact that many states have a combination of *jus soli* and *jus sanguinis* laws governing citizenship, this dichotomy has remained ubiquitous in the description and theorizing of citizenship law.[6] However, to understand change in citizenship laws, a more nuanced mechanism for classifying citizenship is required.

Christian Joppke (2003) provides a different framework to explain citizenship policy, again in the countries of Western Europe. He rejects Brubaker's argument of "national traditions of citizenship" as well as Soysal's (1994) hypothesized relationship between the construction of a "post-national membership" and national citizenship laws. He argues that two factors are critical in understanding states' changes in citizenship policies. The first is the flow of peoples, both immigration and emigration. The second is the political coalition in power. Where immigration and a left political coalition coincide, citizenship laws are eased in response to the liberal democratic tradition that is defined by citizenship participation.

---

[6] But see Howard (2007) for an effort to quantify different levels of citizenship policy. I also proposed a coding scheme to evaluate variation in citizenship laws (Money 2002). Citizenship laws were decomposed into four components: naturalization procedures for non-citizen adults, procedures pertinent solely to women, procedures for granting citizenship to children of citizens (born within and outside the territory of the state), and procedures for granting citizenship to the children of foreigners. Within these four categories, a global survey of laws in 1929 and 1954 (Flournoy and Hudson 1929, United Nations 1954) revealed substantial variation.

Where emigration and a right political coalition coincide, citizenship laws are expanded to retain the membership of the emigrants, even across generations. Joppke's argument is important in that it incorporates migration flows into the equation, as a trigger to change citizenship policy. But the domain of his theory is limited to democratic, presumably European, countries and partisan politics characteristic of those polities. Moreover, even in the carefully selected examples employed to illustrate his theory, some cases do not fit the model.

Marc Howard (2007) proposes an alternative theoretical framework to explain citizenship policy in Europe. Howard distinguishes between the original determinants of citizenship policy and subsequent change in citizenship policy. For the first, there are two key elements in the equation: whether or not the state was a former colonial power and whether or not the country was a historical country of immigration. Where those two characteristics are present (Belgium, France, and the UK), we should see relatively liberal citizenship policies; where the two characteristics are absent (Austria, Denmark, Finland, Greece, Ireland, Italy and Sweden), we should see relatively onerous citizenship policies. Countries that fall into the off diagonal should experience pressures that propel them in one direction or the other.

For the second issue, Howard argues that the presence of strong far right parties prevents a movement toward liberalization, in those countries that were previously restrictive. There are two components to this argument. First, the starting point matters. Countries that are already fairly liberal will not need to liberalize further. Second, the presence of strong far right parties is one indication of the politicization of immigration and citizenship that prevents politicians from responding to the liberal democratic imperatives of citizenship. Howard marshals a quantitative indicator of citizenship based on three factors: jus soli for children of aliens, residency requirement for naturalization and the presence or absence of dual citizenship. Most of the evidence is consistent with his hypotheses.

Howard takes a step forward in distinguishing between the initial basis of citizenship law and the subsequent changes to citizenship law. He also recognizes that the starting point counts. If there are pressures for liberalization of citizenship laws, those are most likely to take place in countries that have restrictive citizenship laws. But Howard only recognizes changes in a more liberal direction, rather than tracing and accounting for changes in a more restrictive direction, as experienced by the United Kingdom (1981), France (1993) and Denmark (2002), for example. Again, the domain of his theory is limited to democratic, presumably European countries. However, migration flows are virtually universal now, in Latin America, Asia, the Middle East and Africa. And citizenship laws are changing in all of these places. We need a more generic theory of citizenship laws to account for this universal process.

I take these three analyses as a starting point in my own theory building. I suggest that citizenship law has less to do with identity than with politicians' incentive structures. I have not yet developed a theory of citizenship, although the Brubaker piece suggests a starting point: the issues of nation building at independence. Here I propose a theory of change in citizenship law.

Theory

Although there is no unique definition of citizenship, most researchers would agree that, in the contemporary context of (nation) states, citizenship offers a set of rights and responsibilities to individuals who meet the criteria of citizenship. These rights may be more or less distinctive from the rights of non-citizens. I argue that politicians evaluate the costs and benefits arising from these definitions and modify citizenship laws accordingly. That is, the incentives that politicians face in making access to citizenship easier or more difficult vary based on potential gains derived from the obligations that citizens must fulfil and the costs generated by offering rights to the new citizens. The important element of this definition for theory building is that the set of rights and responsibilities varies across countries, as does the treatment of citizen and non-citizen, thus providing the basis for a generic theory of citizenship change.

The returns on rights and responsibilities are a function of prior political and judicial decisions. The rights available to resident aliens change over time. West Germany is a case in point, where the guest worker programs implemented in the 1950s and 1960s restricted residence rights of foreigners, rights that were subsequently expanded through both administrative practices and judicial rulings to more closely resemble the rights of the host population (Green 2004). Rights of permanent residence and family reunification in Germany generated larger costs for the state and, because the judicial system was the source of these rights, they could not be easily reduced. In Sweden, on the other hand, the corporatist institutions and tripartite bargaining over immigration helped ensure that resident aliens had very similar rights to the host population, right from the beginning (Green-Pedersen and Odmalm 2008). In Europe, these changes to the rights of resident aliens modified the returns to politicians.

The first implication of this heuristic is that there must be a change in the costs and benefits accruing to politicians to generate a change in policy. It seems logical to assume that there must be a group of resident aliens to trigger reconsideration of the political calculation, and that politicians must see some immediate payoff to the legislative change. I thus incorporate Joppke's recognition of the presence of population movement to trigger the change in citizenship law. However, attention must also be paid to the foreigners' demographics, as changing demographics may also shift the cost-benefit ratio. In the case of Germany, to illustrate this point, had the rights of the resident alien population been expanded but few immigrants were present to benefit, the change in costs would have been small. However, the immigrant population in Germany was large and growing, with a dramatic shift in the dependency ratio, thus generating a need to change the status quo. This generates my first hypothesis.

> H1: The underlying equilibrium is disturbed by the presence of a non-citizen population; change in citizenship law becomes more likely as the non-citizen population grows. That is, the larger the proportion of the non-citizen population, the more likely politicians are to change policy.

The second implication that this heuristic suggests is that the starting point matters. If the benefits of restrictiveness outweigh the costs, a country with relatively relaxed citizenship laws will be more likely to change its policies than a country that already has relatively restrictive policies. Thus I incorporate Howard's insight that the country's starting point matters.

> H2: The greater the distance between the initial policy and the desired policy, the more likely politicians will be to adopt a new policy.

Third, it is the difference between citizen and non-citizen rights and responsibilities that generates the decision function. We can think about differences in rights and responsibilities on these two dimensions as generating four different types of status quo in states (see Table 1). Let us take the position of quadrant 3 – where there are small differences in rights between citizens and non-citizens but large differences in responsibilities. As the number of immigrants grows, the costs of providing rights to non-citizens grow, while the benefits generated by their responsibilities remain stable, because non-citizens have fewer responsibilities than citizens. Politicians experience declining utility from the current citizenship regime. If they are unable to reduce the payouts to immigrants, then the only other solution available is to make them citizens, in order to extract the required responsibilities. Hence, if citizenship is difficult, we would anticipate a relaxation of citizenship laws. This is a situation that, given the extension of the welfare net to the immigrant population, many European countries may experience.

Table 13.1: Interaction between Rights and Responsibilities (between citizen and non-citizen)

	Small differences in rights	Large differences in rights
Small differences in responsibilities	1. Status quo	2. Restrict citizenship
Large differences in responsibilities	3. Relax citizenship	4. Status quo

Conversely, as depicted in quadrant 2, politicians can increase their payoffs by restricting access to citizenship. In this case, there are small differences in responsibilities between the alien population and the citizen population but a large difference in rights. If a state provides easy access to citizenship, aliens could naturalize and gain many rights, but without providing any additional responsibilities. As the alien population grows and naturalizes, this represents a growing cost to politicians and hence an incentive to restrict access to citizenship.

The grid also presents two quadrants, 1 and 4, where there are few differences between the citizen and non-citizen population. Quadrant 1 suggests a country where the non-citizen population has access to virtually all the rights that citizens have, but where non-citizens also have the same responsibilities as citizens. In this case, politicians cannot modify their payoffs by changing citizenship law and the status quo is likely to be maintained, even in light of a large non-citizen population. Similarly, states have no incentive to change citizenship laws if they discriminate against aliens by excluding them from rights available to citizens but also receive few benefits from the aliens. A change in citizenship laws would not modify the payoffs in either situation. Of course, this calculation of payoffs to politicians assumes a fixed status quo ante. The equation could also be changed by changing what immigrants are eligible for and what they contribute to the state. In many liberal democratic countries, however, politicians are constrained by equal treatment under the rule of law, which prevents them from rolling back access of benefits to the non-citizen population.

This theory generates three more hypotheses.

> H3: Where politicians confront small differences in rights but large differences in responsibilities, they are more likely to relax access to citizenship.
> H4: Where politicians confront large differences in rights but small differences in responsibilities, they are more likely to restrict citizenship.
> H5: Where differences in rights and responsibilities are "matching," the status quo is likely to be maintained.

There is an interaction between H3 and H4 and H1 and H2. We can expect the relationships in H3 and H4 to hold only when there is an increasing (or large) non-citizen population, and where existing policies are inconsistent with the desired outcomes. These hypotheses, along with H5, suggest that citizenship policy should be relatively stable – not because of the impact of history but because the incentives to change citizenship policy do not arise frequently.[7]

---

[7] If we want to apply this theory of citizenship more broadly, there are additional hypotheses that may be important. Citizenship also has to do with legitimacy of the government. Non-citizens have less of a stake in the host society than do citizens; they may be able to return to their home countries. In many cases, they send significant resources home to family they left behind, in the form of remittances, thereby taking resources out of the country. They are less likely to want to contribute to the public goods produced by the society. Where legitimacy is important for maintaining societal order, as it is in participatory democracies, the benefits of relaxed citizenship are greater than where legitimacy is not crucial to maintaining societal order, as it is in autocracies. This suggests that democracies are more likely than autocracies to be more open to incorporating non-citizens into their polity. On the other hand, democratic polities may well have to deal with anti-immigrant sentiment on the part of the populace whereas authoritarian regimes

One can think of examples to fit in the different boxes. The example of France comes to mind when thinking about the relaxation of citizenship policy. In the 19th century, the French government was unable to call upon its non-citizen population to serve in the military. This led to the implementation of a "double jus soli" law in 1889, which made children born in France to French-born foreign parents, citizens at birth.

Preliminary Test of Hypotheses

To adequately test these hypotheses, a cross-national time series data set would be helpful. In the absence of that data set, however, it is possible to examine a specific case to determine the plausibility of the argument and to compare the explanatory power of this theory vis-à-vis other contributions to the theoretical literature. I take the case of Germany, as the changes to its citizenship laws have been among the most dramatic in Europe; Germany has turned from a predominantly *jus sanguinis* based law to the admission of *jus soli* in principle for children of foreigners.

Germany

To examine the case of Germany, I trace the level of the foreign population, the changing demographics of that population and the extension of rights to the foreign population. I also examine the efforts of politicians to modify the facts on the ground and their inability to do so. Given these circumstances, I then describe the associated changes in citizenship policy that relaxed the requirements for citizenship. Briefly, as the foreign population grew, gained access to the provisions of the welfare state and other social services, and took advantage of these benefits, pressure grew on the government to make access to citizenship easier. This was true of both governments of the right and governments of the left, and despite opposition from the mass public. Finally, I will compare my analysis with those of Joppke and Howard to demonstrate that this theory of citizenship provides at least equal explanatory power. Given that the theory is more generically framed, it provides a way forward for analyzing changes in citizenship policy over time and over geographic space.

---

may be less attentive to public opinion. If this is the case, one might conclude that democracies have a more difficult time in liberalizing citizenship laws than do autocracies. With these two processes, we do not have a clear idea of which might outweigh the other. Since I am interested here in European democracies, the issue of variation in the level of democracy is moot.

The growth and changing demographics of the foreign population. Tables 13.2 and 13.3 depict just how rapidly the foreign population in Federal Republic of Germany (West Germany) grew (see tables for sources). In 1960, there were just over a half a million foreigners, with 40 percent in taxable employment. Although West Germany had signed labour migration agreements with Italy in 1955 and with Spain and Greece in 1960, flows of foreign workers were relatively small until construction began on the Berlin Wall in August 1961, cutting off the flow of Germans from the German Democratic Republic (East Germany) (Dreyer 1961). Thereafter, foreign migration flows increased rapidly. By 1973, there were 3.6 million foreigners, multiplying the foreign population in West Germany by seven in just 13 years. The foreign population accounted for 6.4 percent of the total population. Before the stop of recruiting in November 1973, as a consequence of the anticipated impact of the rise in oil prices generated by the 1973 war in the Middle East, an astonishing 71.5 percent of foreigners were employed in taxable employment. Unemployment for foreigners stood at a mere 1.8 percent.

Although foreign workers had many of the same workplace and social rights as German workers (Schmitter 1981), they did not make use of them. Contracts were renewed annually, as were residence permits, and the foreign population was predominantly male. Few dependents came to Germany not because they were forbidden per se, but because most workers intended to return home. Moreover, family reunification required adequate housing, which was in short supply in Germany (Dreyer 1961).

This demographic balance was, in fact, a strategy of the Federal Labour Office, the bureaucracy designated to guide the recruitment process. The Federal Labour Office sought to reduce potential costs associated with immigration. Dreyer (1961, 24), a government official, recognized this in his 1961 article on labour recruitment in West Germany, writing, "Large scale immigration of workers with their families would, of course, lead to many other problems such as integration of school children and overcoming the language barrier." A subsequent analysis by Green (2004, 33) confirms this stance:

> "In order to minimize costs for society (which would arise in the form of schools, housing and health care provisions for permanent immigrants and their dependants), the Federal Labour Office usually favoured young single men."

Table 13.2: (West) German Stocks of Foreigners and Foreign Workers

Year	Stocks of Foreigners (in thousands)	Stocks of Foreign Workers (in thousands)	Dependency Ratio	Foreign Unemploy-ment	(W.) German Unemploy-ment
1950	568.0				
1960	690.0	280.0	40.5		
1967	1806.6				
1968		1089.9			
1969		1501.4			
1970		1948.9			
1971		2240.8			
1972		2354.2			
1973	3625.0	2595.0	71.5	1.8	
1974	4127.4	2386.6	57.8	5.4	4.2
1975	4089.6	2226.9	54.5		
1976	3948.3	2027.1	51.3		
1977	3948.3	1977.7	50.1		
1978	3981.1	1961.9	49.2		
1979	4143.8	2025.1	48.8		
1980	4453.3	2115.7	47.5		
1981	4629.8	2096.3	45.3		
1982	4666.9	2029.0	43.5		
1983	4534.9	1983.5	43.7		
1984	4363.7	1854.9	42.5		
1985	4378.9	1823.4	41.6		
1986	4512.7	1833.7	40.6		
1987	4240.5	1865.5	43.9		
1988	4489.1	1910.6	42.5		
1989	4845.9	1940.6	40.0	12.2	7.9
1990	5342.5	2025.1	37.9	10.9	7.2
1991	5882.3	2179.1	37.0	10.7	6.3
1992	6495.8	2360.1	36.3	12.2	6.6
1993	6878.1	2575.9	37.4	15.1	8.2
1994	6990.5	2559.6	36.6	16.2	9.2
1995	7173.9	2569.2	35.8	16.6	9.3
1996	7314.0			19.0	10.0
1997	7365.8	3575.0	48.5	20.4	11.0
1998	7319.6	3501.0	47.8	19.6	10.5
1999	7343.6	3545.0	48.2	18.4	8.8

Sources: OECD (1973-2000), Fassman and Münz (1992).

Table 13.3: German Migration Information

Year	Natural increase of foreigners (in thousands)	Percentage foreigners > 9 (10) years residence (from 1994)	Foreigners as percent of population	Foreign workers as percent of all wage earners	Children >16 as percent of foreign population
1950			1.1		
1968				5.2	
1969				7.0	
1970			4.9	9.0	
1971			5.6	10.3	
1972			5.7	10.8	
1973			6.4		
1974			6.7		
1975			6.6		
1976			6.4	9.4	
1977			6.4		
1978			6.5		
1979			6.7		
1980		37.8	7.2	7.8	25.2
1981			7.5		
1982			7.6		
1983			7.4		
1984			7.1		
1985			7.2		
1986			7.3		
1987			6.9		
1988			7.3		
1989			7.7	6.5	
1990	76.8	60.4	8.4		
1991	79.2	56.7	7.3*	7.0	
1992	88.9	51.9	8.0*	7.8	
1993	91.0	49.5	8.5*	8.2	
1994	88.3	47.4	8.6*	8.3	
1995	86.9	44.5	8.8*	8.3	
1996			8.9*		
1997	93.5	49.2	9.0*		
1998	86.3	51.0	8.9*		
1999	80.9	52.1	8.9*		
2000	35.3	54.7	8.9*		

*Statistics now include the East German population, thereby reducing the proportion of the population that is foreign.

The picture changed dramatically after the stop to immigration in 1973. Workers who had returned home annually for family visits realized that they would not be allowed to return to Germany if they left the country. Given the large wage differential between Germany and their home country, they decided to stay and began to bring family members to live with them. The stock of foreigners therefore continued to grow as the proportion of the foreign population active in the labour market dropped dramatically from 71.5 percent to 57.8 percent in the space of a year, and declined slowly after that.

By 1980, the foreign population in West Germany had risen from 6.4 percent to 7.2 percent of the population and the demographics of the group had shifted dramatically. By comparison to the 1974 level, the foreign population had increased 7.9 percent. The proportion of adult males in the population declined by 5 percent, whereas adult women had increased by 6.5 percent and children under the age of 16 had grown a whopping 46 percent, to comprise more than 25 percent of the foreign population (OECD 1981). Some of this increase in children came from family reunification, but a significant proportion came from births of children to foreign couples living in Germany. The proportion of foreign births was almost three times their proportion in the population; in 1974, foreigners comprised 6.7 percent of the population but accounted for 17.3 percent of the children born that year (Green 2004, p. 37.)

Rights of the Foreign Population

Upon entering West Germany, foreigners found a mixed bag of rights. Entry was governed according to the dictates of the labour market and was precarious, with work and residence permits issued for one year periods. Political and civil rights were restricted. Yet, due to the strong influence of labour unions, once inside Germany, foreigners had labour and social rights equal to those of the native German population.

Foreigners who wanted to work were required to obtain a work permit from the local labour office; these were granted if employment of German nationals was not affected. Employers were required to demonstrate the absence of German candidates for a position by advertising locally for at least three weeks. Work permits were only issued or renewed if the foreigner possessed a residence permit granted by the Aliens Office, and a visa was required. The Aliens Act of 1965 governed the conditions of entry and placed the interests of the German state above the interests of the migrants. The legislation indicated that:

> "…A residence permit may be issued if the presence of the foreigner does not compromise the interest of the Federal Republic of Germany… Secondary legislation prescribed that residence permits should normally be issued for only one year in the first instance" (Green 2004, 73).

Conditions of employment were the same as for comparable German workers, in terms of wages and benefits. Moreover, employers were required to provide housing for workers, which the workers usually chose, as it was cheaper than the local housing market (Dreyer 1961).[8] Immigrants also had access to the same social rights of the German population (Schmitter 1981, Marshall 2000). Included were:

> "…Social and work-related rights and benefits (for example, social security, unemployment insurance, health insurance, accident insurance) and equal access to the social infrastructure, particularly schools for children" (Schmitter 1981: 322).

This legal equality between the native and the foreign populations in West Germany was due, in large part, to the central position of trade unions in the economy. The Confederation of German Trade Unions (Deutscher Gewerkschaftsbund or DGB) was the central trade union actor:

> "[The DGB] officially agreed to [immigrant] recruitment on two conditions: that the Federal Labour Office would be in charge of recruitment and that migrants once recruited would be equal to German workers in all aspects of wages and legal conditions of employment. Later they also stipulated that the employers had to provide for suitable housing" (Schmitter 1981, 322).

Thus German trade unions officially welcomed immigrants and made substantial efforts to organize them. Part of their organizational activity included union offices that catered to immigrant needs. The DGB created an extensive network of offices that provided special services to the newly arriving immigrants, often staffed with individuals from the migrants' home country (Schmitter 1981, 327).

---

[8] According to Dreyer (1961), employer provided housing was 30-50 marks per month per person versus 50-80 marks per month in the open market.

The Cost/Benefit Ratio of the Foreign Population

This demographic shift changed the cost/benefit ratio of foreigners. When the population was dominated by young males who participated in the workforce, there were few costs in terms of unemployment benefits and little in terms of social policies such as family allowances and schooling costs. Employers benefitted from an expanded and flexible labour force. The German state benefitted from the collection of taxes but with few obligations in terms of social benefits. The foreigners tended to be invisible to the rest of society, spending time primarily at the worksite and in hostels that segregated the foreign population from the larger community. As noted above, initially many workers saw their stay in Germany as temporary. "Many [workers] prefer to come to Germany for a limited time to take advantage of the opportunities it offers" (Dreyer 1961, 23). Even those workers who wanted to settle in Germany found the lack of accommodations a real barrier. "It is not possible to provide suitable personal accommodation on a large scale and even less so for families" (Dreyer 1961, 24).[9]

As the demographics of the group changed, so too did the balance of costs and benefits. Unemployment rose quickly among foreigners; in just one year, the unemployment rate of foreigners exceeded that of the domestic population. In 1989, foreigners' unemployment rate was 1.5 times that of the domestic population. By 1999, foreigners' unemployment rate was more than double that of the domestic population. Unemployment benefits paid out therefore rose and income taxes from work declined.

The demographic shift from an adult employed population to one dominated by families also shifted the cost/benefit structure. By 1980, 25 percent of the foreign population was under the age of 16, generating costs in terms of education and family allowances. The demographic changes also made the foreign population more visible, as families moved into the larger community and sent their children to the local schools.

---

[9] According to Dreyer (1961), "The bilateral recruitment agreements provide that foreign workers may bring their dependants after them to Germany, provided they have an official attestation that adequate accommodation is available. As a general rule foreign workers who have given particularly satisfactory service manage after a time to find suitable accommodation with the help of their employers. But with the severe housing shortage in the Federal Republic, they must often wait as long as two years to do so."

One of the dilemmas of German politicians was the provision of benefits to foreigners who could not provide the political support that normally accompanies the transfer of resources to the population. Another issue, which grew over time, was the political instability generated by a population, in particular a young population, which was unattached to the German state.

> "There is agreement that the legal and political exclusion of generations of foreigners had led to a dangerous sense of social isolation, particularly among their younger generation, for which they often compensate by membership in militant ethnically or religiously based organizations" (Marshall 2000).

This cost-benefit analysis was only aggravated by the growing rights of the foreign population. The demographic shift generated changes in the cost/benefit ratio but so too did the extension of rights to the foreign population. The first and, arguably, the most important of these rights was the ability of foreigners to obtain permanent residence rights. This was not granted to foreigners by the government but extracted by foreigners through the courts. In early 1978, the German Constitutional Court ruled that an Indian national, whose residence permit had been routinely renewed, had thereby established a reliance right to permanent residence (Green 2004, Marshall 2000). Thereafter, permanent residence permits were normally issued to foreigners after five years of residence.

A second extension of rights was to family reunification where, again, the German courts, rather than the government, were decisive.

Efforts to Restrict Entry and Reduce the Foreign Population

As the balance between rights and responsibilities changed, the initial reaction of the political class was to attempt to reduce both the numbers and the rights. The initial effort came out of the system of annual work and residence permits. The reduction of the foreign population was believed merely to be a matter of non-renewal. But, as noted above, the foreign population challenged this treatment and in 1978 won a court decision that required the government to provide permanent residence permits to individuals who had a reliance right on the regular renewal of annual permits (Green 2004).

The government reacted by passing legislation or issuing administrative rulings that sought to reduce the foreign population. Since the increase in the foreign population was associated with family reunification, that was the first issue at hand. In 1981, the government issued administrative rulings that limited the conditions under which spouses could immigrate and lowered the age of reunion for children from 18 to 16 years of age, requiring that both parents be normally resident in Germany. A more restrictive proposal, to limit reunion with children to those under the age of six, created considerable controversy and was considered to be in contravention to Article 6 of the Basic Law that protected the rights of the family (Green 2004).

In 1982, the legislature passed a bill that increased the penalties for employing an undocumented migrant. Also in 1982, they passed legislation to encourage voluntary repatriation of foreigners by offering a departure bonus. This second measure failed to achieve its goal of reducing the overall number of foreigners, which failed to decline (Green 2004).

The foreign worker population, supplemented by family reunification, was not the only influx of migrants to West Germany. Starting in the 1980s, West Germany's generous asylum laws began to attract ever larger flows of individuals making asylum claims (see Table 13.4). After the collapse of the Soviet Union and Soviet bloc in 1989, asylum flows increased; these flows were compounded by the civil wars in ex-Yugoslavia. These flows generated a cross-party collaboration to modify the asylum procedures, reducing flows.

Efforts were also made to reduce the number of foreigners dependent of social benefits. The Aliens Law of 1991 decreed that for foreigners with less than permanent residence status, if dependent on social assistance for longer than six months, could lose their right to stay in Germany, leading to expulsion (Marshall 2000).

This laundry list of legislation indicates that the political elite were well aware of the costs of the foreign population and made significant efforts to reduce the flows and the benefits allotted to the foreign population. They made some progress but were constrained in these efforts, particularly by the Constitutional Court that guaranteed the stability of residence and prevented more drastic curtailment of family reunification.

Table 13.4: Asylum Seekers and Naturalization Rates

Year	Naturalizations (in thousands)	Naturalizations (discretionary) (in	Asylum Seekers (in thousands)	Foreign workers as percent of all wage earners	Children <16 as percent of foreign population
1950					
1968				5.2	
1969				7.0	
1970				9.0	
1971				10.3	
1972				10.8	
1973					
1974					
1975					
1976				9.4	
1977					
1978					
1979			51		
1980			107	7.8	25.2
1981			49		
1982			36		
1983			20		
1984			35		
1985	34.9	13.9	79		
1986	36.6	14.0	100		
1987	37.8	14.0	57		
1988	16.6	16.6	103		
1989		17.7	121	6.5	
1990		20.2	193		
1991	27	27.2	256		
1992	37	37.0	438		
1993	45	44.9	323		
1994	62	26.2	127		
1995	72	31.8	128		
1996	86		116		
1997	82		104		
1998	107		98		
1999	143		95		
2000	187		79		

Efforts to Modify the Balance of Rights and Responsibilities

German politicians did not take the changing structure of costs and benefits, and the extension of rights without the extension of responsibilities lying down. Efforts were made to redress the balance.

An initial proposal, by the Social Democratic Party (SPD), to provide second-generation foreigners the right to naturalize was passed in the lower house of the legislature in 1981 but was rejected in 1982 by the *Bundesrat*, controlled by the opposition Christian Democratic Union/ Christian Social Union.

Since one element of citizen responsibility is political support, and given the inability of second generation foreigners to naturalize easily, politicians attempted to generate political support from the foreign population by extending the vote to foreigners at the local level. The SPD led state governments in Hamburg and Schleswig-Holstein introduced local voting rights for foreigners in 1989. This measure was opposed by the CDU/CSU, which asked for a ruling from the Constitutional Court. That ruling was not long in coming. On 31 October 1990, the Court ruled that the Basic Law, the German constitution, reserved voting rights for German nationals. Thus this strategy failed to provide the desired political support.

On the other hand, politicians continued their efforts to roll back rights. Proposals were floated in 1990 to reduce the maximum age for family reunification from 18 or 16 to the age of six. The justification for such a draconian policy of family reunification was that a six year old would be fully educated in the German school system and would therefore be integrated into the German community. However, this proposal created a political uproar which prevented its adoption.

The courts and immigrant rights groups thus prevented politicians from modifying the cost/benefit ratios that resulted from the immigration stop in 1973. And the costs were growing. Refugees and asylum seekers accounted for 4 percent of the social assistance claims in 1983; by 1989, they accounted for 28 percent of the claims (Marshall 2000). Between 1986 and 1992, recourse to social assistance among foreigners increased from 5.1 to 11 percent. "By 1996 foreigners made up 9.3 percent of the labour force but accounted for 23.5 percent of social assistance recipients" (Marshall 2000).

Given that rights of foreigners were similar to rights of citizens, politicians needed to extract additional responsibilities. Loyalty to the state and political support could be generated only by extending citizenship to the foreign population. Thus, the only alternative was to change citizenship laws

The Changes in Citizenship Policy

German citizenship policy, since the creation of the German state, has been based on the principle of *jus sanguinis* whereby citizenship is passed from parent to children (Green 2004; Bauböck et al. 2006).[10] Children of foreigners born in Germany are foreign by birth. Their only opportunity to become German citizens was through naturalization, upon reaching adulthood.

Up to 1990, naturalization was governed by Section 8 of the RStG of 1913 (Reichs und Staatsangehörigkeitsgesetz). Naturalization was discretionary; conditions for naturalization included a fixed place of residence, means of support for the individual seeking naturalization and for his/her dependents, and the leading of an "irreproachable life." According to the law, "naturalization may only be considered if it is in the public interest."

Given the vagueness of the 1913 law regarding the criteria for naturalization, a set of guidelines was developed in 1977, based on a cross-party consensus in which the SPD led government and the CDU led Länder (states) agreed. The guidelines included a 10 years minimum residence and release from former citizenship. The applicant must display a "voluntary and lasting orientation towards Germany" demonstrated by, among other things, a good command of written and spoken German.

As noted above, the SPD proposed an easing of access to citizenship in 1981 but this proposal was opposed by the opposition CDU/CSU and ultimately abandoned. However, as pressures grew, the CDU/CSU, along with its Free Democratic Party (FDP) coalition partner, itself sought to ease access to citizenship and passed a foreigners law on 9 July 1990. This law provided for simplified naturalization for young (usually second-generation) foreigners aged between 16 and 23. The conditions included

[10] The discussion on changes to citizenship law draws on both Green (2004) and Bauböck et al. (2006) throughout the following pages.

eight years' residence and six years in German school, no criminal convictions and renunciation of prior citizenship. Moreover, it also provided a simplified naturalization procedure to first-generation immigrants who had lived in Germany for over 15 years. Requirements included renunciation of previous nationality, absence of criminal conviction and the ability to earn a living. In June 1993, legislation established an individual right of foreigners meeting requirements for simplified naturalization, removing administrative discretion over the naturalization process for these individuals. However, dual nationality was granted only as an exception.

These legal changes were ultimately considered insufficient by both the CDU/CSU and the SPD. It was the CDU/CSU that offered a proposal for double jus soli, that is, to provide citizenship at birth to children born in Germany to foreign parents who were also born in Germany. Similar proposals came from the SPD and Green party when they won the national election in 1998. The passage of the 15 July 1999 citizenship law that came into force in 2000 was ultimately shaped by the preferences of the FDP, whose support was necessary to achieve a legislative majority in the Bundesrat. Rather than adopting a rule of double jus soli, the law provides that children born to foreigners in Germany automatically receive German citizenship at birth, provided one parent has been a legal resident for at least 8 years. These children retain the citizenship of their parents as well, providing for dual citizenship until age 23, at which time the individual must choose which citizenship to retain. The legislation also contains a provision for a 12 month transition arrangements for children born after 1 January 1990. The legislation also provided for simplified naturalization after 8 years residence, as opposed to the 1990 legislation that required 15 years residence.

Comparison to Alternative Explanations

Two theories introduced in the literature review specifically address the case of Germany. The Joppke explanation focuses on the preconditions for legislative change and on the composition of the government in power. Specifically, he argues that governments of the left are the governments that "de-ethnicise" citizenship laws by providing foreigners with easier access to citizenship. Certainly, the historical shift from jus sanguinis to jus soli was accomplished by a government of the left, but earlier reforms of naturalization laws took place under a government of the right, in 1990. Moreover, although the specific legislation passed in 1999 carries the imprint of the SPD and the FDP, the CDU/CSU also brought forward legislative proposals that would have introduced jus soli in the form of double jus soli. Clearly, there appear to be pressures on the governments of the right as well as the governments of the left to facilitate naturalization.

Marc Howard's focus on the politicization of immigration issues stands up better to the German case, as the 1999 legislation failed to include systematic acknowledgement of dual citizenship, in large part due to the politicization of the issue in the Hesse state elections that forced the SPD government to negotiate over the provisions of the law with the FDP and to exclude dual citizenship from the legislation. Nonetheless, there was substantial liberalization of citizenship law in Germany even with the high degree of politicization. Thus both accounts fall short of explaining the specificities of the German case although, on average, they may continue to provide insights into the dynamics of citizenship law.

The model of change in citizenship law outlined above is consistent with the German evidence presented. In line with Hypothesis 1, the growing non-citizen population generated pressures to change the status quo beginning in 1980 when the SPD first proposed changes to citizenship laws. The policies adopted in both 1990 and 1999 reflect the content of Hypothesis 2. German citizenship laws were very restrictive and German politicians faced increasing pressure to liberalize those laws. Politicians of *all* political stripes proposed changes to citizenship law. And, most clearly, as described in Hypothesis 3, as the differences in rights between non-citizens and citizens diminished, the politicians proposed to relax access to citizenship, in an effort to garner greater contribution of responsibilities on the part of the foreign population. Thus, although the model warrants more systematic testing, the illustration of the model using the German case suggests that the models of citizenship proposed thus far have yet to unravel the underlying political incentives that politicians face when considering changes to citizenship laws.

The European Context

Although the model attempts to present a generic model of politicians' incentives to change citizenship law, the case study is applied in the European context. This raises several issues relative to other work presented in this volume.

Maarten Vink addresses the Europeanisation of domestic immigration policies and specifically examines the impact of supranational European institutions on Dutch citizenship policy. The research on "Europeanisation" implies that a second level of analysis is necessary to understand the evolution of citizenship policy, at least in the European context. Whether through legislation adopted at the level of the European Union or "soft norms" generated in the Council of Europe, shouldn't the theory I propose anticipate an international context that somehow modifies the calculus of domestic politicians? The short answer is "not yet." As Vink concludes, "in the cases of asylum and nationality in the Netherlands we saw that although European policies and norms were surely relevant they did not decisively affect domestic politics." The role of supranational organizations is strongest in Europe. If those institutions do not play a major role there, it is unlikely they will play a role elsewhere. That said, the model presented here does not preclude the incorporation of benefits and costs accruing from the international system.

Hubert Peres examines the persistence of national models for the integration of immigrants in Europe. His is a nuanced analysis, examining areas of European convergence as well as the strength of national models to incorporate new principles in a distinctly national manner. He concludes, "the study of these three cases tends to support the arguments of those who are sceptical about the scope of paradigmatic convergences." The model presented here is consistent with this perspective. Each state has a different starting point and distinctive pressures associated with immigration flows. Some states are liberalizing citizenship laws while other states are making access to citizenship more restrictive. If there is any common element to the European states vis-à-vis their immigrant populations, it seems to be the inability to systematically exclude immigrants and to restrict their rights. Thus, politicians may feel similar pressures. But, given the variation in immigration control, the level of welfare provisions, and the access of immigrants to social services, the model presented here predicts that there will be continued variation in citizenship policy across Europe, as well as across the globe.

The model presented here suggests that politicians have a common decision calculus, even within the national context. However, the model, as presented, does not take into account national specificities beyond the rules governing citizen and non-citizen rights and responsibilities and the variation in immigrant stocks and demographics. There are surely additional variables that affect the decision to modify citizenship policy so I make no claims to presenting a fully specified model of citizenship policy.

The European context is important to understand, as this is the domain that has generated most, if not all, of the research on citizenship policy. In testing the model, it behoves us to explore the supranational context, in Europe and elsewhere. Moreover, as Willem Maas' contribution indicates, there are additional domestic variables that should be added to the equation.

Conclusions

One promising dimension of the model presented in the chapter is its generic structure. Issues of citizenship are not unique to western European countries. If our analyses are focused on the specifics of this one region of the world, we may well be overlooking the generic forces that dominate the legislation of citizenship policy and focus on the unique dimensions of the process in Europe. Citizenship and citizenship policy are central to both comparative politics – who participates – and to international relations – the movement of peoples affects issues of national sovereignty. Many states, on all continents, are confronting the issues associated with population movement, whether the flows are associated with labour market migration, family reunification, asylum seekers, refugees, or undocumented populations. Much of the research to date has focused on the admission to territory, the desire to enforce territorial borders and the ability to enforce territorial borders. However, there is a second and equally important dimension of population movement: the admission to the polity. This is an arena that deserves equal examination.

Works Cited

Bauböck, Rainer, Eva Ersbøll, Kees Groenendijk, and Harald Waldrauch, eds. 2006. *Acquisition and loss of nationality. Volume 2: Country analyses. policies and trends in 15 European countries.* Amsterdam: Amsterdam University Press.

Brubaker, Rogers. 1992. *Citizenship and nationhood in France and Germany.* Cambridge, MA: Harvard University Press.

—. 1990. Immigration, citizenship, and the nation-state in France and Germany: A comparative historical analysis. *International Sociology* 5(4): 379-407.

Dreyer, Heinrich M. 1961. Immigration of foreign workers into the Federal Republic of Germany. *International Labour Review* 84: 1-25.

Fassmann, Heinz, and Rainer Münz. 1992. Patterns and trends of international migration in Western Europe. *Population and Development Review* 18(3): 457-80.

Favell, Adrian. 2001. *Philosophies of integration: immigration and the idea of citizenship in France and Britain.* New York: Palgrave in association with the Centre for Research in Ethnic Relations, University of Warwick.

Feldblum, Miriam. 1999. *Reconstructing citizenship: The politics of nationality reform and immigration in contemporary France.* Albany: SUNY Press.

Flournoy, Jr., Richard W., and Manley O. Hudson. 1929. *A collection of nationality laws of various countries as contained in constitutions, statutes and treaties.* New York: Oxford University Press.

Freeman, Gary P. 2004. Immigrant incorporation in western democracies. *International Migration Review* 38(3): 945-69.

Green, Simon. 2004. *The politics of exclusion. Institutions and immigration policy in contemporary Germany.* Manchester: Manchester University Press.

Green-Pedersen, Christoffer and Pontus Odmalm. 2008. Going different ways? Right-wing parties and the immigrant issue in Denmark and Sweden. *European Journal of Political Research* 15(3): 367-81.

Hansen, Randall, and Patrick Weil. 2001. *Toward a European nationality: Citizenship, immigration and nationality law in the EU.* New York: Palgrave.

Howard, Marc Morjé. 2007. Comparative citizenship: An agenda for cross-national research. *Perspectives on Politics* 4(3): 443-55.

Joppke, Christian. 2003. Citizenship between de- and re-ethnicisation. *European Journal of Sociology* 44(3): 429-58.

Marshall, Barbara. 2000. *The new Germany and migration in Europe.* Manchester: Manchester University Press.

Money, Jeannette. 2002. The political economy of citizenship policies. Paper presented at the International Studies Association Annual Meetings, March 24-27, in New Orleans, LA.

Organisation for Economic Co-operation and Development. Multiple years. *Trends in international migration. Continuous reporting system on migration.* Paris: Organisation for Economic Co-operation and Development.

Sadiq, Kamal. 2009. *Paper citizens: How illegal immigrants acquire citizenship in developing countries.* Oxford: Oxford University Press.

Schmitter, Barbara E. 1981. Trade unions and immigration politics in West Germany and Switzerland. *Politics and Society* 10: 317-34.

Seely, Jennifer. 2007. Limiting access to citizenship in Africa: A cross-national comparison. Paper presented at the International Studies Association Annual Meeting, February 28-March 3, in Chicago.

Soysal, Yasemin N. 1994. *Limits to citizenship*. Chicago: University of Chicago Press.

United Nations. 1954. *Laws concerning nationality*. New York: United Nations.

Weil, Patrick. 2002. *Qu'est-ce qu'un français? Histoire de la nationalité depuis la Révolution*. Paris: Grasset.

CHAPTER FOURTEEN

CENTRALIZED AND DECENTRALIZED IMMIGRATION POLICIES IN MODERN FEDERALIST SPAIN

ELIZABETH M. WRIGHT

Introduction

A new phenomenon is sweeping Europe, something that has not happened there for centuries. For the first time in recent history, Europe is becoming the destination for large migrant populations from all over the globe. Historically speaking, Europe has been the origin of a large portion of the migrant population in the world. However, this trend has reversed in recent decades, and Europe has become a desirable destination for migrants fleeing economic and political hardships in developing and underdeveloped parts of the world. As major players in the world economy today, the nations of Europe are having to cope with immigration as never before. Spain is no exception to this rule. For the first time ever, Spain has had to create immigration policies to control the influx and the integration of the immigrants who were arriving in ever-increasing numbers until the recent economic downturn.

I will argue that in a federal system like Spain's, political actors at the central and sub-central levels of government face important political costs and benefits by centralizing or decentralizing certain aspects of immigration policy—specifically, sub-central actors seek to gain control over policies dealing with the social integration of immigrants for both economic and "nation"-preserving reasons (language, culture, identity, etc.), while central actors seek to gain control over policies dealing with immigration control (borders, visas, work permits, security). I will use the Spanish case to argue that there are important reasons for the nation-preserving aspect of the theory taking the lead in Spain as opposed to the economic, market-preserving aspect (Boushey and Luedtke, 2006; see also Weingast 1995, Rodden and Rose-Ackerman 1997, Oates 1999). The Spanish division of responsibility of the different classifications of immigration policy is more firmly rooted in nation-preserving motivations because of the historical, cultural, and linguistic particularities of the individual regions within the federation.

Taking this from the perspective of nation-preserving federalism, this theory can effectively illuminate the case of Spain. The Spanish style of federalism is considered to be a bit different from other forms of federalism.[1] Historically, Spain was divided into many kingdoms, and over the centuries, it has been unified, at least geographically, into the nation-state that we find today. The historical, cultural, and linguistic divisions that are present in Spain today were allowed to continue to exist as such by the post-Franco Constitution, ratified in 1978. The article of the Constitution which provides for the existence and creation of the "Autonomous Communities" was created with the purpose of allowing a high degree of autonomy within the country while maintaining a Spanish identity and sovereignty over the entire geographical entity.

The central Spanish government fights strongly for its prerogatives over not just immigration control (i.e. regulating the inflow of *new* immigrants) but *all* aspects of "immigration policy", seemingly creating a political conflict. The Constitution firmly states that all issues of immigration, like those of national security, national economic policy, etc., are to be under the control of the federal government. Thus, the federal government objects when the Autonomous Communities (ACs, hereafter) refer to their integration policies as the "immigration policy" of the region; they claim that all immigration policies are reserved strictly to the federal government and that the policies implemented by the ACs are for social integration and not related to immigration specifically. But when taken in light of the distinction between immigration *control* policies and immigrant *integration* policies that Boushey and Luedtke (2006) set forth,

---

[1] There are even some scholars who do not consider it to be a federalist state at all (See Ruiz Vietez, 2004; CIA World Factbook; as cited by López Laborda and Monasterio Escudero, p. 448, although they believe Spain is a federal country). I feel that that is clearly not the case. When Spain's internal structure is compared with other federalist states, there are striking similarities, regardless of the exact wording of their respective constitutions.

there is no categorical conflict between the immigration policies governed by the state and those administered by the Autonomous Communities.[2]

I argue that the main motivation of the federal government in allowing a large degree of decentralization in certain types of immigration policies is a cost they have to pay in order to preserve the nation as a whole in its present form. Basque Country and Navarre have especially strong and prominent separatist movements because of the cultural and linguistic differences between themselves and Spain. Catalonia and Galicia, while not having as successful a separatist sentiment and movement as Basque Country and Navarre,[3] also have very strong claims for autonomy based on history, culture and language. The cost of maintaining the integrity of the state is that the federal government has had to devolve power to the Autonomous Communities. One of the benefits it receives is that politicians in the ACs gain political benefits with the power that has been delegated to them, thus mitigating separatist sentiment.

The benefits for the ACs are as Boushey and Luedtke (2006) describe. They avoid the large-scale costs associated with the implementation and enforcement of immigration control policy and are able to focus their resources and energy on integrating immigrants into society in the ways that are specifically attuned to the needs of the society. One of the costs, however, is that the financial burden of these policies lies at the sub-central level. These financial burdens are not equally nor evenly dispersed among the ACs because immigrant populations are concentrated within a small number of the ACs, with Catalonia, Madrid, Andalusia, and Valencia receiving over two-thirds of the nation's immigrants (Balch, 2005). This is partly due to the types of policies that these individual ACs have adopted and implemented, which facilitate and even invite settlement in those particular areas.

---

[2] On the distinction between control and integration policies, see also Hammar, Thomas, *Democracy and the Nation-State: Aliens, Denizens and Citizens in a World of International Migration*, Avebury: Aldershot, 1990.

[3] The Basque Country and Navarre both have separatist movements that have been successful in securing taxing systems and treasuries that are almost completely autonomous from the central government (López Laborda and Monasterio Escudero, 2007). To date, these are the only two ACs that have been successful in achieving such a high degree of fiscal autonomy. Although Catalonia and Galicia have very strong separatist sentiments and movements, they have not achieved the degree of autonomy from the central government that the Basque Country and Navarre have, although their claims to such are essentially the same.

Fig. 14.1

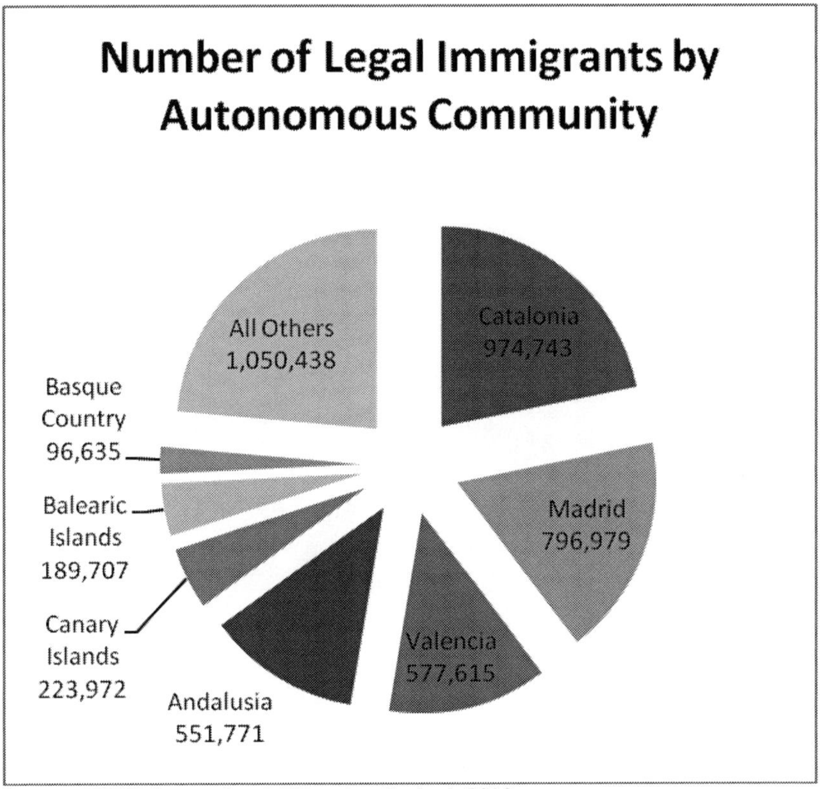

Source: OECD International Migration Outlook 2008.

Fig. 14.2

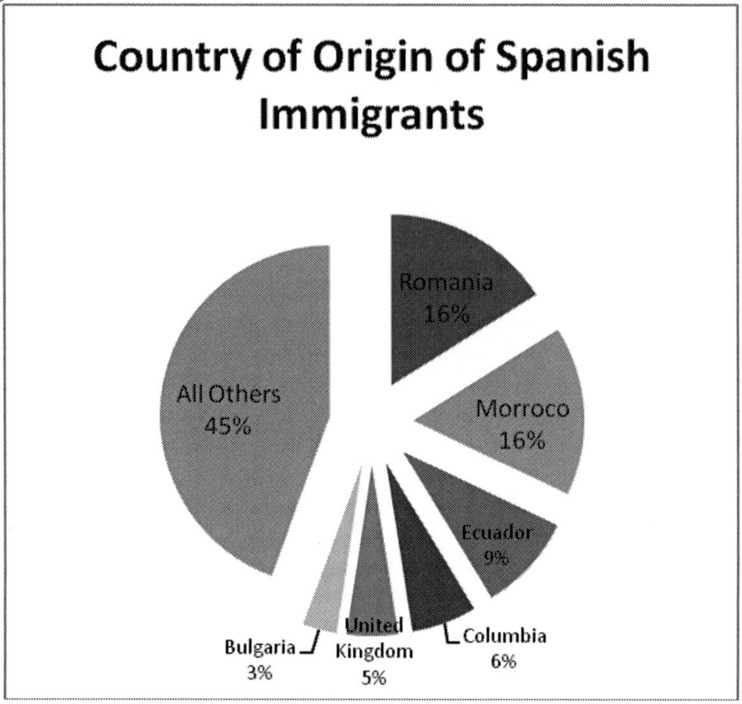

Source: OECD International Migration Outlook 2008.

In this paper, I will first explain the theory as developed by Boushey and Luedtke, touching on the costs and benefits of centralized and decentralized immigration policies in a federal system. I will then look at the basis for Spanish federalism, both historically and actually under the current Constitution. Although Spain is by definition a parliamentary monarchy (CIA World Factbook), the provisions for a federal arrangement between the state and substate levels are clearly provided for in the Spanish Constitution. After establishing the Spanish model as a federal one, past and present centralized immigration policies are examined, beginning with the first Spanish national immigration policy, which was enacted in 1985 and ending with the current immigration policies. This section will also discuss the controversial policy of regularization, a process oft-used in Spain through which illegal immigrants can gain legal status if they meet the specific requirements that are set forth in each round of regularization. The following section looks at the various decentralized policies found throughout Spain in the different Autonomous

Communities, classifying the types of policies into three categories: exclusionary policies, which tend to prevent the integration of immigrants into society; inclusionary policies, which facilitate immigrant integration; and middle-of-the-road policies, which tend to be more neutral, neither making great efforts to include nor to exclude immigrants in society. Despite the efforts of ACs one way or another, the implementation of decentralized policies sometimes backfires, as demonstrated in the case of El Ejido, which is discussed in some detail. Some unanticipated successes can be seen as in the case of Aguaviva, a small town that has embarked on an immigrant integration program at the municipal level. This case demonstrates the economic motivations that are driving some decentralized immigration policies. The paper will then conclude with a brief discussion on how the Spanish case fits and supports the Boushey and Luedtke's theory, followed by some suggestions for further examination of the topic in general.

Fiscal Federalism and Immigration Policy

Federalism is marked by the hierarchical arrangement between different levels of government. The state level is at the apex of the hierarchy, ruling over regional and local governments while allowing them jurisdiction over certain policy areas. At times, this results in policies that fall under the same category, such as the different aspects of immigration, but also fall under different jurisdictions, making them either centralized or decentralized policies. At times, the needs of each substate unit are so diverse within the same policy area, such as immigration, it is difficult to create a universal policy at the state level that will meet the needs of each unit. In its attempts to be equitable, the state ends up providing little in terms of practical policies that meet the wide range of demands from the substate units. For example, in the area of immigration, the state has the tools at its disposal to equitably control the inflows of people. However, because of the unequal distribution of immigrants throughout a country, the state is unable to create a policy for integrating immigrants socially and economically that is universally applicable while being flexible enough to accommodate the demands placed on each substate unit. Thus, it is advantageous to delegate the responsibility of immigrant integration to the substate units, as they are more attuned to local needs and can create the policies that will most likely achieve social and economic integration of immigrants within the country as a whole. This results in a wide range of policies across the country, but it allows each substate unit, whether regional or municipal, to adapt according to the number of immigrants they receive and the local motivations for integration (or lack thereof).

Certain motivations for centralization or decentralization of immigration policies exist within federalist systems, as is seen by borrowing a theory from fiscal federalism (Weingast 1995, Rodden and Rose-Ackerman 1997, Oates 1999). There are costs and benefits of having immigration *control* policies at one level of government while centring immigration *integration* policies at another. The two types of policies (control and integration) will tend to fall under the jurisdiction of different levels of government because costs can be minimized and benefits maximized if immigration *control* policies are centralized and immigrant *integration* policies are decentralized. They define immigration *control* policies as those which "[deal] with keeping out unwanted immigrants," while immigrant *integration* policies are those which "[deal] with the recruitment, selection, welcoming and settlement of desired immigrants" (Boushey and Luedtke, 2006). As will be explained below, state/central governments will seek to control the flow of immigrants into the country, while regional/decentralized governments will seek to integrate the immigrant with policies that aim to recruit, select, welcome, and settle.

There are two ways that jurisdictions can gain from immigration policy—preserving 'national'/regional character, and preserving economic markets. The way policies are divided between the jurisdictions or levels of government, even when those policies are categorically the same, depends on the perspective or point of view of each level of government. Since each level of government has motivations toward market preservation and nation preservation, we are likely to see both centralized and decentralized policies demonstrating those motivations.

In the literature on market-preserving federalism, we find two factors in particular that most likely will yield the centralization and decentralization of certain types of policies. The first factor is that subnational governments generally have primary regulatory responsibility over the economy within their own jurisdiction. Each substate unit will likely choose to regulate their own economy as guided by the economic demands inherent therein. The second factor is that a common market must somehow be ensured. The common market is most likely to be controlled by the central government, thus prevents subnational governments from erecting trade barriers against other units (Weingast, 1995).

In the case of immigration, these two factors speak especially to the movement of labour within the country as well as into the country. Substate governments will tend to regulate the economy and labour force by means of integration policies. Since immigration is not evenly distributed among different substate units, each government will have different needs in terms of the actual policies that are enacted. As noted above, national policies dealing with integration are not always effective, having sacrificed efficiency for equity. As a result, as the first hypothesis states, substate governments are more likely to push for jurisdiction over the integration of immigrants into local markets in order to provide for the needs of their own economy. This is likely to occur because substate governments are more in tune with local needs and preferences and are more able to address them through integration policies. Integration policies, in this respect, are those that address issues such as recruitment of labour, health care, housing, education, and other public services.

The second factor looks at the preservation of a common market within state borders. Because of pressure from the regions containing primary ports of entry for immigrants, governments will push to see that this aspect of immigration policy is centralized. If there were barriers erected that prevent the free flow of labour within the country, the regions receiving all of the new immigrants would soon demand that those barriers be removed to relieve the pressure of receiving so much labour. The common market is most likely to be maintained through oversight from above, in other words, the central government. Thus, the second hypothesis states that due to high costs and inefficiencies that arise with maintaining immigration control policies at the substate level, immigration control policies will be centralized. By controlling the flow of immigrants at the state level, immigrants are able to enter through a single entrance point and are then able to move freely about the state. This reduces costs for the immigrant and each level of government.

As far as nation preservation is concerned, the main point of departure for the state and substate units lies in how the "nation" is defined. At the state level, the nation is defined politically, according to international borders. To the state government, a citizen of the nation is equivalent to a citizen of the state. It seeks to define who can become a citizen and who cannot. According to this perspective, the French state defines who is a French national, the Russian state defines who is a Russian national, the Indonesian state defines who is an Indonesian national, etc. There is no distinction beyond the political. At the substate level, however, the government may have to deal with a different type of nation: the cultural and/or linguistic nation. Especially in regions that are dominated by this type of nation, there often arises the desire to make distinctions about who is a member of the nation and who is not. There may be the desire to exclude outsiders, thus insulating the "otherness" of the nation. In cases where a nation is facing extinction, one may encounter the need to augment the nation with outsiders who are willing to take on the language and culture thereof. Regardless of the desire to include or exclude outsiders, because of desires to preserve the linguistic or cultural nation, the prerogative to define this type of nation generally puts pressure on regional governments and makes this definition of nation the predominant one at the substate level.

The desire to achieve nation preservation is not exclusive to one level of government or another. This desire, however, is defined by the perspective of each respective level of government. The central government, having jurisdiction over the entire state, will define its interests insofar as they concern the entire population. They will seek to define what criteria must be fulfilled in order to be a citizen of the country. Not only that, it will also defend the national borders against attack and intrusion. Thus, the third hypothesis states that the ability to define citizenship and to secure national borders are traditional nation-preserving functions and are thus reserved to the state.

As mentioned, the perspective of substate governments in terms of nation preservation vary from those held at the state level. Pressure from different cultural and/or linguistic groups, especially those which tend to be concentrated in a single geographical region, forces substate governments to respond to their demands and preferences. Thus, the fourth and final hypothesis suggests that since local cultural and linguistic preferences exist, substate governments are likely to control policies that deal with the integration of new immigrants into society. Because of local preferences for either immigrant inclusion or exclusion, substate governments, rather than the state government, receive the pressure to integrate immigrants accordingly. There is more motivation to create these integration policies in substate regions where politicians feel more pressure from citizens to preserve the culture and language common to that area. There has to be some sort of perceived threat, however, in order for this to become a working argument. This argument is especially applicable in a society so fragmented as that found in Spain.

Spanish Federalism as a Basis for the Centralization and Decentralization of Immigration Policy

Spain is a historically fragmented society because it is made up of several medieval kingdoms that were conquered and unified centuries ago. It is a country made up of many different nations of people with distinct histories, cultures, and languages. There are three main regional identities in Spain: Basque, Catalan, and Galician. Each one of these regions has maintained a desire for self-control in spite of years of subjection to the Spanish state. Unable to achieve such autonomy, each region has waited for the opportunity to arise in which they could once again enjoy some degree of self-control (Núñez, 2000). Although the regional identities of these groups are centuries old, the nationalist movements that have emerged from them only date back to the late 19th century (The Economist Special Report). Harsh repression of nationalism and nationalist movements under the Franco regime (1939-1975) led to the reaction against such actions by the national government. The provisions for a high degree of decentralization in the 1978 Constitution represent the will of the people after living for almost three decades under a repressive, highly centralized dictatorship (Ruiz Vietez, 2004).

After the death of Francisco Franco in 1975, work began on a new form of government and a new Constitution for Spain. The new Constitution was ratified on 7 December 1978 by a referendum by the Spanish people, with 59 percent of the population ratifying it (Ruiz Vietez, 2004). Eduardo Ruiz Vietez makes a concise summary of that system of government in Spain. He says,

> Spain is organized politically as a single State, with the 1978 Constitution emphasizing national unity as a basic principle. Nevertheless, the Constitution does acknowledge the existence of nationalities and regions within the State and envisages the possibility of territorial self-government for them, without defining a map or a definitive model. Constitutional development has given rise to the division of Spanish territory in 17 Autonomous Communities, each endowed with broad legislative and executive powers, with legal status of each Autonomous Community defined by its Statute of Autonomy (Ruiz Vietez, 2004, p. 149).

The 1978 Constitution directly addresses the need and desire for some separation of power between central and regional governments. The constitutional provision that allows for this system of government reads, "The State is organized territorially into municipalities, provinces and Self-governing Communities that may be constituted. All these bodies shall enjoy self-government for the management of their respective interests" (Spanish Constitution, Part VIII, Chapter 1, Article 137). Part VIII of the Constitution continues by enumerating the responsibilities of territorial governments.

As Ruiz Vietez states, the Constitution did not formally define the territories that would become the Autonomous Communities that now exist in Spain, with the exception of the Basque Country, Catalonia, and Galicia. These three regions, having historical claims to autonomy, were granted special status in the Constitution as distinct regions within the country, and were placed on a fast track to achieving the status of Autonomous Communities. All remaining regions in the country were allowed the ability to gradually achieve the same status, but lacking the historical claims of the three aforementioned regions, all other regions had to wait longer for the same rights of self-government. According to Article 147 of the Constitution, those regions applying must draft a Statute of Autonomy stating the name of the Community based on its historic claims to autonomy; the territorial boundaries; the name, organization, and seat of the autonomous institutions; and the powers which would be assumed within the framework of the State Constitution, as well as the transfer of services which would then be assumed by the Autonomous Community.

Articles 148 and 149 lay forth the division of competences as they would apply to the state and regional governments. The competences of the ACs are: providing for the well-being of people residing in their territory; country planning; housing; public works; regional transport and infrastructure; farming; the environment; culture; tourism; sport; etc. Article 149 states the competences of the State are: economic stability; income and wealth redistribution; provisions of national public goods and services, including international relations, defence, customs and tariffs, foreign trade, currency system, financial, banking, and insurance systems, and basic Social Security legislation and funding. Most importantly, however, Article 149 section ii gives to the state exclusive competence over nationality, immigration, emigration, status of aliens, and right of asylum. As defined in the theory above, these would all fall under the category of immigration *control*, but it makes no mention of what would be defined as immigrant *integration*. Those areas of policy are implicit in Article 148.

The division of and responsibility over the specific competences in these Articles is by no means unchangeable. Article 150 states that each

AC may apply for increased control over areas governed by the State. The State reserves the ability to confer or delegate additional competences to any or all of the ACs through an organic act, provided the nature of the competences permits them to do so. There is much room for interpretation in this article, but it is clear that the system laid forth in the Constitution is a fluid one by design, allowing both state and regional governments to adapt to circumstances that may arise in the future. Some of the ACs, especially those with large coastal areas such as the Canary Islands and Catalonia, are putting this Article to the test by requesting more competence over border control and the monitoring of territorial waters (Esteban and López-Sala, 2007). It remains to be seen how the State will deal with this request for even more decentralization of immigration policy.

Centralized Policies

As the theory predicts, Spain is motivated to retain immigration control policies as centralized because they are seeking to define who can enter the country and become a Spanish citizen. They are controlling the modern Spanish nation, while giving the ACs the ability to control the historical nations found within Spain by persuading or dissuading immigrants to settle in a particular area. This gives the historical nations within Spain the prerogative to define who can become a member of or be integrated into that nation.

Spain has a relatively short history of immigration policy at the central government level; the first legislation on immigration was passed in 1985. This law was passed without much public discourse, its main purpose being a move to comply with European Community policies before Spain joined the EC the following year. At the time, there were an estimated 200,000 foreigners living in Spain, most of which were Europeans. The 1985 Law was quite restrictive, aiming mostly at expelling irregular immigrants. The law left many areas with no specific legislation and made no mention of the concept of integration of immigrants, although there was an implicit understanding that that would fall under the control of the ACs. The gaps created by this law were left to be filled by administrative regulations, which gradually filled in a few of those gaps (González Enríquez, 2007; Pabón López, 2007).

In 1985 Spain was still a country of emigration, but soon after its admission into the European Community, its economic growth began to increase rapidly, causing the flow of migration to turn from emigration towards immigration. Between 1986 and 1990, over 2 million jobs were created in Spain, which created a demand for cheap immigrant labour. As a result, more comprehensive regulations were needed to control the numbers of immigrants that began to come to Spain, and laws were thus enacted in 2000 to address the issue (Pabón López, 2007). Referred to simply as the Ley Orgánica 4/2000, the first law was introduced in order to address the increasing rate of immigration that the country was beginning to see. The 4/2000 Law was a combined effort by the coalition government as well as the opposition, with major contributions coming from the Catalan centre-right nationalist party and the Socialist Party. This new law was focused on integration more than any previous law, and it was also seen as being more liberal toward the rights of both legal and illegal immigrants (González Enríquez, 2007). It was necessary for the centre-right Popular Party in power to make concessions to the opposition in order to pass the 4/2000 Law. However, with its position in government firmly established, the Party passed the 8/2000 Law, which focused more on border controls and restrictions and less on integration issues.

Another major step forward in immigration policy was the establishment of the GRECO Plan (Global Program on Regulation and Co-ordination of Immigrants and Alien Affairs in Spain). The plan presents immigration as desirable and positive, but at the same time it emphasizes the unavoidability of it. Alex Balch described the attitude of the Plan as “one of welcome through clenched teeth” (Balch, 2005, p. 22). The way he puts it, no one was happy to be dealing with immigration as a permanent phenomenon, but it was something that had to be done.

This plan had several aspects which aimed to address the increasing number of immigrants in Spain. The main aspect of the program focused on legal means of entry through the use of annual quotas in certain sectors, seasonal work permits, and a general system of immigration. The annual quotas applied mostly to the economic sectors which employed the highest numbers of immigrants, those being construction, agriculture, and services, including hotel, transport, and domestic services (Terrón, 2004). Each year, 10,000 work permits were granted to new immigrants under this system. This area of the plan functioned as a permanent regularization system under which illegal immigrants could apply for existing positions and acquire a work permit. In 2002 the quota system was reformed to allow employers to recruit workers directly from their country of origin based on international agreements Spain had made with those countries. Seasonal work permits were a second part of the plan. More than twice as many seasonal permits as annual quota work permits were given each year. These permits were intended for seasonal and temporary work, and were mostly available to the agricultural sector. Together, these two aspects account for only 35,000 work permits each year. The remaining immigrants fall under the general system, which refers to any other means of entry aside from the annual quotas and seasonal work permits. The permits allowed under the general system must be applied for by the employer. He bears the burden of proving that there is no other legal resident (Spanish or otherwise) who is available and qualified for the position. The vast majority of these permits have been granted under the rounds of regularization that have been enacted periodically. This system is slow and inefficient, resulting in many immigrants losing their regular status as they wait for their paperwork to be processed by the state (Balch, 2005).

The Plan also included provisions for co-development in an effort to improve conditions in countries of origin. It was hoped that the program for co-development would encourage potential immigrants to remain in their home country due to improved infrastructure and economic circumstances. It was also seen as a means to train immigrants and then encourage them to return home, taking their newly-acquired skill sets with them, which would also help development efforts in their countries. Unfortunately, the centralized nature of the co-development programs prevented society and individuals from working well within the system. A lack of specific budgetary commitment on the part of the national government also doomed the Plan to failure (Terrón, 2004). Although the GRECO Plan was deemed an overall failure, mostly because of lack of funding, the principles upon which it was based were still attractive to the leaders of the Socialist Party (PSOE). This is evident by the way that the principles were incorporated into the amendments made to the immigration law in 2005. The plan has since been renamed the Fund for the Integration of Immigrants, and has received enough funding from the government to ensure its success (González Enríquez, 2007).

It was the Popular Party who was in power when the immigration laws of 2000 and the GRECO plan were created. The laws 4/2000 and 8/2000 initially spurred yet another round of regularization, but after the 2001 regularization, the party insisted that it would not authorize any more regularizations as long as they were in power. They held firm in this position, but failed to win the following election in 2004 (González Enríquez, 2007). When the Socialists took power in 2004, they reversed the position held by the previous government and proceeded to make changes to immigration laws that had been in place for only a short time. Although there have been no major departures from previous policies in general, there seemed to be a recognition that the existing system needed to be changed if it was going to be effective. In 2005, the immigration law was amended to allow for the consolidation of the existing system found under the GRECO Plan (annual quotas, seasonal labour permits, and the general system) (Balch, 2005). It also allowed for the most recent round of record-high regularization (the largest single amnesty to undocumented immigrants of any industrialized country), which has been the round most criticized by the international community, as well as by certain groups within Spain itself (Pabón López, 2007).

Regularization

Regularization is an important topic in Spain's centralized immigration policy, and as such, merits some attention in and of itself. The use of regularization to control the number of illegal immigrants living in Spain has been one of the main strategies used in the past twenty years. It is also one of the most widely criticized policies that has been adopted by the national government. Regularization is the process by which illegal immigrants are offered the opportunity by the national government to regularize or legalize their status as immigrants in the country. In many of the cases, there are limitations and regulations on who is permitted to apply for regularization, thus avoiding a sort of "blanket amnesty", a term used by detractors of regularization to describe the outcomes thereof.

Since 1985, there have been six rounds of regularization (1991, 1993, 1996, 2000, 2001, and 2005), which have been directed toward different sectors of immigrants. The 1991 round was available to all irregular immigrants. This regularization was valid for only one year, but was renewable if certain requirements were continually met. The following round in 1993 added more requirements and also set quotas in the sectors of agriculture, unskilled construction workers, and various services (including domestic service). Another round of regularization began in 1996. In this case, regularization was only available to those immigrants who had at one time had legal status but had been unable to renew that status. New rounds followed the enactment of the 4/2000 and 8/2000 immigration laws, and the Popular Party claimed that those would be the last rounds of regularization. The most recent round of regularization in 2005 was enacted by the Socialist Party and was, in effect, a blanket amnesty for all illegal or irregular immigrants that were in the country by a certain date. The thinking behind this strategy is to "set the clock to zero," thus, in theory, eliminating all irregular immigrants for the time being. During the assigned time frame for regularization in the 2005 rounds, over 1.1 million residence permits were given to employed immigrants and their immediate family members (Pabón López, 2007).

Regularization has been widely criticized over the years, and in recent years, the criticism has been coming from other members of the European Union. Although Spain is well within its sovereign rights to enact such measures as regularization, other members of the EU, such as France and Germany, have not reacted kindly to the measures taken. Those other members look at regularization as "a form of back door immigration to the European Union" (Pabón López, 2007, p. 6). Regularization is also criticized as having a "call effect", leading current and potential immigrants to believe that they should risk settling in Spain illegally because they will be able to obtain legal status during coming rounds of regularization (Pabón López, 2007). Ultimately, regularization is just a stop-gap measure that does not come near to the solutions that are required and needed in a comprehensive immigration reform. As Adam Balch suggests, regulation of immigration through better immigration control policies has much more effective long-term results than repeated rounds of regularization do (Balch, 2005).

Fig. 14.3

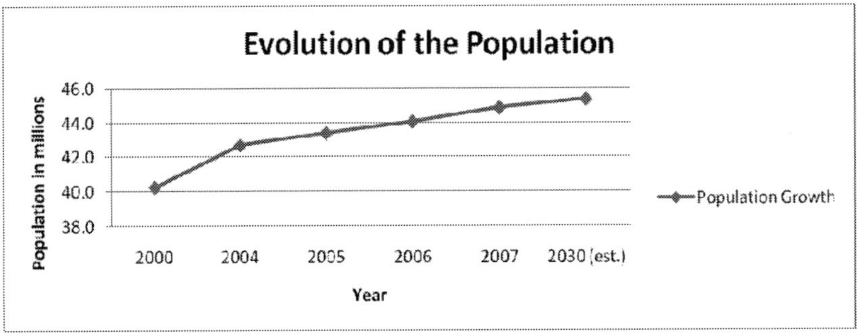

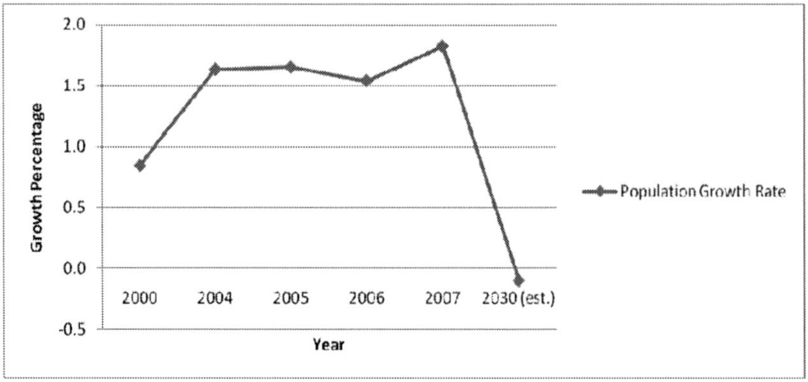

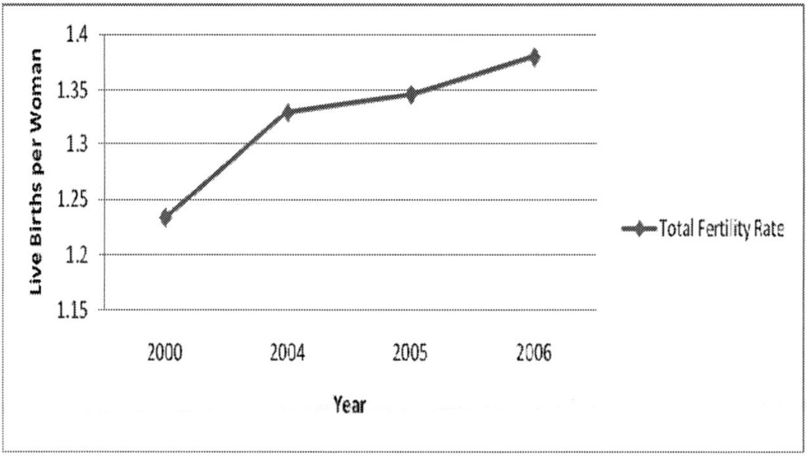

Source: OECD Country Statistical Profiles 2009, Spain.

* Although immigration is not a popular topic in Spain, projections for the Spanish population demonstrate the demographic need for augmentation to the population. With the fertility rate below the rate necessary for long-term population stability, as well as a projected negative population growth by 2030, the need for immigrants or some other stimulus for sustaining the Spanish population becomes clear.

Fig. 14.4

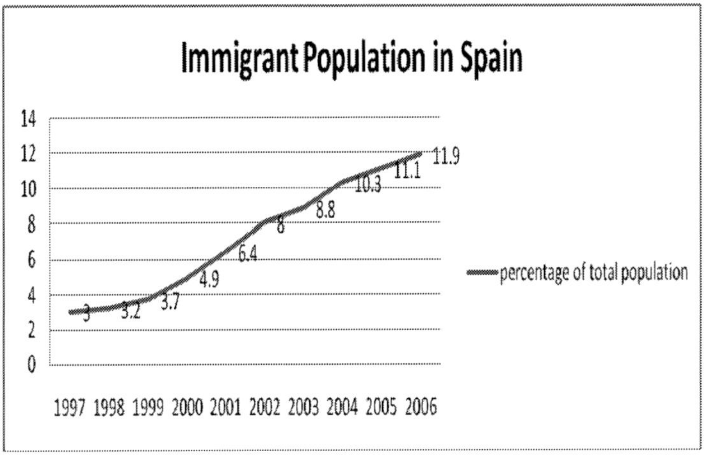

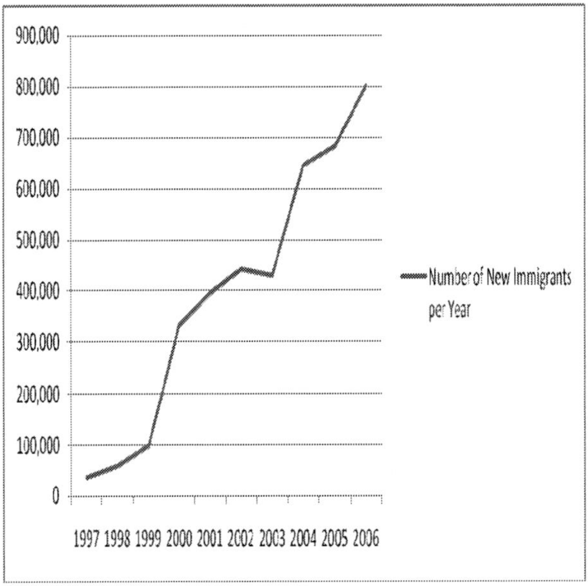

*Inflow data based on population registers
Source: OECD International Migration Outlook 2008.

Even with all of the recent legislation and laws enacted by the government, immigration is an issue that continues to challenge the Spanish government today. According to the most current OECD statistics, Spain continues to receive a significant number of immigrants. In 2006 around 800,000 people migrated to Spain, which represents a 17% increase from 2005. By early 2007, there were 4.5 million foreigners registered to live in Spain, which is nearly ten percent of the total population of Spain (OECD International Migration Outlook, 2008). It is reasonable to believe that while the numbers of immigrants rises yearly, the central government will continue to search for policies that will help them better control the flow of immigration and help them find long-term solutions for a long-term issue.

Decentralized Policies

In terms of nation-preserving motivations, there seem to be two different tactics employed when creating immigration policy at the sub-central level. First there are those ACs who approach nation preservation through the use of what I will call *exclusionary* practices and policies. These practices and policies are those that act to discourage immigrants from settling within a certain area because of the nation's desire to maintain the integrity and purity. Other areas adopt more *inclusionary* practices and policies, which are aimed at integration through helping the immigrant population to learn the language, culture, and history of the nation. In addition, there are also programs in place to help the autochthonous population learn more about the cultures and traditions of the immigrant communities that have settled there. Rather than trying to make a distinct division between insiders and outsiders, inclusionary methods seek to integrate the new elements of society in such a way that does not compromise the dominance of the autochthonous society and culture.

Exclusionary Policies

Nationalistic tendencies are the main driving force in creating exclusionary immigration practices and policies. With the number of nations represented in Spain, especially considering their concentration within certain geographical areas, one might expect to find many policies aimed at the preservation of their culture and language. Indeed, such policies exist, but an interesting point to make is that these policies do not necessarily extend themselves into immigration policies. Within the AC of the Canary Islands, however, such exclusionary policies and practices have been directed at immigration.

The Canary Islands are located about 100 km west of southern Morocco. The Islands have belonged to Spain for over five centuries, and have acted as the crossroads between Europe, Africa, and America. Their location has allowed them to be a hub for flows of commerce and people. Over the centuries, the Canaries have been settled by ethnicities from around the world, making for a very diverse culture. This has never been a problem until recent years when immigration to the Islands has caused a political uproar. The changes that began occurring in the early 1990s have changed political views on immigration and have resulted in the shift toward exclusionary policies toward immigrants.

Historically, the Canary Islands have been one of the major sources of emigration from Spain. Communities of former residents of the Islands sprouted throughout Latin America and the Caribbean. The large Canarian population in Venezuela prompted the people to refer to Venezuela as the eighth island of the Canaries. When migration trends in Spain began to shift away from emigration and toward immigration, the Canary Islands were among the first of the ACs to experience the shift. Much of this immigration was due to return migration by those Canarians who had settled elsewhere for a time and were returning "home". They also experienced increased arrivals from European countries such as the United Kingdom who had long-standing connections with the islands. Up until the mid-1990s, almost three-fourths of the population of the Canary Islands was European. But by 2005, the percentage of the European population of the Islands had dropped below 50 percent. Today, the Canary Islands rank fifth (out of 17) among ACs in the number of immigrants they receive each year. The major change in immigration patterns and the impetus for the changing views and policies on immigration was a massive increase in the number of clandestine arrivals of illegal immigrants from Africa (Terrón, 2004).

Moroccans represent the largest single group of immigrants to Spain (Balch, 2005). They have available to them a number of access points into Spain. The Autonomous Cities of Ceuta and Melilla which are located within Morocco have been a traditional access point, as well as mainland Spain via the Strait of Gibraltar to Andalusia. As surveillance of these access points by the Spanish government has increased, African immigrants have sought other means by which they can enter Spanish territory. These immigrants have shifted their course to the west and are now entering Spain through the Canary Islands. The increased flow of African immigrants into the Canary Islands began in the 1990s and has continued until the present. The situation attracted even more attention in 2006 when more than 10,000 new immigrants arrived in the Islands in the first five months of that year (Esteban and López-Sala, 2007).

The major influx of African immigrants is seen as a threat to the Islands' economic viability and their shared identity as Canarians. Politicians have seen fit to discourage outsiders from settling there and have done so vis-à-vis policies that are aimed at protecting the Canarian nationalistic identity, which has been created by the leading nationalist political parties found on the Islands. Most nations mould their identity around a shared distinct language or culture, as is found in Basque, Catalan, and Galician communities in other parts of Spain. The Canary Islands have no distinct language to bind them; instead they rely on the *hecho diferencial canario*, or the idea that the Canary Islands are socially and culturally distinct from Spaniards living on the mainland. The idea of the *hecho diferencial* dates back to a time before the Franco dictatorship. Even Franco recognized the difference between the Canary Islands and the mainland and allowed them some degree of autonomy, even under his highly centralized rule.

Canarians have also based their distinct nature on the agrarian roots that have existed in the Islands for centuries. In defining the differences that create their Canarian identity, they have succeeded in creating a notion of the "Other", thus helping them define the threat against them. As Valeriano Esteban and Ana María López-Sala (2007) state,

> This is an extremely complex otherness which, in its most extreme versions, not only includes immigrants from the Third World but also Europeans, mainland Spaniards and even Canarians from other islands. The immediate need to defend the territory has obviated the difficulty of reaching a consensus over a highly problematic national narrative. The political minimalism of Canarian nationalism serves as a perfect counterbalance to this extremely effective social closure (p. 103).

According to this argument, their need to defend their territory has, in effect, erased most of the problems usually encountered when attempting to create a common identity among a heterogeneous population.

The dominant political party on the Canary Islands, the Canarian Coalition (*Coalición Canaria*), has been in power for over a decade. During that time they have succeeded in working together with whatever party is in power in Madrid to discourage immigrants from settling in the Islands through a redistribution policy. This policy allows officials from the Canary Islands to transfer illegal sub-Saharan immigrants who arrive in boats to the Islands to other ACs on the mainland. As a result, very few African immigrants are allowed to settle on the Islands. This was an informal arrangement until 2005, when the Canaries-State Sub-commission helped the central and regional governments officially agree to the practice. Attempts have been made to create residence laws that would restrict foreigners and Spanish citizens from other ACs from settling there. In 2003, the Canarian government created a committee to explore the possibilities of such laws. In line with the arguments about centralization of immigration policies, the committee found that such laws would be unconstitutional under the Spanish Constitution, and they would also be in violation of the protection of freedom of movement as established under EU law. Many left-wing Canarian nationalists, in addition to some members of the Canarian Coalition, are still seeking the implementation of these residence laws, arguing that the flow of people seeking to settle on the Canary Islands disrupts the local economy and threatens Canarian identity (Esteban and López-Sala, 2007). Based on these arguments, the debate over residence laws as well exclusionary immigration policies in the Canary Islands may continue.

Inclusionary Policies

In sharp contrast to the exclusionary immigration policies found in the Canary Islands, Catalonia has become a model of inclusionary immigration policies in Spain. Catalonia receives over 22 percent of Spain's new immigrants each year, making it the number one recipient of immigrants among the 17 ACs (Balch, 2005). Over 25 percent of the total number of immigrants living in the country have chosen to settle in Catalonia. This represents about 5 percent of the total population in Catalonia (Obiols i Gras, 2003). Rather than making integration difficult or impossible, the Catalan government has put in place policies and practices that work toward inclusion of immigrants into Catalan society.

Among recipient states, there is evidence of three models of integration: multimosaic, assimilationist, and integrationist (Peres, this volume).[4] The multimosaic model is seen in the United States and the

---

[4] Hubert Peres (this volume) argues against the use of such national models of immigrant integration. He believes that these models are misleading and

United Kingdom, and is represented by the presence of many individual groups within the system which do not regularly or officially interact with other groups. France ascribes to the assimilationist model and embraces the attitude that those coming to France must leave behind who they were and assimilate themselves into French society as soon as possible by becoming like the French are. Catalonia has embraced the integrationist model, which is characterized by the desire for immigrants to keep their own culture, but to integrate into the host society. This is accomplished by facilitating access to society, while impressing on immigrants that Catalonian society has its own rules, values, mechanisms, way of living together, and way to solve problems. Immigrants who want to settle in Catalonia should demonstrate their readiness to help add to the Catalonian lifestyle without radically contradicting it. The success of this model is dependent on work opportunities for immigrants, guarantees of certain rights, fulfilment of certain obligations, and the predisposition to assimilate into a new culture and society (Rigau i Oliver, 2003).

In 2003, Salvador Obiols i Gras, then-Secretary of Immigration for the Catalonian government, stated that the goal of the government of Catalonia was to make Catalonia a place that welcomes foreigners but at the same time preserve Catalonian unity and culture. To achieve this goal, he said, it would require the participation and hard work of individuals and groups, both foreign and native. The main policy that reflects this goal is the policy of accommodation. It is accepted that there is no single, universal way to accommodate every group that wants to settle in Catalonia. It is a long process, and conflicts will inevitably arise between natives and immigrants. The responsibility largely lies with the immigrants to accept the social and cultural norms that exist in Catalonia because the community has offered its hospitality and the existent norms represent the work of many generations of natives working together to achieve certain ends. This does not remove all responsibility from the natives, however. They must also work with the immigrants to ease their transition into the new society (Rigau i Oliver, 2003).

The policy of accommodation that has been adopted and implemented in Catalonia has been accompanied by many social programs that have helped to ensure the integration of immigrants into Catalonian society. These programs range from free education for immigrant children to assistance finding employment to free health care (Obiols i Gras, 2003). It

---

stereotypical when, in fact, there is some overlap between models in their actual policy application.

also includes programs that deal with the cultural integration between Catalan and immigrant cultures. There are programs that help facilitate relations between native and immigrant families at schools. Others address cultural differences specifically. A civic centre program called "Other Peoples, Other Customs" has been enacted to promote community interest in other cultures that surround them. Information about other cultures and customs is made available to the natives in Catalan. Courses are also made available to immigrants to help them learn Catalan, the official language in Catalonia (Rigau i Oliver, 2003). Finally, starting in 2002, the government created and began distributing a pamphlet called *Guía de Acogido* (Welcome Guide) to all immigrants entering Catalonia. It is a bilingual pamphlet, having translations in Catalan and the immigrant's native language (if available), alerting them of all of the policies and programs available to help ease their transition into life in Catalonia (Obiols i Gras, 2003).

Rather than acting upon a perceived threat to their identity as in the Canary Islands, Catalonia has managed to enact policies that embrace the differences inherent in immigrant groups and that promote integration, while strengthening Catalonian identity through the same programs. Catalonia has been able to preserve the language and culture which define it as a nation while accepting the realities of immigration that face it. By encouraging social and cultural programs that help newcomers learn about the dominant identity of the region, Catalonia has managed to preserve its national characteristics without excluding the large immigrant population from them.

Middle of the Road Policies

Some ACs do not show a strong tendency toward either exclusionary or inclusionary policies. They fall somewhere in the middle of the spectrum, according to the needs and desires of their populations. Here is a brief look at some of the policies enacted in other ACs that do not represent either extreme of decentralized immigration policies.

The Balearic Islands approach immigrant integration as an opportunity and tend toward inclusionary policies, although their policies are not as overt as those found in Catalonia. Antonio Sancho Cervantes, who served as the General Director of Social Planning (*Director General de Planificación y Ordenación Social*) for the Balearic Islands, presented the policy areas that most concerned the AC in terms of social integration of immigrants. The government views immigration as an opportunity and a challenge, but not as a problem. They view integration as an effort to achieve equality of the exercise of rights and the access to public services. In order to apply that view to the social structure of the Islands, the government has established policies that address a broad range of social establishments. Since Catalan is one of the main languages used on the Islands, programs in schools as well as in civic organizations are aimed at facilitating the learning of Catalan by immigrants. They view this as one of the key methods to integrate immigrants into Balearic culture and society. The government has also made an effort to publish information that will prove helpful in gaining access to health care, job markets, and housing. Similar to programs seen in Catalonia, the government seeks to diffuse the culture of the Balearic Islands among immigrant populations, thus fostering understanding between native and immigrant cultures (Cervantes, 2003). Although they do not receive immigrants on the same scale as Catalonia, the Balearic Islands have established policies that tend to encourage the prompt integration of what immigrants they do receive.

Basque Country has one of the strongest nation-preserving reputations in Spain. Basque politics have been governed by nationalist and separatist movements for most of recent memory. But something interesting has happened with Basque immigration policy. Rather than enacting strict exclusionary immigration policies as might be expected, Basque immigration policy has been rather neutral compared to other ACs. Basque Country has not been the recipient of large numbers of immigrants, receiving only a small percentage of the nation's yearly flow of immigrants (Balch, 2005).[5] This is due in large part to economic factors. Economic opportunity is heavily concentrated in the Mediterranean coast of Spain. Since they do not receive a large number of immigrants, the nation-preserving motivations found in Catalonia or the Canary Islands are not found in Basque immigration policy.

While the strong nation-preserving motivations are not necessarily present, neither is there a strong movement to integrate immigrants into society. This is particularly evident in the Community's co-development programs which are designed to help encourage development in countries of origin. The idea of the co-development programs is that by helping with development in countries of origin, immigrants will eventually return to their countries when circumstances improve. This program promotes

[5] The top seven receiving ACs received over 80 percent of the total new immigrant population in 2005. Basque Country combined with the remaining nine ACs received only 18 percent of the total new immigrant population in that same year.

the direct involvement of immigrants as trained development agents in their country of origin. The fostering of Basque relations with these countries helps facilitate the processes in place for developmental aid. The Basque government has also eased restrictions on home payments by the immigrant population. On the surface, this program appears as if it would discourage any type of integration by immigrants into Basque society, and perhaps it does to some degree. Similar programs enacted in Catalonia have, in fact, proven to aid in immigrant integration because of the work that they are conducting in close cooperation with the native population. This side effect, however, has not stymied Basque efforts to encourage immigrants to one day return to their country of origin (Terrón, 2004). The result, in the area of co-development at least, is a lukewarm reception by Basques, but not an outright rejection of immigrants that might be expected.

Results of Poor Implementation of Decentralized Policies

The policies themselves may seem to be black and white, but the implementation thereof can have the tendency to stray into gray areas. For example, although the intent of these policies and regulations is not to exclude certain groups specifically, the end result is sometimes the very thing that they profess to avoid. This was the case in the Autonomous Community of Andalusia in the city of El Ejido in the year 2000. El Ejido is a city of about 42,000 people on the Mediterranean coast of Spain in the AC of Almeria. Mainly an agricultural town, El Ejido is a natural draw for immigrants, who traditionally work in the agricultural sector. Greenhouse-related technologies in recent years have allowed for an economic boom to occur, but the new technologies require labour that Spaniards often are not willing to perform. Low wages make the agricultural sector profitable, and only immigrants are willing to work for wages as low as $3.50 an hour, despite unemployment rates hovering around 20 percent. Thus the greenhouses of El Ejido were filled with immigrants, mainly of Moroccan origin.

The living conditions of the roughly 5500 immigrants in El Ejido were especially bad. Only about 25 percent of immigrants lived within the city limits; the remaining 75 percent lived in plastic shacks and renovated warehouses owned by the greenhouse operators. About 60 percent of the Moroccan population lived in what would be considered sub-par housing (no electricity, no kitchen, no running water, and no sanitary bathroom facilities). Employers and citizens alike preferred to have the immigrants out of sight altogether. Although the regional government had implemented policies to combat such conditions for the immigrants, the local governments consistently sidestepped those policies. This removal from society obviously prevented any type of integration into Spanish society from occurring. Not only were the immigrants separated from society, they were also separated from each other in their living situations, which prevented them from forming any type of social connections with other immigrants (Caro, 2001).

In February 2000, a Spanish girl was killed by a Moroccan immigrant who was employed at one of the local greenhouses. This event ignited the riots which the Spaniards referred to as "la caza del moro" [the moor hunt].[6] Moroccan nationals were beaten up, their houses were burned and ransacked, their businesses were looted and wrecked, and their mosques were desecrated and destroyed. Immigrants fled to the mountains to avoid the persecution or hid with other immigrants whose homes had not yet been destroyed. When peace was again restored, between 500 and 700 Moroccans were left homeless; 49 were injured. Of the 158 people ultimately arrested during the riots, 92 of them were immigrants (Caro, 2001).

After the riots subsided, conditions actually got worse for most of the Moroccan immigrants there. As employers had to replace dwellings, they did so by bringing in prefabricated barracks to the sites of the greenhouses. In order to keep them out of the sight of citizens, the greenhouses provided company transportation to take the immigrants to hospitals and malls outside of the city limits. As conditions worsened, over 3000 Moroccan immigrants relocated within the country to find better living and working conditions. Still in need of immigrant labour, the greenhouses hired Eastern European and Latin American immigrants to fill the void left by the Moroccans. The replacement workers were treated much better because they either spoke Spanish already, which helped integrate them into society quicker, or they had whiter skin and shared the same "European" traditions (Caro, 2001).[7]

---

[6] "Moro" is the Spanish word for "moor" and is often used as a derogatory term for Maghrebis.

[7] It is interesting to note how perceptions of national identity change depending on the type of immigrant that is being dealt with. When it comes to dealing with immigrants of non-European origin, the identity claimed by the people is Spanish or European while defining the immigrant as something outside of that identity (in

Decentralized Policies at the Municipal Level: the Case of Aguaviva

Decentralized policies do not exist only at the AC level; they are also starting to form at the municipal level. One very specific case of decentralized policies at this level is found in the small village of Aguaviva in the Autonomous Community of Aragon, located about 175 miles west of Barcelona. This small community has experienced a high degree of depopulation, similar to many of the small towns and villages in Spain and across Europe, due to the migration of residents to surrounding urban areas. The mayor of Aguaviva, Luis Bricio, decided to enact a program to address the problem of depopulation in this small village. In 2000 he went to Buenos Aires, Argentina to invite people to leave Argentina to come settle in his village in Spain. He initiated the program in Argentina first, thinking that the transition would be facilitated by a shared language and heritage. What he had to offer was free airfare, guaranteed employment, education for children, and loans and subsidies that would help the immigrants find housing. The following year he expanded the program to Romania, offering them the same benefits as the immigrants from Argentina. Some of the key demands of the immigrants were that they must be willing to sign a contract to remain in Aguaviva for five years, they must agree to repay any loans given for housing, and they must be under the age of 40 with at least two children under the age of 12. Theoretically, this case illuminates how sub-central jurisdictions can seize upon both market- and nation-preserving motivations to become more involved in immigration policy, as long as centralization of control is not threatened.

As the program progressed and immigrants flowed in from the outside, things did not go exactly as initially expected. Bricio anticipated that the integration of the Argentines would be a much easier process than it proved to be. The linguistic and cultural similarities between the two cultures were not enough to make up for the attitudes that the Argentines had in regards to the village and the integration process. Many of the program's initial participants found that life in a small village was not an attractive prospect and left Aguaviva soon after arriving. Some had no intention of ever staying in the village to begin with. It is estimated that

---

this case, Muslim). It seems that when the basis of their identity is challenged, the people unite under a more general nationality, whereas when there is a shared identity, such as Spanish or European, there emerges fracturing within that shared identity (Basque, Catalan, Galician, etc.).

600 participants eventually left for one reason or another. Some of the villagers were also disenchanted with the Argentine immigrants, saying that they were haughty and expected everything to be handed to them with little or no effort on their part. On the other hand, the Romanians were found to integrate better than the Argentines. It was found in this village that the main determinants of successful integration were a strong work ethic and job skills brought by the immigrants (most jobs offered were in construction); the Romanians exceeded the Argentines in both categories. In addition, they had lower economic expectations in general, which made them more likely to stay in Aguaviva, rather than seeking better economic opportunity in nearby cities.

Another unexpected outcome from this program was the criticism levelled at it from outside the community itself. Some criticize the fact that the mayor was inviting foreigners to enter the country, while other areas in Spain and in Europe are trying to slow the flow of immigration altogether. Although Spain is trying to control the number of immigrants who enter the country each year, they are sympathetic towards those who enter the country through legal channels, as opposed to those who enter irregularly. Another criticism was that the program initiated by Bricio could only serve as a temporary solution and that it does not get to the root cause of the demographic crisis of the town. Now that the program has officially ended, the village of Aguaviva finds that people are still coming to the village because of the notoriety that the program gained over the years in which it was enacted. Not many of the people stay, but with the constant flow of people, every once in a while, a few will end up settling there (Anderson, 2006; Voss, 2003).

The main purpose of enacting this program in Aguaviva was not specifically about autonomy and preservation of the local identity, which demonstrates that national preservation is not always the main motivation in creating a decentralized immigration policy. There are times when market forces act as a stronger motivation when making the policies that will govern immigration (though demography as an issue can obviously have both economic and "national" implications). The autonomy that exists in the ACs allows them to develop plans and policies that are tailored to local needs, rather than forcing them to adapt a generic, universal policy which is imposed from the top down. Specific needs, such as demographic ones, are not apt to rapid change, but the village of Aguaviva is experiencing a gradual reversal that may be the determining factor in the survival of the community. The flexibility for creating appropriate integration policies in the ACs and the municipalities as permitted by the federal arrangement in Spain has allowed for this program and ones similar to it to be implemented in other communities around the country, thus placing the costs for localized and specialized policies at the sub-central level, as the theory predicts.

Conclusion

The Spanish case goes far in supporting the theory of centralized and decentralized immigration policies. At the state level, Spain demonstrates that the national government is willing to bear the costs of controlling their borders and who is allowed to enter by continually drafting new immigration policies. In little more than 25 years, the government has enacted at least five variations of a national immigration policy aimed at tackling a problem that is still very new to the country. More than that, they have also taken steps to define who can legally reside in the country. This is evident thorough the frequent, though controversial, practice of regularization. Although the policy has been highly criticized in recent years, the Spanish government is working to *control* immigration in the best way it is able at this point in time.

Due to the federal structure of the country and the demands of the ACs, Spain leaves the *integration* of immigrants to the substate levels of government. There are no national provisions as to how this should take place, and this becomes evident when examining the different policies that have taken shape within different ACs. On one hand, Catalonia is making an attempt to integrate immigrants into society while maintaining the region's cultural identity. On the other hand, the policies made in the Canary Islands serve to exclude immigrants as much as possible in an attempt to preserve the unique identity that has developed over the years. Each of these ACs demonstrates one end of the spectrum of approaches to nation-preserving behaviours. Catalonia expects its immigrants to adapt their native culture to fit within and contribute to the Catalan culture. The Canary Islands attempt to keep immigrants separate from Canarian culture by enacting policies that discourage any form of permanent settlement on the islands. The ACs that fall somewhere in the middle of this spectrum have policies that neither attempt to include nor exclude immigrants, and this seems to be tempered a bit by the economic or demographic demands within each AC.

It can be seen that nation-preserving motivations, while being the dominant motivation in integration policies, are not the only type of motivations that drive the creation of immigration policy in Spain. The economic demands that vary among the ACs also play a part in what type of policies emerge. This can be seen in the types of policies that are being enacted in ACs such as the Basque Country, where one might anticipate finding policies based on nation-preserving motivations. Instead of finding this type of policies, immigration policies in the Basque Country seem to be more economically motivated than one might expect to find in an area with such prominent nationalist sentiment. Also, as demonstrated in the case of Aguaviva, demographic motivations can also play a role in the types of policies and programs that emerge. These two cases show that there are implications beyond the nation-preserving motivations that are at the forefront of substate immigration policies in Spain. Although the idea of nation preservation is important in this case, it is not universally applicable throughout the country. Specific economic or demographic needs of a substate unit can be a compelling driving force which explains deviations from the types of policy that one might expect to find in any particular region, especially in regions like the Basque Country that have a strong nation-preserving sentiment in most other policy areas.

Although far from perfect, the system of centralized and decentralized immigration policies is succeeding in dividing optimal competences between the competing levels of government. This separation of competences remains in line with the aims of the 1978 Constitution, which marked a major leap from centralization to decentralization of political authority. There is still some progress that must be made, however, as evidenced by the El Ejido Riots of 2000. The ways in which existent policies are applied are not always in keeping with the original intentions of lawmakers.

The country is still a novice in terms of dealing with immigration and the policies that will best represent the long-term need and interests of the country. While it may be helpful to draw from the experiences of other European nations with longer histories, Spain must also draw its own conclusions based on its form of government. The demands of the division of competences inherent in their federalist system make their case unique from most other European countries. Incorporating the demands of the European Union and of the Schengen Agreement's free travel area adds even more complexities to potential reforms that the Spanish immigration system may undergo in the future. This is certainly an area of interest that could benefit from continued research. Despite the challenges that have arisen and are present today, the centralization and decentralization of certain immigration policies in Spain has been a successful venture up to this point, for both the ACs and the central government, with relatively minimal political conflict surrounding the division of powers. If economic recession or separatist sentiment flare up in the future, however, this relative consensus could be called into question as political costs and benefits change for all levels of government.

Works Cited

—. 2003. *Aurrera Goaz: Third World Congress of Basque Communities.* Vitoria-Gasteiz, Servicio Central de Publicaciones del Gobierno Vasco.

Anderson, John Ward. 2006. A global village in Spain. *Washington Post*, June 8, 2006, page A16.

Balch, Alex. 2005. *Immigration as a labour market strategy.* Migration Policy Group. Available online at: http://migpolgroup.socialchange.net.au/multiattachments/2561/DocumentName/SpainImmigrationLabourMarketStrategyBalch.pdf

Boushey, Graeme and Adam Luedtke. 2006. Fiscal federalism and the politics of immigration: Centralized and decentralized immigration policies in Canada and the United States. *Journal of Comparative Policy Analysis* 8(3): 207-24.

Caro, Manuel J. 2001. Tying racism in El Ejido to Spanish and European politics. *Rutgers Law Review* 54: 893-907.

Cervantes, Antonio Sancho. 2003. El desarrollo de políticas de integración de Gobierno Balear. In *Perspectivas de la inmigración en España: Una aproximación desde el territorio.* Barcelona: Icaria Antrazyt.

The Economist Special Report. 2008. How much is enough? *The Economist.* Available online at: http://www.economist.com/specialreports/displaystory.cfm?story_id=12501023

Esteban, Valeriano, and Ana María López-Sala. 2007. Breaking down the far Southern border of Europe: Immigration and politics in the Canary Islands. *Migraciones Internacionales* 4(1): 87-110.

Flesler, Daniela. 2008. *The return of the moor: Spanish responses to contemporary Moroccan immigration.* West Lafayette, Indiana: Purdue University Press.

González Enriquez, Carmen. 2007. Spain. In *European immigration: A Sourcebook*, ed. Anna Triandafyllidou and Ruby Gropas. Aldershot: Ashgate.

Laborda, Julio López and Carlos Monasterio Escudero. 2007. Regional governments: Vertical imbalances and revenue assignments. In *Fiscal reform in Spain*, ed. Jorge Martinez-Vasquez and Jose Felix Sanz-Sanz. Cheltenham, UK: Edward Elgar Publishing.

Losada, Antón. 2000. National identity and self-government in Spain: The Galician case. In *Identity and territorial autonomy in plural Societies*, ed. William Safran and Ramón Máiz. London: Frank Cass.

Majone, Giandomenico. 2006. Federation, confederation, and mixed government: An EU-US comparison. In *Comparative federalism: The European Union and the United States in comparative perspective*, ed. Anand Menon and Martin Schain. Oxford: Oxford University Press.

Moya Milanés, Pedro. 2003. Las políticas de inmigración de la junta de Andalucía. In *Perspectivas de la inmigración en España: Una aproximación desde el territorio*. Barcelona: Icaria Antrazyt.

Núñez, Xosé-Manoel. 2000. Autonomist regionalism within the Spanish state of the Autonomous Communities: An interpretation. In *Identity and territorial autonomy in plural societies,* ed. William Safran and Ramón Máiz. London: Frank Cass.

Oates, Wallace E. 1999. An essay on fiscal federalism. *Journal of Economic Literature* 37(3): 1120–49.

Obiols i Gras, Salvador. 2003. Posición y aportación de Catalunya en materia de inmigración extranjera. In *Perspectivas de la inmigración en España: Una aproximación desde el territorio*. Barcelona: Icaria Antrazyt.

Organisation for Economic Co-operation and Development. 2008. OECD international migration outlook 2008: Spain country note. Available online at: www.oecd.org/els/migration/imo

Pabón López, María. 2007. Immigration law Spanish-style: A study of the regularización of undocumented workers in Spain. *Georgetown Immigration Law Review* 21(4).

Pajares, Migues. 2008. Inmigración y Mercado de Trabajo, Informe 2007. Observatorio Permanente Integración, Ministerio de Trabajo e Inmigración.

Peres, Hubert. 2009. Towards the end of national models for the integration of immigrants in Europe? Britain, France and Spain in comparative perspective. In *Migrants and minorities: The European response*, ed. Adam Luedtke. Newcastle upon Tyne: Cambridge Scholars Publishing.

—. 2003. *Perspectivas de la inmigración en España: Una aproximación desde el territorio*. Barcelona: Icaria Antrazyt.

Rigau i Oliver, Irene. 2003. La inmigración extranjera en Catalunya: Presente y futuro. In *Perspectivas de la inmigración en España: Una aproximación desde el territorio*. Barcelona: Icaria Antrazyt.

Rodden, Jonathan and Susan Rose-Ackerman. 1997. Does federalism preserve markets? *Virginia Law Review* 83(7): 1521-72.

Ruiz Vietez, Eduardo J. 2004. Federalism, subnational constitutional arrangements, and the protection of minorities in Spain. In *Federalism, subnational constitutions, and minority rights*, ed. G. Alan Tarr, Robert F. Williams and Josef Marko. Westport, Connecticut: Praeger.

Schain, Martin. 2006. Immigration policy. In *Comparative federalism: The European Union and the United States in comparative perspective*, ed. Anand Menon and Martin Schain. Oxford: Oxford University Press.

Terrón, Anna. 2004. *International migration and relations with Third Countries: Spain*. Migration Policy Group. Available online at: http://www.supplierdiversityeurope.eu/multiattachments/2573/DocumentName/Spainforeignrelationsfullreport.pdf

Triadú, Joaquim. 2003. Un Reto del presente, lectura de una análisis sociológico de la inmigración. In *Perspectivas de la inmigración en España: Una aproximación desde el territorio*. Barcelona: Icaria Antrazyt.

Voss, Michael. 2003. Rural Spain welcomes immigrants. *BBC News*, June 19, 2003. Available online at: http://news.bbc.co.uk/1/hi/world/europe/3002928.stm

Weingast, Barry. 1995. The economic role of political institutions: Market-preserving federalism and economic growth. *Journal of Law, Economics and Organization* 11(1): 1–31.

Williams, Robert F. and G. Alan Tarr. 2004. Subnational constitutional space: A view from the states, provinces, regions, länder, and cantons. In *Federalism, subnational constitutions, and minority Rights*, ed. G. Alan Tarr, Robert F. Williams, and Josef Marko. Westport: Praeger.

CHAPTER FIFTEEN

RIOTS AND RIGHTS: COMPARING RACIAL POLICY MAKING IN FRANCE AND THE U.S.

JACQUELINE S. GEHRING

In 2005 riots rocked the suburbs of Paris, and spread to other parts of France, shocking the French public and leading to calls for new and different approaches to racial policy making. Integration policies in France were widely called into question as some argued that these *jeunes d'origine immigrée* ("youths of immigrant origin") were not truly French and had remained foreign—thus their very un-French explosion of violence. Others saw the riots as the extreme result of the problems faced by youths of the *banlieues* (suburbs) and the lack of support they have received from the government and the lack of opportunities for them in mainstream French economy and life.

At the heart of the riots was a general discontent among youths of the suburbs with the large gap between the Republic's promise of *liberté, égalité, fraternité* (liberty, equality and brotherhood) and the realities of their lives—marked by inequality, discrimination and problems with the police. Indeed, as a number of scholars have argued, although the problems of racial inequality in France and the U.S. are certainly not identical (e.g. Wacquant 2006 who argues for a division between American ghettos and French banlieues), "the roots of recent uprisings in France are not dissimilar to those that sparked the events of . . . Los Angeles (1992). The institutional racism plus police harassment minus jobs equation is certainly the same." (Murray 2006, 30)

In fact, the 2005 riots in France suggest that although there remain many differences between the two societies with regard to racism, discrimination and inequality, the basic frustration of racialised people in both states is quite similar: that they live in a free and equal state, but that they are often denied the promised freedom and equality of their fellow citizens. Although elites in both societies often ignore these inequalities, violent outbursts such as the 2005 riots in the French suburbs and similar riots in the US, perhaps most recently in Cincinnati (2001) and more historically in the 1960s, have forced elites in both societies to respond. Although both states have reacted with increased policing and imprisonment of minority youths, they have also moved towards other policies that purport to address the inequalities that underlie the frustration expressed in the riots. In the United States policies emerging out of the Civil Rights movement and the riots of the 1960s include affirmative action and anti-discrimination institutions. In France, meanwhile, the riots emboldened the government to strengthen new Anglo-American style anti-discrimination institutions that it had introduced in the previous seven years, and allowed emerging diversity and affirmative action style programs to take a stronger foothold.

In this chapter, I propose that the riots and their fallout are not the only events in France that are similar to historical experiences in the United States. Instead, I argue that there are a number of similarities between current developments in French racial policy and the development of American racial policy in the 1960s and 1970s. By considering some of the similarities and differences between the French and American experiences, I hope to shed light on current debates in France over the efficacy of new anti-discrimination institutions as well as the possible development of other policy changes.[1] I attempt to do so while making as few egregious errors in comparative analysis as is possible when considering two very different states, cultures, legal systems, and time periods.

Although the historical development of race relations in France and the United States are quite different (not the least in that "race relations" as such does not exist as a term in France), both states recognize the problems of inequality faced by racialised people in their societies and attempt to address those problems via public policies. In the last ten years in particular, there have been significant shifts in the fight against racism and discrimination in France. These changes include the introduction of

[1] Although my primary goal is to situate the French experience, I also wish to make clear that I do not think this policy exchange is only a one-way street. Americans have and will continue to learn from the French approach and France's current transformation of imperfect American institutions.

stronger racial anti-discrimination laws, the implementation of affirmative action-style programs that increase admissions of under-represented groups in institutions of higher education, a commitment by major employers to increase diversity in their workforce and the creation of an equality agency (*La Halde*) which attempts to aid victims of discrimination and promote equality. One result of the riots of 2005 was that the government moved to address the problems perceived to be at the heart of the unrest by strengthening these nascent anti-discrimination institutions and by increasing opportunities for youths of the banlieues by introducing short term jobs and by making the job application process more colour-blind.[2]

These changes are, on paper, dramatic ones in light of France's historical approach to racial policy in which France positioned itself "in explicit and self-conscious opposition to the United States" (Calves 2004, 219) and focused on fighting racism and discrimination without turning to litigation, without creating official racial categories, without collecting any extensive statistics on discrimination and without implementing American-style affirmative action. As Tomen (this volume), argues, this unique French approach to issues of diversity has strong historical roots. The conscious choice to avoid these approaches to fighting racism finds its basis in the fear of *communautarisme* which is seen as the source of the disarray that marks race relations in Great Britain and the United States (Calves 2004). *Communautarisme* is difficult to translate, but is often used to suggest a type of multiculturalism gone wrong where people's affiliation with an ethnic (or religious) group surpasses their primary French or American identity, tearing apart the national community and creating divisions that cause social decay and are difficult to heal (Bowen 2006). Unfortunately, the traditional French Republican approach which promoted equality by preventing too much focus on ethnicity or supposed race often amounted to simply ignoring race and proclaiming equality in the hopes that this alone would make racism go away. Ignoring race without other strong policies to combat discrimination or to promote equality has failed, however. As former minister of equal opportunities Azouz Begag (2007, 33) observes: "the incantation of well-worn republican myths is to no avail. Every pore in the skin of French universalism is now coming out."

---

[2] These reforms did not reach full implementation, however. See below.

As the problems with the old model have become acknowledged, France has searched for both new solutions and ways to re-invent its old approach. This has led to a middle ground between reconstructing old institutions and the wholesale adoption of new, often Anglo-American, ones.[3] Indeed, France is at something of a cross-road when it comes to racial policy. It is undergoing what Alec Hargreaves described in 2004 (228) as a "half . . . revolution in "integration" policy," since it "stop[s] short of some of the key features of British anti-discrimination policies." This chapter proceeds with a consideration of some of the major recent innovations in French racial policy making and then compares those developments with the American experience of the 1960 and 1970s where there was also a half, and then a full revolution in racial policy making.

Innovations in French Racial Policy

In this section, I focus not only on the emergence of affirmative action policies but also on the activities of the new anti-discrimination/equality agency, *La Halde*, the push for the collection of racial/ethnic statistics and the emergence of NGOs led by young "ethnic" people. Overall I find that the story of racial policymaking in France during this time is one of both great change and substantial resistance and opposition to change. As Calves (2004, 223) argues, in recent years France has been remarkably open to considering possible changes to its anti-racism policy so much so that

> one can only be surprised by the remarkable speed at which affirmative action rhetoric and policies have been adopted in France. The country is discovering simultaneously the United States of the 1960s (outreach techniques) and that of the 1980s (diversity promotion).

Despite such openness, however, Calves also notes a distinctly French approach prevails (one she supports). In light of the limitations of new Anglo-American style institutions and the persistence of traditional French policies, some observers who had hoped for more significant changes have concluded that racial policy in France has only changed minimally without much substantive reform and that things seem unlikely to change much

[3] Considering that the traditional French evaluation of Anglo-American racial anti-discrimination institutions is so negative and at least partially accurate (racism and discrimination do certainly persist in both states) it may be surprising that such institutions have been adopted at all. For possible answers to this conundrum see Guiraudon, 2003; Geddes and Guiraudon, 2004; and Gehring, 2007.

further in the near future (Chappe 2008; Lepinard 2008). Considering the experience of the United States, where many equality activists had a similarly bleak outlook by the mid-1960s, I venture into possible ways in which the equally bleak image of racial policy currently in France may be misleading, just as it was in the US (to the extent that such institutions are seen as weak and as mere symbols that do not materially aid in the fight against racial discrimination). I then consider some of the possibilities that still may exist for the further development of French anti-discrimination institutions, the seed of which I believe can be seen in the activities of actors such as the Halde and other civil servants and NGOs.

New Anti-Discrimination Institutions

France transposed the European race directive in 2001 implementing a law that looks strikingly like the American Civil Rights Act of 1964. This law outlaws both direct and indirect (or disparate impact) racial discrimination and racial harassment in a number of areas including education, employment and goods and services; requires states to shift the burden of proof in anti-discrimination cases; and protects victims of discrimination from retaliation for reporting discrimination, among other provisions (Council Directive 2000/43/EC). In 2004, France also established a new equality agency, *La Halde* (*Haute Autorité De Lutte Contre Les Discriminations Et Pour Egalité*), whose mandate is to promote equal opportunity and fight discrimination in France.

The Halde's mandate is two-fold. First, to aid victims of discrimination based on a number of categories (eighteen in total) in addition to supposed racial or ethnic belonging, such as women, the disabled, gay and lesbians, etc… which it does primarily through legal counselling of victims, legal training of attorneys and judges, and other law-centred activities. Second, it is expected to promote equality in French society via advertisements, studies of discrimination, and activities with the social partners and non-governmental actors (NGOs). The activities of the Halde are overseen by its director Louis Schweitzer (appointed by former President Chirac), and decisions on individual discrimination disputes are made by a college consisting of representatives from diverse groups including the *Conseil d'Etat* (Council of State), private business, and the president of the NGO *Ni putes, Ni soumises* (Neither Whores nor Submissives). When a victim has a legal claim of discrimination the case is brought before the college who can then issue non-binding opinion on the case which may be introduced into a court of law if an official suit is filed.

Legal Activities of the Halde

By European standards, the Halde is a relatively strong anti-discrimination agency with a budget of over 11 million Euros and a staff of over 50. Yet, considering the size of its workload, these limited resources restrict the agency's activities significantly. In addition to a lack of resources, the Halde also lacks the power to pursue litigation itself, to punish private actors for not complying with their investigations (although it may appeal to the courts to compel action) or to demand compliance with anti-discrimination law from private enterprises (although it may impose limited fines). Furthermore, French courts thus far seem resistant to strongly enforcing racial anti-discrimination provisions. Despite its limitations, the Halde is expected to address a large number of areas of discrimination in French society. It received over 14,000 claims the past two years (2007-2008) and had only 27 lawyers and 5 extra interviewers whose job was to work with these cases. Furthermore, claims to the Halde are on the rise with a 57% increase in 2007 as compared with 2006 and an additional 25% increase in 2008. Of the claims filed, racial and ethnic discrimination is the most oft cited ground and the majority of claims are made in the area of employment (The Halde). Overall then, the Halde has been given a massive mandate, but almost none of the powers or resources necessary to achieve the goals set before it.[4]

Despite these limitations the Halde assists thousands of victims of discrimination each year by giving them legal counselling about their cases. Yet, one of the major criticisms of the Halde's work is that very few of the victims who bring claims to the Halde actually end up taking their cases to the courts. Less than thirty percent of the claims fielded by the Halde actually make it through its claim process with many being discarded for lack of evidence or being closed by the person who filed the complaint. Of those processed, only a handful result in legal victories within the nation's courts. Critics, such as Malek Boutih, former head of SOS Racisme, argue that the small number of court cases suggests that the Halde may be actually achieving very little justice for victims of discrimination.

---

[4] It should be noted that despite these limitations, businesses in France have criticized the Halde for having too many investigatory powers. "La Halde, nouvel arbitre dans le monde du travail" La Croix http://www.la-croix.com/article/index.jsp?docId=2361956&rubId=4079.

Yet the limited number of cases and the Halde's own limitations (including a lack of real power to pursue cases directly and the limited budget for legal counselling) can too easily obscure the fact that the Halde has developed a focused strategy of anti-discrimination litigation which seeks to create a French anti-discrimination jurisprudence that will influence the legal interpretation of anti-discrimination cases in the future. Faced with so many limits on its power and budget, the Halde has made an explicit choice to not focus on achieving justice for individuals, which is the aspect of its work its critics find most disappointing. Instead, by selecting good cases that can help create precedents in the area of anti-discrimination law it hopes to make a difference in individuals lives over the long-term: by establishing for French judges, lawyers and litigants a cohesive anti-discrimination jurisprudence. This is very similar to the way in which the EEOC limited its focus to creating precedent when it faced limited resources, focusing those small resources in major fights instead of spreading them too thin among the many individuals with claims (Lieberman, 2002). The Halde is working at a "construction of anti-discrimination law in France" so that everyone knows that "anti-discrimination law will have to be dealt with in France—even if it goes against the legal culture" (Latraverse personal interview, 2008).

The Halde also depends on cooperation with civil society in order to make these few cases a success, asking NGOs to help them find better data, to train and inform court experts, and to send promising cases to the Halde, etc… The emergence of NGOs who do support some of the Halde's efforts will be discussed below.

Testing Activities of the Halde

The criticism of the Halde does not end with its lacklustre record in getting cases into the courtroom to secure justice for individuals. In 2008, the Halde released a CV (curriculum vitae) "testing" study of 15 of the top 40 companies in France in which it found pervasive discrimination based on race across the companies against those with North African and African sounding names (they were 23% less likely to get a phone call for an interview even though their CVs were identical to others with "white French" names who did receive such calls). This finding is striking even though it is much lower than the rate of discrimination that has found by other studies, perhaps because hiring discrimination is more common in small and medium sized firms [for example a study by the International Labour Office in 2007 which focused on small and medium sized firms found that they chose white candidates over North African and African candidates 80% of the time]. Borrowing a page from other nations' equality agencies, the Halde then publicly declared that ACCOR Jobs, the hiring body for the major hotel and hospitality company ACCOR, was the most egregious discriminator in the area of ethnic origin and denounced its hiring practices.

The singling out of ACCOR (along with two other firms for age discrimination) was the first major controversial act of the Halde and put it in all the newspapers where it—not the companies—was attacked widely for its methods and for the way in which it made its accusations so "public". There was almost no discussion of the implications of such discrimination in the French labour market in the media coverage of the testing (although some papers cited business representatives who wondered if such tests have any validity since the ILO test results were so different from those of the Halde). Instead of a discussion of discriminatory hiring practices, the companies accused of discrimination have reacted strongly accusing the Halde of poor methodology and disparaging the institution. For example, the former president of SOS Racisme Malek Boutih called the testing "amateurish" and wondered why a government agency was only doing something (anti-discrimination testing) that SOS Racisme has been doing for years (*Le Parisien* online). The irony of this statement is that Boutih (and SOS Racisme) has led the fight against the collection of racial statistics—which would provide the data needed for less 'amateurish' studies. Boutih argues that he is simply protecting the Republican tradition.[5] Current leaders of SOS Racisme have seconded Boutih's critiques of La Halde challenging it to stop talking about discrimination and instead do something about it (http://www.20minutes.fr).

In response to the uproar over the CV testings, the Halde has stood its ground. Instead of being defensive about the vociferous response to the Halde's public outing of ACCOR the deputy legal director at the Halde responded by dismissing the strong response arguing that "it's normal for them to fight, but they know. They know we're right . . . yes we could

---

[5] Although the next president of the Halde will not be chosen until 2010 there are rumours that Boutih is a possible choice of President Sarkozy. Obviously, if Boutih were to be chosen the direction of the Halde would most likely be significantly altered.
(http://www.lefigaro.fr/politique/2008/12/21/01002-20081221ARTFIG00155-malek-boutih-interesse-par-la-presidence-de-la-halde-.php

have done some things better, but the results stand . . . they all know it's true." (Latraverse Personal Interview 2008). In addition, the Halde plans similar investigations of large employers in the future. Thus, despite, or because of, its limited resources the Halde is working to put issues of racial discrimination on the public radar and to use the limited coercive pressure it has to influence the actions of private employers unhappy with such scrutiny. This is a strategy that the EEOC in the US used to great effect as the agency gained more and more legitimacy. It remains to be seen how much legitimacy the Halde will be able to muster in future public hearings and reports against private businesses.

Advertising

In addition to its litigation and discrimination testing strategies, the Halde has also been putting forward a particular agenda in its spots on television, radio and in cinemas. These advertisements are meant to publicize both anti-discrimination law and the services of the Halde for those who experience discrimination. Such advertisements can no doubt be seen as positive measures generally, but their actual impact is quite difficult to measure. Regardless of their measureable effect, the advertisements do tell observers about the Halde's goals and priorities at the same time that it puts those goals and priorities into the public sphere hoping to influence both the minds of victims and of the perpetrators of discrimination. The publicity efforts include a somewhat typical television spot that advertises the Halde's services by showing a door being closed in the face of a job candidate. At the end the words "If you are a victim of discrimination, call the Halde. Equality: Act on it, apply it." appear (http://www.halde.fr/-Spots-televises-.html) suggesting to the viewer not only that discrimination exists but that there are remedies to be applied for such behaviour (even if in reality the agency is very weak in its ability to enforce those remedies). In this way the Halde is suggesting a much stronger set of laws and actions to be taken than it can actually deliver in most cases currently—a false promise perhaps, but also a consciousness raising promise that could have an impact on both victims and discriminators.

The Halde has also produced a series of television and cinema spots that depict actual victims of discrimination talking about their experiences. In one spot that plays in the cinema, a man talks about his experiences looking for a job as a baker

> "I'm training to be a baker. I have called employers who tell me to stop by. I stop by and then they say "You're black." And I said "No, I'm not black, I'm mixed race." "Yeah, OK, but you're still black. You have an African name, and you're black. It's all the same." I called another one, and I told him my name, and he said "You have an African name." "Yeah," I said, "I am African...and so?" He never called back. And so, I lived with the feeling of failure, but I told myself, this is who I am and I want to be a baker. I'm not going to stop here..." http://www.halde.fr/-Spots-cinema-.html (Film 1)

The spot ends with the simple message of "Discrimination: Call the Halde" followed by its phone number.

The advertisement appears quite straightforward—it is an effort by the Halde to inform the public about what discrimination is and to let individuals who are victims of discrimination know that they can go to the Halde for assistance. Yet, there is much more going on in this advertisement, especially when one considers the great debate over Republican ideology that is taking place in France when it comes to racial categories. The young man is instantly identified with a racial category by all the possible employers he contacts. And he does not immediately turn to the Republican ideology and say "no I am French." Instead, he engages in the racial categorization that is a part of his job application experience by saying "no, I am not black, I'm mixed race" as if this categorization is different, better, more acceptable—as if this categorization and the one of black are accepted terms in everyday interactions in France. Later it is his name that is the offending feature and he readily agrees that he is "African…and so?" It seems that for him being put into categories is part of his everyday experience and this occurs even when possible employers do not see him—even if they only read or hear his name. Finally, the young man concludes by talking about how he lives with "a fear of failure" suggesting the personal implications of discrimination, humanizing the face of the racialised (instead of just seeing a hooligan throwing rocks at police in the suburbs), and creating the possibility that the viewer may indentify with the unfairness of the young man's situation.

Such an experience was no doubt chosen by the Halde because it was a clear example of discrimination. But it also puts into the mind of the viewer the pervasiveness of existing racial and ethnic categories in French society and points out how those categories are used to maintain systems of inequality. This is a striking message to communicate in the midst of the debate over ethnic identity in France. As the debate over collecting ethnic statistics develops in France [see below], this ad's suggestion also takes on a much larger meaning. Perhaps, it is not the collection of ethnic statistics which will construct or reify ethnic categories, but instead that those categories already exist and have enough power to be taken for granted by the young man and his prospective employers. If that is true, then collecting ethnic statistics might be more easily seen as a mere reflection of the pre-existing categories in French society and such statistics may pose less of a threat of additional harm at the same time that they could be used to fight racism.

In addition to ethnic statistics, the advertisement also highlights the importance of the job candidate's name as an indicator of his supposed ethnicity during the application process. This element directs the French viewer of the commercial to the debate over CVs and whether or not they should be anonymous (in order to prevent employers from assuming ethnicity) without actually making the point directly. The debate over anonymous CV's has gone on for a number of years in France and will be discussed below in the section on the equal opportunities law of 2006. In sum, ads like this not only put a human face on discrimination and give voice to victims of discrimination, they also are opportunities for the Halde to make political and policy statements and to subtly shape the public's consciousness.

Collecting Ethnic Statistics

Moves to begin to collect ethnic statistics in France can be characterized in two general ways. One is that such statistics help to better understand the nature and extent of racial discrimination in French society, to better tailor responses to such discrimination, and to better prove discrimination in order to more effectively enforce anti-discrimination law, etc... The other is that such statistics are a major step towards more *communautarisme* and are much too similar to how Jews were marked leading up to the Holocaust. This debate also allows one to observe the fault lines of French racial policy and to see more clearly where the push for and resistance to new anti-discrimination policies lie. Many of the policy entrepreneurs behind the implementation of European anti-discrimination law are also those who are calling most strongly for the collection of ethnic statistics, while those who oppose the collection of such statistics are often the more established elite. I argue that this debate is so intense not only because both sides truly believe so strongly in their position, but also because collecting such statistics may open the door to other, potentially significant transformations in French racial policy.

The Halde wants to be able to demand racial or ethnic statistics about hiring practices because then it would not have to conduct the above cited methodologically "questionable" CV testing that it now employs in order to establish the reality of employment discrimination. Yet the collection of racial or ethnic statistics is widely seen as unconstitutional and very un-Republican in France. In fact, France's high court (*Cour de cassation*) threw out a provision of a 2007 immigration law which purported to collect ethnic statistics, putting the constitutionality of the production of any ethnic statistics into question. The deputy legal director of the Halde emphasizes that the court's ruling did not completely rule out such statistics, but suggested that the collection of ethnic statistics would violate the constitution unless they met very particular standards (such as 'objective' categories) that many commentators think are impossible (Latraverse 2008).

Furthermore, the deputy legal director of the Halde does not believe that the high court's suggestions are the last word on the matter. After admitting that "there's no reason to be heroes and contradict the cour de cassation" she went on to cite the European Union's race directive claiming that "European law requires that a person can make their case and this directive is not limited by the French constitution." By invoking Europe into this debate she is also pointing out how racial policy making in France is no longer the exclusive property of the strong and centralized French state, but must also respond to European imperatives. In this example, one can see how Europe and European spaces introduce more possibilities for action—more entry points for policy and interpretation and more possible sources of power. That is not to suggest that a showdown between Europe and France on the issue of such data collection is a likely possibility (it is not), only that it exists. Instead of pursuing this point further, the deputy legal director returned to domestic law and noted that "the French law on sensitive data has an exception for evidence that is for judicial cases. Disparate impact is a comparative issue and you need to be able to collect data to make your case." She concludes with optimism stating that although she understands that many people in France do not want racial categories in the census, but she does think they may support the Halde's efforts to identify "visible" groups in litigation efforts. (Latraverse, 2008) There are two very important elements of this tour of French and European law on ethnic statistics. First, ethnic statistics are a top priority for this Halde employee so much so that she is trying to consider every single possible avenue to achieving this goal despite the limited resources at her disposal. Second, the invocation of Europe, of an embryonic type of federalism, is a noteworthy development in France where the strength of the central state has rarely been questioned and will be important to consider in the comparison with the US below.

As the comments from the Halde official suggest, the high court's ruling has done little to damper the push for some type of racial or ethnic statistics. Instead, officials from INED (Institut national d'etudes demographiques/National Institute of Demographic Studies) and INSEE (Institut national de la statistique et études économiques/National Institute for Statistics and Economic Studies) have decided to go forward with their survey of discrimination that includes the selection by individuals of an ethnic category, arguing that it is virtually impossible for them to meet the current demands for information about the problems of racial and ethnic discrimination in France without also asking about ethnic identity.[6]

The announcement of plans to collect ethnic data quickly led to duelling editorials in two of France's major newspapers. *Liberation*, the leading daily of the left issued its "Republican Pledge Against Discrimination" after the possibility of collecting ethnic statistics seemed to be looming, taking a strong stand against the collection of any racial or ethnic statistics. *Liberation* maintained that discrimination can already be identified by using proxies such as first names instead of ethnic origin. It went on to argue that "ethnic statistics are . . . dangerous [and would] fuel intercommunity conflicts" (Sabbagh 2008). *Le Monde* (the most read daily in France) responded to *Liberation's* pledge with its own take on the matter "Statistics Against Discrimination." In its editorial the paper argued that "no research tool . . . should be prohibited on the ground that it would conflict with the . . . French republican model of integration." The editorial went on to argue that "the prevalence of discrimination indeed demonstrates that this model has not fulfilled its promises." "How" the

[6] Interestingly, the demographers have been doing test surveys in order to better understand how to measure ethnic discrimination, asking individuals different questions about origin/ethnicity/race in order to better understand the nature of such identity/such discrimination in France. Reflecting traditional French ideas about race the people surveyed have objected strongly to having to choose a "ethno-racial" category, but accept approaches that ask them their ancestry reflecting the current French predilection to refer to 'young people of immigrant origin' despite the fact that many of them are French from birth (Simon, 2008).

paper then asks, "can it be decreed that it is 'dangerous' to know who is affected by discrimination? Today, "ethnic statistics" are not a threat to social cohesion—discrimination is" (Sabbagh 2008).

SOS Racisme, perhaps the leading anti-racism organization in France, did not agree with *Le Monde's* conclusion. Instead, it reacted vehemently to the proposals to collect ethnic statistics and issued a petition in which individuals could declare that "I refuse to be asked about the colour of my skin, my origin or my religion. . . I refuse that the attention and investigation be focused on the victims rather than the perpetrators of discrimination." SOS Racisme's petition concludes by suggesting that data needed to fight discrimination should be established in "individual in situ investigations of racist conduct" not through the collection of racial statistics that will only reinforce racial and ethnic divides (Sabbagh 2008). Ethnic statistics are, in and of themselves in this view, racist. This perspective stands in stark contrast to that of those who support gathering ethnic statistics in order to show the extent of discrimination and disparate treatment which they hope will be used in efforts to fight discrimination beyond the individual level. As the debate over ethnic statistics continues, though, there has no doubt that those that resist the production of ethnic statistics are part of the established Republican tradition and those that are pushing for their collection are challenging France's established approach to racial policy.

In contrast to SOS Racisme, the CRAN (*Conseil Représentatif des Associations Noires*), an association of black French that was founded just after the 2005 riots, has come out in support of what it calls "diversity" statistics. Diversity statistics are not racial or ethnic statistics because the CRAN agrees that race, as such, does not exist. However, the CRAN does believe that voluntary and anonymous statistics based on one's own feeling of belonging (*ressenti d'appartenance*) should be allowed (www.lecran.org). In choosing different words the CRAN hopes to stake out a middle ground in this debate, although it is not clear how influential its suggestion has been.

In a similar tactic, the director of INED, Francois Heran, also tried to fit the collecting of ethnic statistics with the Republican tradition. He argues that collecting ethnic statistics may in fact be in keeping with the principles of the Republic at the same time that it contradicts the traditional Republican approach to race and ethnicity when he writes that

> there are two ways to defend the Republican model. The first is to restrict oneself to an ideal by refusing to measure what separates it from the reality. The second respects the principle of equality, but enhances it by emancipation through knowledge. Lucidity is better than blindness. The INSEE and the INED experience this every day through the feedback their publications receive: French society has a profound need for self-knowledge. (Le Monde Nov 15 07 "There are no Sorcerer's Apprentices at INED" translated in Sabbagh, 2008)

Whether or not such appeals will be successful is unclear. What is clear, however, is that a loose network of academics, civil servants and NGOs has placed this goal at the centre of their efforts. And, it seems that they may have gained a very important ally which may transform their position into one of authority. The often confusing President of the Republic, Nicolas Sarkozy, has frequently shifted his positions on matters related to racial policy. He has condemned the rioters, but answered their actions with an equal opportunities bill, supported and then opposed affirmative action (*la discrimination positive*), appointed visible minorities to his cabinet, but then left them to wolves, and recently has shown signs that he may be ready to support collecting ethnic statistics. In early 2009, President Sarkozy appointed Yazid Sabeg to bring together a commission to propose ways to identify and measure diversity and discrimination. Sabeg's commission then came back with a report recommending the collection of ethnic statistics in May 2009. As a group of French academics opposed to the collection of ethnic statistics (Commission alternative de réflexion sur les "statistiques ethniques" et les discrimination/CARSAD) suggest, this conclusion of Sabeg's commission was not a surprise (in part, they claim, because Sabeg's commission only included those who support collecting ethnic statistics). In retort to Sabeg's report, CARSAD has issued a book length report of its own on ethnic statistics, The Return of Race: Against Ethnic Statistics (*Le retour de la race: Contre les statistiques ethniques).*

Obviously the debate over ethnic statistics is not near dead. If the President chooses to publicly support the collection of ethnic statistics that would immediately change the power positions of those seeking this policy. Even without a final conclusion to this policy debate, however, it is clear that traditional French racial policy is in flux, challenged by sum, defended by others and re-imagined in the process.

Diversity in Education and Employment

In addition to the new anti-discrimination law, the activities of the Halde and the debate over ethnic statistics, a number of new initiatives have been undertaken in France to "increase diversity" in higher education and the workplace in the last seven years. In the area of higher education the elite *Institut d'etudes politiques de Paris* (*Sciences Po*) has implemented a type of affirmative action (or what is known as positive discrimination in France) program admitting, since 2001, a number of students from disadvantaged areas of France. Although this program recruits students from *zones d'education prioritaire* (educational priority zones) which are zones of disadvantage identified by the government for extra support and are, therefore, race-blind, the not overly hidden goal of the program is to increase the number of racialised students in the student body of *Sciences Po*—to diversify one of the least diversified institutions in all of France. This program brought with it strong opposition from a number of quarters (which Sabbagh (2004, 246) notes is another "deep similarity" between the French and American policies), yet it is thus far perceived to be a success and continues to operate. Furthermore, *Sciences Po* is not alone—other institutions of higher education are also undertaking similar efforts to 'diversify' their student bodies. This all leads to the possibility that the elite schools of France which are largely the haunts of "white" and upper/upper-middle class French may begin to be resemble the population at large.

Of course, even those graduates of elite institutions who are racialised often face discrimination in hiring when looking for internships and jobs after graduation. Despite the new laws against such discrimination, there have not been many cases of hiring discrimination brought before the courts because of the difficulty of proving such discrimination in individual cases. One positive step that has been made in the area of employment, however, is the emergence of a commitment to "diversity" from a large number of major French firms. This commitment can be seen in the widespread signing of a 'diversity charter' (authored by Yazid Sabeg who was the commissioner for the study of ethnic statistics) in which firms pledge to not discriminate in recruitment, training and promotion, as well as in a number of individual programs to employ youths from economic priority zones that have been set up by a variety of firms in conjunction with the government (which offers special incentives for such programs). Most major French employers now have a 'diversity' page on their websites proclaiming their commitment to this principle as an important part of their overall employment policy. Although such proclamations are just that for many companies at this point (as can be seen in the uproar over the Halde's CV testing), the widespread embrace of diversity in employment makes France unique among the vast majority of its European neighbours. Thus this commitment can be seen as a major step towards the American model even if it is largely rhetorical thus far.

A final example of changing French racial policy (and the limits of such change) can be seen in the equal opportunity law of 2006. The riots of 2005 led the government to pass the equal opportunity law which gave every indication of being a concrete statement of France's commitment to fighting racial discrimination and to increasing opportunity for racialised young people. The National Assembly noted that in the riots "that which we knew, but at times did not want to see, appeared clearly" including "shocking discrimination" which the law hoped to combat by further empowering the Halde and by increasing employment opportunities for the youths of the suburbs through short-term contracts, by giving employers incentives to employ those from economic priority zones and by introducing new 'anonymous' hiring procedures (Suk 2007, 100-101). Overall the law seemed to be a good first response to the problems highlighted by the riots.

Two elements of the law that are especially interesting are the short term contracts and the anonymous hiring procedures, both because they would probably have had the most impact and because they were rather quickly discarded. The new 'first contracts' (CPE) provision of the law allowed employers to hire youths for short (2 year) contracts without long-term job security in the hopes of encouraging employers to take risks on young 'ethnic' employees without the fear that they would have to keep employing them their entire career if they were not satisfactory. Economists have noted that France's labour policies which favour extreme levels of job security exacerbate existing discriminatory tendencies and this law was supposed to encourage firms to consider employing young people that they might not want to risk giving a long-term contract to, such as the racialised youth of the suburbs (e.g. Salanie, 2006).

This element of the law fell quickest and with the loudest thud. That is because the primarily "white"/"French" young people who are set to become the next generation of "haves" in French society took to the streets in protest against this element of the law. With their parents and labour unions they denounced the attack on French labour laws and demanded that their futures be secured and protected from the dangers of short-term employment. An example of this point of view can be seen in an advertisement from Force Ouvrière, a major French union, which claims that working without a secure contract, is like having sexual intercourse without wearing a condom (on file with author). In the face of this fierce opposition the government backed down and scrapped the CPE. What is perhaps most interesting is the minimal amount of self-reflection in France about the racial and class implications of this protest and change in law. It could leave no doubt that racial inequality is directly tied to economic and power differentials in French society.

In addition to the short-term contract provisions, the equal opportunity law also called for the acceptance of anonymous CV by firms with more than 50 employees. This would allow racialised young people an opportunity to get their foot in the door of the hiring process and would have been especially valuable given that discrimination in hiring seems to be rampant in France. A number of businesses, however, despite their commitment to diversity protested this provision after the defeat of the short-term contract law (there was little opposition prior to that occurrence), in part, no doubt because they were scared of giving long-term contracts to 'risky' candidates. It should be noted, though, that despite the repeal of the anonymous CV provision of the law there are some large French companies that have gone forward with this provision on their own.

This backtracking makes clear the challenges those who wish to reform French racial policy face at the same time that it shows how limited the progress has been for those young racialised French who face not only racial discrimination, but a system of education and employment/labour law that reinforce and exacerbates racial discrimination. Nonetheless, even though many of the changes in French racial policy have been limited they *are* real developments that show a shift in French racial policy and the underlying struggle in French society over racial and class inequality. Resistance from the French elite and the non-racialised middle and upper classes (with regard to economic reforms in particular) has limited some reforms, but it has not silenced the debate over racial policy or cancelled out the changes that have occurred. Instead, young ethnics (as Begag has termed them) and the discrimination that they face continue to be a source of contention in France. In fact, by 2006, 79 percent of the French public reported that fighting discrimination based on supposed racial or ethnic origin was a "top priority" (HALDE annual report, 2006).

In an address to the French public in late 2008, President Sarkozy seemed to be resurrecting some of these provisions calling for a testing of the blind CV program and increases in special incentives to get private employers to hire youths from priority zones (essentially under-privileged neighbourhoods, like the educational zones mentioned above). He also said that he no longer believed in affirmative action, but instead did want to increase the number of seats for those from under-privileged neighbourhoods in important elite university programs (Ollivier 2008). Such measures may finally start to put some teeth into his long list of promises to improve the life of young racialised people in France at the same time that they would give life to some of the weak anti-discrimination institutions discussed here.

A Civil Rights Movement?

A comparison of France with the United States of the 1960s and 70s that excludes the extreme importance of the organized civil rights movement in the US would be impossible. After all it was the civil rights movement in the US that

> advanced deeply critical reviews of and challenges to the realities of U.S. life by measuring the realities with the yardstick of the nation-state's highest principles. The result was the exposure, yet again, of the enormous and brutal gaps between the principles of justice and the realities of injustice lived daily by those who were the victims of racism (Outlaw 2005, 122).

A similar movement has failed to appear in France despite efforts as early as the 1980s (e.g. the marches for equality staged by the beurs) to engender such action in civil society. Considering that identifying racial groups, and even self-identification of an ethnic identity, is often seen as an affront to the Republican model, the lack of organization around such identification is not surprising.

Some developments on this front have occurred however. First of all, it is important to not deny the impact the *beur* movement of the 1980s had on France in that it for the first time really put issues of discrimination and racialisation on the agenda and gave the French their first pseudo-hyphenated identity "*beur*" (a play on the French word for Arab). The riots of 2005 and similar unrest in 2006 are also important shifts towards a type of civil rights mentality in France. At the heart of those riots was the very contrast that Outlaw (2005) identifies as the heart of the civil rights movement in the US—the difference between a democracy's goals and the realities faced by those excluded from those possibilities by discrimination. Out of the riots have sprung a number of grassroots groups that may emerge to form a larger movement, though institutional factors in France make a movement on the scale of the US unlikely.

This does not mean, however, that NGOs who prioritize the fight against discrimination do not exist in France or that they are totally excluded from power and political influence. For example, *ni putes ni soumises* (neither whores nor submissives) a group founded by a young woman of the suburbs in response to the discrimination faced by women of immigrant origin in both the larger society and within the sub-culture of the suburbs has become a powerful actor in France. Although I will focus on their identity as racialised others here, it is important to note that *ni putes ni soumises* also represents Muslim women in particular. (For more on the emergence and co-option of Muslim organizations as a way for the government to control French Islam see Gardner, this volume). Many critics have argued that by becoming active in the government and supportive of some of its policies, the organization has sold its soul to President Sarkozy and the centre-right (e.g., it supported the head scarf ban in schools). Despite its status as a "sellout", I think it is interesting to consider the positions of the current leader of *ni putes ni soumises* on French racial policy making—not the least because she is one of the eleven members of the college of the Halde and because the former president of ni *putes ni soumises* (Fadela Amara) is now a member of the Sarkozy government. The current president, Sihem Habchi actually considers herself to be closer to the Socialist party on the left, but claims to try to be independent of both political parties (she argues that this is not difficult to do because they are both elite clubs that exclude people like her—young (Muslim) women of immigrant origin from the suburbs).

Habchi (2008) argues that her group and other young people must get more involved in pressuring politicians because "you can't be far away from these powers if you are too far away you will always be neglected. We have to always be in the face of the men or the women in power—telling them to change our lives." She goes on to argue that if those in power will not change things then it is time for them to pass the baton of power because France needs to reinterpret Republicanism (an argument that is in line with the arguments from representatives of groups such the Halde and INED outlined earlier in this paper). Habchi (2008) proclaims that

> If we want to progress we need to focus on universalism that respects difference, a universalism that is not blind—I am not talking about this kind of universalism—that has been used to maintain the people in the ghetto. That is why we say to the politicians "you don't know how to use equality, democracy—you've had enough, you're tired, I'll take your place. Don't worry I will defend the Republic, defend universalism, defend laïcité, better than you because you don't believe in it and that is the problem."
>
> The fight in France is fighting against privilege. The left and the right share privilege, they share business, they replicate themselves, so you cannot enter. They are le grand bourgeoisie.

Habchi concludes that current leaders are not willing to do the hard work needed to create equality in France. She also believes that in order to fight discrimination and create equality ethnic statistics are necessary. These are the words of someone who leads an organization committed to changing the current do nothing nature of racial policy in France. *Ni putes ni soumises* and other young organizations like it that are currently emerging in France may begin to provide the NGO support that is necessary to transform the recent developments in French racial policy into substantive changes.

Like *ni putes ni soumises*, the CRAN, an association representing the interests of black French, is also an important NGO that could play a role in an emerging civil rights movement. The CRAN is a fairly new organization and has less of a "sold out" reputation in France when compared to *ni putes ni soumises*. The CRAN's organization around a perceived racial category is an important development for a French NGOs. By organizing around a perceived racial identity the CRAN is echoing the *beur* movement and pushing past the stigma of organizing around any particular supposed racial or ethnic category. The CRAN has been especially active in pushing for diversity statistics and encourages it followers to sign the petition published in *Le Monde* in favour of such statistics.

The CRAN and *ni putes ni soumises* are just two examples of new NGOs that have emerged during France's recent grappling with racism and discrimination. Along with other NGOs they have yet to initiate a civil rights movement like that experienced in the U.S. and they still have a limited impact in French politics, but they have increased activism on behalf of racialised peoples in France. In sum, as Peres notes in this volume about the CRAN, "both the difficulty of the movement to rally people under the label "black" and its rhetorical emphasis on the defence of Republican values" demonstrate that those wishing to change French racial politics significantly still face a very uphill battle.

In the next section I consider the history of the development of racial policy in the US as a possible tool for better understanding the current French situation.

Comparisons with the US

How can the development of American racial policy be used to understand the current situation in France?

Although explicit comparisons between the US and France pose challenges and require qualification (Lieberman 2001 and 2002; Wacquant 2006), it is possible that we might be able to employ the American experience with similar racial anti-discrimination institutions and America's own struggle with colour-blind and race-conscious policies in order to better interpret recent developments in France.

France's current debate over ethnic statistics and the possibility of positive discrimination resonates with the strong and heated debate over race-blind versus race-conscious policy in the US in the 1960s. The Civil Rights Act of 1964 seemed to resolve this debate by "refus[ing] to recognize so-called "statistical discrimination"" and by "refus[ing] to sanction group-based remedies for discrimination, such as targets or quotas for the hiring of minorities." (Lieberman 2002, 705). Thus, the current predominance of the colour-blind model in France and its policy implications, which so many French racial equality activists, academics and civil servants criticize as much too limited, mirrors the beginnings of racial anti-discrimination policy in the United States. Likewise, the U.S.'s equality agency, the Equal Employment Opportunity Commission (EEOC), began as an emaciated institution that was "given no effective enforcement power and was relegated to a sideline role as conciliator and investigator" without the power to "order remedies for discrimination nor file lawsuits" (Lieberman 2002, 705). In France, the Halde finds itself in the same situation—having been given a strong mandate to fight discrimination and promote equality and very little with which to fulfil its duties.

Despite this lacklustre beginning in the U.S. for both race-conscious policies and the EEOC

> within 10 years of the act's passage [the Civil Rights Act of 1964], the United States. . . developed an extensive set of race-conscious, group-based policies and practices that offer compensatory advantages to members of historically or currently disadvantaged groups—known collectively as affirmative action (Lieberman 2002, 705).

It also "proved surprisingly effective at . . . enforcing anti-discrimination law." Lieberman (2002, 705) concludes that "neither ideas (the apparent triumph of colour-blindness in 1964) nor institutions (the apparent weakness of the civil rights enforcement apparatus) predict the emergence" of race-conscious and effectively enforced racial anti-discrimination policies.

Lieberman goes on to note that the ideology of colorblindness was powerful and entrenched in the United States and it counted among its most fervent supporters many who were active in the Civil Rights movement, just as those in SOS-Racisme hold on to the promises of a colour-blind Republicanism. As Lieberman observes, in a passage that could just as easily apply to French anti-discrimination institutions

> although the Civil Rights Act certainly counts as dramatic political change, it was in many ways consonant with much that had come before, both in its embrace of colorblindness and in its withholding of strong coercive enforcement power from the state (2002, 707).

Lieberman argues that the "strong, race-conscious anti-discrimination enforcement mechanism" which emerged came about precisely because the "strong expectations that the federal government would act to combat employment discrimination" were combined with exceedingly weak levels of enforcement (as can be seen in the weakness of the EEOC) (2002, 707). Some politicians ignored this gap, while others, such as President Nixon took initial steps to close the gap in order to gain political leverage against the left with its strong minority vote without actually significantly changing track (Skrentny 1996). Meanwhile in France, it was the Chirac government that transposed the EU's race directive, established the Halde and first submitted and then withdrew the equal opportunities law after the 2005 riots. Perhaps the centre-right was undertaking a similar strategy of creating institutions to fight discrimination while giving weak enforcement powers to them so that actual change was limited. It is still unclear what President Sarkozy's contribution may be to racial policy making although glimpses of political manoeuvring not entirely different from Nixon can be seen in Sarkozy's constant balancing of strict immigration and crime measures with the promotion of ethnic minorities in government and his on and off support for positive discrimination measures or his new found interest in ethnic statistics.

In addition to the political arena, Lieberman notes that the civil servants at the EEOC "found themselves in a nearly impossible position. Expected to enforce the law but left essentially powerless to do so, the EEOC had to find other outlets to fulfil its enforcement mission" (2002, 708). Because of these limitations, Lieberman claims, "the EEOC sought to play what role and forge what alliances it could as it sought pragmatic rather than ideological or coercive solutions to the problem of fulfilling its mandate in constrained environment" (2002, 708). Lieberman concludes that because the EEOC lacked strong powers and sufficient resources it could not effectively fulfil its race-blind mandate of enforcing individual violations of the Civil Rights Act and, instead, turned to other possible policy solutions. With that in mind it might not be surprising to learn that actors at the Halde are at the forefront for calling for the collection of ethnic statistics and are also using publicity techniques, such as shaming ACCOR and other companies about their discriminatory hiring practices, and pointing out the pervasiveness of racial categories in its advertisements, instead of enforcing case by case instances of discrimination that the Halde lacks both the power and resources to pursue. They are, in fact, following the EEOC's similar path for similar reasons.

Lieberman goes on to argue that the EEOC's success in becoming more influential despite its initial institutional constraints had much to do with alliances with African-American political organizations such as the NAACP and its legal defence fund. Such an alliance in France between the Halde and racialised political organizations seems unlikely at best considering that political organizations related to ethnicity are few. Nonetheless, some political activists, such as those mentioned above, have appeared claiming to represent racialised people. Possible alliances between *ni putes ni soumises*, the CRAN or the more established MRAP (*Mouvement contre le racisme et pour l'amitié entre les peoples* and the Halde provide possibilities for new action, but overall France lacks NGOs that place significant resources towards litigation efforts like the NAACP's LDF did in the US.[7] Furthermore, labour unions which became an ally of

[7] All of these groups currently lack the resources necessary to engage in long-term strategic litigation.

the EEOC in the US, have not risen to the occasion thus far in France, perhaps reflecting the links between labour and the establishment in France that did not exist in the US were labour represented a much less elite section of society.

In addition to litigation, however, the EEOC also adopted other alternative routes that are more available to the Halde and the NGOs that support its work, such as public exposure of "egregious cases of discrimination" in the hopes of "pressuring employers to change their personnel practices" (Lieberman 2002, 708). Lieberman also suggests that the shift in American policy from a colour-blind approach to a race-conscious one had much to do with the fact that the EEOC was so limited to these few activities and lacked much real implementation power. It was because the EEOC was so weak that it could lead a movement for race-conscious measures while all the while arguing that such race-conscious measures were essential to enforcing the colour-blind law on the books (just as the Halde is arguing currently in France):

> "institutional incentives and opportunities in which key actors were embedded allowed them to mount a challenge to this [race-blind] approach even while claiming to maintain it. . . In fact, had the EEOC been given greater coercive powers at the outset to enforce the colour-blind vision of anti-discrimination law, it is likely that the impulse for affirmative action would have been weaker, because the EEOC would have turned its attention to an apparently more fruitful set of tasks" (2002, 709).

This is not to suggest that simply because the Halde is as weak as the EEOC that France will shift towards race-conscious policies, but instead to propose that perhaps the institutions in France that appear so weak may actually be playing a more substantive and important role in policy making than currently seems to be the case. Or, that they may be able to do so in the future.

It will be clear to anyone who has read Lieberman's own comparisons of France and the US that I am adopting his analysis of the US to make arguments that he has never supported in relation to France. Indeed, Lieberman has written in 2001, 2003 and again in his recent book *Shaping Race Policy* (2005) that despite strong similarities between France and the US in the 1960s and 1970s, French and American policy diverged because of differing state structures (strong and centralized in France and weak and decentralized in the US). In particular, he argues that the French state's strength and centralization limits the avenues available to minority groups who attempt to challenge traditional policies (Lieberman 2001).

Besides the strong and centralized structure of the French state most of the reasons Lieberman cites for as limits on movements for more minority rights include: the lack of a "dedicated anti-discrimination agency;" the lack of civil anti-discrimination law; the lack of the power of precedent in a civil law system (which he says means that anti-discrimination cases have "no cumulative force and little policymaking function" (2001, 50)); and the lack of equal opportunity officials within private businesses to influence hiring are no longer true obstacles. The transposition of the race directive created stronger civil (not only criminal) law anti-discrimination mechanisms, France has created a dedicated anti-discrimination body, precedent has been and only continues to be increasingly important in France and other civil law countries despite theoretical suppositions to the contrary and many companies now prioritize diversity in the hiring process and are putting more resources towards these efforts. Perhaps, as in the US, the new creation of the anti-discrimination body may also create new avenues for those seeking change, such as the CRAN and *ni putes ni soumises*.

There is one last possible point of convergence to consider when looking at France and the United States. Lieberman's key argument is that the major divergence in French and American policymaking occurs because the structure of the two states is so different: the US is a weak and de-centralized state and France is a strong and centralized state. What Lieberman's arguments fail to consider is the increasingly important role that the supra-national European Union plays in nation-state policymaking. Racial policymaking, in particular, is now not only formulated and enforced by the strong and centralized French state, but also by European-level actors. In the US the de-centralized and weak state meant that racial policy makers like those at the EEOC had to seek out differing venues and different points of access in order to put forward an agenda for change. For France, the presence of the European Union as an additional source of policymaking opportunities and possible power in domestic policy making may be currently providing the Halde and other actors with more possibilities than existed historically in France when Europe was still very weak and when Lieberman notes that the centralized and strong state in France prevented the development of more race-conscious policies.

Overall there is no doubt that the two states have different historical trajectories and different state structures in addition to significant variation in the strength of civil rights groups. Despite these differences, however, there are significant similarities between French racial policymaking of the last ten years and similar policy developments during the 1960s and 1970s in the U.S. The American experience shows that significant institutional and ideological change can occur in a short period of time and that initially weak or "half" measures may become stronger policy initiatives under certain circumstances. Thus, the criticism of recent developments in French racial policy as being too weak, or that they are simply window covering and that the old French Republican model continues on unchanged, may be underestimating the powerful effects these nascent institutions can have on French racial policy and society. Furthermore, this comparison might serve as an interesting source of inspiration for current French actors who hope to push France beyond old ideas in the area of racial equality. Perhaps there are many more possibilities that can be squeezed out of the new 'weak' anti-discrimination institutions. Finally, the comparison suggests that the next ten years in France could be years of transformation and should be watched closely. If anything, what the American experience tells us about France is that we can expect that racial discrimination will be a social phenomena and political issue that will not go away easily and that no one policy approach is likely to eradicate this problem quickly.

Works Cited

20 Minutes Online Edition. 2009. Available online at: http://www.20minutes.fr/article/324821/Politique-Le-rapport-Sabeg-mise-sur-l-emploi-et-l-education-pour-lutter-contre-les-discriminations.php

Begag, Azouz. 2007. *Ethnicity and equality.* Lincoln: University of Nebraska Press.

Bowen, John. 2006. *Why the French don't like headscarves: Islam, the state, and public space.* Princeton: Princeton University Press.

Calvès, Gwènaële. 2004. Colour-blindness at a crossroads in contemporary France. In *Race in France*, ed. Herrick Chapman and Laura Levine Frader, 219-226. Oxford: Berghahn Books.

CARSED. 2009. Le retour de la race. June 2009. Available online at: http://www.millebabords.org/spip.php?article11712

Chappe, Vincent-Arnaud. 2008. La construction publique du problème des discriminations à travers la genèse de la HALDE: La création d'un consensus a minima. Master's Thesis. Institut d'étude politique de Paris.

European Council Directive 2000/43/EC. Available online at: http://europa.eu/eurlex/pri/en/oj/dat/2000/l_180/l_18020000719en0022 0026.pdf

Geddes, Andrew and Virginie Guiraudon. 2004. Britain, France, and EU anti-discrimination policy: The emergence of an EU policy paradigm. *West European Politics* 27: 334-53.

Gehring, Jacquleine. 2007. Race, Law and Politics in Europe. PhD diss., University of California, Berkley.

Guiraudon, Virginie. 2003. The Constitution of a European Immigration Policy Domain: A Political Sociology Approach. *Journal of European Public Policy* 10: 263-82.

Habchi, Sihem. 2008. Interview by author. Digital recording. Telephone. 5 August 2008.

La Halde Annual Report 2006, 2007 and 2008. Available online at: http://www.halde.fr

Hargreaves, Alec. 2004. Half-measures: Anti-discrimination policy in France. In *Race in France*, ed. Herrick Chapman and Laura Levine Frader, 227-245. Oxford: Berghahn Books.

Latraverse, Sophie. 2008. Interview by author. Digital recording. Paris, France, 3 July 2008.

Le Parisien. 2008. Discrimination: Malek Boutih tâcle la Halde" 11 June 2008. Available online at: http://www.leparisien.fr/politique/discrimination-malek-boutih-tacle-la-halde-11-06-2008-3298560306.php

Lépinard, Elénoare. 2008. Gender and Multiculturalism. In *Developments in French politics,* ed. Alistair Cole, Patrick Le Galès and Jonah Levy. London: Palgrave Macmillan.

Lépinard, Eléonore and Patrick Simon. 2009. From integration to antidiscrimination. . . to diversity? *French Report for European Approach to Multicultural Citizenship* ELIAMEP. Available online at: http://emilie.eliamep.gr/wpcontent/uploads/2009/02/antidiscrimination - politics-and-policies-in-french-workplaces2.pdf

Lieberman, Robert. 2001. A tale of two countries: The politics of colour blindness in France and the United States. *French Politics, Culture & Society* 19: 32-59.

—. 2002. Ideas, Institutions, and Political Order: Explaining Political Change. *American Political Science Review* 96: 697-712.

—. 2005. *Shaping race policy: The United States in comparative perspective*. Princeton: Princeton University Press.

Murray, Graham. 2006. France: the riots and the Republic. *Race and Class* 47: 26-45.

Ollivier, Christine. 2008. Sarkozy acts for ethnic diversity. Associated Press. Available online at: http://abcnews.go.com/International/wireStory?id=6482132.

Outlaw, Lucius. 2005. *Critical social theory in the interests of black folks*. Lanham, MD: Rowman and Littlefield.

Sabbagh, Daniel. 2004. Affirmative action at Sciences Po. In *Race in France*, ed. Herrick Chapman and Laura Levine Frader, 246-256. Oxford: Berghahn Books.

Sabbagh, Daniel. 2008. The collection of ethnoracial statistics: Developments in the French controversy. *Policy Report, French-American Foundation*. Available online at: http://www.frenchamerican.org/cms/files/policybriefs_pdf/Policy%20Brief%20-%20Ethnic%20Statistics.pdf

Salanié, Bernard. 2006. The riots in France: An economist's view. *Social Science Research Council Online*. Available online at: http://riotsfrance.ssrc.org/Salanie/

Simon, Patrick. 1996. Beyond assimilation: The second generation debate in France. Available online at: http://cas.uchicago.edu/workshops/immigration/events/PatrickSimon_slides.ppt

Skrentny, John. 1996. *The ironies of affirmative action*. Chicago: University of Chicago Press.

SOS Racisme. 2008. Encore Warsmann. Available online at: http://www.sos-racisme.org/Encore-Warsmann.html

Suk, Julie Chi-Hye. 2007. Discrimination at will: Job security protections and equal employment opportunity in conflict. *Stanford Law Review* 60: 73-114.

Wacquant, Loïc. 2008. Ghettos and anti-ghettos: An anatomy of the new urban poverty. *Thesis Eleven* 94: 113-18.

—. 2006. French "banlieues" and black American ghetto: From conflation to comparison. *Qui Parle* 16: 5-38.

LIST OF CONTRIBUTORS

Roger Andersson is professor in social and economic geography at Uppsala University, Sweden.

Alessandra Beasley Von Burg is Assistant Professor in the Department of Communication at Wake Forest University. Her article "Public Discourse and Cosmopolitan Political Identity: Imagining the European Union Citizen," published in *Futures*, was the winner of the Emerald Management Reviews Citation of Excellence Award.

Ana Paula Beja Horta is associate professor at the Universida de Aberta, Lisbon, Portugal. She is affiliated with the Centre for the Study of Migration and Intercultural Relations (CEMRI).

Maria Berger is a political scientist and a research advisor for the city of Delft in the Netherlands. Before joining the city of Delft, she was affiliated with the Institute for Ethnic and Migration Studies (IMES), University of Amsterdam.

Alexander Caviedes is assistant professor in political science at the State University of New York at Fredonia. His publications include *Prying Open Fortress Europe: The Turn to Sectoral Labour Migration* (Lexington Books, 2009) and an article on the Open Method of Cooperation in EU immigration policy in the *Journal of European Public Policy*.

Meng-Hsuan Chou is a post-doctoral fellow at ARENA – Centre for European Studies, University of Oslo (Norway), working on the project "The Transformation and Sustainability of European Political Order" (EuroTrans). She recently completed her Ph.D. titled "Historical Institutionalism and the Evolution of European Union's Asylum and Immigration Acquis (1992-2004)" at Cambridge.

Mario Diani is professor of sociology at the University of Trento, Italy. He is co-editor of the book *Social Movements and Networks: Relational Approaches to Collective Action* (0xford University Press, 2003).

Rhonda Evans Case, J.D., Ph.D., is an Assistant Professor in the Department of Political Science at East Carolina University. She has published in the *Australian Journal of Political Science*, *Congress and the Presidency*, and the *Journal of Common Market Studies*.

Amparo Gonzalez Ferrer is lecturer in sociology at the Universitat Pompeu Fabra, Barcelona, Spain. With Hector Cebolla she recently wrote the book *La Inmigración en España (2000-2007): Del Control de Flujos a la Integración de los Inmigrantes* (Centro de Estudios Politicos y Constitucionales, 2008).

Kathryn Gardner is a PhD candidate in the Department of Political Science at the University of Notre Dame. She is the author of "Fighting Terrorism the FATF Way" *Global Governance* (2007) as well as "De-fanging Terrorist Financing: The Financial Action Task Force (FATF) and the Fight against Terrorist Financing" in *Strategies Against Terrorism* (2007).

Jacqueline S. Gehring is Assistant Professor of Political Science at Allegheny College. She has written about the "hidden connections" between citizenship and anti-discrimination policy in Europe (in *Citizenship Policy in an Age of Diversity: Europe at the Crossroads*, edited by Ricard Zapata-Barrero. Published by Monografia CIDOB, Barcelona, 2009).

Marco Giugni is associate professor at the department of political science at the University of Geneva, Switzerland. He recently edited the book *The Politics of Unemployment in Europe: Policy Responses and Collective Action* (Ashgate, 2009).

Terri E. Givens is *an* associate professor at the University of Texas at Austin. She has written the book *Voting Radical Right in Western Europe* (Cambridge UP 2005) and edited the volume *Immigration Policy and Security* with Gary Freeman and David Leal (Routledge 2009).

Laurie Hanquinet is research fellow of the National Fund for Scientific Research (FNRS-FRS) at the Université Libre de Bruxelles, Belgium.

Carrie Humphreys is a Ph.D. candidate at the University of Utah in Salt Lake City, USA. Her Master's Essay was titled "Explaining the Rise and

Decline of Single-Issue Environmental and Anti-Migration Parties: A Study of Seven Western European Countries."

Dirk Jacobs is professor in sociology at the Université Libre de Bruxelles, Belgium.

Adam Luedtke is a visiting fellow at the Niehaus Centre for Globalization and Governance at Princeton University, and an Assistant Professor of Political Science at Washington State University, Vancouver. He is the author, with Thad Hall and Lina Svedin, of the 2010 Palgrave book *Risk Regulation in the United States and European Union: Controlling Chaos.*

Willem Maas holds the Jean Monnet Chair at York University, Toronto, where he is Associate Professor of Political Science at York's Glendon College and the Glendon School of Public & International Affairs, and Director of York's European Union Centre of Excellence. Maas is the author of *Creating European Citizens* (Rowman & Littlefield 2007).

Jeannette Money is an Associate Professor at the University of California, Davis. She is author of *Fences and Neighbours: The Political Geography of Immigration Control* and other articles on comparative immigration policy.

Miruna Morariu is assistant in political sciences at the University of Geneva, Switzerland.

Hubert Peres is Professor of Political Science at the University of Montpellier and Director of the CEPEL (South European Centre of Political Studies). Among his latest publications are "Comparing the Dynamics of Identity : the Cases of Spain and France", in M.S Darviche & W. Genieys, *Multinational State-Building. Considering and Continuing the Work of Juan Linz*, Pôle Sud, 2008.

Katia Pilati is post-doctoral researcher at the National Science Foundation (FNRS) at the Université Libre de Bruxelles, Belgium. She obtained her Ph.D. at Trento University, Italy.

Paul Statham is professor in sociology at Bristol University, Bristol, UK. Together with Ruud Koopmans, Marco Giugni and Florence Passy he wrote the book *Contested Citizenship: Immigration and Cultural Diversity in Europe* (Minnesota University Press, 2005).

Marc Swyngedouw is professor in sociology at the KULeuven, Belgium.

Raymond Taras is visiting fellow at the European University Institute in Florence, Italy. His recent books include *Europe Old and New: Transnationalism, Belonging, and Xenophobia* (2009), and *Islamophobia and Europe's Values* (2010).

Eiko Thielemann is Senior Lecturer/Associate Professor in the Department of Government and the European Institute at the London School of Economics and Political Science. He is also Director of the LSE Migration Studies Unit, and is currently completing a book on the international politics of refugee burden-sharing.

Bihter Tomen is currently pursuing her doctoral studies at Southern Illinois University, Carbondale. She completed her previous studies in Canada where she became politicized as an immigrant. Her areas of interest include issues of identity, immigration and nationalism in Europe and Turkey.

Véronique Vandezande is research fellow of the "Prospective Research in Brussels" Program at HUBrussel and KULeuven, Belgium.

Maarten P. Vink is Associate Professor at the Department of Political Science, Maastricht University, and FCT Post-Doctoral Research Fellow at the Institute of Social Sciences, University of Lisbon. He is the author of *Limits of European Citizenship* (Palgrave Macmillan, 2005) and co-editor of *Europeanisation: New Research Agendas* (Palgrave Macmillan, 2007).

Elizabeth Wright recently graduated from the University of Utah with a Master's of Political Science. She is currently working in the private sector for a non-profit organization, focusing on intellectual property issues.